China's Third Revolution

China's Third Revolution

Tensions in the Transition towards a Post-Communist China

*Ian G. Cook and
Geoffrey Murray*

CURZON

First Published in 2001
by Curzon Press
Richmond, Surrey
http://www.curzonpress.co.uk

© 2001 Ian G. Cook and Geoffrey Murray

Typeset in Sabon by LaserScript Ltd, Mitcham, Surrey
Printed and bound in Great Britain by
Biddles Ltd, Guildford and King's Lynn

British Library Cataloguing in Publication Data
A catalogue record of this book is available from the British Library

Library of Congress Cataloguing in Publication Data
A catalogue record for this book has been requested

ISBN 0–7007–1307–7

Contents

Contents

Preface

During July, 1921 (officially the 1st July), a few people met secretly in the old French Concession of Shanghai to plot the overthrow of the government and discuss plans to replace it with one dedicated to the interests of workers and peasants. Thus was held the First Congress of the Communist Party of China (CPC).

In 1949, after 28 turbulent years of wars, strikes and rebellions that left tens of millions dead, the party achieved its aim. It promised its members, the poor and landless, equality and fairness, and confiscated property from the rich and foreigners. On the 1st of October, Mao Zedong stood atop Tiananmen (Gate of Heavenly Peace) – only thirty-eight years before, a symbol of imperial power – to declare the foundation of the People's Republic of China (PRC).

In a rich history stretching back at least five millennia, the Chinese have been witnesses to many tumultuous times – decades, if not centuries of internecine war, the rise and fall of dynasties, appalling natural disasters, such as floods and famines, in which millions have died. And yet, the twentieth century can surely lay claim to being among the most chaotic. It began with China in the grip of a dying, feudal imperial system, a virtual corpse being dismembered by the rapacious European colonial powers, Britain, France and Germany, as well as Russia and Japan. It ended with China emerging as the third largest economic power on earth after the United States and Japan, with a voice that can no longer be ignored in the leading political and economic forums of the world. In between, lies the great, sometimes flawed experiment with communism.

It is perhaps hard now to imagine the upheavals of the 1950s and 1960s when Mao inspired the Great Leap Forward and, later, the Great Proletarian Cultural Revolution. Such events had a remarkable effect, for good and ill, and each proved to be a step too far towards the Maoist vision of a better tomorrow. Millions of lives were blighted, many permanently. But the Chinese are a remarkably resilient people. They picked themselves up and began rebuilding – with results that are evident to every visitor to the mainland today.

To see the new China, walk along Chang'an Avenue, the main Beijing east-west thoroughfare, turned into a 'green corridor', complete with trees and flower beds, for the fiftieth anniversary of the PRC. Wander into one of the many up-market department stores on the mainland, offering top-of-the-range cosmetics, of which the average annual salary of a peasant farmer in 1998, namely 2,160 yuan would buy possibly three or four items. But, walk further along the street and the 'green corridor' becomes 'beggar's row'. An elderly woman in filthy clothes brings forward her blind husband, pointing to her mouth. 'Money, money,' she says. A boy of about eight follows, clutching the legs of passers-by. Nearby others are selling fake compact discs for about 10 yuan, Mao badges and copies of his Little Red Book, as well as vases, embroidered bags and T-shirts, all laid along the pavement on cloth that can be wrapped up in a few seconds when the police appear. Thus, one sees the essential contradiction of China today.

The late Deng Xiaoping, had an explanation for this. In his final years, he reportedly declared that: 'While the final goal of communism remains wealth for all, it is necessary for some to get rich before others.' And that is now certainly the case. At the top of the ladder are those who run successful private businesses, managers of large and powerful companies (state or partially state-owned), film stars and other performers and officials who trade their power for money. At the bottom are the unemployed, those who work for unprofitable companies that do not pay wages and those who have lost out in the transformation brought about by 20 years of reform, who receive neither the pensions nor the medical or social benefits they thought they were entitled to.

Even in the 1980s, it would have been impossible to imagine the *People's Daily*, staid mouthpiece of party orthodoxy, declaring in a commentary, as it did in mid-June 1999, that to buy shares was glorious and that rising shares would bring 'hope and happiness'. Within hours, the two official stock exchanges in Shanghai and Shenzhen, languishing in the doldrums for many months, went ballistic. The party leadership has been traditionally suspicious of share markets and their-justifiable-reputation in China as casinos. So why the change of tune? Desperate times, it seems, demanded desperate measures.

At the time, China had been in the grip of deflation – consumer prices falling for eighteen straight months. Facing an uncertain economic future, households refused to spend. What was missing, the leadership suddenly discovered, was what Americans call the 'feel-good factor'. Savings piled up in state banks. But the banks, under pressure to improve their performance, were loath to lend to the state enterprises, their main customers, many of which continue to lose money. Thus, the stock market suddenly became a possible saviour of China's 118,000 industrial state enterprises. What banks were unwilling to offer, investors might, was the logic. Thus, newspaper readers, long conditioned to 'good news' stories about record harvests and the heroic exploits of model workers, can now get analysis on 'good share' buys and 'companies to watch'.

This seems a far cry from what the CPC's founders set out to achieve. Despite talk of 'socialism with Chinese characteristics', it is becoming increasingly difficult to find anything that can truly be described as Communism on the mainland today. So, can China still be regarded as a communist state? If Marxism and Maoism are dead, what is taking its place for the twenty-first century? Whatever it is, there is a very real sense of China undergoing a cataclysmic social and economic revolution that is already beginning to spill over into the political arena. Our contention is that this is China's third significant revolution of the twentieth century, following the 1911 upheavals that brought an end to imperial rule and the long civil war that created the PRC in 1949.

It is from this premise that we have embarked on the writing of this book at a crucial turning point in Chinese history. No one book could possibly encompass every aspect of modern Chinese life. We have, therefore, identified a selection of key areas to illustrate our thesis. Some topics of importance, such as the food situation, the problem of an ageing population and international security issues, were dealt with at some length in Murray's recent work *China The Next Superpower* (1998) and Cook's co-edited volume *Dynamic Asia* (1998), and therefore are not repeated here.

Two chapters deal with the crucial issue of state-owned enterprise reform, seeking to turn round the chronic debilitation of the sector unable to cope with the demands of a market economy due to the legacy of the contradictions inherent in central planning. Two further chapters deal with the issue of regional disparities, especially in the rural interior, where the bulk of the population still lives, and where the sharp contrast between have and have-not remains so apparent. A further related chapter then deals with the issue of ethnic minorities, especially Xinjiang and Tibet, where separatism creates a source of continuous tension.

The focus then switches to the cities and a rapidly growing urban population, a source of a whole new range of problems, including the difficulty of housing the new influx. Finally, the severe and growing problem of environmental degradation which not only affects all Chinese, but many of their neighbours, is dealt with.

The opening and closing chapters were written jointly, while the first draft of the remaining eight chapters were divided equally between the two authors based on their specific interests and specialities. The format largely involves a case study approach, with each chapter containing a number of boxes where a specific issue is dealt with in more detail.

This collaborative effort has emerged from a shared interest in China, especially through the Centre for Pacific Rim Studies at Liverpool John Moores University. Thanks are due to Ron Noon of the School of Social Science for introducing us, and to David McEvoy, professor emeritus of

JMU, and other friends and colleagues for their helpful support over the years. This collaborative effort has proved an enjoyable experience as each author has brought to it specific teaching and research experiences stemming from different backgrounds. Professor Cook brings a particular perspective to this work through having been a regular visitor to the PRC ever since 1980, presenting papers at international conferences and bringing groups of final year undergraduates annually to China for fieldwork. Geoffrey Murray, meanwhile, has spent the majority of the time since 1990 living and working in Beijing as a business researcher and editorial training consultant.

As these words were being written, a new Tiananmen Square, of pink granite and green carpets, opened to media fanfare. The preparations for the PRC's fiftieth anniversary, symbolised by the dust and noise from 5,000 work sites, many related to refurbishment, have been amplified by the strain of coping with record temperatures and soul-destroying traffic jams. The dense dust and traffic exhaust fumes are making Beijing one of China's most polluted cities in China. But amid the gloom, there is hope. The relentless drilling and hammering is also because natural gas pipes are being laid to ease the pollution caused by coal fires in winter, and for new subway lines that should cut road use. Many landmarks have emerged from decades of grime. Beijing's first railway station, dating from the Boxer siege of the old Legation Quarter on the south-east corner of Tiananmen Square, is now resplendent in pink and white. The smelly rubbish-filled moat around the Forbidden City has been drained, repaved and cleaned – part of a billion-yuan project to clean up Beijing's antique waterways and canals.

In such ways is China renewing itself, prepared to put up with inconvenience today in the hope of a brighter tomorrow. But there are many tensions in this transition to a better future, and this is very much the theme of this book.

Ian Cook and Geoffrey Murray

List of Abbreviations

ADB	Asian Development Bank
CCB	China Construction Bank
CET	Chinese Economic Triangle
CPC	Communist Party of China
CPPCC	Chinese People's Political Consultative Conference
CSRC	China Securities Regulatory Commission
FAW	First Automotive Works Group
FDRS	Factory Director Responsibility System
GDP	Gross Domestic Product
GNP	Gross National Product
HEP	Hydroelectric Power
MOFTEC	Ministry of Foreign Trade and Economic Co-operation
MTR	Mass-Transit Railway
NEPA	National Environmental Protection Agency (now SEPA)
NGO	Non-Governmental Organisation
NIDL	New International Division of Labour
NPC	National People's Congress
PRC	People's Republic of China
RMB	Renminbi (Chinese currency, the Yuan)
SAR	Special Administrative Region
SEZ	Special Economic Zone
SEPA	State Environmental Protection Agency
SETC	State Economic and Trade Commission
SOE	State-Owned Enterprise
SSB	State Statistical Bureau
TSP	Total Suspended Particle
UNDP	United Nations Development Programme
WWF	World Wildlife Fund For Nature

List of Maps and Illustrations

Illustrations appear between pages 112 and 113

List of Boxes

List of Tables

NOTE: The majority of currency figures refer to the Yuan (Renminbi), which normally converts at approximately 8.3 to the US Dollar and 13.0 to the Pound Sterling.

CHAPTER 1

China's Three Revolutions: Achievements and Setbacks

Arguably, during the twentieth century, China has undergone not one but three revolutions. The first was led by Dr. Sun Yat-Sen in 1911, and freed China from the Imperial Dynasty. The second was led by Mao Zedong in 1949, and freed China from the worst depredations of poverty and famine. The third revolution was begun by Deng Xiaoping in 1978, and despite his death in 1997 is still ongoing under his successor Jiang Zemin. This revolution is seeking to give China a new era of wealth and prosperity. It may, ultimately, provide an alternative government to the present one of Communism. This book uses case studies of key topics and issues to focus on the stresses and strains in this third revolution. In the twentieth century, change in China has been truly remarkable. In 1999, the Communist Party of China celebrated fifty years of tumultuous rule over the People's Republic of China. On October 1, 1949, the late Chairman Mao Zedong stood on top of the Tiananmen Gate in Beijing to proclaim the beginning of an unprecedented experiment in achieving a complete economic, social and political transformation of a giant country encompassing almost a quarter of the world's population. It has since undergone some of the most astonishing changes ever witnessed by a major society in such a short space of time.

This opening chapter will focus on the following themes:

- A century of dramatic change
- Policy oscillations; from *shou* to *fang*
- The Maoist legacy: moving the mountains
- China's Third Revolution: Deng transforms the dream

A century of dramatic change

Henry Kissinger, on one of his periodic visits to Beijing, in 1979, observed that Britain had launched its industrial revolution at a time when its population stood at 15 million, Japan's parallel Meiji Restoration drive for modernisation involved a population of thirty million, while the United States and Russia had created their industrial economic underpinnings in the late nineteenth century when their populations stood at sixty to seventy million. China, however, was trying to carry out its own industrial revolution among a billion people, then around a quarter of the human race – a task of monumental proportions (Short, 1982, p.75). Since then, and despite the demographic success of the Single Child Family Programme (which, of course, has its critics in human rights' terms), officially the population reached nearly 1250 million in 1998 (see Table 1.1) and more likely 1270-1300 million allowing for unregistered births, problems of data collection and so on. The monumental task is now even greater, with more than 300 million aged less than 0-14 years as well as a rapidly expanding elderly population, as the Table shows.

Further, the Chinese also seek to telescope this task into a relatively short time. And, while past attempts to speed up the process of change led to disastrous setbacks such as Mao Zedong's 'Great Leap Forward' in the late 1950s, they also have much to be proud of. According to the World Bank, economic development has been so rapid in recent years that, if China's thirty provinces and autonomous regions were counted as separate states, the twenty fastest growing economies in the world between 1975 and 1995 would have been Chinese. Over the next 25 years, the Bank expects the Chinese economy to undergo a transformation which it claims took about sixty-five years in Latin America and eighty years in the world's most advanced economies (World Bank, 1997a).

Table 1.1 Key Population Indicators in 1998

	Population (millions)	Percentage
Total population	1,248.1	–
Urban population	379.4	30.4
Rural population	868.7	69.6
Net population growth	11.8	–
Population aged 0–14	320.8	25.7
Aged 15–64	843.7	67.6
65 >	83.8	6.7

Source: State Statistics Bureau, *Annual Report 1998*, Beijing.

And yet, only two decades ago, most Chinese had no distinct concept of living in comfort, which then leader Deng Xiaoping was putting forward as the focus of reform, namely: '[to quadruple] the gross national product by 2000 to attain a moderately high standard of living'. Few people then could have conceived of a situation where grain would no longer be rationed; they would enjoy the luxury of the unhurried choosing of food amid a dazzling array of commodities; they would have large-screen colour TV sets on which they could see the newest fashions and famous-brand products in Paris and Hong Kong, and then buy these selfsame articles in mainland shops, via the telephone or the Internet. During the 1970s, a newly-wedded couple cherished three items – wrist watch, sewing machine and bicycle. In the 1980s, these changed to TV set, refrigerator and washing machine. Now, they have become a motor car, apartment and foreign tour. In 1978, almost 36 per cent of urban and rural residents still had an annual average income below 100 Yuan. Two decades later, official figures suggest the number of people lacking self-sufficiency to buy food and clothing had shrunk from 250 million to less than fifty-eight million. In 1997, the yearly income budgeted by each urban resident was 5,160 Yuan, compared to 2,090 Yuan in the countryside. Their total bank savings deposits exceeded 450 billion Yuan (*Annual Reports*, State Statistics Bureau).

Twenty years ago, the words 'mobile phone' and 'information super-highway' formed no part of the vocabulary, while today, even in outlying areas, a mobile phone is a regular fashion accessory, and, in urban areas, the public is coming to grips with the Internet (more than four million users at the end of June, 1999, according to the China National Internet Information Centre survey, *China Daily*, 15-7-99). A survey in March 1998 indicated that in 12 major cities, such as Beijing and Shanghai, 97 per cent of families had TV sets, 88 per cent refrigerators and washing machines, about 60 per cent hot-water heaters, automatic rice cookers, air conditioners and cameras; 36 per cent had a pager and 12 per cent a cellular phone (Xinhua, 14-5-98). In the late 1980s, an expressway, for most Chinese people, was only a concept learned from TV and newspapers, and in many rural areas in particular the bicycle or the mule cart remained the dominant means of personal transport. Now, the country produces over a million passenger cars a year in joint ventures with the world's giants like General Motors, Toyota and VW (Murray, 1994, Chapter 6), and nearly 4,000 km of high speed highways have been built, with longer term plans for a latticework of such roads linking all major population centres. Work will start by 2000 on the country's first high-speed railway, similar to the French TGV and the Japanese Shinkansen, between Beijing and Shanghai.

The achievements of the Chinese industrial revolution have been substantial. During the 1950s, the country paid a heavy price for striving to reach a target of producing 10.7 million tons steel a year. Now, its annual steel output exceeds 100 million tons, largest in the world (see Chapter 3).

Western manufacturers of space satellites increasingly come to China to have them carried aloft by Chinese-developed rockets like the Long March 3B which has the capacity to carry 5,000 kg payloads into space. By the beginning of the next century, these could be putting a Chinese astronaut on the Moon. A latecomer to the IT revolution, lagging at least thirty years behind the United States in technology, China is now beginning to export computers to the American, Japanese and European markets.

In 1998, China's foreign trade was approaching US$400 billion, placing it in 10th place overall among the world's major trading nations; it would be even higher if Hong Kong's trade, now calculated separately, was added to the mainland figure. By 2010, it is predicted the mainland's exports alone will reach $435 billion, quadrupling the 1994 figure, and by 2020, it could have tripled its share of world trade to 10 per cent from the three per cent prevailing in 1996 (World Bank, 1997b). These figures become even more impressive when one considers that over the whole of the Maoist era, China's share of world trade fell from 1.4 per cent in the mid-1950s to just 0.4 per cent in the mid-1970s (Xu, 1982, p.168). Indeed, 'Under Mao ... international markets were regarded as economically anarchic systems from which China's domestic economy should be insulated' (Nolan and Dong, 1990, p.8).

In judging where China stands today, however, it is also important to go back further in remembering where she came from. A nation proud of its ancient civilisation and its achievements in the advancement of learning, it suddenly found itself in the nineteenth century slipping far behind other countries long regarded as its inferiors. The Qing Dynasty which finally expired in the first revolution of 1911, presided over a nation so sunk in feudal lethargy – but still gripped by a giant superiority complex – that by 1792, Lord Macartney, the British envoy sent to try to put relations with China on a proper footing could already discern a 'backward state of scientific and medical knowledge, the indifference of the literati class to material progress, the backwardness of the army which still used bows and arrows and lacked modern firearms, the poverty of the masses, and the widespread graft and corruption in the government' (cited in Hsu, 1990, p.207).

Macartney further observed that, 'China is an old, crazy, first-rate Man of War, which a succession of able and vigilant officers have contrived to keep afloat for these hundred and fifty years past, and to overawe their neighbours merely by her bulk and appearance. She may, perhaps, not sink outright; she may drift some time as a wreck, and will then be dashed to pieces on the shores; but she can never be rebuilt on the old bottom' (ibid., pp.207-8). The eighteenth century German philosopher Johann Herder was similarly colourful: 'The empire is an embalmed mummy painted with hieroglyphs and swaddled in silk; its circulation has a sluggish vitality of animals in hibernation' (cited in Wiethoff, 1975, p.13).

By the mid-nineteenth century, the country was ripe for invasion, exploitation and the carving up into spheres of influence by the European powers, and, to a lesser extent, the United States (Hughes, 1937). From the 1840s to the 1940s, the country was in chaos. The decline of the Qing Dynasty was marked by major rebellions. In striking contrast to Meiji Japan, the Qing resisted modernisation almost to the bitter end, finally accepting its necessity only after defeat by Japan in 1898. Following the dynasty's collapse in Dr Sun's revolution of 1911, China was riven by fighting between rival warlords ruling different parts of the country, some of which collapsed into banditry. By the 1930s, it was a desperately poor, underdeveloped country exploited by a small wealthy elite of Chinese and foreigners, especially in cities like Shanghai which became known euphemistically as 'The Paris of the East' and more damningly as 'The Whorehouse of Asia', a city of glaring contrasts between:

'the hundred dance halls and the thousands of taxi dolls; the opium dens and gambling halls; the flashing lights of the great restaurants, the clatter of mah-jongg pieces ... the sailors in their smelly bars and friendly brothels on Szechwan Road ... the innumerable shops spilling with silks, jades, embroideries, porcelains and all the wares of the East [and] the beggars on every downtown block and the scabby infants urinating and defecating on the curb while mendicant mothers absently scratched for lice' (Snow, 1970, p.503).

Under Guomindang (Nationalist) rule from 1927, the country was largely reunified, but there was a persistent civil war waged for most of the following two decades with the emerging Communists, complicated by Japanese take-over of Manchuria in the 1930s and full-scale war with Japan from 1937, that caused a virtual economic collapse. When the Communists finally marched into Beijing in 1949 and Mao Zedong, the country's new 'emperor' declared the founding of the People's Republic of China atop the famed Tiananmen Gate of the former imperial palace, the country was in a state of utter prostration. '[It] was a shattered, ruined land, a 'blanket torn and full of holes', commerce bankrupt or paralysed, administration non-existent, cities haunted by starvation, misery and crime, beggared villages, famished millions' (Han Suyin, 1976, p.24).

Little industry existed – what there had been before the war was almost exclusively located in the Lower Yangtze Valley around Shanghai, where it was looted by the Japanese invaders (Snow, 1941, p.80) and in Manchuria by the Russians in 1945 (Schaller, 1979, p.293). One noted China scholar suggested that the country's late industrial development stemmed from the intensive agriculture, demanding intensive labour, which shaped the emergence of Chinese society and its culture. For the dominant class (landlords/scholars/bureaucrats), 'in order to keep rentals up and wages down, the social system demanded not merely enough people but too many people. Those whose vested interests lay in the control of manpower discouraged the development of alternatives to manpower [discouraging] the development of mining, industry (except local handicraft industry) and all other activities that might threaten the supremacy of the irrigation-controlling, land-controlling, manpower-controlling classes who were the real rulers of China at each successive stage of history (Lattimore, 1998 (1940), pp.40-1).

Policy oscillations; from *shou* to *fang*

During more than a century of violence, from 1840 to 1949, through political upheaval, civil wars and foreign conquest, the Chinese people experienced profound social change, which has continued unabated since the foundation of the PRC. The past fifty years, in fact, in many respects merely mirror the recurrent experience in the country's long history, in which it has oscillated between strength and weakness, war and peace. Under Communist rule, for example, this oscillation has been between restriction (*shou*) and liberalisation (*fang*). When one aspect became too extreme, the other aspect would act as a partial antidote. In the 1950s, for example, the newly victorious CPC set about establishing a Stalinist-type totalitarian system, eliminating real or potential opposition, reorganising the masses into new party-led associations and removing from them the resources to mount autonomous activities. The Great Leap Forward was a period of intensified direct party control over society, emerging in the wake of the 'Hundred Flowers' movement of 1956, a *fang* interlude during which intellectuals were encouraged to criticise excessively tight party-state control – suffering greatly for their boldness as Mao launched a vicious anti-rightist campaign.

The disastrous legacy of the Great Leap Forward – in which an estimated 20 million died or remained unborn due to the neglect of agriculture in favour of industrialisation, coinciding with a severe drought (Chen, 1965; et al) – brought about another spell of relaxation, but this was short-lived. The decade of the Great Proletarian Cultural Revolution (1966-76) represented a renewed policy of *shou*. Following this disaster – a million dead, the lives of another thirty million blighted by political disgrace, the economy in tatters as industrial production was neglected in favour of playing at revolution, and education in ruins (Goodman, 1994; Han Suyin, 1976; Salisbury, 1992; Spence, 1982; Terrill, 1984 among others) – another period of *fang* in the economy, arts, scholarly inquiry, religious belief, personal relations and contacts with the outside world began from 1978.

Nevertheless, even within this general trend of careful liberalisation, there were three distinct periods of *shou*: the 1983-4 Anti-Spiritual

Pollution Campaign, the 1987 Campaign Against Bourgeois Liberalisation and the 1989 Tiananmen Square 'incident'/ 'massacre' and subsequent witch hunt of those who challenged party rule. At the time of writing, the country would seem to be in a period of *fang* although with some *shou* undertones (Murray, 1998, pp.17-18). The key question now, therefore, is: where is Communism (or, socialism) heading in the twenty-first century? What, in fact, does Communism mean in the Chinese context? Does it bear much resemblance to the nineteenth century doctrines of Marx or Lenin – or, in the Chinese context, Mao? Firstly, what are the ideological underpinnings of mainland China today?

> 'Ever since Mao assumed the leadership of the Chinese Communist Party – indeed, ever since its foundation in 1921 – its raison d'être has been class struggle in one form or another. The Third Central Committee Plenum held December 18th-22nd, 1978 decreed that large-scale class struggle was over. More than any other single factor, this marked the end of the Marxist system. Implicit in it was the view that man could not be transformed through revolution, as Mao had believed, but must work to transform his country through production, so that this economic transformation would bring about the transformation of man' (Short, 1982, p.284).

In a key speech in 1979, Zhao Ziyang, later to become premier until his dismissal at the height of the Tiananmen disturbances in 1989, set out the basic principles of the post-Mao (Deng Xiaoping) era:

> 'The major principles of socialism are: first, public ownership of the means of production, and second, a system of 'each according to his work'. When we talk about the socialist principle of public ownership we mean [public ownership] of the principal part of the economy, not the whole of it. By the principle of each according to his work, we mean we must not exploit others or use capital to exploit others. As long as we adhere to these two conditions, we should adopt any system, structural policy and measure that can promote the development of productive forces. We must not bind ourselves like silkworms in cocoons. On this issue we really have to emancipate our thinking vigorously' (Xinhua News Agency 9-11-1979).

This was the pragmatic viewpoint justified by the need to drag China out of backwardness, summed up by Deng's oft-repeated aphorism that 'it doesn't matter if the cat is black or white as long as it catches mice'. Thus, even aspects of out-and-out capitalism could be adopted if they achieved the rights results for China. Against this was set a more conservative ideological approach, typified by Hua Guofeng, immediate successor to Chairman Mao but shunted aside by Deng in 1980, who told an army conference in 1980 that:

'China is a socialist country. The socialist system dictates that primary attention should be paid to raising the ideological consciousness of the people in solving economic problems and doing all kinds of work. No good results will be achieved if undue emphasis is placed on economic methods and material rewards while political work and efforts to raise the people's ideological awareness are relaxed. Indifference to the weal and woe of the people is wrong, but over-emphasis on improving the people's living standards beyond the growth of production is unrealistic. It is necessary to raise the people's political consciousness and encourage the revolutionary spirit of building the country through diligence and thrift' (*People's Daily*, 8-5-1980).

Those who survived the Maoist era and took over the running of the country after the death of the 'Great Helmsman' as he was known in 1976, went through several years of political contortions in trying to disown some of the worst excesses of Maoism without calling into question the whole basis for the Communist Party's right to rule. Abandoning Maoism meant abandoning virtually the entire ideological underpinnings of the PRC. It took some years, before Deng Xiaoping felt secure enough to begin wholesale debunking of the alleged infallibility of Mao Zedong Thought. Now, with Deng gone, the current third generation of party collective leadership feels the need to establish its own credentials by 'holding high the banner of Deng Xiaoping Thought' – which might be summed up as, 'to get rich quick is glorious, but challenging the right of the Communist Party to rule is not'. As will be considered in later chapters, there is a very real sense of a national leadership grasping at anything which can fill the ideological void created by the disappearance of the all-embracing, all-dominating Maoist dogma. To search for a new political credo seems to have descended to the level of education in patriotism as an important part of promoting 'socialist ethical and cultural progress.' In the course of socialist modernisation, the emphasis is on instilling a strong sense of pride in every Chinese in both past and present national achievements (for which the party should be given due credit).

As President, Jiang Zemin declared in a speech to a party meeting in October 1996:

'Our motherland is a great, unified, multi-national country. For more than 5,000 years, the Chinese nation has worked and lived on this land, and various nationalities have united and learned from each other. With their diligence and wisdom they have jointly developed the beautiful rivers and mountains of the motherland, and created the splendid Chinese civilisation. A large number of great thinkers, statesmen, military strategists, scientists, men of letters and artists have emerged. The Chinese civilisation has not only exerted profound influence on the Orient, but also made indelible contributions to the civilisation of the whole of mankind. The Chinese people have never yielded to invaders, and they have the glorious tradition of ardently loving freedom, seeking progress, and safeguarding national dignity and state sovereignty. It has become our precious national character to bitterly hate foreign invaders, boundlessly disdain the nation's scoundrels who sought power and wealth by betraying the country, and show great reverence for the noble-minded patriots who waged a constant struggle against foreign bullying.'

Jiang said the establishment of the Communist Party of China marked the historic turning point in the struggle, moving it from failure to final victory, national rejuvenation and prosperity. Chinese Communists were the staunchest, most thorough patriots who set a supreme example to the nation:

'People have come to realise from their own experience that only socialism can save China, only socialism can develop China and patriotism and socialism are one. In the course of reform, opening-up and modernisation drive [started by Deng Xiaoping in 1978], a large number of heroic and model people have sprung up from various walks of life, who have won honour for the country and created glorious merits, making the patriotic tradition of the Chinese nation shine out with new splendour. To continue promoting our cause, education in patriotism, especially among the younger generation, must be further strengthened.'

It may be a losing battle. One sign of changing times, for example, is the fact that a political textbook studied by 200 million children has now been changed so they learn less about Lenin and more about the market economy. The lessons on ideology have been altered at least 10 times since 1950. But, from autumn 1998, youngsters began learning about shares, stocks, corporations, finance, taxation and labour contracts. Professor Cheng Shuli, chief editor of *The Basic Knowledge of Economy*, said previous editions were too theoretical and included too much about class struggle, land reform and 'long live Leninism'. 'They tried to lead the reader to the conclusion that capitalism is doomed and the victory of socialism is inevitable', Professor Cheng said. He described the old textbook as a piece of 'hard tack, very dry and hard to digest' (*Economic Daily*, 7-5-1998).

Before the present decade, such a statement would have risked a long jail sentence in one of the labour camps scattered around the outer limits of China's remote western borders. Similarly, the eight democratic (non-communist) parties permitted to exist in China startled many in the government when they produced a report in 1997 based on studies and public opinion polls showing growing popular demand for quickening

9

political reforms. Political liberalisation would help defuse worsening social contradictions, they stated flatly. For all his boldness in the economic arena, Deng Xiaoping never countenanced similar liberalisation on the political front.

Reform over the past 20 years has given rise to a whole set of contradictions to which all possible resolutions are costly. It has brought China to the point at which the interests of some large constituencies must be threatened. Official propaganda repeatedly stresses appeal to individual interests as the effective motivator of human energy. Luxury consumer goods are dangled on television before the populace, and tales of the emerging wealthy fill the media. 'Developing the forces of production' is treated at the sole criterion for choosing social policies.

Belated attempts are being made to revive the old utopian values such as solidarity, co-operation and equality, but it is an uphill struggle given the teachings of the past two decades that tend to oppose and discredit these values. It seems, in fact, that the leadership has still to find a new model and a new vocabulary to describe what they seek to create. 'Socialism with Chinese characteristics' invented by Deng Xiaoping, and still promoted by his successors, is essentially a catch-all concept. Similarly, the idea that China is at the 'primary stage of socialism' which the leadership use to lend Marxist legitimacy to reform policies, does not seriously confront the issue of preserving the core of the socialist enterprise through a long historical detour.

The best-selling books in China at the time of writing reflect this search for a new direction. There is a great demand for works that seek to examine where China stands today, and, more importantly, where it is going to be in 20 years time. Among liberal Beijing intellectuals, for example, especially those hoping for a more open debate on constitutional reform and freedom of information, the great excitement in 1998 was over *Political China: Facing the Era of Choosing a New Structure* – thirty-nine essays written by thirty-two scholars, journalists and former government officials who were dismissed for pro-democracy leanings. In it. Jiang Ping, former head of the University of Political Science and Law, writes: 'Discussing political structural reform is not just an armchair strategy, but will build up psychological anticipation for the reform in society.' However, the party leadership quickly countered with a firm rejection: no parliamentarianism, no multi-party system and no separation of legislative, executive and judicial powers.

In the first three decades of the PRC, there was an intense struggle at the centre between those like Mao who sought a fast track to a Communist utopia, and men like one-time head of state Liu Shaoqi, who believed it would take a 100 years to achieve that goal, and that a long period was necessary in which there would be a continuation of various economic systems that were essentially capitalistic. One theory about the causes of the

Cultural Revolution was that it was essentially Mao's way of eliminating Liu – who subsequently died a broken man in prison – and all those, like Deng Xiaoping, who insisted on taking the 'capitalist road' (see Han Suyin and Terrill, op.cit., for example). Liu, was posthumously rehabilitated (and the subject of lavish public praise on his 100th birth anniversary in 1998) when Deng regained power, and his views on the long hard road to socialism have been borne out by the repeated statements of the present party leadership.

The Maoist legacy: moving the mountains

Notwithstanding the notable contributions of others, it was Mao Zedong, who played such a tremendous part both in developing the dream of a communist alternative for China and also leading the country towards it. Born in Hunan province on December 26, 1893, Mao's upbringing was during a time of incredible upheaval in the old order. The humiliations to which China was subject by outside powers arguably peaked at the turn of the century, including the 'Boxer' rebellion and its aftermath, and the Qing dynasty proved powerless in the face of internal and external threats. Mao was influenced not only by his conventional education in the Confucian texts and classical language, which were to bear upon his thinking and chosen examples throughout his life, but also the ferment of revolutionary ideas which he found at the new Teachers' Training School in Changsha.

Upon graduation, in 1918, Mao worked as a library assistant at prestigious Peking University, the first of China's universities, founded in 1898. If Changsha had been a ferment of ideas, then Peking University was the epicentre of the earthquake which was eventually to shake China to the core. The crucial May Fourth [1919] Movement, formed to oppose Japan's claims on China at the Versailles Conference, was led by the students and staff of this university, including the librarian for whom Mao worked. Impressed by the success of the Soviet Communist Revolution, and unimpressed by attempts at democracy, the Communist Party of China (CPC) was founded soon after, holding its First National Congress in 1921 in Shanghai and environs. Mao Zedong was there, as one of the thirteen present.

During the 1920s Mao worked mainly in Hunan, spreading revolutionary ideas and preparing the peasantry for revolution, leading in 1927 to his influential 'Report on an Investigation of the Peasant Movement in Hunan' for the CPC. He analysed the newly founded peasant associations which, although being dismissed by outsiders as 'terrible' in their activities he viewed as 'anything but 'terrible' ... what they are doing is absolutely right; what they are doing is fine!' (Mao Zedong, 1971 (1927), p.28). To him the peasantry was like a 'mighty storm', a 'hurricane' of overwhelming and irresistible force that 'will sweep all the imperialists, warlords, corrupt officials, local tyrants and evil gentry into their graves' (ibid., p.24).

11

Again and again, in his writings and, more importantly, in his practice, he would demonstrate this belief in the peasantry and entrust them with upholding the revolution, as when, in 1945 in the closing speech to the Seventh National Congress in Yan'an he retold the fable (*'The Foolish Old Man Who Removed the Mountains'*) of the old man who was so determined to remove the two mountains which obstructed his way that he worked by hand to do so, dismissing the objections of his critics by saying that task could be carried on by future generations until finished. Eventually, this endeavour moved the gods to send two angels do the job.

> 'Today, two big mountains lie like a dead weight on the Chinese people. One is imperialism, the other is feudalism. The Chinese Communist Party has long made up its mind to dig them up. We must persevere and work unceasingly, and we, too, will touch God's heart. Our God is none other than the masses of the Chinese people. If they stand up and dig together with us, why can't these two mountains be cleared away?' (ibid., p.320).

The first part of the dream was the ridding of China of these two mountains. To accomplish this prompted Mao's theory of 'People's War', a doctrine which was to prove successful not just in China, but later in Vietnam and other overseas revolutionary situations. Controlling the countryside rather than the cities was the key, in 'base areas' of the peasantry from which the PLA would strike out at the armies of its opponents, but avoiding large-scale pitched battles, at least until later stages when conditions were such that success could be more-or-less guaranteed. This attritional 'War of the Flea', as it became known, first proved to be highly successful in the Anti-Japanese War when the CPC left command of the cities to Japanese forces, contested the 'grey areas' immediately around the cities, and controlled the surrounding 'liberated areas' of around ninety million people (Fitzgerald, 1977, Chapter 3). More than a guerrilla war; the CPC organised the peasantry and built up their strength in such a way that the war 'would develop towards an advanced stage, so that they will gradually change into a regular army and regular warfare' (Mao Zedong, Volume Two, 1954 (1938), p.280). What was to become the *People's* Liberation Army (PLA) was a key element in the rapid fall of China to the communist forces in the late 1940s.

The masses of China, the peasantry, had been brutally exploited for centuries, but especially so in the upheavals of the nineteenth and early twentieth centuries (see Chapter 5). Landlessness and indebtedness increased markedly, famines and floods became especially widespread and devastating, and the country had been almost destroyed by years of internal warfare plus the war with Japan. The CPC worked hard in the base areas to develop models of good practice, working with, not against, the peasantry, which paid off in 1949. During what was known as the 'years of development', however, antagonisms and dissent surfaced within the party leadership, over matters of strategy and tactics. One which eventually turned out to be a running sore was between Mao and Liu Shaoqi, who, no less staunch a communist, had greater contact with the Soviets and according to Fitzgerald was 'more of the 'apparatchik' type; a firm believer in hierarchy, discipline and strict obedience to the line laid down by the central organs of the Party' (Fitzgerald, 1977, op.cit., p.123). His protégé was Deng Xiaoping.

A command economy was quickly established, to be developed via a series of Five-Year plans. Based on the Soviet model, it included heavy investment in the development of raw material extraction and processing industries; large-scale, capital-intensive technology in industry; high rates of saving and investment institutionalised through agricultural collectivisation (extracting a surplus from the peasantry); and an under-emphasis, by contrast, on agricultural investment, consumer industries and social 'overheads' (Buchanan, 1970). In agriculture, the landlord class were eliminated, literally or figuratively, via criticism sessions led by the local peasantry with the assistance of cadres, and the process of collectivisation was set in train via mutual aid teams and producers' co-operatives. Tensions grew within the leadership, however, over the nature and pace of change.

Mao, drawing upon his vast experience of peasant conditions, realised that the Soviet model was appropriate for Soviet conditions, in a country that had already achieved considerable industrial development, but could not readily fit the peasant situation of China. The Maoist model of economic development, therefore, came to the fore during the life of the First Five Year Plan when he called, in speeches in 1955 and 1956, for rapid collectivisation to accelerate agricultural progress. His call was heeded to such an extent that by year-end 1956, 91 per cent of the peasant population was in Elementary Producers' Co-operatives. More dramatically still, nearly all of the peasants were in 680,000 Advanced Producers Co-operatives by the end of 1957. 'Thus a revolution planned to take fifteen years was completed in little more than one' (Howe, 1978, op.cit., p.xxvii)

The Soviet model, therefore, was beginning to be questioned and modified at the *diktat* of Mao Zedong. Soviet-style characteristics, of heavy industry, of large-scale projects, of morphological transformation in cities towards blocks of featureless mid-rise flats and mega-scale prestige projects, with immense boulevards, would continue, and have an impact in later decades. But from the late 1950s it was the Maoist model, and reaction to it, rather than the Soviet one which became dominant, attempting to mould socialism to fit the Maoist view of Chinese conditions. Mao felt that even more dramatic progress was called for, and unleashed the concept of the Great Leap Forward in 1958. This famous/infamous attempt to transform the political economy of China was multi-faceted. The first, major, plank of the policy was to move rapidly beyond the Agricultural Producers' Co-operatives to Communes. These were designed to transcend and envelop social, economic and political forms of organisation, moving beyond the factory or the village as the centres of pre-commune life.

The first commune was set up as the model in Mao's home province of Hunan, and entitled 'Sputnik' for inspiration. From there, the commune concept rapidly spread until 99 per cent of the population was in 26,500 communes throughout rural and urban areas. Each commune would be comprised of around 20,000, or in some cases, up to 50,000-60,000 people. Their task was to transform the economic landscape of China, no more, no less. The pace was frenetic, the hype amazing. This was the era of the 'blue ants', where the people, dressed in their blue Maoist uniforms, would work without sleep for 24, 48 and in some cases 72 hours straight, building with bare hands if necessary the irrigation ditches, canals, levees and ponds which would transform China's agriculture.

In the industrial sector, the 'backyard furnace campaign' attempted to catch up with Britain in steel production in 15 years. Around sixty million untrained peasants were set to work to build the kilns and furnaces, to dig the ore and obtain the power supply, to produce steel. And steel, of sorts, was produced, demonstrating that human ingenuity can indeed overcome many obstacles. Then, there was the 'barefoot doctors campaign' in which paramedics were given rudimentary training in traditional herbal medicines and acupuncture, plus more modern techniques, and sent into the rural areas to improve the health levels of the peasantry. There was also the 'Walking on Two Legs Policy' which was applied in different areas of the economy, such as hydroelectric power projects, where a few large-scale projects were counterbalanced by smaller more localised projects in rural areas, or iron and steel production where the large integrated plants of Anshan, Shijingshan, Wuhan, Baotou and others were counterbalanced by up to two million backyard furnaces.

Inevitably, this incredible pace could not be maintained. The party cadres who were overseeing this process lacked the expertise to effectively oversee such a wide-ranging transformation of life (not just economic conditions) in the communes. The more radical communes attempted to pool all land and other resources, 'and there was a widespread campaign to limit incentives by paying incomes in relation to need as well as to effort' (Howe, 1978, op.cit., p.xxviii). The peasantry resisted, and they quickly had their small private plots restored to them. The communes proved unwieldy, therefore the locus of planning and accounting was at first moved to the smaller Production Brigade (about 12,000 people, 4-500 workers), and later to the smaller Production Team of about 150 people (50-60 workers). Communes increased to 78,000 at one time, but by 1980 these stood at '54,183 communes ... with an average population of 14,967 people belonging to 3,262 households' (Leeming, 1985, p.31).

These average figures of course, belie considerable variation throughout China. Some localities were more radical in their degree of collectivisation, some were less so; some were more prosperous, others less so. Local conditions would determine the nature and shape of the commune, and in many areas the 'production brigade' would merely be the old 'village'. Ian Cook visited Zhou Lu Tain commune in November 1980. Lying 25 kilometres north-west of Guangzhou (Canton), it comprised 115 production teams, in 15 production brigades; 8,300 households with a total population of 33,000. The main crops were rice and peanut (80 per cent production) plus 20 per cent vegetables, fruit and herbs. The commune also contained 49,000 pigs and 100,000 chicken, ducks and geese.

In pre-revolutionary days, adversely affected by the dry season, and requiring great effort, production was 150 kg per *mu* (Chinese unit of land, approximately 15 to the hectare). By 1962, this figure had increased to 400 kg, up to 500 kg by 1972 and 550 kg by 1979. Incomes were 400 Yuan per head by 1979 (750 Yuan 'per manpower') plus 200 Yuan per manpower from private plots, which would make this a wealthy commune, relative to many in North China, for example. Each production brigade had a health centre, a small hospital and 140 medical workers (working in rather basic, but clean, conditions). It cost 10-20 cents per month for medical treatment, while each farmer paid 36 cents per month for the 'mutual aid system'. Eight years education was compulsory, five years primary plus three secondary, and each year the commune would send five students to college or university. The leader of the commune, Mr. Mu, when asked about the GLF summed it up by saying that 'it was good with regards to water conservancy and so on, but not with regards to the 'spirit of the people" because it had been too quick.

The 'spirit of the people' then, had been severely dented by the GLF, which was followed by bad weather conditions and several years of famine and suffering. Production figures, in both the agricultural and industrial sectors were inflated for propaganda reasons, but it rapidly became clear that this Maoist experiment had become unstuck. For example, Buchanan states that the backyard furnaces produced 4.2 million tons of pig iron and 3.1 million tons of steel, but the quality was, understandably, poor, and they had to be abandoned. The 'Walking on Two Legs Policy' continued as regards steel, but the smaller units were medium-sized blast furnaces of 200-800,000 tons capacity.

In agriculture, although it was known for many years that suffering had been caused by the harvest failures of 1959-61 (when the harvest fell to perhaps 150 million tons compared to perhaps 200-210 million tons in 1958 (Schram, 1967, p.317), it was felt by most observers that via grain imports and the organisation of the commune system, which initiated a rigorous system of rationing, China had managed to avoid the death rates of pre-Revolutionary days. It was not until the Dengist era that the Chinese authorities released figures which show that millions of deaths took place (and more millions of people were not born) as a result of the hardship of this time.

The loss of Soviet support in the Sino-Soviet split of 1960 exacerbated this situation but the Chinese economy and society recovered (albeit slowly) and the early 1960s became a period of retrenchment and rehabilitation. The worst excesses of the GLF were ameliorated, commune structures amended and China recovered reasonably effectively from this audacious experiment. Agriculture was henceforth to be the 'leading link' in economic development, with industry to be focused on the support of agriculture, producing tractors and other farm machinery, for example. Mao's power was truncated and 'moderates' came to the fore. Mao, however, saw these 'moderates' as 'rightists' or 'capitalist roaders' and saw China as backsliding from revolutionary ideals. The differences between Mao and Liu had become public after the response to Mao's 1956 campaign to 'Let a Hundred Flowers Bloom, Let a Hundred Schools of Thought Contend'. This was part of his project to develop a truly socialist culture, in his belief that criticism would help to improve government practice and overcome 'bourgeois' tendencies from the past. The criticisms turned out to be far more than Mao or others expected, so the dissent was quickly crushed. It seems clear that Liu Shaoqi disapproved of the whole campaign, and his disapproval became especially marked as problems emerged from the Great Leap Forward of 1958.

Under attack from Liu Shaoqi and others, Mao stepped down from the Presidency of the PRC but retained his Chairmanship of the CPC. Amid speculation his power had been drastically curtailed, he then laid the groundwork for the 'Socialist Education' movement from 1962-64, which in turn was to form the basis for the 'Great Proletarian Cultural Revolution'. In this, Mao swept aside party opponents by appealing directly to the young people to carry the revolution forward against the entrenched power of the bureaucracy and, indeed, the (other) CPC elders themselves. The Great Proletarian Cultural Revolution was begun in 1966 with the unleashing of the 'Red Guards', young people fortified by the thoughts of Chairman Mao, flourishing his '*Little Red Book*' and calling their parents, teachers, managers and other authority figures to account for their bourgeois misdeeds. This period was one of tremendous chaos throughout China. Economic imperatives took a back seat to ideological ones

The Cultural Revolution was part of the Maoist doctrine of permanent revolution. To avoid the danger of the CPC 'changing its colour' through being taken over by counter-revolutionaries, it was necessary 'to train and bring up millions of successors who will carry on the cause of the proletarian revolution' (Mao Zedong, 1963, cited in Schram, 1967, p.324). This was first done via the PLA who in 1964 were issued with the

Quotations from Chairman Mao, the '*Little Red Book*' as it became popularly known, and then via the Red Guards. From this time the cult of the personality would reach unprecedented heights. 'To rebel is right' was one of the key slogans, as was Mao's personal call to 'bombard the headquarters' (Blecher, 1986, p.83). The young people involved were encouraged not only to criticise Mao's enemies in the party but to subject them to vitriol and opprobrium. Thus Liu Shaoqi was denigrated as the 'Chinese Krushchev' and 'many thousands of Red Guards marched past his official residence, shouting offensive slogans, displaying insulting banners and demanding the expulsion and degradation of the chief 'revisionist taking the capitalist road" (Fitzgerald, 1977, op.cit., p.141).

At first there was no violence, with 'mass psychological pressure' being used to humiliate these 'revisionists'. Later, the movement degenerated, with parents, teachers, CPC members, officials, professors and others with 'bourgeois tendencies' (perhaps owning Western books or records, or antiques for example) being dragged from their homes, paraded through the streets wearing dunce's caps with derogatory slogans written upon them, and on occasions beaten so severely that they died of their injuries, or, if not, of the humiliations to which they were subject. One of the legacies today is that a whole generation of scholars lost their posts and there is a clear gap in research and higher education institutions between those in their mid-60s who are on the point of retiring and those in their late thirties, with relatively few in between.

Mao's last years were marked by jockeying for position of his potential successors. He himself had encouraged the rehabilitation of many of those, such as Deng Xiaoping, who had been disgraced in the early years of the Cultural Revolution, but who were opposed by the 'Gang of Four' which coalesced around Mao's wife, Jiang Qing. Mao's achievements had been vast, in keeping with the vastness of China. His failures too, had been great, but to the authors and to many in China itself, the former outweighed the latter, as was seen by the wave of nostalgia and reverence displayed during the centenary of his birth in 1993. But after his death in 1976 China was ready for an end to the 'shared poverty' of the Maoist period. It would shortly be time for that arch-survivor, Deng Xiaoping, to come into his own.

China's third revolution: Deng transforms the dream

While Mao certainly developed 'Maoism', which has had an impact beyond China's borders as a approach to revolutionary practice, it is less certain that Deng developed an equivalent approach which could be similarly labelled as 'Dengism'. His writings do not possess the grand sweep of the Maoist vision, for example, but he always had a clear vision about China's progress – economic development and material progress had to take precedence over political mobilisation. Nonetheless, the other side of the coin was his belief in the paramount role of the party, of the need to debate in order to determine policy, but once policy was decided by the collective leadership, to support it wholeheartedly, or face party disciplinary action. In the late 1950s and early 1960s Deng came to increasingly despair of Mao's 'maverick' line, and a rift grew between them. However, Goodman's biography, for example, makes clear that for many years previously, Deng Xiaoping had been a Maoist loyalist, and even after this schism the two men did not fall out at the personal level, as was true of Mao's relations with Liu Shaoqi for example. Deng was referred to as 'the number 2 person in authority taking the capitalist road' rather than being referred to by name, as was Liu Shaoqi (ibid., p.91).

Indeed, Mao seemed to admire Deng to a greater extent than many other of his contemporaries, pointing him out to Krushchev during a State visit, as 'highly intelligent' and someone who has 'a great future' (ibid., p.61). This admiration went back at least to the 1930s, when Deng was subject to party discipline as a surrogate for Mao himself (deemed to be too powerful to criticise). Years earlier, Deng had already worked with Zhou Enlai while working and studying in Europe. His revolutionary career took him from France to Moscow and then, especially, to South West China (Bose, in Guangxi province) before joining the Jiangxi Soviet and then the Long March. Himself from a peasant background (a fairly prosperous one, in Sichuan province), he proved adept as a political organiser, and strongly supported Mao's ideas of peasant-based revolution. He was sent from the Yan'an base area to the Taihang Border Region as political commissar to the 129th Division which he and Liu Bocheng eventually expanded to the 2nd Field Army, which was to play a key role in the defeat of the Guomindang.

Conditions were quite different in this Revolutionary Base Area, compared to Yan'an, with a population of five million in the Base Area alone, and sixteen million (8–30 million depending on the state of the Anti-Japanese War) in the wider border region (of Shanxi-Hebei-Shandong-Henan provinces). Goodman documents the importance of the economic and political ideas which Deng developed and applied here, for economic production (in this very poor area) was seen to be so important, while 'a parallel with the reforms Deng introduced in the 1980s, was that individuals were taxed according to their average production in previous years and allowed complete control over any surplus' (ibid., p.51). Not only did Deng demonstrate good organisational and political abilities, but he also proved to be a brave and able general, thereby establishing excellent credentials with the PLA, which were to stand him in good stead in the 'difficult years' of the 1970s and, indeed, the late 1980s.

In all, Deng was disgraced three times, in 1933, 1966 and 1976, and if this had been Stalinist Russia he would have been unlikely to survive one, certainly not two and most definitely not three of these setbacks. His contacts supported him on each occasion (in any case, re-education and rehabilitation is more a feature of the CPC than execution, at least for party discipline). He opposed Maoist concepts of mass political mobilisation, was against the repetition of the mistakes of the Great Leap Forward and objected to the thrust of the Cultural Revolution, allegedly showing his opinion of one of Jiang Qing's operas by falling asleep during the performance! In contrast, when he came to power from 1978 he was in favour of 'smashing the iron rice bowl' of work and support for life in state enterprises, of individual responsibility, realised at a household or enterprise level and of such policies as the 'Four Modernizations' and the 'Open Door Policy'. He developed a reputation abroad as a favourite-uncle character; an image which was stood on its head after Tiananmen when it became clear that he opposed Zhao Ziyang's liberal views and was the person most responsible for unleashing PLA units on the demonstrators. To many foreigners he became the 'Butcher of Beijing' instead.

This negative image was somewhat erased following his South China tour of 1992, which gave the green light for a massive surge in overseas investment, leading to the 'China Fever' which has been so important ever since. So what are we to make of his legacy to his successor, Jiang Zemin? Maoism was based on a dream of a socialist future. Deng transformed that dream; he was committed to 'building socialism with Chinese character-istics', but some have seen him as 'building China with socialist characteristics', in that he was such a strong nationalist (Parker, 1987, op.cit., p.22). Nevertheless, he *was* strongly socialist, but it was a socialism centred on the party and the State. He emphasised the 'four cardinal ['basic'] principles' which emphasise 'leadership by the Party', the 'core' of these principles (cited in Petras, 1988b)), the importance of the 'Socialist Road', the 'Proletarian Dictatorship' and 'Marxist-Leninist-Maoist Thought'. Thus, there is no desire for democratisation in the Western sense, and 'Contrary to Western views, the Chinese bureaucratic elite views political and ideological authoritarianism and market socialism as complementary' (ibid., p.240).

Deng was a key contributor to this perspective; being a rational, party-centred, state-centred, nationalistic, economic reformer. Although his daughter subsequently suggested that her father lived to regret his stance over Tiananmen, there was, to him, no contradiction between such a hard political line and the soft economic line which he promoted. As a Chinese vice-minister, Li Baoku, once put it at a visit to Sun Yat –Sen's birthplace, during an International Symposium on Urbanisation in 1995, 'Sun Yat-Sen gave the Chinese people the idea of freedom, Mao Zedong helped them to achieve it, and Deng Xiaoping gave them the money to spend when they had it'. To many, if not most Chinese, the money he gave them to spend will outweigh any concerns about Tiananmen, or about choosing leaders via the Western system of the ballot-box.

Deng Xiaoping died in February 1997. His revolution continues, and the transition to the leadership of Jiang Zemin has to date been remarkably smooth, reflecting China's political maturity, and Deng's lack of day-to-day involvement in government during his last years. Jiang is General Secretary of the CPC, State President and holder of other powerful posts. Zhu Rongji is another key figure, but at the moment the leadership has a more collective hue than it had in the heyday of Mao and Deng. Jiang Zemin (and Zhu) is one of the 'Shanghai boys', those who built their reputation primarily on running that great city as Mayor, in his case from 1985-88. His background was in Mechanical Engineering and *The Cambridge Handbook of Contemporary China* states that he was first identified publicly as director, North-East Military Engineering Department 1950 (Mackeras and Yorke, 1991, p.88). This post was followed by a range of others in engineering or electronics, import-export activities or investment, before he was appointed Minister of Electronics Industry in 1983, and soon after Mayor of Shanghai.

Jiang was elected to the Twelfth Central Committee in 1982 and the Thirteenth Party Congress Presidium and Politburo in 1987. His final breakthrough came after Tiananmen, when he replaced Zhao Ziyang as General Secretary and Deng Xiaoping as Chairman of the CPC Central Military Commission. He later became President. At first his appointment seemed something of a stopgap measure, but he has steadily built up his power base in recent years and he seems more strongly entrenched than before, drawing to different factions in the party. In large part Jiang's policies follow logically from those of Deng Xiaoping, who in turn has heavily influenced his direction. From a technocratic background he is representative of the urban modernisers who seek to continue China's development towards being a sophisticated modern society, with a strong economy.

Jiang is credited with expanding the scope of the reforms to make the programme 'a grand social systems project for the establishment of a new economic structure' (cited in Yang, 1994, p.84). It would seem that he also showed political nous in that he (and Zhu) visited personally many provincial leaders who would be likely to oppose the reforms for they sought to re-centralise the resource base, away from the province level, and persuaded them on a one-to-one basis to accept these fundamental changes. Some key leaders, as in Jiangsu for example, were sacked because they opposed the reforms (ibid., p.86). Note, however, that despite these changes being associated with Jiang that they were very much at the instigation of Deng Xiaoping, concerned lest the East European demise of communism [as it seemed at the time] would be repeated in China (ibid.).

Another aspect of the changes which he has encouraged are reforms to the state bureaucracy, via 'administrative streamlining', which was necessary because the administrative structure had to be aligned with the needs of the economy, the cost of this administration was too high, and 'with genuine political change ruled out, bureaucratic streamlining appears to offer quick results with no destabilising effects' (Saich, 1995, op.cit., p.48). These are themes with which we are familiar in the West; in China they are largely being followed through via merger of organisations, changing functions and so on, reducing the number of ministries, commissions and other bodies from eighty-six to fifty-nine, for example, and attempting to reduce the numbers of government employees, at all levels by 25 per cent, State Council personnel by one-third (ibid.). Clearly, such objectives create considerable tensions, as we shall illustrate in this book.

In October 1996, the Plenum of the Central Committee was held in Beijing. The emphasis was very much on 'control – in this case, party chief Jiang Zemin's bid to consolidate his power by dominating political discourse' (Forney, 1996, p.28), via the slogan 'socialist ethical and cultural progress'. In practice this means censorship of the media and the arts, the promotion of patriotism, and of traditional culture, which includes 'family virtues', and opposition to 'leftism'. The emphasis, as already noted, is on Confucian values as part of 'Jiang's 'spiritual civilisation' campaign, which is heavily influenced by neo-conservative ideas: pro-business but wary of markets, nationalistic, favouring strong central control over provinces and promoting an ill-defined spiritual purity to block the influx of Western ideas and values' (ibid., p.28). If this report is accurate, and there is little reason to doubt it, then Deng Xiaoping has been able to depart in peace.

The purpose of the remaining chapters of this book will be to examine key areas of Chinese life – both economic and social – for clues as to how China today is tackling the immense task of creating a socialist state, and the problems and tensions which this is throwing up. Throughout the remaining chapters, the reader would be well advised to bear in mind one lesson from 5,000 years of Chinese history – namely, that repetition tends to rule the course of events (or, more colloquially, 'there is nothing new under the sun'). The rise and fall of the various imperial dynasties displays a pattern of recurrent phases that cannot be ignored. The progress, as Owen Lattimore, for one, described it, is:

'First, increasing returns as the result of concentrating people in favorable areas in order to organize them in water-conservancy works on a large scale and for the practice of agriculture. Second, apparent stability, as production reaches its peak by means of those activities, and those who controlled the order of the state settled down to maintain the working of the order and to discourage all initiatives that trended away from it. Third, diminishing returns because the social system emphasised large families while the economic system resisted new kinds of activities to employ the surplus manpower. An oversupply of human labour was a condition of prosperity of those who lived by the control of law, order and tradition.

Out of this was bred agrarian depression and collapse, and more and more intolerable contrasts between the few who were literate, sophisticated, well-to-do and ordained to rule, and the illiterate, many of whom, were ordained to live by their muscle but who were denied the right to work and life if the market was oversupplied with muscle. Fourth, agrarian uprisings, which destroyed the state' (Lattimore, op.cit., p.45).

Many of the conditions which have just been described can be discerned today, and will be dealt with in due turn over the next nine chapters. We consider the tensions around the revitalisation of China's State-Owned Enterprises (Chapter 2) and in particular the steel industry (Chapter 3). In Chapter 4 we examine the serious issue of regional disparities which have potent rural (Chapter 5) and ethnic minorities (Chapter 6) dimensions. China's urban explosion is the focus of Chapter 7 and within cities, the concern to provide adequate supplies of affordable housing (Chapter 8). Chapter 9 focuses on the environmental deterioration which is fast-developing as another hindrance to China's development trajectory. Finally, we pull the different themes together in Chapter 10 via consideration of alternative scenarios for the future of China. China faces a wide range of internal and external threats. How the country, government and the people respond to these will have a marked impact in the twenty-first century, not just in China but due to its growing importance, also at the global level.

CHAPTER 2

Reforming the Public Sector

The Chinese Government has identified revitalisation of the state-owned sector as crucial to the country's future economic direction, raising the question of whether, having moved from a centrally-planned economy to a market-oriented one, the continuation of a broad state-run sector is justified. There has been a continuous search for ways to reform the system that creates efficiency, but retains the State-owned sector as the industrial core – with the oft-repeated statement by party and government leaders that without state-owned enterprises there can be no socialism. Because various weaknesses of the former planned system which have survived represent the most difficult link in the transformation process to a market economy.

This chapter will examine the following elements:

- The need for reform
- The initial experiments
- 'Grasp the big and forget the small'
- Coping with excess labour
- Increased management powers a myth?
- Success stories

This will then lead into the following chapter, where the experiences of a specific sector – the steel industry – will be examined.

The need for reform

In the 1950s, China rapidly constructed a Soviet-type planning system, replacing the 'anarchy of the market' with a state-administered plan. Almost all the means of production were nationalised or transferred to ownership by 'collectives', which operated mostly as de facto state-owned institutions. Planners directly determined all significant variables, including

23

enterprise inputs, output levels, product mix and prices. Competition, entrepreneurial activity and the pursuit of profit were eliminated; no longer would enterprises compete with each other; the factories, workshops, mines and other productive institutions would, in effect, become 'sub-divisions of one vast people's workshop' (Bukharin and Preobrazhensky, 1969, p114).

But, as Soviet planners first, and their Chinese counterparts later, discovered, this has fundamental flaws. Plans can only be as good as the information on which they are based. Enterprises have strong incentive to provide false information in order to obtain easily attainable targets – understating true productive potentialities and inflating input needs to make output goals easier to attain. The number of decisions in even a simple plan is astonishingly large because of the feedback effect of one decision on others. This can engender conservatism, as it is easier to work incrementally from the previous plan than attempt major changes of direction. To determine centrally all decisions is well-nigh impossible, as China soon found during its First Five Year Plan (1953–7), so that a great deal of detailed planning had to be done at lower administrative levels, with only the simplest of exchanges of major commodities occurring between regions. This reinforced other pressures towards regional and sectoral self-sufficiency, with all the resulting costs in terms of opportunities foregone for trade and specialisation. Big was considered best. By the 1970s, for example, around 26 per cent of China's industrial output was produced in a small number of large plants, 18 per cent produced in medium-sized plants and 56 per cent produced in small-scale, mainly urban and state-run (Nolan and Dong Fureng, 1990, pp.4–5). In each of the subsequent Five-Year plans another difficulty in central planning emerged: achieving a balance of inputs and outputs. What usually happened was simultaneous shortage and surplus throughout the system. In the 1980s, for example, there were severe shortages of iron ore, non-ferrous metals, construction materials, transport equipment and energy. However, in 1980, the value of stockpiles of machinery and equipment was greater than the year's total capital produced in unneeded varieties (ibid.).

The fact that enterprises were uncertain about receiving inputs created a tendency to hoard, exacerbating shortage. Thus, there was a high level of capital accumulation wastefully tied up in stocks. If a plan is to balance at all, output must be the key success indicator by which enterprises are rewarded. But, of the many difficulties this creates, none is more fundamental than trying to stimulate enterprises to innovate. The primacy of output targets combines with the unreliability of material supplies tends to produce a powerful anti-innovation bias. Because Chinese economic planning originally followed the Soviet pattern, the emphasis was nearly always on substantial growth in heavy industry with only secondary attention to other parts of the economy. For example, 'at some periods the machine-building industry produced machine tools but insufficient equipment for agriculture, food processing, manufacture of consumer goods etc. Steel mills produced semi-finished products that light industry was not equipped to process further, but produced no materials for steel window frames or wire and nails. Heavy industry received large appropriations for new facilities and products, while light industry could secure little in the way of materials, funds or facilities' (Etheridge, p.83).

Specialised ministries traditionally dealt with each industrial sector, with various subordinate administrative units dealing with specific aspects of the business, such as finance, materials or labour. In the early 1990s, there were at least 100 separate central government departments employing forty million people, although an organisational reform programme adopted in 1993 reduced the number of administrative bodies to forty-one (*Beijing Review*, 16-8-1993), and a further drastic reduction took place in 1998. For many key products, there are a minimum of six levels of authority required to rubber-stamp the decisions taken at factory level. One major industrial project required the seals of 860 offices at central, provincial and local level before final approval could be achieved (Murray, 1994, p.35).

At the bottom of the ladder, individual enterprises tended to receive insufficient attention because the administrative units above them had their own interests, as well as other enterprises to worry about. This created the ludicrous situation, cited by the director of a large Shanghai research institute, of management not even being able to buy something as simple as a packet of tea (ibid.). Factory managers also faced further official interference at shop floor level. From 1956, when the Communist Party began to extend its grip to all aspects of daily life, a party committee was installed in each enterprise to which its directors were responsible. The committee had to approve all decisions, so that it was the in-house party secretary who really controlled the enterprise. And, while the former might be skilled in political manoeuvring he did not necessarily have much idea about how to run a business. Ideology – and preservation of the status quo – tended to triumph over business common sense.

The initial experiments

It is crucial to understand the important role state enterprises still play, despite the reforms which will be described in due course. There are still 79,000 of them across the country. The proportion of taxes handed in by state enterprises, the proportion of state enterprise staff to total urban employment, and that of fixed assets of state industry in total industrial fixed assets are all around two-thirds. The SOEs dominate the raw material, heavy chemical and other basic industries. For example, they have a 70–100 per cent share in oil, metallurgy, electric power, chemical raw materials and medicine, and a 30–50 per cent share in food processing, machine-building, electronics and machinery, textiles, paper-making, electrical machinery

(Prime Minister Zhu Rongji, March 1998). Table 2.1 shows the top 25 SOEs in 1998 as calculated by the government, from which it can be seen that they are concentrated in three industrial sectors – automobiles, iron and steel, and petroleum-petrochemicals.

By the early 1980s, it was already apparent that economic reforms instituted a few years earlier by Deng Xiaoping could not achieve the expected results. Hence, Deng opted to give the factory director full responsibility for the day-to-day running of the enterprise, relegating the party secretary to a secondary role. But, with bureaucrats and party activists fearful of their power being diminished, it took four years before the Factory Director Responsibility System (FDRS) gained sufficient support to be introduced on an experimental basis in six cities – although it was subsequently adopted rapidly throughout the country. Yet, continuous decline in overall SOE performance into the 1990s clearly showed this was not the best way to achieve efficiency. The economic growth rate of the non-state economy has been consistently faster than that

Table 2.1 Top 25 Industrial Companies in 1998

1	Shanghai Automobile Industry Corp.
2	Daqing Petroleum Administration
3	Anshan Iron & Steel Co.
4	China No. Motor Vehicle Group
5	Baoshan Iron & Steel Complex
6	Dongfeng Automobile Co.
7	Capital Iron & Steel Corp.
8	Shengli Petroleum Administrative Bureau
9	Shengli Petroleum Administrative Bureau
10	Wuhan Iron & Steel Co.
11	Yanshan Petrochemical Corp.
12	Liaohe Petroleum Exploration Bureau
13	Xinjing Petroleum Administration
14	Qilu Petrochemical Corp.
15	Fushun Petrochemical Corp.
16	Shanghai Petrochemical Joint-Stock Co., Ltd
17	Panzhihua Iron & Steel Corp.
18	Daqing Petrochemical Complex
19	Jilin Chemical Group
20	Maoming Petroleum Industrial Corp.
21	Tianjin Motor Industry Co.
22	Baotou Steel & Rare Earth Co.
23	Jinling Petrochemical Corp.
24	China Heavy Automobile Group
25	Shanghai Gaoqiao Petrochemical Corp.

Source: China Internet Information Centre, www.chinanews.org.

of the state economy ever since the reforms were begun, as shown in Tables 2.2 and 2.3.

The key factors for this poor performance appear to have been:

1. Firms relying too much on the government rather than seizing the chances offered by various management responsibility systems;
2. Producers slow to react to the market;
3. Bureaucrats reluctant to give managers full responsibility to make individual decisions which would allow factories to reduce stockpiles and production cost;
4. The market mechanism unable to work because state enterprises are not really businesses but welfare societies;
5. Management and workers unwilling to accept that wages and bonuses were not a divine right but closely linked to performance.

Admittedly, the proportion of industrial fixed assets in the state economy has declined – from 88.9 per cent in 1981 to 80.7 per cent in 1990, and 68.8 per cent in 1995 – while the proportion of employees has fallen from 51.5 per cent in 1978 to 45 per cent in 1990 and 40 per cent in 1995 (CASS, 1995). Yet, it does not appear that the rapid growth of the non-state sector will be enough to mop up surplus labour from the inefficient state sector, nor the vast army of unemployed peasants now pouring into the cities in search of jobs, so that more pro-active measures are needed.

The first stage in the reform process in the 1980s was to separate the relationship between ownership and management of enterprises, giving them more autonomy in the day-to-day running of their business operations – responsible for their own profits and losses, product mix and production

Table 2.2 Performance of State Industrial Sector 1985–95

Year	Profit Rate (%)	Loss-makers (%)
1985	13.5	9.7
1990	3.2	27.6
1995	1.8	33.8

Source: Chinese Academy of Social Science (CASS), 1995, Beijing.

Table 2.3 Growth Comparisons State/Non-State Sectors 1978–95

	State	Non-State
Growth of Total Output Value 1978–90 (%)	7.6	20.1
Average Annual growth 1991–5	8.3	31.1

Source: CASS, 1995, Beijing.

levels. By the late 1990s, the main aim was to create a number of state-run conglomerates transcending the whole narrowly-defined industrial boundaries of central planning – spreading not only across different sectors but also erasing provincial boundaries and even national boundaries. The government promised to pump in as much money as was needed in order to ensure the success of these corporate groups, while cutting adrift the smaller and medium-sized enterprises to find their own niche, perhaps through worker buyouts to form co-operatives or through acquisition of the weak by the more successful, and even by allowing foreign investors to buy into and even control them (Murray, 1998). Especially since 1994, great changes have taken place. Due to the fast-track development of the non-state economy, state enterprises have lost the super-profit reward for products out of the state plan. The price changes of most means of production from former planned or double-track prices to market prices have also deprived state enterprises of the low preferential treatment they previously received. Reform of financial and monetary system, and the development of the capital market and monetary system, further deprived state enterprises of the previous fund supply which was lower than market cost. The development of the labour market and the reform in the social security system have increased labour costs.

There are many problems in the operation of state enterprises that don't suit the market economy. Some are natural, some habitual and others formed during operation. Major problems include the fact that state enterprises:

- bear the industrial distribution costs left over from the era of a planned economy;
- have a high capital liability rate caused by lacking reasonable amount of capital and funds;
- have a heavy social security burden;
- have difficulties identifying the property rights of the enterprises and in assuming sole responsibility for its profits or losses.

SOEs with various heavy burdens and all kinds of defects cannot expect equal competition with their essentially burden-free flexible non-state counterparts. For instance, many have had to retreat from the clothing manufacturing industry or announce bankruptcy, and now occupy less than seven per cent of the sector (*China Daily*, 3-5-1998).

The operational environment of state enterprises recently has experienced much change in terms of products, market factors, prices and trade, which have adopted ways suitable to a market economy. They have been set free to a large extent from state control and have entered the market. Production and overall operational decision-making of enterprises are mainly or completely in accordance with market changes. Firms can enjoy the increased income brought along with the enhanced operational interests, and must undergo ever-increasing competitive pressure and bear the over-clarified responsibility for operational loss as well.. But many companies have been hobbled in their attempt to compete by an expanding debt burden left over from the former operational system (see Box 2.1).

Box 2.1 Main Causes of State Owned Enterprise Debt

The excessive debt burden of SOEs emerged while the old system was being replaced. Six key problems can be identified:

1. Low economic efficiency detrimental to the debt-equity ratio. Enterprises consistently reporting profits between 1991 and 1995 had a debt-equity ratio of 65.1 per cent; those making losses had a ratio as high as 99.65 per cent.

2. Policy Changes. After the State began providing loans instead of appropriating funds in 1983, some newly-established SOEs lost their sources of state funding. Some of those established in the early years of reform borrowed heavily and started life heavily in debt.

3. Imperfect capital fund system. The state has been drawing funds from enterprises over a long period. The main source is a 'depreciation charge' which must be handed over from the enterprise's capital funds. Without any new investment from the state, enterprises have to rely on loans for renovation. With outdated equipment, factories cannot renovate; renovation, however, brings new debts.

4. Poor profit retention and heavy social burden. For quite a long period of time, the SOEs have had a low level of profit retention, while at the same time bearing a heavy burden for the social security of their staff and funds for the construction of educational and medical facilities. Being in a poor position to accumulate funds themselves, the enterprises have to rely on loans to expand their production scale.

5. Excessive enterprise investment and duplication of projects. Since China implemented the reform policies, SOEs have been granted more power in making decisions concerning their management, including investment. But the problem that they are only responsible for their profits and not their losses has not been solved, resulting in a strong desire to increase investment which tends to lead to more debt. Many enterprises have adopted a blind attitude towards investment without thinking about the cost of raising capital, the efficiency of the investment and their ability to pay back loans. The former close relationship between banks and enterprises encouraged increased investment and led to project duplication and losses for everyone.

Source: CASS, op.cit., 1995, Beijing.

Since 1994, the state specialised banks, who provided the bulk of funds for the state sector by lending under government instruction (currently the main cause of bank indebtedness from non-collectible loans) have changed their role to become commercial banks and the division by specialisation has been eliminated, creating more competition. In addition, about a dozen commercial banks have been established, while dozens of city Cooperative banks and foreign-owned banks are attracting deposits. The changes in the banking system have brought about a change of fund supply relations between banks and enterprises and strengthened the lending-borrowing relationship. The banks now consider risk, and lend money to market-oriented and promising enterprises. The Industrial and Commercial Bank of China, for example, has implemented a loan management system based on investment risk in order to strengthen the management of loans and improve their quality. The banks have devoted great efforts to promoting mortgage and guarantee loans and reduced the amount of credit loans, with the former now accounting for about four-fifths of off lending activity. They have established a post-lending auditing and examination system. There is a trend towards linking increased loans with the economic operation of undertakings.

Banks offer preferential treatment for those enterprises with good production and sales, a high recovery efficiency of sales, rapidly increasing profits and tax payments, and a low equity-debt ratio. They also link new loans with the results of enterprise efforts to increase profits and reduce losses, and increase existing loans based on fulfilment of management targets, capital turnover, increase of circulating funds and repayment of loan capital plus interest. They have also begun linking increased loans with enterprise efforts to clear up their debts and decrease product stocks. Banks refuse to provide loans to those enterprises with poor payment records, and the tardy acceptance of bills and payment of old debts. Finally, banks insist that enterprises first demonstrate they have tried to increase their circulating funds by their own efforts before seeking further loans. Thus, as the economic system is shifting to the market economy the relationship between banks and enterprises is changing. But it is very difficult to establish a normal relationship between banks and enterprises when the latter are burdened with debt. As a result, the commercialisation of state-owned banks has been held back.

'Grasp the big, forget the small'

In March 1998, the struggling rust-belt city of Shenyang, with an unemployment rate approaching 29 per cent, made investors an offer it hoped they couldn't refuse: own a former state-owned company for just one Yuan. Fifty medium and small state-owned enterprises were put on sale (Xinhua, 21-3-1998). Those firms whose net value had been assessed at nil or in the red would cost one Yuan. Buyers of the defunct firms received breaks on settlements with employees, debts and taxes. They would not have to repay debts to banks for up to two years, and other creditors would have to be flexible. Buyers who agreed to take on a firm's old work force could expect further relief, city officials promised.

This is part of a central government policy described as 'grasping the big and forgetting the small.' Since the initiation of reform, SOEs have gradually changed from being controlled by and relying on the government to entering the market on their own. One of the key steps is to sweep away the thousands of small factories responsible for billions of dollars in wasted production, while seeking a variety of ways to salvage those that still have some potential after a complete revamp and under new ownership. In 1999, the government ordered party and administrative organs to break their links with enterprises operating under their umbrellas, following a similar order the previous year to the army, armed police and public security organisations to divest themselves of all business operations and turn them over to civilian control. More than 500 large enterprises under the direct control of government organisations were to be supervised and co-ordinated by the 'Large Enterprise Work Committee' set up under the State Council in late 1998. Finance and investment companies tied to the bureaucracy would be temporarily administered by the Ministry of Finance and the People's Bank of China. Smaller enterprises will be taken over by related local industrial authorities.

This is a crucial step. Vested interests in some government institutions have prevented the reform of State enterprises from deepening. 'We would lose some big contracts usually guaranteed by our parent ministry if our company were separated,' lamented one company official. For years, many enterprises subordinate to government organisations took advantage of their unique privileges in applying for loans, gaining quotas for listing on stock exchanges, soliciting foreign investment, and receiving tax breaks. The government sees the move as helping set up a fair and transparent market competition mechanism.

Many of the enterprises no longer wanted were mostly created during the Mao era. They have accumulated massive stockpiles of unsold consumer goods, from men's shirts to women's bicycles, and are a growing liability. The National Council of Light Industry, for example, proposed to merge all the manufacturing of consumer goods into 100 publicly-traded conglomerates by the turn of the century with the help of government funding. Industry should become more competitive by merging larger enterprises and annexing weaker ones. It calculated that most of China's 2,046 counties are home to 'food, beer, shoe, plastic and paper factories,' with excess capacity, sloppy production and warehouses full of unsold goods.

Hu Nan, the National Council's chief planner, lamented that the sector had 'long been plagued with poor structure'. Most state manufacturers of consumer products operated at less than half capacity in 1996. Yet factories still reported stockpiles of 1.5 billion men's shirts, 10 million watches, tons of cosmetics, 20 million bicycles, 678,000 motorcycles, at least 116,000 cars and millions of dollars in unsold appliances. According to Hu, many companies had blindly invested in low-tech products without considering the whole market and existing production capacity, resulting in a market glut of low-tech products. For example, of 800 breweries operating nation-wide, only 10 per cent are capable of annually producing more than 50,000 tonnes of beer; all but 15 of China's 200 motorcycle manufacturers are incapable of producing 100,000 motorcycles a year; more than 6,000 rural paper mills have average yearly production of 4,000 tonnes, less than a 10th of the world average in the paper sector; thirty 'hopeless' state-owned car-makers have a total output of four vehicles a week, on average. Mainland factories have stockpiled a record $60.2 billion worth of goods, the equivalent of more than a quarter of the nation's 1996 industrial output (author interview, 1997).

Of all the business ventures gone awry, none ever mastered the concept of futility like Qingdao's Textile Mill No. 9. At the state-owned mill, workers and managers produce garments nobody needs at a price no one can afford – that is, when they make anything at all. In pre-communist China, the mill ran at a profit for thirty years. Now, as a state-run enterprise, the company bends all the laws of economics to breaking point. Xie Siliang, director of the mill, explained: 'It has been a very heavy burden for state-run factories (since the 1979 reforms). We are facing some difficulties.' The factory has 3,000 workers, a further 2,000 employees on pensions, plus the cost of a health plan and schooling to cover. Monthly production costs include $210,800 in wages and $192,800 for interest charges on old debts at a state-owned bank. Management has spent nothing on new equipment since 1985.

Mr Xie admitted: 'All our products are very ordinary, and not competitive.' Allied to this, government-fixed prices for labour, cotton and electricity have risen steadily in recent years.' Even a 10-year contract to supply uniforms to the PLA was not enough to get the No. 9 mill back in the black. Management was desperate to score another bank loan to upgrade the plant's antique looms and perhaps to merge with a slightly less inefficient mill in Inner Mongolia (author research).

The World Bank describes the state sector as a 'drag on growth and employment creation' (World Development Report 1996), with combined debts of more than $620 billion, and insists 'heavy losers, with little future, need to be closed down'. Yet China's mines, mills and factories received more than $10.6 billion in loans in the first half of 1996. Annual write-offs on bad debts would average $20 billion by December, the Bank said.

Qingdao, an old German-built port in Shandong Province, is typical of the country's heavily subsidised industrial regions. Seventy per cent of the work force is employed by state enterprises. Yu Zhengsheng, Qingdao's Party Secretary, said that in the heyday of state planning, 'We preferred that everybody worked. But we paid no attention to efficiency. It will take a fairly long time for Qingdao companies to get in a better situation'. Of 20 factories run by Qingdao's Municipal State Assets Commission in 1992, all but four remained in business in late 1997 despite marginal operations. Bankruptcy is not a genuine option. Instead, mergers are common. Thus, in Qingdao, the managers of a failing State-owned pencil factory were appointed to run a failing State-owned hotel. Nobody seemed to mind, least of all the workers guaranteed 80 per cent of their salary while awaiting reassignment. 'The performance has been very satisfactory,' boasted one city official.

With the reform and opening policies, the government has gradually relaxed its control over the planning of enterprises. The quotas of government planned output of the key enterprises during the 1990s dropped from a quarter to less than a fifth; more than 95 per cent of product prices are decided by the market, and only about 30 per cent are influenced by the government in any way (CASS, op.cit, 1995).

The major competition comes from the non-state sector, and it is the main market force promoting the need for change. The competition among state-owned enterprises is definitely greater than before, but there are still about a third still regarded as 'not having joined the competition' (ibid.). Faced with increased competition, 35.4 per cent of SOEs in the 1995 CASS survey felt they were worse off than before, especially with regard to the changes in the provision of raw materials and prices, while 43 per cent believed they were not quite adaptable. The traditional 'bottlenecks' from scarcity of raw materials, electricity and energy seem to have been mitigated to a large extent, and many enterprises feel they are getting on top of the redundant worker issue. It is the change in the environment regarding the provision of capital that is the major problem – whether it is the short-term circulating funds, long-term investment loans, defaults on fund movements among enterprises, or heavy debts incurred by enterprises. More than half of the enterprises felt their situation was worsening, especially given the government's inflation-battling budgetary restraints instituted from 1994.

Having gone through more than a decade of reform, most state-owned enterprises now have some understanding of how to deal with market competition. Therefore, the question of change is not that simple, in the sense that as long as there is market competition, the problems of the SOEs could in theory be solved. To know how to compete, and whether one has the internal motivation to do so, however, are two different matters. Any improvement in the efficiency of enterprises in recent years, most managers believe, is due to the improvement in the autonomous decision-making and management powers of managers. Secondly, it is related to the improvement in the enthusiasm of workers and staff. Thirdly, it is due to the role played by market demand.

The *Law of the People's Republic of China Concerning Industrial Enterprises Owned by the Whole People*, promulgated in 1988, stipulated that state-owned enterprises have decision-making power in 13 fields of management. *The Regulations on Shifting Operating Mechanism of Industrial Enterprises Owned by the Whole People* published in 1992 listed 14 items of decision-making power that state-owned enterprises would have in regard to their management. But the main sticking point was that the state, as owner or the main holder of the assets, should have control, which continues to limit managerial decision-making powers. There were many differences over what kinds of power the state should retain.

Among the problems that quickly emerged was the legal position of enterprises. The 14 fields in which the enterprises had decision-making power did not contain the full rights needed as an 'independent legal person' as defined by the law to compete in the marketplace. So, the *Regulations on the Supervision and Management of the Property of State-Owned Enterprises,* promulgated in 1994, explained the concept of the property rights of the legal persons of the enterprise, while still leaving somewhat unclear the managerial decision-making powers.

Enterprises are granted the property rights of legal persons and they have the right to budget independently the property to whose management they have been entrusted by the state according to the law. The government and supervisory department have no right to budget directly the property rights of the legal persons of enterprises, are prevented from drawing from the capital fund in any form, take away the property of the enterprises and ask for any expenses from them under any name. The state bears the duty for the debts as it invests in the enterprises, while the latter bear a civil duty for their debts with the total property. These are grey areas that continue to be a source of contention between bureaucrat and businessman.

To most SOEs, however, the importance of the reforms is that they have begun to achieve independent decision-making power, no matter how imperfectly, moving step by step from a passive entity dictated by a rigid plan to become a mainstay of the market able to take initiatives to optimise their on interests and benefits in terms of day-to-day production management, namely on production volume, variety of products, sales and prices (although there has been both forward and backward movement in this area).

To draw together the various complex strands of SOE organisation reform, Box 2.2 provides a brief chronology of the policy changes.

Coping with excess labour

How independent are State enterprises in reality? In the area of labour, enterprises have much less power over recruiting and discharging their staff,

---

Box 2.2 An Outline of State Enterprise History

In the 1950s, State enterprises contributed 40 per cent of the country's gross industrial output.

In the 1960s, their share of industrial output rose to 90 per cent. The government planned everything and took all the profits.

Between 1978 and 1983, the central government let State enterprises decide on their own operations and keep part of profits they made.

Between 1983 and 1986, State firms began to hand in 55 per cent of their profits in taxes.

Between 1987 and 1993, they were allowed to adopt leasing and contract responsibility systems to stimulate production.

Since 1993, the government has begun to restructure the State enterprises according to the modern enterprise system, selling off small firms, introducing shareholding and joint stock systems, and establishing large conglomerates.

Source: Author research.

---

and the pace of loosening up is also much slower, with only about half estimated to have been given this power by the mid-1990s. Since this is related to the questions of social security and unemployment, the power exercised by enterprises seems to depend to a large extent on the establishment of a social welfare system.

Generally speaking, the state-owned enterprises now have the power to discharge staff who have violated discipline or factory rules and regulations, but these represent an infinitesimal number and can be largely ignored. But those staff who have no disciplinary problems and are merely redundant, must first be laid off. Those laid off for a long period tend to find a more suitable job and will not wish to return to the previous enterprise. Through this process, enterprises can then formally discharge them, hopefully easing the tension that might arise from more typical Western practices. But this still tends to leave enterprises with the burden of supporting surplus workers whether on the premises and idle, or staying at home.

At the same time, there are social pressures not to get rid of workers simply because they are surplus to requirements. This is partly a hangover from the Mao era, when work units provided the only social security available. Managers, therefore, find themselves pulled both ways. They are urged by their government masters to slim down, become efficient, by trimming the payroll. At the same time, they are under pressure not to exacerbate the rising social tensions caused by more jobless workers with little or no hope of ever being employed again.

China, in 1997, claimed an urban jobless rate of three per cent, but these figures exclude redundant state employees or its 134 million surplus farm workers. Western analysts have calculated true unemployment at anything from 11 per cent, according to the World Bank, to a high of 20 per cent. Many laid-off workers are sceptical of the official unemployment figures, believing the government understates them for fear that it would reflect badly on communism and encourage social disorder. What also distorts the figure is that many workers are laid off by their companies but are still officially 'on the books' so that technically, at least, they aren't 'unemployed'. According to Deputy Minister of Labour and Social Security Wang Jianlun, the mainland planned to lay off another seven million workers from state enterprises in 1999, one million more than the previous year, which would cost it 24.5 billion Yuan in welfare payments (*China Daily*, 14-4-1999).

The government officially says that with readjustment of the economic structure, it will be hard 'to avoid the flow of personnel and lay-offs' and 'all workers should change their ideas about employment and improve their own quality to meet the new requirements of reform and development'. Table 2.4 illustrates the impact on jobs of the rationalisation plans for selected key industries, while Box 2.3 looks at the issue from the viewpoint of a key industry – textiles.

There is recognition that one of the most intractable problems in the state sector is featherbedding. Firms traditionally took on far more workers than they really needed more as a form of social welfare, safe in the knowledge that they would be subsidised by the government. There is growing recognition such benevolence can no longer continue. The State sector can only prosper if the lame ducks are allowed to cease business, if the work force is dramatically cut, or vast amounts of money injected so that millions of new jobs are continually created year after year. If the government were to carry out this programme with the ruthlessness required, millions more inevitably would be thrown out of work, with many probably remaining unemployed long-term.

Table 2.4 Targets for Workforce Rationalisation by 2000

Sector	Current Workforce	Planned Cuts
Iron and Steel	3.3 million	700,000
Coal Mining	5.2 million	1 million
Aviation	560,000	150,000
Shipbuilding	300,000	60–120,000
Railways	2.25 million	240,000
Petrochemical	660,000	218,000

Box 2.3 Textile Industry Restructuring

Some 1.2 million workers were due to lose their jobs between 1998 and 2000 in the troubled textile sector, as part of the government's attempt to salvage this former pillar industry of the Chinese economy. Of this number, 600,000 jobs were scheduled to go in 1998. The State Economic and Trade Commission said that to cushion the blow, unemployed textile workers would be given priority in obtaining new jobs ahead of workers to be made redundant in other industries.

It is a sign of the seriousness of the textile industry's difficulties that the government is willing to risk urban social unrest by ending the job-for-life guarantee for so many workers in one sector concentrated in key cities like Shanghai. In fact, government officials concede it has become the most difficult state sector to bail out. According to official statistics, it saw five straight years of growing deficits – from 1.9 billion Yuan in 1993 to 10.6 billion Yuan in 1997. It is reckoned that loss-making textile companies, with 1.8 million employees, account for almost one-fifth of the nation's loss-making companies. Apart from the redundancies, the China National Textile Council (CNTC) plans to scrap 10 million outdated spindles over the three year period, including 4.8 million this year. The scrapping drive will start in the coastal areas (*Business Weekly*, 16-11-1997).

At the same time, the government is taking steps to revive the slimmed down industry. One key step is the increase in export rebate rates from nine to 11 per cent, retroactive to January 1998, which will mean an extra three billion Yuan in refunds. This is an obvious move as textiles have been the engine driving China's exports for many years, with more than half its output intended for overseas markets. Since 1996, however, the industry has lost its leading position. Its export volume in that year dropped to 38 billion Yuan, lagging behind shipments of machinery and electronic products (*China Daily*, 17-2-1998).

Although there was a slight upturn in 1997, the major increase came from exports of goods made from imported materials, while general exports (from domestic raw materials) actually declined. But only the latter enjoy export tax rebates, so the increased rate may have a positive impact. In 1996, the government refunded a total of 82.8 billion Yuan to exporters through the rebate scheme, but cut this to 43.2 billion Yuan in 1997 as part of the program to eliminate budgetary deficits. Besides the export tax rebates, the government plans to offer preferential policies on export quotas and financial subsidies. The reserve fund available to eliminate companies' bad loans was expanded from 9.73 billion Yuan in 1997 to 19.73 billion Yuan in 1998.

At the national working conference of textile industry officials, co-sponsored by the State Economic and Trade Commission (SETC) and

CNTC in December 1997, Vice-Premier Wu Bangguo said the industry's deficit would be cut by three billion Yuan in 1998. Companies are also being encouraged to engage in mergers and restructure their capital structure (i.e. become shareholding entities) to become more efficient. In 1996, more than 280 companies were merged to form 100 conglomerates (*Business Weekly*, 21-11-1997).

Another alternative is diversification. Suffering from rising costs and a slumping market, many cotton mills in Shanghai, for example, are gradually retreating from their core business and moving into the service sector. One such plant is the Shanghai No 6 Cotton Mill, a State-owned enterprise that once worked more than 80,000 spindles to produce cotton yarn and other primary textile materials. Now, it has teamed up with the Shanghai Lianjia Supermarket Co Ltd to open a supermarket employing about 150 laid-off workers. The plant has already started a real estate project in co-operation with a property firm from Hainan Province in the far south. It began the diversification in June 1996, at a time when it had accumulated debts of 129 million Yuan. To date, it has set up five companies dealing in trade and catering services. Its textile trading company alone generated around US$100,000 in profits last year. Meanwhile, the plant has also acquired five township textile enterprises near Shanghai valued at 50 million Yuan. Currently, the plant's debt-asset ratio had fallen to 65 per cent from 84.1 per cent in June 1997 (*Shanghai Liberation Daily*, 3-11-1997).

Sources: *Business Weekly*, 16-11-1997, 21-11-1997
China Daily, 17-2-1998
Shanghai Liberation Daily, 3-11-1997

One leading economist has warned that this will lead to soaring unemployment on an unprecedented scale in the coming years. Feng Lanrui predicted the jobless rate could approach 28 per cent by the end of the century, adding that his forecast was in line with international trends and showed the mainland's unemployment problem was far more serious than the Government admitted. 'I did my calculation basically using statistics provided by the Ministry of Labour,' he said. 'The finding may be a little shocking but I feel a responsibility to society' (author interview, 15-3-1998).

The issue of just what constitutes the real level of the country's jobless rate dominated discussions at the first session of the Ninth National People's Congress (NPC) in March 1998, where Labour Minister Li Boyong sought to quell delegates' fears by expressing his confidence that China could tame unemployment. He said more jobs would be created as the country's economy continued to grow. But Feng said the official predictions did not take into account 214 million surplus rural labourers who would be seeking work in cities. According to him, it was likely the Government would find work for 77 million of these, leaving 137 million out of work. In addition, he estimated about 15 million workers would be laid off from state-owned enterprises. To this figure, at least temporarily, it was necessary to add four million civil servants losing their jobs in a massive government organisation involving the disappearance of 11 ministries.

Despite Labour Minister Li's optimism, the structural aspect of the unemployment problem is the most worrying. Typically, laid-off workers are older and have a low educational level, making it hard for them to be re-employed in an increasingly high-tech economy. According to State Statistics Bureau 1997 figures, 28.9 per cent of laid-off employees had been out of work between six and 12 months, 16.9 per cent for one to two years, and 14 per cent had been idle for more than two years.

> 'Most laid-off employees are eager to find new jobs. But there is not much hope for them of doing so, or of getting back their former jobs because of their relatively older age and low educational and technical levels. Many also have a traditional view of employment. They are accustomed to the planned economy in which jobs were assigned by the State. They still think that only working in the State sector and being permanent workers or long-term contract workers can be considered employment. Instead of actively looking for employment opportunities, they hope that the State will assign them jobs again' (*China Labour News*, 12.2.98).

According to a joint investigation in 1997 by four government organs in Wuhan, capital of Hubei Province, 48.5 per cent of laid-off employees were aged from 36–45. In the same year, Beijing Statistics Bureau made an investigation among 2,500 laid-off employees and found that 52.9 per cent of them were aged 36–45. According to the State Statistics Bureau, 56.8 per cent of laid-off employees in 1997 had junior high school education and 13.8 per cent only primary school education, or less (*Outlook*, 22.2.98). The number of laid-off employees is especially high in economically backward regions. For example, in West China where the economic development level is comparatively low, many laid-off employees have had difficulty finding new jobs. But in richer, coastal provinces in South and East China, there are more employment opportunities. In addition, redundant employees there tend to be more accustomed to the market-economy mechanism and can cope better with redundancy and finding a new job. This issue will be considered later in this book in connection with the issue of regional inequality.

Laid-off employees are largely from struggling sectors such as the military industry, coal industry, forestry, machinery manufacturing and textiles. They seldom come from new sectors, such as high-tech industry, tourism, real estate, finance and insurance, said the newspaper. And many are in financial difficulties. The Wuhan investigation previously cited found 50.2 per cent of retrenched workers in the city's industrial sector lived on monthly allowances of less than 120 Yuan, lower than the city's guaranteed minimum level standard of living. Given all these facts, what then of socialism that promised so much?. After all, job insecurity was one of the worst aspects of the bad old days that the Communists pledged were gone for good with the liberation of 1949.

There is also a gender inequality operative. A few years ago, the proportion of laid-off female employees was not much higher than that of males. But in recent years, the proportion of laid-off females has been markedly higher than that of the males. In addition, the proportion of laid-off women who later find new jobs tends to be much lower than that of men. Box 2.4 illustrates some of the problems facing the most vulnerable working group of all – middle-aged women. Women can feel somewhat betrayed in that it was Chairman Mao himself who urged them to abandon the home and gain equality at the workbench with the men. Equality, however, seems to go out of the window when it comes to retrenchment.

Increased management powers a myth?

Investment decision-making is obviously a very important management power to any enterprise. But in early 1997, three-quarters of some 750 leading enterprises still did not have this power (*Beijing Review*, 16-6-1997). Despite some relaxation, enterprises must still go through a series of complicated programming, scrutiny and approval procedures if they want to get a large investment loan. Enterprises may have quite big decision-making power with regard to small technical renovation projects which require an investment of hundreds of thousands of Yuan.

But when it comes to big investment projects, they still have no major power. At the very least, they need to consult and make decisions together with the competent department, local government, and banks, while bigger investment projects may need to be scrutinised and approved by the relevant departments in the central government first before bank loans are sought. Typically, only about half the applications seem to succeed. But an enterprise without investment management power often cannot adapt to and cope with the changes in market demand, thus causing product overstocking, a common problem in the state sector. Not much progress appears to have been made in asset management power, namely, the power to buy and sell assets, which is closely linked with investment power. What this means is that enterprises cannot adapt to fluctuations of market demand, because they are unable to adjust their product structure. Though the enterprises have the decision-making powers as regards the variety of goods they produce, they do not have the power to adjust the asset structure which is needed to make the necessary changes in the product structure.

Box 2.4 Impact of Job Cuts on Women

The workers of Factory 3501 used to work on an assembly line, endlessly stitching one pile of military uniforms after another. It was hard work for modest wages, but, at least, it guaranteed the women a semblance of security. But at the end of 1997, about two dozen of these women found themselves out of work – cast out with millions of other workers who have been laid off from struggling state-run factories. Their plight illustrates how decisions to downsize are setting some of China's most vulnerable workers adrift. It also shows how embattled workers are daring to lobby for better treatment despite the government's fear of public dissent. 'We all worked very hard for 15 or 20 years and it took its toll physically. Now, for the factory to cut us loose is unreasonable,' argued Zhu Ru, a one-time political activist who led the protest.

The women got a one-time severance payment ranging from 2,880 to 9,600 Yuan – roughly nine months' to two years' wages – and were told to expect nothing more. What they wanted was a small monthly stipend of about 200 Yuan and medical care. The mainland is still struggling to establish a reliable social welfare system, so what helps tide over many laid-off workers are meagre stipends and limited medical care from their state-owned workplaces.

The women of Factory 3501 lost their jobs when their one-year contracts expired. Many state factories have started giving workers contracts instead of lifetime employment and benefits that prevailed during earlier decades of Communist rule. The 80-year-old plant once employed 3,000 workers, but began trimming its staff by not hiring new workers to replace those who retired, followed by involuntary retrenchment. Ms Zhu's group was the first to leave. At factories in Beijing and elsewhere, older women often are the first to be let go under this. The seamstresses, all in their late thirties, and with little education and no other skills, had limited opportunities for re-employment. Ms Shu needed a new job to support herself and her 13-year-old son. Her ex-husband had also lost his job and could not pay child support

Source: Associated Press, 25-1-1998.

Therefore, the enterprises cannot produce products that are suitable for the market because they don't have an asset structure suited to market needs.

Government departments also continue to exercise virtually full power over the appointment of managers. According to the CASS survey already cited, about 86.6 per cent of the managers are appointed by the relevant departments, who play a very important role in the removal and discharge of 95.5 per cent of managers, which is tantamount to full control. The internal managerial staff and workers also play a role in the discharge of about half the managers. Next, is government legal entities who have invested in the enterprise, and their role accounts for about 40 per cent. What is worth noting is the role of banks. At present it is small (11.8 per cent), but it may well become more important in the years ahead. Such a modality of appointment by the government makes the enterprises unable to rid themselves of control by the bureaucratic hierarchy. Enterprise managers are unable to distance themselves from the preference of their superior leaders and cannot fully face the market. They are not able to replace the value criterion of their superior government leaders with the optimal market value. There is also a tendency for managers of enterprises performing badly to be transferred or even promoted rather than being forced to take responsibility for failure, through either demotion or dismissal. CASS found that except for those who retired, about 37.57 per cent of the managers were promoted, 41.66 per cent were transferred to head other enterprises. Those demoted or removed to other ordinary posts accounted for only 9.79 per cent and 9.65 per cent respectively.

Then, there is the issue of the profit distribution relationship with the government. According to policy, enterprises are no longer required to pay over their profits and surpluses as in the past, but are now liable only for value-added tax and income tax. This includes stock exchange-listed companies who are not required to pay dividends for the government-owned equity for the time being. In theory, this should give enterprises comprehensive power over their surplus cash. In reality, they are under varying degrees of control by the competent government departments at local and central levels, to whom they must pay 'deal fees' in order to survive and develop – in essence a cost to be paid to maintain the original enormous planned management system.

One of the most obvious is a management fee paid to the competent government departments and usually fixed as a certain percentage of sales revenue, regardless of whether it has incurred a profit or a loss. Apart from this, firms are often asked to pay after-tax profit dividends to certain state-owned holding companies or asset management companies. These are, in essence, the original competent departments turned into a fake company. After that, comes the turn of local governments and local organisations, so that in total the fees may exceed gross profit. And, in fact, the fees have to be paid even if the enterprise makes a loss on the year.

There are also many other payments which have not been clearly identified. For instance, in order to obtain capital for development, companies must apply for a bank loan. For certain investments, they will need to set up a specific project and get it approved by the superior department. In order to get into a new market, they must have the support of the local government. They also need to deal with various activities by their superior departments, such as promotion, inspection and evaluation.

All these require payments of deal fees, meaning further division and distribution of their profits often before any actual surplus has materialised. Thus, state-owned enterprises with independent management power over daily production and operation, still lack sufficient internal initiatives and capability to deal with an intensely competitive external market. This incompatibility results in a downward turn in the rate of return, threatening enterprise survival. An important reason for this failure is that state-owned companies have not yet become real enterprises. The most important element, independent management power is still under strict government control – e.g. power over personnel, investment, assets and income etc. This control causes the diversion of profits, ensuring that the production structure cannot adapt to the fluctuations of market demand and discourage enterprises from seeking maximum value. Accordingly, the drop in the rate of accumulated funds leads to a weakening capability to develop. Under government control, enterprises have no space to seek their maximum values, thus being deprived of the basic motivation to compete.

What is still to be recognised by some bureaucrats is that enterprises are part of the horizontal network of the market, not a unit of the vertical administrative system. Therefore, only when managers obtain completely independent power can they gain sufficient motivation and capability for competition.

Faced with this contradiction, the central government then declared the orientation of reform would shift to incorporated enterprise, allowing a mix of limited liability stock companies, limited liability companies and wholly-owned state companies depending on individual circumstances. Even so, there are still problems, especially through the ban on state-held shares, whether they are listed or not, are forbidden to be circulated in the market. Critics argue this is not good for optimising allocation of resources and increasing the value of state assets, which are also exposed to unnecessary stock exchange risk. However, in compensation, listed companies do benefit from a lower tax rate – 15 per cent compared to the 33 per cent imposed on unlisted companies.

At the same time, while the state-held shares and those held by the enterprise employees receive the same dividends, the workers enjoy priority in distribution (in addition, they receive a dividend even if the enterprise's results are not good or there are no results at all, while the state-held shares are linked with economic results), which removes some of the element of incentives for higher productivity. There is also confusion in the fact that the holders of the state-held shares are not clear. In general, state assets administrative departments hold such shares, or they entrust certain institutions with the right. But the departments in charge of enterprises and other institutions demand the right. In this way, the incorporated state-owned enterprises retreat back into old ways without a clear representative for their state assets.

Box 2.5 Incorporation Route to Restructuring

The Feiyue Acoustics Company established by Shanghai Shengdian General Factory in 1984 was the first limited liability stock company, but after the Shanghai and Shenzhen stock exchanges opened in November 1990 and April 1991 respectively, more incorporated enterprises appeared rapidly. By the end of 1995, there were 2,400 limited liability stock companies and 17,500 limited liability companies including wholly-owned state ones. To become an incorporated enterprise, the SOE has to reorganise itself, becoming the holding company of a newly-established limited liability company. This tends to produce an immediate change in thinking represented by the fact that the production and management targets, in order of ranking, of state-owned incorporated enterprises are: (1) profits, (2) marketing, (3) control of production costs, (4) effective use of capital (return on investment) and (5) technical innovation (*Beijing Review*, Issue 38, 1996).

Establishing a modern enterprise system means conducting means clearly defining the property rights of state assets. The ownership is divided into ownership of the state contributor and the enterprise corporate property right. The state's ownership control over the portion itself funded and its involvement in the process of enterprises are carried out in accordance with the management regulations of a modern company system; expanding enterprise decision-making power is being carried out under the condition that the rights and interests related to ownership of state assets are not impaired.

Between 1984 and late 1991, 708 SOEs were restructured into shareholding enterprises. The shareholding system met strong opposition in the process of trial implementation. According to the opposing view, the shareholding system would lead to division and even privatisation of state-owned enterprise, the rights and interests concerning the property rights of state assets would be impaired, and speculation would emerge in the transaction of stocks. But Deng Xiaoping, in a speech in early 1992 during his famous South China inspection tour, pointed out that 'we should resolutely conduct the experiment with the shareholding system'. Deng's speech removed the political obstacles to implementation of the shareholding system. The Corporate Law published in December 1993 brought the transformation and development of state-owned enterprises in line with the company system and legal orthodoxy.

In November 1994, the State Council selected 100 large companies to experimentation, which was later followed by more than 2,000 pilot enterprises in various regions. Eighteen cities were selected as pilot cities for optimising the enterprise capital structure and comprehensive co-ordinated reform. In accordance with the stipulations of the Corporate Law, pilot cities made a general check-up on the fixed assets, settled claims and debts, delineated property rights and organised company management institutions. By the end of 1996, of the 100 pilot enterprises, apart from one that was disbanded and another merged, the remaining 98 were respectively reorganised into exclusively nationally-funded companies, limited liability companies and joint stock limited companies.

The work of pilot enterprises was concentrated mainly on solving the problems such as excessive debts and too heavy social burdens on enterprises. In reorganising debts, the debt funds resulting from state financial loans to enterprises and 'change of allocation into loans' are turned into state investment with capital funds; in clearing old accounts, the profits and taxes owed by enterprises to the state over previous years and funds turned into the state's capital funds; that part of profits and taxes actually paid by enterprises to the state is returned to enterprises, part of the profits which the enterprise should turn over to the state is retained as increased state capital fund investment in the enterprises; the laid-off or redundant enterprise employees and early retiring personnel are transferred to other work units; the function of running social welfare undertakings is separated from enterprises.

Source: *Beijing Review*, Issue 38, 1996.

One expert has suggested that the government should sell part of its equity stake in some listed companies and use the funds raised to increase the capital of debt-ridden state enterprises. Zhou Daojiong, the former chairman of the China Securities Regulatory Commission (CSRC), argued that such a sale could be handled without affecting the state's controlling role in the enterprises. Although hundreds of state enterprises have issued listed shares, the state still holds a majority stake in them for fear of losing control of the economy. Mr Zhou said most state firms were burdened by high asset-to-debt ratios, threatening the health of state banks. The government should choose more state enterprises with relatively good earnings records to list shares domestically or abroad to raise funds for restructuring. It should also allow more state firms to issue corporate bonds and convertible bonds and to allow the establishment of more mutual and industry funds (Reuters, 5-4-1999).

In June 1999, the central government decided to remove the debt burden of the Dongfeng Motor Corp., one of the country's 'Big Three' carmakers, by turning its unpaid loans worth nearly 4 billion yuan into State equity. Dongfeng Automotive Co. Ltd, a subsidiary of the Dongfeng Motor Corp., issued A shares (Yuan-denominated shares for domestic investors only) to raise an expected 1.49 billion Yuan for upgrading technology and building a plant with an annual capacity of 100,000 light trucks. In an organisational restructuring, the number of departments in Dongfeng's headquarters was reduced from thirty-seven to eleven, with the number of employees trimmed from 2,224 to 300. As many as 10,000 people were to be laid off in 1999 on top of the 6,000 jobs cut in 1998. At the time of writing, Dongfeng had about 100,000 employees. Under a new board of directors, five divisions are being formed, including a car and truck manufacturing division, a components group comprising 14 producers, and an independent logistics company. Officials sent by the central government assumed a supervisory function, overseeing whether the State's assets appreciate or not (*China Daily*, 26-6-1999).

Similar moves were underway in other State enterprises – First Automotive Works Group (FAW), for example, was exempted from debts worth 6 billion Yuan (ibid.) – and it seems likely this will be the main form of attempt SOE revival for some time to come. Managers of many ailing enterprises have been sacked and replaced with younger men considered more open to the ideas of a market economy. But reshuffling the management teams at State enterprises has become one of the toughest issues for the government, with the difficulties ranging from lack of qualified candidates to lack of incentives for new managers to remain. Low salary levels and rigorous performance requirements have made entrepreneurial spirits in State enterprises seek quick operational results in order to be promoted to higher government posts.

To further accelerate the reform process, the government has been encouraging mergers or bankruptcy, although preferring the former. Enterprises doing the annexing, however, have to take over all the debts of enterprises being annexed, and are responsible for relocating its employees – firms losing money for three consecutive years can be exempted from interest on bank loans of annexed enterprises, and have five years to pay back the principal. Annexing enterprises facing difficulties in repaying loans in time years can negotiate an extension of one or two years.

The first high tide of mergers appeared in 1988, four years after the process began in 1984, with the scale extending from one-to-one merging in limited trades and areas to cross-trade merging of multiple enterprises nation-wide. The priority was also changed from eliminating loss-making enterprises to optimising economic structures. But there was a slowdown in the second half of 1989, as the entire national economy entered the stage of comprehensive rectification. The second high tide appeared in 1992 following the central authorities' decision to establish a 'socialist market economic structure'. Property right reform became an important component through the trade of property rights and the cultivation of a trading market.

Along with the development of the stock and property rights trading markets, the form for merging and purchasing of enterprises became more diversified. A distinctive feature is the merging and purchasing of state-owned enterprises by listed or overseas companies, and cross-border mergers by Chinese enterprises. Local governments are also now allowed to dispose of small state enterprises by selling them to their own workers and creating shareholding co-operatives. 'Workers can volunteer to invest in the enterprises they work for and hold shares. Through holding shares, workers are also responsible for these enterprises' debts' (Xinhua, 6-8-1997). A circular issued by the State Commission for Restructuring the Economy urged all workers in small enterprises to become shareholders, although no-one would be forced to join. Workers would decide if the firms would keep some shares as state-owned shares, although only as a minority.

The document said shareholding co-operatives would hold the key to boosting the fortunes of small firms in cities. Despite the controversy over ownership rights and a reluctance to allow debt-stricken enterprises to go bankrupt, local governments have tried to relieve themselves of financial burdens by selling and renting small and medium enterprises to private investors, letting them merge or fall into bankruptcy as a last resort. The circular argued that shareholding co-operatives should practice 'democratic management' and all shareholding workers would be considered equal in the enterprise. Boards of directors would be established to look after daily operations of the company and be accountable to shareholders (ibid.).

Yet, there are some who feel the existing bankruptcy and acquisitions policy has cost the government dear and failed to achieve the desired results. One bankruptcy expert told the official *China Daily*, for example, that between 1994 and 1997, the central government earmarked 97 billion Yuan in emergency funds to write off bad debts owed to banks as a result of SOE acquisitions and bankruptcies. The rationale behind the funding was that bankruptcies and acquisitions were originally considered the best way to cure their chronic illnesses of mismanagement and snowballing deficits. 'But of the 512 key SOEs propped up by the government, 156 were still running in the red. For some enterprises, deficits have hit 50 million Yuan or more for two years in a row,' the expert said. 'A high rate of bankruptcies and acquisitions may worsen banks' asset-debt structures and lead to higher unemployment' (*China Daily*, 14-12-1998).

On the left of the party, die-hard Maoists also see the policy as a disaster, but from the aspect of its erosion of socialist principles. Leading ideologue, Deng Liqun, former party propaganda chief, accused party reformists of abandoning socialism. In a speech reprinted in *Zhong Liu* (Midstream) magazine, Deng, declared: 'In their hearts, it's no longer 'only socialism can save China' but 'only capitalism can save China'.' Addressing the Society of Research on the History of the People's Republic of China, he cited one unidentified city which, he said, had sold 1,771 state enterprises, or more than 90 per cent of its total. The role of the state sector in the economy had been reduced to one-third this year (1998) from 76 per cent last year. 'This situation cannot be ignored. Public ownership should be the mainstay and non-public ownership supplementary.' (*South China Morning Post*, 31-12-1998).

And even though, at the time of writing, the government remained committed to the policy, some of its frustrations at the lack of results spilled out into the open when Premier Zhu Rongji, using a soccer analogy, warned State managers they would be shown the 'yellow card' after one year's bad performance and 'sent off' the following year if they fail to turn business around. Central government auditors would '*vigorously examine*' accounts of loss-making enterprises. Managers found to be responsible for bankrupting the companies would be '*fired without mercy*'. Bosses who 'lived off the enterprises and profited themselves' and those who took bribes would be punished to the 'utmost of the law. We cannot be soft on them' (Xinhua, 29-11-1998)

The government also became worried at the random selling of small and medium-sized SOEs, and, in fact, began to slow down the process of offloading the minnows in early 1999. Haphazard selling had caused 'losses of State assets and difficulties in recovering the bank debts and the unpaid taxes,' the State Economic and Trade Commission (SETC), Ministry of Finance and the People's Bank of China said in a joint circular (*China Daily*, 24-2-1999). Smaller enterprises account for 99 per cent of China's registered 10 million firms and employ three-quarters of the country's rural workers, according to statistics of the SETC's newly-created Small and Medium-Sized Enterprises Department.

The circular said there were many ways for them to compete and survive in the market and be responsible for their own profit and loss. During the years of reform, shareholding co-operation and other non-State ownership systems have been chosen by many small enterprises. However, some regions had adopted a single solution: selling off the smaller firms, and wiping out all their responsibilities, even though it would be detrimental to the interests of the corporate workers, the circular noted. The circular did not say how many smaller firms had fallen into non-state hands. 'Government departments at all levels should have a more accurate understanding of the central government's principles regarding reforms in smaller State firms, and should implement various practical measures to invigorate the enterprises.' No smaller firms in the social welfare sector should be sold (ibid.).

Success stories

Much of the above focuses on problem cases, but it should also be stressed that there are success stories, especially via the merger and acquisition route. By solely relying on its own efforts, for example, Three Gun, a Shanghai-based underwear manufacturer, expanded its assets, sales revenue and economic returns by 10, 12. and 100-fold in six years to 1996. Its products have constantly enjoyed brisk sales on the domestic market for their variety, quality, prices, credit and services, despite the acute competition of over 100 Chinese and foreign brand-names.

Three Gun's success lay in taking advantage of its famous trademark to merge seven loss-making enterprises, taking over debts of 358 million Yuan and making up historical losses of 150 million Yuan. Arrangements were also made to protect the economic interests of 9,000 employees and retirees. According to General Manager Su Shounan, without the merger, construction of new factory buildings would not only have soaked up much capital, but lost the firm a golden opportunity to expand its market. Three Gun has attached high importance to enhancing its reserves for development. It has increased the amount of circulating capital from 90 million Yuan in 1990 to one billion Yuan six years later. The value-added of state-owned assets of the Shanghai No. 9 Knitwear Mill, predecessor of the Three Gun, surged by 66.7 per cent in 1996 on the basis of a dramatic rise of 528 per cent in 1995. Three Gun's development indicates that merger is not only an important measure for enterprise reform, but also an effective way to readjust industrial structure, preserve state-owned assets, invigorate dead bank loans and rejuvenate inferior enterprises (author research).

In June 1996, the TCL Group in Guangdong Province bought a 60 per cent of the shares of the loss-making Shekou-based colour TV factory owned by the Lu Group, an old Hong Kong business. Before the merger, colour TVs under the trademark of TCL had been manufactured by the Hong Kong Colour TV Great Wall Electronic Group and sold by TCL's own marketing network. With competitive prices, TCL's widescreen colour TVs constantly clawed back domestic market shares held by foreign makes. In 1995, TCL came sixth among Chinese manufacturers in terms of domestic market share. Lu Group, an experienced colour TV producer, possessed great overseas market development capacity. TCL Electronic Co. Ltd. was established in Shenzhen, and heavy investment made to re-equip the old factory. This enabled it to develop more than thirty new products and raise its annual output to a million sets.

In December 1994, Tu Guoshen, a private entrepreneur, bought the loss-making Taihe Combine Manufacturing Plant for 6.2 million Yuan and established the Taihe Jiuding Industrial Development Co., which is now the largest private business in the Jinggangshan area of Jiangxi Province. In April 1997, Tu used 29.89 million Yuan to purchase four other small and medium-sized SOEs – Jishui Reeling Mill, Jian Electrical Appliances Factory, Ganzhong Electronic Components Factory and Taihe Black Chicken Winery. By the end of May, all the four loss-making enterprises had revived production, enabling their 600 laid-off employees to return. Through merger, Jiuding owns nine exclusively- and jointly-funded enterprises, initially forming a conglomerate integrating trade with industry and agriculture.

Box 2.6 Changhong: Making the Fortune 500

Faced with stagnant domestic demand in 1988, Chinese colour television manufacturers reduced their production of the prevailing standard 14-inch set one after another. But Ni Runfeng did the exact opposite. As a result, his Sichuan Changhong Electrical Appliances Co. Ltd. in 1997 accounted for a third of all colour TV set sales in China. Due to the downturn in production generally prevailing in the 1988 slump, cathode ray tubes (kinescopes) piled up in the producing factories. But from his vantage point in south-west China's remote Sichuan province, Ni saw things differently. His logic was that farmers would obviously increase their income as the government had raised the price of grain and cotton. Few rural families then had a colour TV, but that was bound to change when they got more money.

Thus, he went out and bought all the stocked 14-inch colour tubes from the country's largest producer at bargain prices. And, he expanded his production. At the time, other TV manufacturers were vying with each other in the cities for the sale of 28-inch colour televisions. Not until Ni had begun placing 14-inch sets in the hands of farmers in a steady stream, did other factory directors realise the potential of the large rural market. And by then, 14-inch colour kinescopes were in short supply and the prices soared.

The company was formerly known as the State Changhong Machinery Factory. Founded in 1958, it was one of the key military industrial enterprises in China. But in 1973, with military orders beginning to dwindle, the company began to manufacture monochrome TV sets for the civilian market to stay alive. By 1985 even this lifeline wasn't enough. With orders dwindling for an outdated product, the factory was on the verge of closure – until the 41-year-old Ni, then one of the youngest major factory directors in the electronics industry, took a bold step.

With money borrowed from the provincial government, he imported colour TV technology and production lines from Japan, and, combined with the right marketing instincts, it was an instant success. Talking now of his approach, Ni describes how he made two crucial decisions: to concentrate on producing nothing but colour televisions, and to stay close to base in Sichuan Province, China's most populous. 'It was difficult for Changhong to go into the whole country as a spring chicken. But, we could be the king of Sichuan'. Dominating the provincial market after his coup in cornering the CRT supply, Changhong in 1989 unleashed its sales force on the rest of the country.

For eight years in a row, the company has ranked first in sales volume in the domestic market, and its profit has grown 100 times. Annual production was 4.8 million in 1996, rising to 5.5 million in 1997, and an expected eight million in 1998. Exports are flourishing to Russia, Southeast Asia and Africa. In 1989 and again in 1996, Changhong took the lead to lower its prices, causing a sensation in both business and media circles, and drawing muttered complaints from some of its domestic counterparts. But one of the direct results of this price reduction is that the proportion of imported colour televisions in the Chinese market has dropped from the previous 50 per cent to 15 per cent.

In 1997, it began a controlled program of mergers and acquisitions, taking over two ailing rivals in Nantong, Jiangsu Province, and another in Changchun, Jilin Province, where export bases are about to be built. In 1998, Changhong planned to invest two billion Yuan to build a 'household electrical appliances city' in the Mianyang High-Tech Development Zone. It will produce 37-inch colour TV sets and frequency controlled air conditioner and other electrical products. It is working hard on development of digital colour TV and digital and video disc products.

Ni keeps his company 'lean and mean' and forward-looking. To ensure his executives stay on form, they face an annual performance assessment, and the bottom 30 per cent get the sack. But with salaries above average, there are no shortage of potential replacements, largely recruited from the country's top universities. In 1996, sales volume was 12.55 billion Yuan. According to Ni's analysis, from now on to 2010, the sales volume of large-screen colour televisions in China will be about 300 billion Yuan, of which Changhong's share should be half. At that time, he calculates, Changhong would enter the ranks of world's top 500 companies.

Source: Author research.

The Gaosen Group in Wuhan, capital of Hubei Province, is a private business with 60 million Yuan registered capital. In November 1995 and March 1996, it merged Wuhan Synthetic Leather Factory and Wuhan Knitwear Factory, two collective enterprises. The synthetic factory, with 574 employees, had debts of 15 million Yuan and assets of only 13 million Yuan. The knitwear factory, with 701 employees and 5 million Yuan in total assets, piled up a debt of 8.5 million Yuan. Before the merger, both factories had suspended production. To reduce social burden and seek self-development, Gaosen Group reached agreement with the two factories on a merger on condition it took over all their debts, employees and pension payment. With several million Yuan pooled by Gaosen, and efforts to change their operational mechanisms, the two factories quickly revived.

The Changzhou Diesel Engine Co. Ltd. in Jiangsu Province and the Changchun Tractor Plant in Jilin Province are both on the list of China's top

100 machine-building enterprises and among China's top 500 industrial businesses. Though standing more than 2,000 km apart, in June 1995 the two pooled 20 million Yuan to establish a joint venture in Yushu City, Jilin Province – the Changchai Changchun Diesel Engine Co. Ltd. The venture, with 350 employees, yielded 39.31 million Yuan in sales revenue and 2.5 million Yuan in profits and tax payments in five months after it started trial production in late July. In 1996, it raised its sales revenue and profits to 162 million Yuan and 8.8 million Yuan respectively, with per capita profit and all-labour productivity hitting 23,700 Yuan and 470,000 Yuan. The venture annually now produces more than 100,000 Changchai-brand diesel engines which sell well in north-east China.

The government cites these companies as examples that retention of a state-run sector is viable and that the reform procedure is on the right track. But they stand out because they have been carefully nurtured by the government and given every assistance possible in order to achieve their goals. This same treatment cannot be adopted for the whole of the state sector because the financial cost would be enormous. Thus, it seems that the state sector which will eventually emerge will contain a few core groups in a few strategic industries, while the rest will either founder or be allowed to become quasi-privatised concerns. This, however, will not necessarily solve the issue of whether a state-owned industrial core is the best way for China to progress.

CHAPTER 3

Case Study: The Steel Industry

China's iron and steel industry was a key element in the Maoist vision of the new China. Large-scale plants such as Anshan (Angang) became symbolic of China's revitalised industrial path. At the micro-scale, the 'walking on two legs' policy of the Great Leap Forward included steel production as one of its main planks, with the Backyard Furnace Campaign being an amazing, and costly, experiment in social engineering. By the Dengist period, steel was viewed as more of a dinosaur than a shiny symbol of a better today or tomorrow. Steel plants throughout the country were obsolete or obsolescent, they were dirty, polluting blots on the landscape, badly constructed and badly run. Steel workers and their families, as in other state enterprises had a job and support for life. Each SOE had thousands of mouths to feed, far more than in the equivalent plant in other countries.

The new transformation began with the construction of Baoshan (Baosteel) on the mouth of the Yangtze. This plant may, however, be the last of the huge steelworks to be built in China. It has become a major success story, well suited to the needs of the modern era, with a modern management structure and high operational efficiency. More of a corporation than an SOE, Baoshan is leading the necessary changes in China's massive iron and steel sector. New methods are being developed, and a new flexibility is becoming apparent. However, in other plants there is a long way to go. As with other SOEs, redundancies in the steel sector are set to be massive. Equivalent job losses were large in countries like Britain, Germany, the USA and the former USSR, but these pale into insignificance compared to China. This chapter will consider the burgeoning success stories (examples of Angang, Baosteel, Hangang and Hougang), and also the costs of the changes which are being made in this still-vital sector.

The format is:

- The rise of the steel industry in China
- Pressures for change: global, national, local
- Transforming the steel industry: the drive for efficiency
- The costs of change: economic, social, political

The rise of the steel industry in China

In China, the first steel plant was the government-run Hanyang Iron Works, containing two blast furnaces and two converters, bought from Europe, and established in Hubei province, at Hanyang on the Yangtze in 1894. This was 'two years before Japan built its first iron and steel works at Yawata' (Tregear, 1980, p.232). The venture was established on a poor financial footing, however, and the lack of sufficient capital combined with transport difficulties, bad management and poor supply of coking coal led to its privatisation in 1908. Although the coking coal problem was solved via discovery of good quality deposits in Hunan province, the transportation costs proved too high, and the new company was supported by many loans from Japanese banks. Eventually, the Japanese took control of the company, being keen to obtain the company's good quality iron ore for their own Yawata steel plant. High demand during World War I kept the company going, but after the war production declined rapidly until it ceased in 1925.

In the meantime, China's iron and steel production achieved take off via the development of the first plant in Manchuria, at Benxi, in 1910, and the establishment of the great steel works, also in Manchuria, at Anshan, in 1919. Raw materials were important in the location of the latter, but its tremendous growth also reflected the wider industrialisation of Manchuria under the Japanese occupation from 1931–45. Steel production was 344,000 tons by 1936 and peaked at 837,000 tons, from nine blast furnaces, in 1943 (ibid., p.233), but the Soviets dismantled and removed most of the plant during their period in control in the late 1940s.

Since the Communist Revolution, steel production has been a central component within China's Centrally Planned Economy, as part of the drive for industrialisation via, initially, heavy rather than light industry. China's international isolation during and after the Korean War encouraged the target of self-sufficiency, whereas in the inter-(world)-war period imports rather than home production had underpinned the industrial growth of Shanghai, for example. Writing in the late 1970s, Howe wrote:

'Steel is an essential ingredient of industrial growth, and the potential scale of China's industrial sector ensures that this is an industry for which the ambition of self-sufficiency is logical' (Howe, 1978, p.114).

This point about self-sufficiency is one which will be discussed further below. Despite the opening of other centres, Angang remained the main focus of production, and by the 1970s had been rebuilt (initially with Soviet assistance in the 1950s) to the scale of 10 blast furnaces. Byrd provides further information on its development and contemporary role (1992). Table 3.1 summarises output statistics during the Maoist period, while Table 3.2 shows the relative output of the main centres. These tables are based on Western sources of the 1970s, including the CIA *Handbook of Economic Indicators*. It is interesting to speculate how they compare with official Chinese sources for that period, and any subsequent revisions by the Chinese authorities, given that the then secret 'third front' industrial development centred on Sichuan province had begun in the late 1960s (Cannon, 1990, and Linge and Forbes, 1990 provide further details).

Table 3.1 shows the gradual expansion in output during the 1950s, when the Soviet-style period of heavy industrialisation was in full swing. If we consider the ratio of Finished Steel to Crude Steel Output as a measure of efficiency, we can see that efficiency levels climbed steadily to a peak of 0.80 in 1957. Then came the Great Leap Forward of 1958, when the drive towards *'walking on two legs policy'* and the *'backyard furnace campaign'*, among other features of this amazing socio-economic experiment, sought to dramatically expand China's industrial output to previously unprecedented levels. Hence Table 3.1 shows the very high production figure for 1960, but note also that the efficiency level had slipped back to 0.60, an indication that all was not well with steel production at that time. It quickly became clear that much of the steel produced in the backyard furnace campaign was of poor quality, often being produced in poor locations. Further, it proved impossible to sustain this high level of output, therefore steel production declined dramatically in the early 1960s, recovering eventually to a Crude Steel Output of 17.8 million tons in 1970. By this time, although efficiency levels did not recover to the 0.80 ratio of 1957, a steady 0.75 was sustained,

Table 3.1 Steel Production in China During the Maoist Era

Year	Crude Steel Output (million tons)	Finished Steel Output (million tons)	Ratio of Finished Steel to Crude Steel Output
1949	0.2	0.1	0.50
1952	1.4	1.1	0.79
1957	5.4	4.3	0.80
1960	18.7	11.3	0.60
1962	8.0	6.0	0.75
1965	12.5	9.4	0.75
1970	17.8	13.4	0.75
1975	26.0	19.5	0.75

Source: Production Data, Howe, 1978, p.116; Ratios, Authors' calculations.

and Finished Steel Output surpassed that of 1960 by 1970, with a figure of 13.4 million tons.

In many ways the Great Leap Forward failed. Two features which are worthy of further consideration, however, are the 'walking on two legs policy' as well as the related decentralist tendency of this period. The walking on two legs policy had a number of aspects, but one feature was the attempt to balance the construction of a few large scale plants (in a range of industries, including energy production and chemicals, as well as steel) with a larger number of smaller ones. The benefits of this policy would be firstly, strategic. Smaller plants would be more difficult to knock out in time of war (during this period of the Cold War, the perceived threat of attack from the United States, and, later, from the Soviet Union, was an important factor in decision-making). Smaller plants also offered a flexibility of production and of location (nearer to raw materials or markets as the case may be, or to energy sources), and a counterbalance to the dangers of overconcentration in a few larger scale plants. Disadvantages might include, in contrast, the loss of economies of scale in the smaller plants; the difficulty of ensuring availability of skilled management and labour in a range of locations; and the difficulty of ensuring profitability of a wider range of plants with varying requirements for capital investment and technology. The strong element of decentralisation tended to give greater autonomy to local cadres, who, on the one hand would be better placed to respond to local needs, but, on the other hand, might lack the specialist training to run or direct a specialised steel plant effectively.

Table 3.2 gives the contrast between production in the peak efficiency year of 1957 and 1973, by which time steel had progressed to a high output, fairly efficient, industry. Note that Anshan's share of output declined significantly from 54 per cent in 1957 to 23 per cent in 1973, while remaining the largest single steel plant. Its relative decline came via the opening of new, more modern, plants in Wuhan (on the Yangtze), Baoutou (Inner Mongolia) and Shijingshan (Beijing), as well as expansion of steel plants in Shanghai and the opening of the smaller plants around the country. Wuhan Iron and Steel Corporation began production in 1958 and was completed in 1961 with a capacity of 3,000,000 tons p.a. (Treager, op.cit., pp.236–7). The iron ore was local high quality ore, but the coal at first came from further afield, from Hunan and Anhui provinces, at a high cost in transportation. Baotou was also completed in 1961 and was reliant on local supplies of ore, coal and limestone. Shijingshan is unusual in that it is located on the outskirts of a major capital city. Dong Liming notes that by the early 1980s there were 20 steel mills within the inner city of Beijing, as well as petrochemical works and other noxious industries around the capital due to a strong investment emphasis on heavy industry, a pattern of development which was, to him (and to many others) 'incongruous' (Dong

Table 3.2 Location of Steel Production in China During the Maoist Era

Location	1957 Output (million tons)	1973 Output (million tons)	% Share of Total Output, 1957	% Share of Total Output, 1973
Anshan	2.9	5.9	54	23
Shanghai	0.5	4.2	9	16
Wuhan	–	1.8	–	7
Baotou	–	1.6	–	6
Shijingshan	–	1.6	–	6
Other Modern Plant	2.0	7.2	37	28
Small Scale Plant	minimal	3.2	0	13

Source: Howe, 1978, p.116.

Liming, 1988, p.76). The Shijingshan Iron and Steel Works, begun in 1920, was considerably expanded in 1958 to include a blast furnace, a steelworks, an electric furnace and other features.

In the Dengist era, the major steelworks became Baoshan, near Shanghai. It is a significant symbol of this period, being a new plant built with modern machinery originally imported from Japan and Germany, on a coastal site at the mouth of the Yangtze. Table 3.3 shows the output pattern of this era, with the near quadrupling of output from 1975 to 1994. The figures are certainly impressive, and China marginally outproduced the United States by 1993, to become the world's second largest producer, behind Japan. By year end 1996, China's steel output reached beyond the 100 million tonnes mark for the nation to become, for the first time, the world's number one producer of steel. In 1997 output reached 107.3 million tonnes, nearly three million tonnes more than Japanese output.

Table 3.3 Steel Production in China During the Dengist Era

Year	Crude Steel Output (million tons)
1979	34.5
1985	46.8
1990	66+
1994	92.6
1996	100.0

Sources: 1979–90, Zhao Songqiao (1994), p.98; *China Statistical Yearbook 1994*, Beijing: China Statistical Publishing House, 1995, p.417; *Financial Times*, 3rd January, 1997.

Pressures for change: global, national, local

In common with other steel industries around the world, and despite the undoubted success in raising output to such high levels, China's steel industry is under intense pressure. Globalisation continues apace, for example, heightening the need to be competitive at the global rather than just the national or local level. Although China's steel industry has been relatively insulated in the past, its immunity to the imperatives of the global economy is weakening. Also, China's need to join the World Trade Organisation will weaken its protective trade structure further. Modifying previous work by Cook, pressures on the industry can be identified as:

- global
- scale and type of plant
- national consumption issues
- new regionalism
- the need for sustainability
- socio-economic and political imperatives

Considering each in turn, global pressures on the steel industry are summarised in Table 3.4, based mainly on a close reading of the *Financial Times* plus other sources. And so, with regards to competition, this is more internationalised than ever before, with British Steel for example increasing sales to China among other Asian destinations, and new players such as China itself or South Korea entering the global marketplace. Labour shedding began from the 1960s in the United States, and continues apace across the world. The US steel industry lost two-thirds of its production workers from 1967 to 1987 (434,000 to 147,600), while Iscor (South Africa) reduced its workforce from 85,000 in 1985 to 48,000 in 1995, and British Steel in June 1998 announced further losses of 10,000 jobs over the next five years, even though the company now employs only 43,000 people in the UK (plus 10,000 overseas) compared to 200,000 in the early 1980s. Companies are growing larger, with Posco in South Korea, until the Asian Financial Crisis, aiming to have a capacity of around thirty million tonnes by the year 2000, and Nippon Steel's being even greater than that. At the time of writing, British Steel has just announced merger with Hoogovens, the Dutch steel company, to become the world's third largest, raising further fears of unemployment among the workforce (Bannister, 1999). In all, mergers continue apace, state subsidies are being withdrawn across the globe, and older plants are being continually demolished or completely rebuilt.

The scale and type of plant is another pressure. China has more than 1100 iron and steel enterprises, but 12 major ones accounted for more than 60 per cent of total steel production in the early 1990s. As with other SOE's, conventional wisdom suggests that wastefulness and duplication is found at the provincial or county level, such as in Wuxi county where seven

Table 3.4 Globalisation and the Steel Industry

Globalisation has led to an *increase* in:

International Competition
Rate of Acquisition of New Technology
Restructuring and Labour Shedding
Privatisation
Joint Ventures and Alliances
Protectionism in Supranational Blocs and 'Anti-Dumping' Suits
Exchange Rate Volatility and Subsequent Impact on National Production and
   Export Levels
Large Companies and Rationalisation
Flexible Specialisation (arguably)

There has also been a *decrease* in:

State Subsidies
Proportion of Outdated Plants
Plus, note the considerable debate on Agglomeration effects

Source: Based on Cook, I.G. (1997), *Contextualising Steel: Changing Locational Factors in the Steel Industry*, International Symposium on Steel Industry Development and Management, Baoshan, May 1997 (details omitted, these are available from the author).

separate township-owned plants specialised in the rolling of steel (Kirkby, 1994). Hodder has concluded that 'Clearly there is an urgent need in China for a firm policy to encourage mergers, consolidation and concentration, whatever the type of industrial ownership' (Hodder, 1994, p.123). Certainly, this will fit well with the global pressures noted above. Cook has sounded a cautionary note in a previous paper, however (Cook, 1997). There is a need for reduction of numbers, but China is a vast country and transport and energy bottlenecks are widespread. Minimills, therefore, might be an important alternative at the local level.

'A minimill recycles steel scrap rather than making it from scratch using iron ore and coal' (D'Costa, op.cit., p.108), and this type of plant is proving extremely popular in the United States and India. Minimills have greater flexibility, require much lower capital investment per ton of capacity, and their operators 'have exhibited adaptability to new technologies' (ibid., p.108), while their main disadvantage is that 'they are not generally equipped to produce most flat products' (ibid., p.108). Miller, suggests that not only do minimills allow smaller scale operation, but also that:

'It would appear that most new technologies allow a reduction in the economic scale of production from at least four or five million tons of output annually to one or two million tons with a blast furnace and basic oxygen furnace combination' (Miller, 1991, p.39).

Given that these minimills also have economic and environmental advantages via not only their use of scrap steel, but also via their lesser use of water and energy than larger plants they might well offer a flexibility of location particularly appropriate for such a vast country as China.

If there is to be a growth of minimills, largely replacing the inefficient older plants at the local level, quality and customer care will have to be ensured. National consumption issues are set to increase. As noted above, a major disadvantage of the Great Leap was the shoddy quality of steel produced. Until recently, Chinese consumers, at all levels including enterprises themselves, have tended to take what they are given rather than press for improved quality. This perspective is changing, however, and as shown in the next section, the blithe disregard for customers exhibited by many steel producers, including the then largest, Angang, has had to be changed. Better steel is needed, better steel for the construction industry, better steel for vehicle production, and better steel for 'white goods'. Unless enterprises keep up with the demand for improved quality, and also for better coatings for specific tasks, then they will be outstripped by their competitors, at the national or global level.

New regionalism is another source of pressure for change. Globalisation is continually creating new economic spaces as a result of such trends as the increase in Foreign Direct Investment (FDI) noted above, migration of industry and management expertise, the New (or Newer) International Division of Labour (NIDL), new information linkages especially between large urban centres, new flows of ideas and so on, across national boundaries. Many of such spaces are in South East Asia and East Asia, including the Hong Kong-Guangdong-Shenzhen Triangle, the Singapore-Johor-Riau Triangle, the Northeast China-Korea-Japan Triangle and many others, often pulling together the labour and raw material resources of one country with the managerial expertise of a second, and the capital and technological capabilities of a third (Liu, 1996). If steel production can be the national symbol noted above, then it can also be a symbol for new, self-confident regionalisms, which seek to project themselves more strongly on the international stage. D'Costa has already speculated that: 'In the changing geography of steel production Southeast and East Asia will be the growth centers for both steel production and consumption' (D'Costa, op.cit., p.122). Cook has suggested that their precise location, further down the scale, will be discernible within these new spatial entities, either as completely new steel plants or considerably expanded and modernised old ones, as central features of their burgeoning regional economies. Within China, therefore, the Guangdong-Shenzhen-Hong Kong area has room for expansion, as does, arguably, the Fujian-Taiwan economic space, and also the newly reshaped Chongqing. In contrast, in other areas there is probably little room for expansion, unless via the minimills noted above.

Sustainability issues are on the increase, in China as elsewhere, reflecting the environmental pressures discussed below in Chapter 9. At some point, hopefully sooner rather than later, auditing of the steel industry among others will fully incorporate environmental as well as conventional economic costs, focusing in an holistic way on the integration of the steel plant *into* its environment, not separate from it, possibly employing the concept of *industrial metabolism* to do so (Taylor, 1996). Perhaps, in the longer term, auditing will incorporate social costs also. The consequences of such incorporation are difficult to predict. A plant like Baosteel, China's largest, for example, could benefit via such wider criteria through being able to achieve energy efficiencies, levels of cleanliness and care for its employees that might prove impossible for smaller, and especially older, enterprises. In the short term at least, it is unlikely, however, that such (new) audits will be taken widely enough to consider the cost to the environment of building and running the huge ships which transport the ores which are extracted, again at a high environmental price at the point of extraction, to a steelworks such as that at Baoshan. A full audit would also consider the cost of energy production to fuel steel plants, and, even, the potential impact on the local community of closure, as and when the plant outlives its usefulness. As these issues are more widely discussed and debated in China, it is likely that the pressures on the older and environmentally unfriendly plants will increase even further.

China's socio-economic and political imperatives will determine which of these and other pressures are responded to by the steel industry. Although the dominant thrust of policy is currently towards efficiency on strictly economic criteria, the violent reaction to unemployment detailed in the final chapter serves as a timely reminder that there are many people throughout China who will be unwilling to accept capitalistic strictures should these entail too much unemployment and poverty of the workforce. The conflicts in other countries during the reshaping of their steel and related industries have been substantial, and the social costs have been high. British society for example was nearly torn apart by the pressures of such job loss in the 1980s. Chinese society will face even greater pressures, and a neoMaoist response to this cannot be completely ruled out.

Transforming the steel industry: the drive for efficiency

With these contextual points and caveats in mind, this section presents case studies to show how steel SOEs are seeking to transform themselves into modern and efficient firms. Angang, for example, sustained massive losses in the last two months of 1994 after suspending production of three furnaces due to an overstock of more than a million tons of rolled steel. The complex, which had fixed assets of over 10 billion Yuan, faced unprecedented and rather grim challenges. Giant state-owned enterprises such as this have faced the threat of extinction during China's transition from a planned economic structure to a socialist market pattern.

In 1995, Angang's new leaders initiated effective transformation measures in terms of both ideology and methods to ensure economic growth. Results in the following year suggested that Angang will not become a dinosaur. Instead, the complex is continuing to create a better economic environment to ensure its existence and enhance prospects for development. Ideological transformation is a key element. Angang's ideological breakthrough was partly the result of the swingeing cutback in its order by Changchun No.1 Automobile Manufacturing Plant (see Box 3.1). Ensuing consultations with the Changchun management forced Angang to compare its products with those of its competitors – the Baoshan Steel Complex (Baosteel), in particular. The subsequent analysis provided Angang with valuable insight and a close inspection of Baosteel products revealed the absence of quality defects, a fact quite different from the inferior quality of Angang products. Moreover, Baosteel would strictly abide by contracts regardless of rising prices. Angang, however, simply ignored contracts and stopped shipments at will. This study convinced Angang officials that their problems stemmed from a total disregard for customer service and quality, a habit fostered under the centrally planned economy. Such disdain had caused Angang to lose a long-term customer and any failure to alleviate the situation would lead to the flight of many more.

Management initiated a period of introspection and self-scrutiny in line with the requirements of the market economy. Angang's 100 plus secondary production units previously operated under a pure service relationship that required no calculation for costs, profits and losses. Workers viewed the distant market as simply the realm of salesmen. The complex has now introduced overall market management, with each secondary unit acting as a legal entity exercising independent accounting and assuming responsibility for its own profits and losses. For example, strict contract relationships have been established between iron and steel smelting and rolling workshops, with the quality and price of products examined in accordance with national standards. Units involved in later stages of production retain the right to refuse to purchase poor-quality, high-priced goods from suppliers. This new practice has taught employees that each production process is directly linked to the credibility and competitiveness of Angang's products on the market.

Before, the complex lacked a sense of contract responsibility, simply waiting for overtures from customers during periods when iron and steel were in short supply. In 1994, Angang produced more than three million tons of steel, with no contracts for 40 per cent of the output. Today, Angang's steel production is based on signed contracts. Since 1995, its production contract rate has remained at 100 per cent. The complex strictly adheres to arranging production in accordance with the needs of customers. For example, the Supply and Marketing Co. under Angang now decides on the variety and quality of products in accordance with data provided by the marketing section. In addition, Angang has endeavoured to expand information exchanges with its clients, and now directly supplies numerous enterprises in north, north-east and south China, including once again the Changchun No.1 Automobile Manufacturing Plant; these together purchase another one-third of Angang's annual output at concessional rates. These types of outlet have erased Angang's worry about an unstable market.

For many decades, Angang officials believed that output alone would yield returns. However, the fallacy of this quantity concept was shown as the complex moved confidently towards its goal of producing 10 million tons of steel annually. The fact that returns under the market economy depend not on quantity but quality became apparent. A large enterprise does not necessarily yield substantial returns. Therefore, Angang officials abandoned the simple extensive mode of production growth and embarked on the road of intensive development via strengthening internal management. The complex recorded losses of over 200 million Yuan in the first eight months of 1995, with the plan for reaping an annual profit of 330 million Yuan appearing to be rather grandiose. The losses were addressed via provisional measures, such as making full use of stockpiles and recovering and recycling waste materials. The value of scrap iron and steel collected by workers in the plant alone exceeded 50 million Yuan. In one case, several dozen tons of rusted steel were found in a large pit. 'This truly represented the chaotic management prevalent at Angang, an enterprise which was previously a national model of strict management', said an elderly worker at the plant.

Box 3.1 summarises key elements of the reforms that were made. For instance, Angang targeted per unit costs for 1,450 types of products and relevant economic indices for relevant production units. As a result, costs were slashed. Similarly, mill director Dr. Mu (see Box 3.1) showed that the mill had the capacity to turn losses into gains regardless of current conditions. Consequently, each workshop formulated its own plan and measures for reducing consumption and costs. The effort in turn enabled the mills to attain its profit targets in the first half of 1996.

Angang's innovative technological transformation plan was approved by the State Council in May 1996, reducing the mill's original targeted output from 10 million tons to 8.8 million tons, with priority placed on renovating key equipment, increasing the proportion of products with high added value, and improving the quality and grade of products. Although the production targets are less, projected economic returns are expected to greatly outstrip those in the original plan. The aim is that more than 60 per cent of Angang's main technological equipment and products will reach

---

Box 3.1 Steel Under Reform: Angang

Established in 1919, in Manchuria, Anshan Iron and Steel Complex (Angang) was for many years the largest steelworks in China, being rebuilt in the 1950s with Soviet assistance, to 10 blast furnaces, as noted in the text. In the early 1990s it typified the problems faced by the state-owned sector, with its legacy of large-scale outdated plant, inefficient production techniques and lack of quality controls resulting in poor quality products and a wilful disregard of the need of the customers who bought these. Production was determined by output targets rather than demand, and by year end 1994, faced with huge losses, the management was required to suspend production in three of their blast furnaces due to an overstock of one million tons plus of rolled steel, in part due to the loss of one of their major customers, Changchun No. 1 Automobile Manufacturing Plant which drastically reduced its annual order for several *hundred* thousand tons to several thousand tons only. The complex had reached crisis point, and 'faced unprecedented and rather grim challenges' (Jing Can, 1996, p.10).

Reforms were introduced as a matter of great urgency. These included the introduction of a new management team prepared to consider innovative proposals to be customer-oriented, quality-focused, to make full use of the stockpile, and to recover and recycle waste materials. Internal contracts have been introduced, at different stages in the production process, with the purchaser having the right to refuse poor-quality, high-priced products, thus disseminating awareness of the rigours of the market among the workforce. 20 sales agencies have been established to market Angang's wares, and by 1996 these agencies accounted for one-third of output (ibid., p.11). Market prices now rule, therefore unprofitable lines are no longer supported. A new mill director, Mu Shicheng, freshly returned with a PhD gained in Germany, has been credited with presenting proposals for more workshop autonomy which resulted in realistic targets being set at the local level, overturning the old model of high-level input/ consumption/ pollution yet low output, into one where the emphasis is on quality, value-added and modernisation of plant.

Losses, which continued into 1995 were turned into profits by 1996, and the plant has begun to tackle its enormous welfare burden, which including children and the elderly totals an amazing 400,000 mouths to 'feed'! The enterprise is seeking to reduce the number of employees directly employed in iron and steel production to 50,000, having reduced the number to 74,000 by 1996, and hiving-off parts of the complex into separate enterprises which must operate according to profit-and-loss principles. Thus, 110,000 redundant workers and 180,000 employees have been 'diverted' or 'transferred' respectively into thirty-four separate factories and seventeen subsidiaries (ibid., p.12–13). Stability is guaranteed by Angang's acting as guarantor for losses over a three-year period, until solvency is achieved.

Clearly, such massive changes within a short time-span are not without problems, but the initial picture is encouraging, with output reaching a record level in 1996, and the stockpile being reduced to zero. As a further indication of the introduction of modern methods, in mid-1997 Angang New Steel as it is now known sought an overseas listing in Hong Kong in order to raise funds US$226 million for the purchase of a new smelting plant, upgrading of products and buying into a German joint venture to make galvanised steel products (Lucas, 1997). An independent profit forecast suggested that the profit of 407 million yuan in 1996 would be increased to 479 million yuan in 1997.

Sources: Jing Can (1996), 'Resurrection of a Dinosaur: Angang Thrives', *Beijing Review*, Oct.28-Nov.3, pp.10–13.

Lucas, L. (1997), 'Angang Seeks HKDollars 1.75 billion', *Financial Times*, 10th July.

---

advanced global levels. The rates of consecutive casting, plate and tube steel, and comprehensive synthetic products – the three major indices indicating the level of a modern iron and steel industry – are expected to rise from 30 to 72 per cent, 57 to 62 per cent, and to nearly 3 per cent, respectively. Angang's comprehensive competitive capacity will equal that of the most advanced domestic iron and steel enterprises.

Prior to reform, Angang had a high liability rate of up to 67 per cent, annual bank interest payments of 1.7 billion Yuan and a high dependency ratio. Box 3.1 shows how many surplus workers have been 'diverted' or 'transferred' to separate factories and subsidiaries. With the workforce being reduced, productivity by the end of the century is set to grow fivefold and the annual per capita output of steel is aimed to reach the advanced national level of 200 tons. Angang officials have attempted to keep repercussions of these changes to a minimum by adopting the principle of attaching equal importance both to reform and to stability. Loss-making enterprises are granted subsidies subject to annual reductions, and are required to turn losses into gains within a three-year period. Angang's Mining Co., Gongchangling Mining Co. and Machine Building Co., which were in the first group of businesses separated from Angang, recorded total losses of over one billion Yuan in 1995. These were covered by Angang and reduced losses by more than 100 million Yuan during the first half of 1996.

According to 1995 statistics, compiled by Angang's financial department, the entire complex yielded 18.6 billion Yuan in sales revenue and 2.38 billion Yuan in profits and tax payments, including 330 million in profits. All taxes were remitted during the year according to stipulated payment schedules. Capital income for the year totalled 12.59 billion Yuan, up 5.38 billion Yuan on 1994, with the sales rate topping 99 per cent. All of the complex's major economic indices hit all-time highs. During the first six months of 1996, Angang's rolled steel output soared to an historical peak, with sales revenues increasing by more than one billion Yuan on the same period of 1995. The complex's sales rate of 100 per cent reduced its stockpile to zero.

Although some of this data may be exaggerated by plant officials, it is nonetheless clear that Angang has made great progress in reform. The significance of this case study is that Angang faces almost all the difficulties and problems impeding large and medium-sized state-owned enterprises as they make the transition to a market-orientation. SOEs can be invigorated, as this example shows, provided that the problems are faced up to, and not ignored, as in the past. SOEs need to learn from the examples of others, avoiding the inward-looking, parochial outlook that used to predominate. Angang, for instance, adopted a formula for change from a smaller plant in a neighbouring province. The formula appeared to be based upon textbook clichés of cost controls and worker incentives, but has been shown to be effective. It was the Ministry of Metallurgical Industry which persuaded the complex to take on this model, that of the Handan Iron and Steel Corp. (Hangang) in Hebei Province. Hangang, which teetered on the edge of losses a few years ago, adopted a 'market simulation and cost veto' mechanism in 1991. After establishing the market price of a product, costs are calculated backwards and targets assigned to workers, who are motivated by bonuses. Further details are given in Box 3.3. The Hangang strategy was adopted by the Communist Party in 1996 as a model for industrial enterprises. In October 1996, with the help of the Central Committee propaganda department, Hangang held exhibitions in Beijing, Xian and Taiyuan. Hangang general manager Liu Hanzhang, mastermind of the measures, said the primary problem facing state-owned enterprises was their high costs, so stringent cost management was the answer. Over the past five years, Hangang has boosted its profits from one million Yuan to 710 million Yuan, making it the third most profitable steel plant after Baosteel and Wuhan Iron and Steel.

The drive for a more commercial approach, is also seen by the various attempts which steel companies are making to raise money on the Hong Kong Stock Exchange. Box 3.1 refers to 'Angang New Steel', for example, which will comprise three of the group's profitable offshoots that make cold rolled sheet for cars and electrical appliances, fast-speed wire rods for construction, and thick plates for shipbuilding. However, elsewhere, plunging steel prices and soaring production costs have hampered the planned Hong Kong flotation of Wuhan Iron and Steel. Angang hopes to alleviate market concern over China's steel sector by separating the profitable downstream operations from upstream operations, which are generally pig iron and steel smelting. The smelting operations will remain under the control of the parent company. The decision to split the operations also means that the H-share company will differ fundamentally from rival Maanshan Iron and Steel Co., the only listed mainland steel plant in Hong Kong, which is an integrated producer. Angang New steel will employ 4,000, compared with the group workforce of 160,000. It is understood that the new company has an agreement with the parent which will supply it with pig iron and steel at discounts on market prices.

Among the 110 large enterprises and business groups with annual sales exceeding 500 million Yuan which have emerged from the latest reforms, Baoshan Iron and Steel Corporation (Baosteel) ranks first. Located on the south bank of the Yangtze River estuary in north-east Shanghai, Box 3.2 provides summary details of this modern plant, now the largest in China. Begun with 30 billion Yuan in government investment, it is different from most domestic iron and steel complexes in being far from raw materials but close to market. The first and second-stage projects began operation in September 1985 and June 1991 respectively. By the end of 1996, the complex had produced a total of 58.53 million tons of steel, yielding 32.7 billion Yuan in profits, 19.5 billion Yuan in tax payments and US$1.74 billion in export value. Its sales revenue and profit in 1996 alone hit 27.22 billion Yuan and 3.14 billion Yuan respectively. Plans call for Baosteel to become a transnational enterprise group by 2010, integrating industry with finance and trade, and entering the ranks of the global top 500 businesses.

Baosteel has endeavoured to create products which the country was unable to produce or turn out in large quantities, products which can replace imports, or those for export with high-technology and added-value. Since 1991, at least 10 per cent of its annual output has been exported to Japan and the Republic of Korea.

The designated number of employees for Baosteel's first and second phases was 40,000, a relatively limited number for an extra-large iron and steel complex with a then annual output of 6.71 million tons of steel. Company officials say that this showed that the enterprise had even then achieved high labour-productivity. In 1988, it began to promote the 'full-load work system', cancelling or merging all posts with a daily workload under 6.5 hours and all repair workers were required to master at least one other related skill. From that year, the group cut its employees by 2,000 annually, reducing the number to 13,000 by August 1996, with even less on the production side (see Box 3.2). Labour productivity on major iron and steel production lines increased from 120 tons per person in 1990 to 655 tons in 1996. Note the chairman's warning, however, that even this level is not sufficiently competitive internationally (Box 3.2).

Today, the group is introducing the 'operational area worker' method which, breaching the boundaries of different posts, employs the smallest number of workers to complete diversified tasks within each set production area. For instance, in the electric furnace steel works, only 120 workers are

Box 3.2 Steel Under Reform: Baosteel

Baosteel, most recent and perhaps last of the mega-scale steel producers in China, is now the largest plant in terms of production. Situated near the mouth of the Yangtze, approximately 16 miles north-east of Shanghai, Baosteel produced 7.2 million tons of steel in 1996. Its development has been in three phases, each with its own blast furnace, with the emphasis moving from imported equipment, mainly Japanese, in Phase 1, through to 90 per cent indigenous equipment in Phase 3. The plant is built in the modern idiom, with its own iron-ore wharf, unloading facilities for coal and limestone, and coal-fired power station. The site has been attractively landscaped, with vegetation cover, including trees and shrubs covering one-third of the area, and even camels, deer and sheep grazing in its own mini-zoo! Number 1 Hot Rolling Mill Plant contains German equipment, has 4 million tons capacity and is 1 kilometre long. The entire capacity of the plant is now 8 million tons, growing to 11 million tons at the end of the soon-to-be-completed Phase 3.

Baosteel is now widely recognised to be a success story, but Cooke (1993) notes that it was plagued with problems during its construction phase, including subsidence on the previously marshy site, the shallowness of the estuary and the cost of the foreign equipment. These problems resulted in, respectively, 100,000 concrete piles being driven into the ground to stabilise the foundations, a long wharf being built out into the Yangtze, and the starting date being delayed by three years until 1985. Since then, the demand for its products, which aim for quality, has been continually high, fuelled by the needs of the Shanghai Volkswagen plant, for example, and the construction boom in Pudong, as well as exports (around 20 per cent of production). Phase 2 was completed in 1991, and Phases 1 and 2 cost the Chinese state a total of $5.5 billion. Phase 3 is reliant on the company raising its own finance, a total of $3.6 billion. According to the company, in the 10 years 1985–95, 'Baosteel has realised total outputs of 50.84 million tons of steel, 100.4 billion RMB of sales, tax payment 17.6 billion RMB' (Cheng Guang, 1997, p.27), and Phases 1 and 2 have now been paid for, including interest.

Baosteel's success comes from its sophisticated corporate structure, skilled management and workforce, and from being built later than plants such as Angang, therefore having less of an historical burden to bear, in terms of plant and social welfare. At the end of 1996, only 10,542 staff worked in the production system (compared to 12,835 the year before) and output reached 655 tons per head (*Baosteel Annual Report 1996*, p.3). Output levels compare well with competitors, but Baosteel executives are well aware of the gap which remains – for example, Pohang, South Korea reached 800 tons per head in 1993, and

New Nippon 694 tons per head in 1992–3 (Cheng Guang, op.cit., p.29). Li Ming, the Chairman, has warned of the external and internal challenges which exist: 'The equipment and technology in China Steel across the Taiwan strait can compete with those of Baosteel's. Aiming at Baosteel, many counterparts in the mainland are quickening their steps of new construction and technical renovation. They are forging ahead in applying new technologies and developing new products, forming a pressing threat to Baosteel' (*Baosteel Annual Report 1996* p.5). The objectives of Baosteel, supported strongly by government, to become one of the world's top 500 enterprises, integrating industry, finance and trade around the core steel production, can only be met if the company successfully meets such challenges, including a possible forced merger with the loss-making municipal-owned Shanghai Steel (Harding, 1997). 'Who manages the business?' – central government, municipality, Baosteel itself – is the key question for the future.

Sources: Baosteel Annual Report 1996, Baoshan Iron and Steel Corporation, Baoshan.

Cheng Guang (1997), 'Baosteel Business Strategy in Market Economy', in Guan Zhian and Liu Kexun (eds), *International Symposium on Steel Industry Development and Management Proceedings*, Metallurgical Industry Press, Beijing, pp.27–32.

Cooke, K. (1993), 'Baoshan Steelworks: Leading Supplier of Quality Products, *Financial Times*, 2nd June, p.34.

Harding, J. (1997), 'Chinese Steelmaker Takes a National Role', *Financial Times*, 11th June, p.4.

employed to operate one 150-ton electric furnace, one continuous casting machine and two refining furnaces. This reduction was achieved by gradually separating auxiliary departments from the main production lines and permitting them to exercise independent management and assume responsibility for their own profits and losses, similar to the Angang example noted above. The first department to be separated was the rear service sector. In 1986, Baosteel established the Enterprise Development Corp. to exercise concentrated management of the group's canteens, regular buses, sanitation, dormitories and housing. Since 1990, a number of auxiliary departments having close relations with the market have been gradually separated from mainline production. For instance, the steel ingot and mould workshop has been separated from the Baosteel Steel Smelting Factory to establish the Baosteel Casting Co. Soon afterward, the metal processing workshop was turned into the Shanghai Machinery Processing Factory, and the transportation department into Baosteel Transportation Co.

Redundant employees are mainly siphoned off to the New Career Co., the Enterprise Development Corp., newly founded subsidiaries or joint ventures. The New Career Co., known as the 'labour power reservoir', is the transfer station for redundant employees. Baosteel has stipulated that this company must unconditionally accept all the group's redundant employees and unconditionally provide workers for units in need. It must also play the transfer role by setting up training and re-employment mechanisms. The New Career Co. and Enterprise Development Corp. have set up a number of waste-materials processing factories, an engineering labour service team and other service businesses.

Baosteel attaches great importance to identifying future strategic clients, in an effort to turn a potential market into a substantial one. For example, the group has made the No.1 Automobile Group its strategic client. Hearing that the latter was eager to use domestically-made parts for its Red Flag sedan cars and yet simultaneously lacking confidence in domestic steel plates, Baosteel quickly sent the car maker 300 tons of plates for trial use and promised to bear all costs if these failed. The trial was a success, enabling the factory to dispense with imports for its needs.

Two other case studies, of Hangang and Shougang, are summarised in Boxes 3.3 and 3.4 respectively. The importance of the Hangang model to Angang's reforms has been noted above. Internal accounting and bonus systems were completely reshaped by Hangang, to introduce more realism into the response of the complex to the external environment. The overemphasis on quantity has been reduced; so too at Shougang, where projects have now had to be shelved, and a greater emphasis on quality been made. Referring to China breaking the 100 million tons barrier in 1996, Luo Bing-Sheng, Chief Executive Officer (CEO) of Shougang, warned that:

> ' ... we must clear-headedly understand that 100 million tons steel is only a superiority in quantity. China can be called as a large steelmaking nation, but it is not a country of steelmaking power yet. Compared with many developed countries, we still have a long way to go in respect of quality, variety, benefit and structure of our products' (Luo Bing-Sheng (1997), p.78).

It is via such clear-headedness that the essential changes to China's steel industry must be made.

The costs of change: economic, social, political

This chapter has considered pressures for change on China's steel industry and the response to these pressures. Not only is the steel industry in China faced by the same global pressures as the steel industry elsewhere, but it is also required to respond to such pressures within a unique spatial political economy in which the *political* must be more heavily underlined than for most of its competitors. There is no doubt that the announcement in 1997 and 1998 of dramatic changes to SOEs represent the influence of

Box 3.3 Steel Under Reform: Hangang

Handan Steel Works (Hangang) in Hebei Province, established in 1958, is now one of China's 11 largest iron and steel complexes. In 1990, however, the works was on the brink of bankruptcy due to high operating costs and a soft market for its products. At least 26 of the company's 28 products were unprofitable. Nonetheless, subsidiary plants continued to release production statements and reports which indicated profitability of all products. The sharp contrast between these two situations was a direct result of an internal accounting system based on planned prices. This system failed to accurately reflect the real costs of products and actual product efficiency. In 1991, Hangang initiated internal reform via an unique operating method based on analogue cost accounting. Subsequent intensified technical renovations and improved internal management have further encouraged dramatic growth, with total profits and steel output between 1991–6 exceeding the respective totals in the previous thirty-two years.

Hangang's analogue cost accounting was also combined with 'bonuses linked to cost quotas'. The initial step in reform was to target costs. The original cost calculation method based on the prime cost of raw materials was replaced with the new accounting method which focused on the lowest acceptable market price. Introduction of the new method enabled the company to calculate costs and profits for various production processes in accordance with changing market supply and demand. At the same time, the company surveyed existing advanced standards of steel enterprises, scrutinised its own record, and analysed every component of costs to tap the greatest potential.

The limitation of target costs were considered inviolate. In 1990, No. 2 Steel Plant, a subsidiary, fulfilled production quotas calculated by the original accounting method based on planned prices, but incurred a deficit of 15 million Yuan in terms of the new accounting method. In 1991, use of the new system dictated that this plant reduce its per ton production costs for steel by 24.12 Yuan. The director insisted that this target was impossible and repeatedly requested readjustment. His pleas failed to alter the thinking of higher level managers who were fully aware of the highly competitive market. Therefore, the plant also used the analogue cost accounting method to determine the maximum limit of per ton production costs for steel and introduced a strict cost-management system. As a result, the No. 2 plant effectively reduced costs by 22.5 million Yuan from the previous year to earn 2.5 million Yuan in profits. In 1994, it succeeded in reducing target costs by 34 million Yuan, while at the same time increasing target profits by well over 46 million Yuan.

In line with bonuses linked to cost quotas, target cost quotas are allocated to each subsidiary plant, workshop, working group and individual worker. Each of Hangang's 28,000 workers is assigned a cost quota. The contract responsibility system, with remuneration linked to profits, has closely integrated the responsibilities, rights and interests of various sectors and individual workers with the overall economic benefits of the enterprise. Workers exceeding assigned cost quotas fail to qualify for their monthly bonuses, regardless of whether or not they fulfil other quotas. Units failing to accomplish set goals for three successive months face delayed wage increases. Monthly inventories are conducted of raw materials and fuel stockpiles of each unit, plus a general quarterly audit of financial statements and goods on hand. Cost and profit quotas are readjusted for units submitting balance sheets which indicate inconsistencies in goods on hand. Units exceeding cost quotas and failing to fulfil target profit are deprived of all bonuses. Up to mid-1996, subsidiaries had been denied monthly bonuses 79 times, with wage increases cancelled for 69 plants and divisions.

The total number of subsidiaries and managerial divisions were also reduced, from 503 to 389 between 1990–5. In addition, the proportion of management personnel in the total work force dropped from 14 per cent to 12 per cent. Hangang has also augmented its finance, quality inspection, marketing, planning, budgeting and auditing departments, to become a potent model for other industrial enterprises in China.

Sources: Author research.

Box 3.4 Steel Under Reform: Shougang

The Capital Iron and Steel Co. (Shougang) is the largest enterprise in Beijing, employing some 240,000 people. By early 1995, it was faced with a dire situation. Overstocked, and suffering an acute funds shortage, it was unable to pay its debts, including taxes owed to the state. The situation was so bad that maintaining normal operations was virtually impossible. After taking stock of its crisis, the company's leadership decided to 'strengthen capital operation, accelerate scientific and technological progress and improve the quality and efficiency of economic growth'. By mid-1996, the company had made impressive progress.

Designated by the state as one of the eight pilot enterprises for reform in 1979, Shougang began with a profit-sharing system with the state that was changed in 1982 to a profit-increasing contract system. This meant that with the profit returned to the state the previous year as the base figure, an annual 7.2 per cent additional profit to be turned over to the state should be guaranteed, with any excess retained by the enterprise. In 1994, the state initiated tax reform and introduced a new tax system. Shougang, however, continued its contract system, thus enjoying special policies unavailable to others.

China's iron and steel policies have always focused on expanding output, and this is true with Shougang. In addition, since it was one of the country's 10 largest state-owned enterprises, it established ambitious goals. To achieve the target of producing 10 million tons of steel and joining the ranks of the world's top 10 companies, it inappropriately stressed output, arbitrarily expanded its business scale and operated numerous social welfare undertakings. This led to many financial problems. As a result, in 1995, the company introduced a new tax system and implemented market-oriented reforms.

Under the old contract system, a senior company official explained, the emphasis was purely on output with little consideration given to market demand, causing overproduction, shortage of funds and management impasse. The plant was also embroiled in a corruption scandal. To extricate itself, management changed the operational principle and, after reducing stock, began to promote sales. They also decided to keep expenditures with the limits of income and reduced the scale of capital construction. The savings were used to pay taxes, invest in programmes to protect the environment and establish welfare programmes for the workers. Since then, major production fluctuations have been eliminated and stability achieved. Since 1995, Shougang has suspended the construction of 10 major projects and reduced investments in fixed assets totalling 10.7 billion Yuan.

'In the past, Shougang practised a highly centralized planned economic system', said Hai Qing, a strip steelworks leader. 'There was only one independent legal person for the whole company and 240,000 people 'ate from the same rice pot.' Prompted by the erroneous policy which led people to shout 'Long Live 10 Million Tons of Steel', our joint venture factory, which should have operated in line with the social demand, lacked decision-making power over production and operations and was drawn into a vortex of blindly pursuing high output. In order to fulfil the goal of high output imposed on us from the higher authorities, we had no alternative but to risk equipment and manpower. As a result, equipment was damaged and management chaotic. As a result of being enclosed in a small circle of centralised power and paying no attention to the demands of the social market, there was product overstocking and a scarcity of funds; production and operations were on the brink of an impasse. Grouping reform is the inevitable trend of enterprise reform. It has enabled the enterprise to become a legal entity, characterised by independent management, self-responsibility for profits and losses, self-development and self-restraint, and to be the mainstay of market competition. It has also enabled the enterprise to directly enter the market, providing an excellent opportunity for sound development.' These improvements were supplemented further via announcements in 1998 of major environmental improvements to the year 2000.

Sources: *China Daily* (1998), 'Shougang Moves Mill for Capital's Environment', 18th June.

economists such as Gao Shangquan and Chi Fulin who have argued strongly for 'macro-level' as opposed to 'micro-level' reform of the State sector. And so, for example:

> 'In accordance with the market mechanism of letting the successful survive and having the unsuccessful eliminated, it is essential to boldly adjust the structure of state firms to let those that cannot survive die and those that can survive live.
>
> ... Developing the guiding role of the state-owned sector does not mean invigorating every state firm, which in fact is both unnecessary and impossible. Therefore, enterprises that suffer long-term losses and are unable to turn themselves around should be declared bankrupt in accordance with the pertinent law' (Chi Fulin, 1996, p.113).

Given such strong sentiments (see also Chi Fulin, 1997), it is perhaps little wonder that there are those in China and elsewhere who are concerned that the price of reform may in some cases be too high. The successful case studies noted above have in large part been successful because the workforce has been drastically reduced, via 'hiving off' to subsidiaries or other enterprises. The previous chapter noted the threat of unemployment, and, as has happened in other countries, the 'defeminisation' of manufacturing as male jobs are protected first. Nonetheless, global pressures, and the inexorable logic of capitalistic development demand large-scale labour-shedding in manufacturing. The Asian Financial Crisis has hit China's steel exports as it has hit other exports to South East Asia, reducing them by 26 per cent in the first 11 months of 1998, for example (*Straits Times*, 5-4-1999). Output at the same time peaked at 114 million tons, and so the government has called in 1999 for a reduction in output to 104 million tons. Also, as shown above, deindustrialisation is about to hit China's SOEs, as it hit Europe, North America and other countries in a similar process but a different way. Given the sheer size and scale of China's steel industry, the number of lay-offs could easily outstrip equivalent job losses in the United States or Russia. By 1994 alone, 3,460,000 employees worked in 'Smelting and Processing of Ferrous Metals' while another 220,000 worked in 'Ferrous Metals Mining and Processing' (*China Statistical Yearbook 1995*, p.376). Many of the jobs of these workers will be under threat, officially 700,000 as noted in Chapter 2, but possibly 1.5 million, or even more than two million if the US scale of job loss is found here.

In China itself, the threat of labour unrest will grow as restructuring continues apace. Even by 1996, the authorities admitted more than 3000 incidents of worker protest, and given that as many as thirty million employees may be 'cut loose' from the SOEs, the potential for protest is enormous, notwithstanding the power of the party and state machine. To underscore this, as we have noted elsewhere:

'The reaction of the workers has been far from passive. According to the Chinese Academy of Social Science's annual report on social issues, an average of nine explosions rocked the mainland each day in 1998 as part of a growing crime wave. By early March 1999, there had been 13 bomb explosions this year, killing thirty-three people and injuring more than 100. The report blamed rising crime on joblessness, widening income disparities and anger at rampant corruption for this trend' (Cook and Murray, 1999, p.4)

Also in 1999 came the news that 46,000 workers had not been paid for 2–6 months at the prestigious Shougang complex in Beijing (*Straits Times*, 1999, op.cit.). To these and other issues of SOE financial problems and potential unemployment must be added the many millions of people now surplus to needs in rural areas as spatial transformation occurs throughout the country. Given the great drift to the cities in recent years, it is in the urban areas that disruption is most likely. No doubt there are some who would welcome such disruption in China's body politic, as a necessary step towards liberalisation and eventual democratisation, but the danger is that China would lurch towards increased authoritarianism in response to the threats of internal fragmentation which widespread labour unrest would bring. Such issues will be discussed further in the concluding chapter 10 below.

CHAPTER 4

Regional Disparities

Although the PRC has made considerable attempts to reduce disparities between the wealthier coastal provinces and those of the interior, this chapter argues that disparities are now rapidly increasing. In part, the knock-on effect of rapid urbanisation, discussed below, exacerbates regional tensions and raises a number of issues concerned with the governance of China and the 'China deconstructs' scenario. The implications of such issues are considered and questions raised about alternative regional futures for China. Notwithstanding periodic attempts to ameliorate the differential spatial impact of development, China still contains poor provinces which share some or all of the following characteristics: interior province, high proportion of ethnic minorities, low levels of urbanisation, low levels of industrialisation, low levels of GNP per capita and, low proportion of exports per capita. These broad contrasts are introduced in this chapter as a prelude to more detailed work on poverty and minorities, and on the urban realm, respectively.

In analysing the context in which regional disparities emerge, it is, in part, the unevenness of the economic reforms, both in time and space, which are so perturbing. Over time, they proceed, as Hussain notes (1994), in stop-go cycles, and these normally follow periods of intense debate within the Chinese Communist Party, with the rapid expansion of the market reforms in the early 1990s, for example, following Deng Xiaoping's personal intervention via his Guangdong tour and speeches in the first half of 1992. Over space, it is very much the coastal provinces which are benefiting most from the reforms, while other parts of the country are lagging behind. Also, of course, China's population is vast, and its generally high economic rating at the national level, is not replicated at the per capita level. Yabuki notes that China is 103rd in *per capita* GNP (Yabuki, 1995, p.82), and although a purchasing power parity calculation would raise this figure, China as a whole has a long way to go in its development trajectory. China is a relatively rich *country*, therefore, but it still contains many poor *people*. These people are especially concentrated in specific parts of China. The economic growth has been phenomenal, and China is to be congratulated on the successes so far achieved; the pressures of development remain great, however, and it is on their regional aspects that we now focus.

The chapter is organised into three sections:

• Legacies of uneven development
• Growing regional disparities
• The implications of regionalism: Greater China, Smaller Chinas

Legacies of uneven development

The Chinese space has always been unevenly developed, as has the space of most countries. The 'cradle area' of Chinese civilisation thousands of years ago was the confluence of the Huang He, Wei He and other rivers. This is the area of the loess plateau, loess being a fine wind-borne deposit which is easily tilled, and civilisation gradually spread from there into the valley of the Huang He and then many centuries later south to the valley of the Chang Jiang (Yangtze). For example, during the southern Song dynasty, based at Hangzhou and Nanjing from 1127 to 1280, a fast-maturing strain of rice was introduced from Indo-China, leading to easier double-cropping, expansion of the ecumene, and terracing, laying a solid base for the future prosperity of the Yangtze basin. The Han people expanded continuously both in numbers and over space, pushing other peoples further West or South especially, and/or upland into higher altitudes.

In spatial terms, China was (and even today to a large extent still is) a rural country in which most people earned their living from the soil. 'Industry' was poorly appreciated in Chinese society, and it was the scholars/intellectuals rather than the merchants who had the high status in society, although the latter could become very wealthy, recompense no doubt for their lack of standing. It was the foreign powers, in the nineteenth century and after, who stimulated industrial development, mainly in coastal cities and especially in Shanghai. The Japanese take-over of Manchuria in the 1930s added to this coastal imbalance, for the Japanese developed their puppet state of *Manzhouguo* as an industrial centre, concentrating on heavy industry and mining, geared for export back to Japan. The other foreign treaty ports and concessions were focused more on light industry. At the dawn of the Communist era China was poorly industrialised, and much of what industry there was, had been destroyed in the Civil War, in the war with Japan, or had been removed by the Soviets (in Manchuria) or by refugees from Communism, to Hong Kong in particular.

The Chinese space was, prior to the revolution, highly unevenly developed, with huge inequalities between wealthy Western-dominated enclaves in the cities, or rich rural regions, contrasting with poverty-stricken urban or rural areas. Especially in the north of China, poverty was widespread, and the 'Yellow River' (the Huang He) had become known as 'China's sorrow'. It is estimated that by the early 1930s, one third of China's vast peasantry were tenants only, with the average peasant earning 10 taels per annum, compared with the official civil service rates of 33–180 taels, but the latter would be expanded via expense accounts, bribery and corruption to between 30,000–180,000 taels (Blecher, 1986, p.7). The appeal of Communism owed much to the feeling that such inequalities would be overcome via such policies as Land Reform or Industrial Development. Population was, and is, concentrated into high densities in the main river valleys and delta regions. In contrast, vast tracts of the Chinese ecumene were virtually uninhabited, and uninhabitable, therefore pressures on agricultural land were acute in riverine or coastal regions. The pressures within the system of inequalities, of humiliation, of the struggle for a decent life for one's family and for China itself reached a peak in the early years of the twentieth century and heralded the success of the CPC. The party would be required to tackle these inequalities, which were spatial as well as structural.

In spatial terms, the early Five Year Plans, therefore, sought to further develop the existing industrial centres, but also to extend development towards the interior, not just what was called the 'rich fringe' (on China's ancient and fading garment) of the coast. Thus, the Manchurian industrial heartland, centred on the integrated steelworks of Anshan, for example, received heavy investment, not just in steel but also in coal mining, machine-building and power production, and there was considerable investment also in the Beijing and Tianjin areas, plus areas in and around Shanghai. In Beijing, for example, the infrastructure was developed for the subsequent expansion of the Shijingshan (now Shougang) Iron and Steel Works, while industrial satellite towns were established around Shanghai, and other, lesser, industrial developments took place in other pre-existing urban centres. Buchanan suggested, some years ago, that more than two-thirds of above-average industrial projects were in the West and North-West (Buchanan, 1970). This spread of investment was due to such factors as the desire to reduce regional disparities, both in a spatial as well as a social sense, to locate heavy industries near to raw material supplies and/or consumer centres to reduce transport costs, but, probably above all, to achieve a strategic decentralisation of industry, in case of attack from the United States. The groundwork was laid, therefore, for, *inter alia*, the subsequent construction of the iron and steel works at Baotou in Inner Mongolia, the petrochemicals complex in Lanzhou, and exploitation of the oil deposits of Xinjiang plus other resources of the interior, during this period (Freeberne, 1971).

Although policies varied during the Maoist era, for much of the time there seemed to be a genuine concern to reduce, or at least not to encourage, regional disparities. However, policies were often developed in secret, as shown most spectacularly in the example of the Third Front (Sanxian) region of the interior, developed for strategic reasons, as noted in the chapter three. Cannon suggests that 'The dispersal of enterprises and institutions under the sanxian policy had little at all to do with bringing about spatial equality. Interpretations which assume that Chinese policy had been concerned with this are misguided. (Cannon, 1990, p.39). Instead, the main objective was to 'strengthen and preserve the country, not to equalise consumption or welfare between provinces' (ibid.). The Dengist era heralded a relaxation in security issues, and less concern for such geostrategic policies. The Dengist reforms had many features and affected agricultural and industrial production alike, rural and urban areas. 'Growth Pole Theory' seems to have explicitly or implicitly guided investment. For example, the 'growth points' known as the 'Special Economic Zones' (SEZs) – Shenzhen, Zhuhai, Shantou in Guangdong province, plus Xiamen in Fujian province – were opened in 1980, then the 14 'Coastal Cities' opened in 1984 (shown in Map 4.1). At a later stage, Hainan island attained province status (was separated from Guangdong province) and, in April 1988 it became the fifth SEZ (Phillips and Yeh, 1990). These offered preferential locations, with exemptions from customs duties, tax breaks, infrastructure advantages including good communications and other features designed to attract foreign investment in joint venture companies. More locations were opened up in 1992, in border cities and provincial capitals for example, as Map 4.1 illustrates. These latter shall be dealt with further in the next section. For the present we can note the spatial dimension of economic development, with these areas of focused development being, until the 1990s, almost exclusively coastal. Once again the 'fringe' was being embroidered, and although the garment was less faded than before, the fringe still stood out from the rest of the cloth.

Growing regional disparities

The urban stresses in China's transformation will be discussed in chapter seven, but for now it must be noted that these interweave crucially with those at the regional level. When discussing regional disparities in China, for example, 'when the urban dimension of development is added there is an even greater divergence between the highly urbanised coastal zone and the poorly urbanised interior as urban economic growth continues apace' (Cook and Li, 1996, pp.203–4). Map 4.2, for example, shows the high levels of GDP per capita in 1996 in the three municipalities of Shanghai, Beijing and Tianjin, plus such coastal provinces as Guangdong, Liaoning,

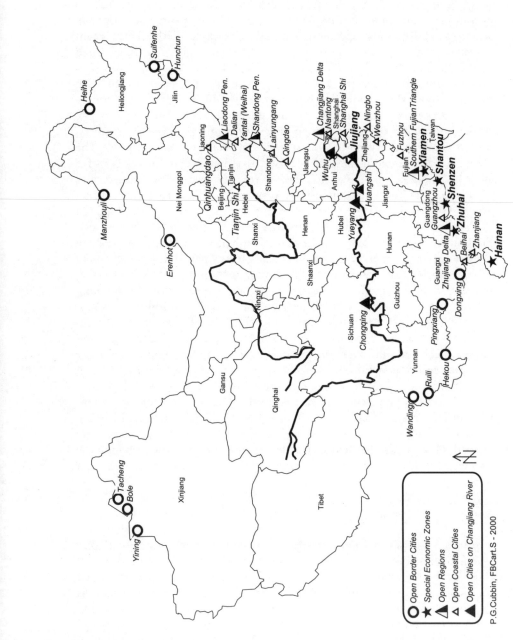

Map 4.1 Spatial Development Initiatives, Dengist Period

P.G.Cubbin, FBCart.S - 2000

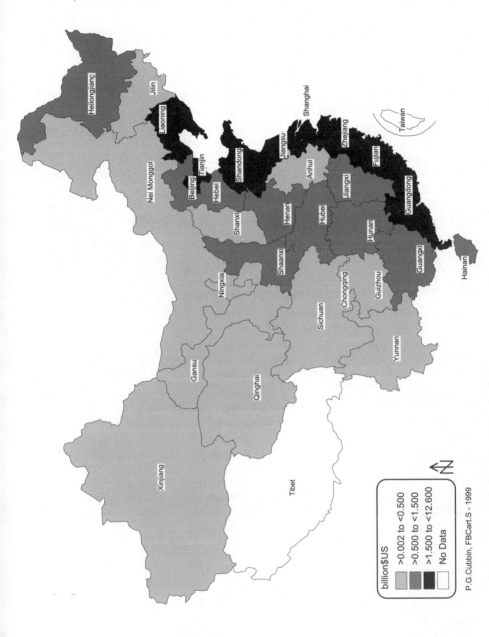

Map 4.2 Utilised FDI, Provincial Level, 1997

billion$US

>0.002 to <0.500
>0.500 to <1.500
>1.500 to <12.600
No Data

P.G.Cubbin, FBCart.S - 1999

Heilongjiang, Shandong and those in the Shanghai delta, Zhejiang and Jiangsu. The use of mean GDP per capita can mask the sheer starkness of spatial contrasts, therefore Map 4.3 which illustrates foreign investment per capita (a major driver of change) portrays a sharper and, to us, more realistic distinction between most of the coastal provinces compared to the interior. Such contrasts are confirmed further, by the total amounts of utilised FDI at the province level, for 1979–97.

Consideration of Table 4.1 shows that, of the nine provinces with utilised FDI of one billion dollars or more, *all* are coastal, with the next being the interior province of Sichuan, 'the rice bowl of China' which is the exception which proves the rule. Conversely, for those with utilised FDI of 100,000 dollars or less, *all* are interior provinces. To us, there is little doubt of the cyclic nature of both regional wealth and poverty, and of the dependence on state intervention of those provinces in the latter category. Cannon and Zhang summarise the internal policy debates concerning the need to balance growth to a greater extent, and refer to a policy document which 'suggested that the state should further develop its regional compensation policy, improve its existing policy of 'aid to poor areas', strengthen policies for minority nationalities, and continue fiscal subsidies to compensate regional interests' (Cannon and Zhang, 1996, p.88). Officially, for example, there are now fifty million regarded as being in poverty, but the true number may be nearer 100 million, many of them

Table 4.1 Utilised FDI by Province, 1997, US$billion

Province	Utilised FDI	Province	Utilised FDI
Guangdong	12.6	Shaanxi	0.6
Jiangsu	5.4	Jiangxi	0.5
Fujian	4.2	Anhui	0.4
Shanghai	4.2	Jilin	0.4
Shandong	2.8	Chongqing*	0.4
Tianjin	2.5	Shanxi	0.3
Liaoning	2.4	Sichuan	0.2
Beijing	1.6	Yunnan	0.2
Zhejiang	1.5	Xinjiang	0.2
Hebei	1.1	Nei Monggol	0.1
Guangxi	0.9	Guizhou	0.05
Hunan	0.9	Gansu	0.04
Hubei	0.8	Ningxia	0.01
Hainan	0.7	Qinghai	0.002
Henan	0.7	Tibet/Xizang	n.d.
Heilongjiang	0.7		

Note: * Chongqing newly created as a municipality under the Central Government, 1997.
Source: China Statistical Yearbook 1998, State Statistical Bureau, Beijing, p.642.

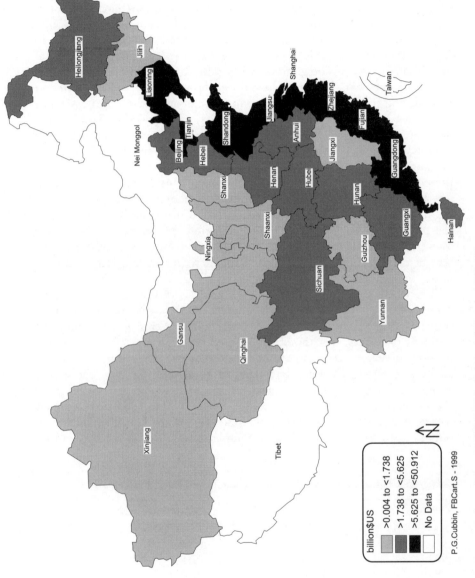

billion$US

>0.004 to <1.738
>1.738 to <5.625
>5.625 to <50.912
No Data

P.G.Cubbin, FBCart.S - 1999

Map 4.3 Cumulative Utilised FDI, Provincial Level, 1979–97

resident in the poorer provinces noted here, or comprising the migrants who move from these provinces to the perceived attractions of the cities.

A recent analysis of the incomes of rural residents in different regions of China confirms that inequalities are increasing rather than decreasing (Zhang Ping, with the Institute of Economics, Chinese Academy of Social Science, 1998). The author suggests that since the contract responsibility system, with remuneration linked to output, was introduced in China in 1979, different economic regions have experienced different levels of development and disintegration, with differing natural resources. 'An increasing imbalance has emerged in the economic development of different regions, and this has led to a big gap in rural incomes' (ibid., p.1). A range of studies by Chinese and foreign scholars, including the World Bank, describe the trend of sharpening inequality in per-capita income of households in different rural areas, and basically come to a common conclusion that the existence of off-farm sources of income, especially the presence of township enterprises, is the main cause. This contrasts with international experience, such as in Taiwan, where in the period 1964–80, the income inequality of Taiwan residents did not intensify, but dropped sharply during the process of industrialisation. The fast-growing labour-intensive industrial enterprises on the island contributed a great deal to the income balance, in mainland China similar activities have led to a widening rather than a narrowing income gap.

It is worth considering Zhang Ping's analysis of this situation in some detail. His data comes from two sources. One is material released by statistics bureau concerning rural household per-capita net income of different provinces, and the other is based on 1988 and 1995 disposable income surveys by the Institute of Economics of CASS. Table 4.2 shows changes in regional income inequality of rural residents over the period 1980–95. The Gini Coefficient measures inequality, ranging from values of 0 (total equality) to 1 (total inequality). From 1980 to 1985 rural incomes increased dramatically, following the reforms, but the Gini coefficient rose only slightly, from .14 to .15, as the Table shows. This is because, in that

Table 4.2 Changes in Regional Income Inequality of Rural Residents 1980–95

Year	Per capita net income	Gini coefficient of rural provinces	Gini coefficient of farmers
1980	184.50	0.14	0.24
1985	348.96	0.15	0.26
1990	401.74	0.20	0.31
1995	501.53	0.23	0.34
Increase 1980–95*	2.7	0.64	0.42

Source: Zhang Ping (1998), Chart 1, pages 2–3 (selected years only). *Our own calculations

time period, income changes were due to increased incomes via agriculture only. From 1985, however, off-farm activities increased considerably, and in the 1990s, since 1992 especially, rural industrial reform has led to a quickening of off-farm economic activities and rural labour transfers, plus a resumption of rural income growth which slowed in the late 1980s. Such changes are fundamentally uneven spatially, with some regions being better placed than others to benefit from them. The Gini coefficient increased considerably, therefore, at the provincial level, from 1985 to 1990, and further still to 1995. For the farmers themselves, the increase in the coefficient was relatively less, from .24 to .34 by 1995. In all, incomes increased markedly, by nearly three times, 1980–95, but provincial inequalities increased by 64 per cent compared to 42 per cent for farmers' incomes. 'The regional income gap has had greater influence on the general income difference in rural areas, and this is probably because off-farm development in China is characterised by regional expansion' (ibid., p.2).

A detailed model is constructed by Zhang Ping of the Institute of Economics 1995 survey which, among other results, shows that, in Beijing for example a household will have on average 137 per cent more income than its counterpart in Gansu, the poorest province, while in Zhejiang a household will have 82 per cent more income than in Gansu. For farm incomes such contrasts are far less, with an average Beijing farming household having only 16 per cent more income than in Gansu, and Zhejiang 46 per cent. More developed areas have much more non-farm income than underdeveloped areas, therefore the non-farm income in a Beijing household is 211 per cent of that in Gansu, and 122 per cent for Zhejiang. The model also reflects the fact that the off-farm incomes of developed areas are more significant than their farm incomes and the off-farm incomes of Liaoning, Hebei, Shandong and Shanxi provinces are higher than their total income. The off-farm figures do not show much difference in Jilin, Anhui, Jiangxi, Henan, Sichuan and Shaanxi provinces, and the locations of other provinces are less influential for their off-farm incomes than for farm incomes. Except for the four most developed areas in the survey: Beijing, Guangdong, Jiangsu and Zhejiang (for some reason some provinces, such as Shanghai, were not included in the survey), the income of most provinces are from farming.

Zhang Ping also shows that geographical elements greatly affect total income and farm income, with total income in the plain areas being 23 per cent higher than that of the mountainous regions, and the total income of hilly land being 9 per cent higher than that of mountainous regions (see Table 4.3). For farm income alone, on the plains this is 29 per cent higher than for mountainous regions, while that of hilly land is 10 per cent higher than for mountainous areas. These variations are higher than those for total household income, showing that geographical elements have a greater effect on farm income. But, not surprisingly, these factors have little influence on off-farm income, indicating there is no direct relationship between the two. The analysis also considers other spatial or policy entities, and so for example the 'old liberated areas' have obviously low income compared with other areas, as do 'frontier areas' and 'ethnic minority areas' with the latter suffering from low off-farm income in particular. 'The latter is the key problem. The poor areas have three negative symbols in the models, showing their backwardness compared with other areas' (ibid., p.4). The gap in farm income is 15 per cent, while that in off-farm income is as high as 39 per cent.

Table 4.3 Income Functions of Rural Residents in 1995

	Name	Household total income	Household farm income	Household off-farm income
P1	Beijing	1.37	0.16	2.11
P2	Hebei	0.29	0.17	0.71
P3	Shanxi	0.12	−0.06	0.29
P4	Liaoning	0.25	0.19	0.62
P5	Jilin	0.12	0.19	−0.12
P6	Jiangsu	0.94	0.59	1.42
P7	Zhejiang	0.82	0.46	1.22
P8	Anhui	0.41	0.37	−0.04
P9	Jiangxi	0.52	0.56	0.19
P10	Shandong	0.34	0.32	0.39
P11	Henan	0.24	0.29	0.12
P12	Hubei	0.35	0.50	−0.53
P13	Hunan	0.49	0.57	0.35
P14	Guangdong	1.26	0.95	1.65
P15	Sichuan	0.13	0.26	−0.12
P16	Guizhou	0.36	0.48	−0.13
P17	Yunnan	0.10	0.19	−0.27
P18	Shaanxi	−0.01	−0.09	−0.08
P19	Gansu	–	–	–
B401_1	Plains	0.23	0.29	0.02
B401_2	Hilly land	0.09	0.10	−0.03
	Mountains	–	–	–
B403_1	Old liberated areas	−0.15	−0.06	−0.23
B404_1	Frontier areas	0.04	0.08	0.07
B405_1	Minority areas	−0.05	−0.02	−0.43
B406_1	City suburbs	0.10	−0.11	0.16
B407_1	Poor counties	−0.22	−0.15	−0.39
Adj-R square		0.37	0.26	0.23
F-test		139.94	85.00	85.00
Samples		6929	6894	5873

Source: Zhang Ping (1998), Chart 3, p.5; t-test columns and some other data omitted.

Focusing on the well-known division between China's eastern, central and western regions, Zhang's analysis displays similar findings, with the geographical elements of eastern and central China having a positive effect on the total local income. At this scale, his model shows that:

'With all other factors remaining the same, the influence of eastern and central regions to their total incomes is 68 per cent and 29 per cent respectively, compared to the western region, while the figures are respectively 41 per cent and 27 per cent for farm income and 135 per cent and 24 per cent for off-farm income respectively. The gap between the eastern and western regions mainly lies in off-farm income, while the gap between the central and western regions mainly lies in farm income, complying with the effects on total income by different locations of different provinces. The advantages of central regions to western regions lie in land resources, while besides good land resources, the eastern part benefits from greater industrialization of the countryside' (ibid., p.6).

Comparison of the Institute of Economics surveys for 1988 and 1995 (Table 4.4) shows that inequalities in rural areas increased by 44 per cent between 1988 and 1995, with the Gini coefficient rising from 0.18 to 0.26. The main reason for this expansion between regions is a 57 per cent increase in waged incomes, from 0.35 in 1988 to 0.55 in 1995; this replaced business revenue as the leading source of household income. The contribution of household business income dropped from 49 per cent in 1988 to 31 per cent in 1995, indicating a basic change in the traditional business pattern of rural households. By 1995, the primary income source was wages, followed by property, house rental and household business. Zhang Ping notes that the total increase of these items will enlarge the inequality income, especially the incomes of wages and property, thus forming an important structure in future income development when the differential income will be further expanded.

In more sophisticated areas, increased market competition emphasises capital inputs and high- or medium-technology. These require higher skilled workers, including highly-educated staff with rich working experience. As there is a shortage of such persons in the rural areas, those who do possess the necessary skills have seen their wages increase rapidly. Thus if more advanced industry exists in one place then wage levels will rise fast. However, if an area is dominated by labour-intensive enterprises that only need simple skills, with a ready availability of labour, then wage levels will be relatively low, with little increase witnessed over a long period. We concur with Zhang's analysis that it is this factor that results in different wage levels between township enterprises in different regions.

The difference in income between rural industry and farming is based on the opportunities of participating in the industrial process. In more

Table 4.4 China's Regional Rural Industrial Employment and Wages

	1988		1995	
	Rural Industrial employment rate (%)	*Average monthly wage of township enterprise workers*	*Rural Industrial employment rate (%)*	*Average monthly wage of township enterprise workers*
Beijing	28.91	125.11	27.83	326.75
Tianjin	31.34	100.77	27.83	326.75
Hebei	10.45	94.03	12.63	100.25
Shanxi	11.25	92.53	13.00	91.05
Inner Mongolia	3.06	83.76	3.02	71.43
Liaoning	12.56	102.49	9.74	155.84
Jilin	4.79	95.86	3.76	76.40
Heilongjiang	5.29	107.37	5.81	86.32
Shanghai	49.08	123.14	46.01	384.20
Jiangsu	20.51	91.10	19.18	240.44
Zhejiang	20.59	102.95	21.33	204.22
Anhui	5.39	70.32	6.69	152.24
Fujian	6.84	102.78	9.13	160.65
Jiangxi	7.52	78.43	6.37	87.10
Shandong	9.71	86.15	10.02	137.46
Henan	5.48	69.43	7.03	117.43
Hubei	7.37	75.85	7.23	114.65
Hunan	5.56	81.53	6.16	103.33
Guangdong	10.64	146.87	13.99	229.61
Guangxi	2.36	70.76	3.05	153.17
Hainan	2.78	73.70	2.96	79.16
Sichuan	4.81	67.17	4.71	90.60
Guizhou	3.01	87.64	3.03	54.45
Yunnan	2.27	70.58	2.59	84.74
Shaanxi	5.09	68.14	5.03	64.59
Gansu	3.48	109.67	3.98	69.34
Qinghai	2.82	71.34	3.67	125.45
Ningxia	2.49	79.22	2.77	151.52
Xinjiang	2.38	92.79	2.50	138.33
Gini coefficient between provinces	0.48	0.12	0.46	0.28

Source: Zhang Ping, p.10, from *China Statistics Year Book 1996*, China Statistics Press, Beijing.

developed regions, the high-level of township industry offers many employment opportunities, so that household income from industrial sources is much higher than from farming. However, in less developed regions, such employment opportunities are limited, so that farmers experience difficulty in obtaining any income from industrial work. In Taiwan, the rapid development of its industry and limited land area, meant that its industrial expansion could attract sufficient rural labourers after four years or so. The employment opportunities for rural labourers were fairly equal, workers in labour-intensive enterprises enjoying equal wages. Therefore, industrialisation in general has led to more equal income. For China, however, the contrasts in opportunity for relatively skilled off-farm work are too high for equalisation to develop.

Table 4.4 highlights provincial contrasts of rural employment and wages of township enterprises between 1988 and 1995. The employment rate exhibits little change in Gini coefficient between the two dates. What is quite different, however, is the Gini coefficient for wage levels, which have become more uneven in the 1990s. This analysis confirms, therefore, the work of other analysts, such as Uri Dadush and Dong He (1995) who considered exports per capita, Bramall and Jones (1993) who examined other rural income data or Chai (1996) who focused on labour productivity and value-added per worker. Along with others (see Cook and Li, 1996, p.203), and although coming from different directions, with contrasting data sets, they are united in one stark message: China's regional disparities are on the increase, with richer regions becoming relatively richer still, and poorer ones relatively poorer. Zhang Ping concludes, in line with a World Bank study of 1997, 'China is one of the worst countries in Asia in regards to regional inequality' (ibid., p.10). It is to some of the implications of this that we now turn.

The implications of regionalism: Greater China, Smaller Chinas

This section draws partly upon an ongoing research project by Ian Cook and Rex Li on Chinese regionalism (Cook, 2000; Cook and Li, 1994b, 1996; Li, 1997). China developed historically as a strong, centralised, state under imperial control. Nevertheless, the strength of the Empire waxed and waned over time and space, and 'The centre in China has never been able to exert complete control over the provinces' (Cook and Li, 1996, p.202). Therefore, provinces such as Sichuan and Guangdong (see Boxes 4.1 and 4.2) became associated with opposition to the imperial writ and the centre of what can be called 'old regionalisms', in which localising identities and allegiances could come into tension or even conflict with centralising ones. Then there were peripheral regions inhabited by the Miao, Tibetans, Uygurs and other peoples who were largely assimilated into the Chinese Empire by force of arms, and so would only patchily owe allegiance to the Emperor, if at all. As we have seen in Section One above, during the nineteenth century, such 'alternative regionalisms' were overlaid and distorted by the Western powers who forced China to surrender control to them in the extra-territorial treaty ports, and, in the twentieth century, to the Japanese puppet state of *Manzhouguo*. New ideas, of modernisation, of democracy, of nationalism, of industrialisation and urbanisation, were introduced to present powerful alternatives to the *status quo*, and led eventually to the Communist Revolution itself.

Since the Revolution, although the central government has consistently sought to exercise strong control over the country, it has at times done so by decentralist rather than centralist policies. The recent Dengist policies, for example, have had a strongly decentralist element, as control has been devolved to the provincial governments, albeit often with a veneer of deference to the centre, in which 'the centre pretends to rule and the provinces pretend to be ruled' (Cannon and Zhang, op.cit., p.85). Old regionalisms have been reasserted, and 'new regionalisms' (see previous chapter) have been developed. The new regionalisms owe much to the heady mix of increased local autonomy, rapid economic growth and a proliferation of new external linkages to the global economy. New elites are emerging, comprised of local party officials, entrepreneurs, intellectuals and others who may challenge or subvert the government writ of Beijing. Cities have a key role in this process of regional change, one which is occurring throughout Pacific Asia and elsewhere (see Cook, Doel and Li, 1996, for other examples). It is these new regionalisms which largely give rise to the 'China Deconstructs' scenario (Goodman and Segal, 1994), which in turn is largely fuelled by growing Western concerns about the growing economic and military might of China. Cook and Li have explored different scenarios for the future of China (1994b and 1996, op.cit.) and these are: 1. no substantial change, 2. China shrinks, and 3. China expands.

Summarising each briefly, a situation with no substantial change would be one in which there is a relatively smooth post-Deng transition of power, and Hong Kong is assimilated without conflict. Problems within the country would continue, and 'Social inequality and corruption within the CPC and government might remain serious' (Cook and Li, 1996, op.cit., p.211), but continued economic growth and consumerism (see Chapters 5 and 7), plus the power of the PLA if needs be, would be employed to defuse internal tensions, and an element of regional autonomy would be tolerated. Western concerns over human rights and copyright infringements would be muted by business opportunities. 'China would remain as a unitary state and the Communist regime would continue in control; the borders of the PRC would remain sacrosanct' (ibid., p.211). At the time of writing, and notwithstanding the tensions within China, this scenario still seems the most probable, but will be considered again in Chapter 10.

The second scenario, in contrast, is one in which the erosion of sovereignty via such combined pressures as globalisation, new regionalism (based partly on newly emerging elite groups) and ethnic dissent, would lead to China fragmenting. Goodman and Segal, among others, have

Box 4.1 Old Regionalism: Sichuan

The ancient Chinese saying, 'the mountains are high; the emperor is far away' might have originated in Sichuan, given its remoteness from the capital, whether it was in Nanjing, Beijing or elsewhere. A modern geography text notes another old saying that 'travelling to Sichuan is as difficult as travelling to heaven' (Zhou, 1992, p.365)! It is only in recent times that the isolation of this province has been to an extent overcome. Given that it is a relatively fertile, self-sufficient area, with a substantial population (now well over 100 million), it is hardly surprising that, as Zhou Enlai for instance noted, it was often said that Sichuan 'always was the scene of turmoil before other provinces, and that order was always restored in that area later than the rest of the country' (cited in Cook and Li, 1996, p.202). Sichuan was one of the centres of 'old regionalism' in China, therefore, with potential for rebellion or upheaval centred upon its ancient cities such as Chengdu (the capital of the province) or Chongqing. The province even proclaimed a 'Declaration of Independence', in 1921, although Goodman explains that this was *pro-tem*, according to the concept of *pian an* (partial peace). 'As a purely transient expedient, when there is imperial disorder, order can be restored in only part of the Empire on condition that it is then extended to the country as a whole, and that restoration is itself a duty incumbent on the partial ruler' (Goodman, 1994, p.8).

Although a fertile agricultural area, industry was only weakly developed, and it was the anti- Japanese war which caused the relocation of factories (and government) to the province from coastal areas. As noted earlier in this chapter, a modern twist to this geostrategic imperative was added during the sanxian policy of the 1960s and 1970s, the revelations about which 'show an astounding scale of investment, involving billions of yuan on several key projects. That China's fifth largest iron and steel works today is at Panzhihua, on the borders of Sichuan and Yunnan in a very mountainous area, gives some idea of the scale and nature of the policy' (Cannon, 1990, p.39). Such investment would have reduced old regionalism in the province via reduction in one of its main drivers, namely the feeling of being neglected by the centre. Later, this driver would have been still further undermined by Zhao Ziyang, who in 1978, as party secretary of the province, used it as the experimental model for enterprise reforms and the introduction of market forces into the management of the state sector. With that dynamic son of Sichuan, Deng Xiaoping, attaining power, the old regionalism of Sichuan would be even further reduced. Sichuan, partly due to its large population, as well as fairly high levels of previous investment now has quite a large sub-economy. Nonetheless, in a post-Deng era there is always the possibility of resurgence in the desire for greater autonomy, especially given that per-capita incomes in the province remain low, and some way behind the well-off coastal provinces.

Sources: Cannon, T. (1990), 'Regions: Spatial Inequality and Regional Policy', in Cannon, T. and Jenkins, A. (eds), *The Geography of Contemporary China: The Impact of Deng Xiaoping's Decade*, Routledge, London, 1990, pp.28–60.

Cook, I.G. and Li, R. (1996), The Rise of Regionalism and the Future of China, in Cook, I.G., Doel, M., and Li, R. (eds) *Fragmented Asia: Regional Integration and National Disintegration in Pacific Asia*, Avebury, Aldershot.

Goodman, D.S.G. (1994), 'The Politics of Regionalism: Economic Development, Conflict and Negotiation', Chapter 1 in Goodman, D.S.G. and Segal, G. (eds) (1994), *China Deconstructs: Politics, Trade and Regionalism*, Routledge, London, pp.1–20.

Zhou Shunwu (1992), *China Provincial Geography*, Foreign Languages Press, Beijing, Chapter 22.

Box 4.2 Old-New Regionalism: Guangdong

Another province which was very much associated with old regionalism is Guangdong, 'which is born largely out of its distance from the various northern capitals rather than any local movements for political separation. Provincial histories often take pride in the fifteen or so independent governments or de facto regimes established in Guangdong since the province's incorporation into the Empire in 214 BC. However, almost all of these represented alternative national governments, rather than movements for an independent Guangdong' (Goodman and Feng Chongyi, 1994, p.179). It is this 'alternative national government' which makes some observers feel, however, that pressures might once again arise in which such a scenario is revisited. In the recent historical era, Canton (now Guangzhou) was of course *the* point of entry for the 'foreign devils', who stimulated such change in China itself. Today, with the Open Door Policy, Guangdong is in a crucial transition between its old, and new, regionalism. Variously termed, the Chinese Economic Triangle (CET) between Guangdong, Hong Kong and Taiwan is a contemporary exemplar of new regionalism.

Here the common ethnicity of the Han has transcended the barriers of political regimes and dialect to integrate Taiwanese and Hong Kong capital, management expertise and technology with the labour force and other resources of South China in a now classic case of transborder development aimed at promoting export-led growth. Growth rate of GDP reached a world record 30% in Guangdong Province in the early 1990s, and is levelling out at double-digit scale of around 15 per cent, with Guangdong being predicted to be the 'fifth tiger' of Asia (Fu-Kuo Liu, 1996). There is a massive expansion in infrastructure, including new expressways, a new subway system in Guangzhou, and new and expanded airports across the region. Cook's most recent visit to this region was (twice) in 1995, contrasting with his first research visit in

1980. The contrasts between then and now are considerable, with the pace of life being nearly as fast in Guangdong itself as it always has been in Hong Kong, and the perennial development problems of congestion, environmental quality and social cohesion being equally in evidence with the pluses of new buildings, economic prosperity and material progress.

Hong Kong has been the main location through which the foreign investment to fuel this boom has flowed, but while much of this is from Hong Kong companies in their own right, much has also been from Taiwanese investors during the period before they were allowed to invest overtly in China, while non-Chinese investors have utilised the services of Hong Kong entrepreneurs as 'middlemen' with the expertise to deal with Chinese bureaucracy and culture. It is estimated that Hong Kong firms now employ 4,000,000 people directly in South China, especially in Guangdong Province (inclusive of the three Special Economic Zones (SEZs) in the Province). Local county or province officials, managers and CPC members have been key players in building the alliances and partnerships with these foreign investors. Often such people have been criticised for graft or inefficiency, but given their previous lack of training or expertise in the ways of business, especially foreign business, their input has been remarkable. The dynamism of these people, and of the CET generally, could drive the desire for independence, free of the remote control and perceived autocracy of Beijing, where relatively few Cantonese reach positions of power and influence.

Sources: Author research.

Goodman, D.S.G. and Feng Chongyi (1994), 'Guangdong: Greater Hong Kong and the New Regionalist Future', Chapter 6 in Goodman, D.S.G. and Segal, G. (eds) (1994), *China Deconstructs: Politics, Trade and Regionalism*, Routledge, London, pp.177–201.

Fu-Kuo Liu (1996), 'Industrial Development and the Impetus to Regional Economic Integration in Pacific Asia', Chapter 6 in Cook, I.G., Doel, M.A. and Li, R. (eds), *Fragmented Asia: Regional Integration and National Disintegration in Pacific Asia*, Avebury, Aldershot, England.

considered this in some detail (1994). In this possibility, what we would call a host of 'Smaller Chinas' might emerge, in which:

> 'Rich regions like Guangdong and Fujian might attempt to break away from the centre to form a South China state with Hong Kong and Taiwan in order to maintain their economic prosperity, while poor regions would become poorer with the possibility of social unrest and even civil war' (Cook and Li, p.213).

Tibet and Xinjiang, perhaps largely encouraged by foreign powers, would secede (Chapter 6 considers this in more detail), and China proper would return to a rump centred on the Huang He – Yangtze deltas, similar to how it has been at some periods in the past. Some western observers might be quite sanguine about, even desirous of, such a scenario, viewing it as a means of restricting the potential threat of China. Cook and Li, however, regard this possibility as a 'nightmare scenario' in that the potential upheaval could lead to enormous loss of life, due to the possibility of nuclear conflict and widespread migration which would make the flow of Kosovan refugees seem tiny in comparison. There would be serious consequences for the international community, especially in Pacific Asia.

The final scenario which Cook and Li considered was that of an expanding China, in which not only Hong Kong but also Taiwan were successfully assimilated into a new 'Greater China'. Such simmering tensions as the spat over the Taiwanese leader's reference to 'state-to-state' relations in 1999, may have further delayed such a possibility, but it nonetheless remains plausible. In this situation, China returns to its maximum spatial extent historically. The combination of Taiwan's wealth and economic dynamism and China's vast population and resources could be formidable. The potential outcomes would be more unpredictable, depending upon whether China chooses to reassert militarily its historic claims in the South China Seas, and Cho Khong for example, discusses this further (Cho Khong, op.cit., p.178). Such a move would add to latent or not so latent fears of China in South East Asia and Japan who would seek US support to ward off the threat of an increasingly powerful China. This scenario would see the ratcheting up of arms expenditure in Pacific Asia (there are already signs of this occurring) and could also be dangerous, 'potentially destabilising the entire international system' (Cook and Li, 1996, op.cit., p.215). Although Tsang feels that 'The fear of an awakening superpower, ready to bully Asia and the West, seems to have been overplayed' (1996, p.41), the perceptions of others may not be so reassuring. The potential unpalatability of the potential outcomes are, therefore, what makes the study of regionalism so crucial to the contemporary New World Order.

At present, the post-Deng transition has been smooth, but the knock-on effect of the Asian financial crisis of 1997–8 is still rumbling on uncertainly. Hong Kong has suffered financially to an extent, and it may be that there is some regional destabilisation in South China as a result. Whichever of the future scenarios eventually unfold, the growth of regional disparities summarised above will severely limit the room for manoeuvre of the regime(s) in power. It seems to us that, as Cook has noted elsewhere (2000), unless the Chinese government develops and facilitates a series of effective regional-level responses to the pressures of urbanisation, industrialisation and general economic growth, the entire fabric of Chinese society could be unstitched.

However, in the face of such potential threats to the stability of the state, the Chinese government has not been idle. They have sought, for instance, to promote new spatial zones of development, around the edge of China and also in the interior. Many of these are still in the coastal region, however. Clockwise from the North East, the new, sometimes overlapping, regions are the Tumen River Regional Triangle [sometimes Tumen River Delta Project], the Bohai-Sea Rim Region, the Yellow Sea Economic Zone, the Beijing-Tianjin conurbation, the Dragon Head of Shanghai, the Fujian-Taiwan region, the Guangzhou-Hong Kong region [sometimes Hong Kong-Guangdong-Shenzhen Triangle], with both the latter being subdivisions of the Chinese Economic Triangle [sometimes Greater China Bloc], the Mekong River Regional Triangle or 'Golden Quadrilateral' [sometimes Golden Quadrangle], and a potential Pan-Islamic Zone in the North-West. These new entities may be the products of top-down political or investment decisions to stimulate investment in or around regional growth poles, bottom-up economic, social and cultural interactions and flows which often have a cross-border dimension, or some combination of the two.

Box 4.3 briefly explores some of the ramifications for regionalism of the new border zones, and Box 4.4 the ambitious plans for the Tumen River area. The future success of these and other initiatives depends on whether the old ideas of Hirschmann concerning the 'trickle down' effect of development are more plausible, or whether it is the contrasting ideas of Gunnar Myrdal and others as regards 'circular and cumulative causation' which are more likely. The evidence of this chapter suggests that it is the latter which will hold sway, with the capitalist dynamic actively producing, indeed thriving on, regional disparities, to such an extent that the state cannot keep up with this process despite the ameliorative effect of state policies. The next few chapters will explore this issue further, with respect to ethnic minorities, rural areas and the urban dimension of development.

Box 4.3 Potential New Regionalisms: Border Zones

Part of the response of the Chinese government to the regional disparities noted in the previous section has been to declare certain Border Cities open, from 1992, other cities along the Yangtze, by 1995, and also provincial capitals in both border areas and interior areas. The broad aim was to ensure that by 1995 these cities would adopt open city policies, similar to those introduced to the coast in 1984, with preferential tax rates and/or custom duties. Those cities in the border areas were specifically 'encouraged to develop processing trade and agriculture capable of generating foreign exchange' and those meeting 'certain requirements' to 'establish economic co-operative zones ... Enterprises with domestic investment and enterprises with foreign investment within such zones can freely sell goods which they import from countries near Guangxi Zhuang Autonomous Region and Yunnan Province, as well as from the Commonwealth of Independent States (the former Soviet Union) through barter trade' (*Investment in China*, 1993, p.210).

As examples of these openings, cities and towns along the borders of Burma and Vietnam are becoming the conduits for a growing cross-border trade between China's provinces of Yunnan and Guangxi respectively with their international neighbours. Thus, Yunnan's growing light industry is providing factory exports to Burma in exchange for such (Burmese) commodities as timber and jade, and even East Asian motor cars (Bray, 1996, p.190). This trade has grown to between US$800 million to US$1 billion since the late 1980s, with the bulk of the trade (80 per cent) being channelled through Dehong Prefecture in Yunnan Province, especially via Ruili and Wanding (Chen, 1995). Similarly, Dongxing in Guangxi Province is the focus for nearly one fifth of cross-border trade with Vietnam, including such innovations as hosting (with Mong Cai city in Vietnam) the first joint trade conference between China and Vietnam, in 1994, and cross-border tourism via cruise ships docking on both sides of this border (Chen, op.cit., p.610). Further afield, in the North East, 'Cross-border trade through the Chinese cities of Hefei and Suifenhe and the Russian city of Blagoveshcensk ... accounts for more than 20% of the total trade between China and Russia' (ibid., p.611).

The percentage trade figures shown here indicate the growing importance of these key urban centres in the developing cross-border interaction around China, an interaction which is, for most, overland rather than over sea. Nonetheless, their importance should not be overstated, and are miniscule in comparison to the huge trade centres of the coastal zone. They are interesting, however, in terms of the 'bottom-up' nature of their trading patterns, with small private companies and individuals leading this cross-border trade rather than the TNCs and other big players of the coastal region. They are also interesting in that they might contribute towards new regionalism. Where cross-border linkages encourage cultural interchange and commonality of interest, desire for autonomy may be fostered, separate from the Han. However, they are channels for an interaction which is not universally popular, for as Bray notes, 'China's economic expansion into northern Burma has alarmed many Burmese. For example, it has become a common complaint that Mandalay is increasingly dominated by Chinese businessmen, many of which are recent immigrants who have purchased Burmese papers illegally ... Economic development is contributing to racial tensions' (Bray, op.cit., p.190). New regionalisms, therefore, are by no means a foregone conclusion.

Sources: Bray, J. (1996), 'Burma: Prospects for Regional Integration', Chapter 8 in Cook, I.G., Doel, M.A. and Li, R. (eds), *Fragmented Asia: Regional Integration and National Disintegration in Pacific Asia*, Aldershot, England: Avebury.

Chen, Xiangming (1995), 'The Evolution of Free Economic Zones and the Recent Development of Cross-National Growth Zones', *International Journal of Urban and Regional Research*, 19, pp.593–621.

Foreign Investment Administration and China Economic and Trade Consultants Corp., Ministry of Foreign Trade and Economic Co-operation (1993), *Investment in China*, Beijing.

Box 4.4 Ambitious New Regionalism: Tumen River Regional Development

The Tumen River Regional Triangle is potentially the most ambitious of the new regions. It involves international cooperation from not only Russia, North Korea and China which are located in the Tumen River delta and would provide natural resources (such as minerals and natural gas) and labour, but also investment and expertise from South Korea and Japan. Mongolia is also involved, via its natural resources. The project is supported by the UNDP (United Nations Development Programme), ADB (Asian Development Bank), academics and businessmen rather than governments, which have their own agendas, but driven by the 'enormous potential regional market [which] 'could encompass nearly 300 million population, have a collective GNP of almost US$3 trillion, and account for nearly one-third of world trade' (Manguno, 1993, cited in Fu-Kuo Liu, 1996, p.159). The countries involved at last agreed, in 1995, to set up a joint committee to 'resolve policy differences in regard to the introduction of foreign capital, trade promotion, and so on' (Hook, 1996, p.23).

Given the potential problems of co-ordination and conflicting objectives, it remains to be seen whether this ambitious mega-project (projected to take 20 years or more and cost US$30 billion) can ever fully succeed, and the Asian Financial Crisis of 1997–8 will have dented its prospects further. If it does, then a new international city, perhaps named 'Tumenjiang City' with 1–2.5 million people will be a central element, along with good transportation facilities. The city would have freeport status, and rail links across to Mongolia and beyond, as part of a new Asia-Europe Continental Bridge. The combination of the skills and resources of the different countries involved is the plus for this project; the negative is the sheer scale of cooperation involved. The political will to succeed will be the key.

Sources: Fu-Kuo Liu (1996), 'Industrial Development and the Impetus to Regional Economic Integration in Pacific Asia', Chapter 6 in Cook, I.G., Doel, M.A. and Li, R. (eds), *Fragmented Asia: Regional Integration and National Disintegration in Pacific Asia*, Avebury, Aldershot, England.

Hook, G. (1996), 'Japan and Contested Regionalism', Chapter 1 in Cook, I.G., Doel, M.A. and Li, R. (eds), *Fragmented Asia: Regional Integration and National Disintegration in Pacific Asia*, Avebury, Aldershot, England.

Ye Shunzan (1997), '*Building a Cross Border International City at the Mouth of the Tumen River*', Institute of Geography, Chinese Academy of Sciences.

CHAPTER 5

Bridging the Gap in Rural Areas

Around 70 per cent of China's population still lives in the countryside. If the nation is to achieve its full economic potential – as well as providing a vast market for foreign manufacturers – greater efforts will have to be made to enhance rural incomes. This chapter, therefore, will look at these efforts, particularly in narrowing inequalities between different regions. The sections are as follows:

- Ending the embarrassment of low living standards
- Bridging the income gap
- Changing the direction of poverty relief
- The contribution of township enterprises
- Moving development inland

Ending the embarrassment of low living standards

Mao Zedong, investigating Hunan Province in 1927, produced a report for the party leadership expressing shock at the appalling living standards of the peasantry. Seventy per cent were poor, divided into 'utterly impoverished' (20 per cent) and 'less impoverished' (50 per cent). The former, he said, had neither land, nor money, were without any means of livelihood, and were forced to leave home and become mercenary soldiers, hired labourers or itinerant beggars. The latter, with a little land and a little money, weren't much better off, 'living amid toil and worry all year round' (Mao Zedong (1927/1954), pp.31–2).

In the words of another writer:

'[...] the poor were only peasants, passive, illiterate, abysmally ignorant, and there to be used. Lost in great tracts of land, where the only roads were rutted cart tracks, and where score on score of villages might be on land owned by one family. In 1927, few if any of them would ever have seen, let alone used, trains, radio or electric light ... They just lived the best they could trapped in the steel jaws of Confucian orthodoxy and the network of hatreds it engendered at every level of life. Men and women from other lands who saw their plight were staggered at their apathy' (Grant, 1988, p.27).

American author Edgar Snow quotes a commune chairman he met on a visit in 1960 who recalled his childhood when 'we were hungry every winter. If there was a flood or famine we had to go into debt to survive. My mother died of starvation during the Japanese occupation. At 14, I became an indentured labourer for a local landlord. Landlords and rich peasants owned 80 per cent of our land. We belonged to the six families in ten who owned no land and were sharecroppers or labourers.' (Snow, 1963, p.426).

By the time the Communists took control in 1949, the lot of the peasantry was not quite as bad, although leaving a lot to be desired. Under the Nationalists, the land was still largely controlled by absentee landlords, whose demands often left their tenants feeling like well-squeezed lemons. The yoke was lifted when the landlords were amongst the first groups to be purged after the communist take-over, many of them being executed. Relief, however, was tempered by the fact that under the collectivisation of agriculture enforced by Mao, life in the countryside remained spartan and often difficult (Hinton 1966 and 1983).

Peasants worked as part of production teams, sharing the work to be done as well as the rewards through 'work points' earned during the year. There were advantages to collectivisation, but there were also many imperfections. Some members of the group did not work as hard as others and some did not work at all, if unwatched. Management of the group by the team leader was sometimes poor. The day-to-day work of the team might be interfered with by higher authorities who had no knowledge of local situations but who issued detailed directives of such matters as crop varieties to be planted, output expected, planting schedules, and the methods of sowing, manuring, irrigation and harvesting.

Under Deng Xiaoping, criticisms of the commune system grew, especially of 'all eating from the same big pot' (Gao Shangquan and Chi Fulin, 1997, p.6), which was seen to be stifling individual initiative. Radical farm reforms were begun which raised the permitted size of private plots and allowed free markets for farm products to develop. Under the new 'household contract responsibility system', families agreed to provide the government with a specified amount of produce each year at a fixed price (to be sold through state-run markets in the urban areas at low cost), with any surplus then available to be sold at a higher price on the 'free market' (where most urban residents now do their shopping; prices are higher, but the quality is better).

Farmers were encouraged to start sideline businesses to further enhance their earning potential. The village or township authorities were responsible for providing the overall facilities, pest prevention and control, and other services of communal value, while the household was responsible for product selection and for carrying out cultivation and field management. Peasants were allowed to keep all income from their production after paying various taxes and contributing to funds for capital construction, operating expenses, welfare, education and so on. Under the reforms, productivity soared. In the 'bad old days', some villages sought to placate the central planners with grossly inflated harvest figures, and the best were hailed in the official media as models for the entire nation to follow. In the mid-1980s the truth finally matched the fiction. But this created a fresh problem. The fields needed to be tended by far fewer people than in the past, creating a vast surplus work force. Rural development experts proposed three methods to try and overcome the problem: intensive farming – growing more crops on the same plot by introducing new techniques; rural enterprises – those started by township authorities, village communities and private investors; and migration to urban areas.

On the surface, therefore, life has improved for the vast mass of the peasantry. As one of the authors has observed elsewhere:

'Since China began to adopt the new policy of reform and opening to outside world, the invisible system barrier between urban and rural areas has gradually dissolved, due mainly to two factors: abandoning limitations on farmers working and opening business in cities, and bringing the price of all major foodstuffs under market regulation. However, the management system separating the urban and rural areas has by no means changed fundamentally. In cities, in particular, people still enjoy rights in employment, housing, health care, welfare, insurance, and education according to their permanent residence registration. While the main cities are home to the nation's political, economic development, commercial and cultural centres, gathering most of the social wealth, they remain a dream beyond the reach of most rural youngsters. The boom in mass media, however, has enabled the rural population to share the same information with their urban siblings, and it has finally begun to occur to them clearly how unfair the existing society is in regards to dispersion of social wealth' (Murray, 1998, p.48).

Movement around the country is no longer restricted by the authorities (until a few years ago, transferring to the city was almost impossible unless one could produce evidence of a job waiting and accommodation, although in the early years of Communist rule rural migration to urban areas was common, adding 23 million to the urban population between 1950 and

1955 (Snow, op.cit., p.427), but there are still limitations imposed by a system of residence permits on which subsistence benefits are based. Rural job seekers are like second class citizens when they come to the cities, putting up wherever they can for the night and entitled to no welfare benefit, while putting great pressure on urban infrastructures. Such people are usually nicknamed 'mangliu' (blind migrants), because they travel around the country without a definite aim, taking up any job that is going. But despite grumbles about their presence, much of urban life now depends on the 'muddy legs' who build all the high-rise apartments and office buildings, sell vegetables, provide the bulk of the maids and nurses, repair shoes and collect garbage.

According to a State Statistical Bureau (SSB) survey of 150,000 labourers from 60,000 farming households, and the most recent agricultural census, in 1997 China had an official floating rural population of eighty million, thirty-four million of whom had worked in cities for more than half a year. In major cities like Beijing and Shanghai, farmers run breakfast stands, sell produce and work in the construction and sanitation sectors. Only 18 per cent of them have received senior high school education. They take up arduous unskilled jobs in the construction, textile, garment, sanitation, and mining industries. The SSB survey in Beijing showed that 94 per cent were engaged in such occupations. The migrants generally live in old, rented houses or shanties they construct themselves. Their income level is low, but it tends to be higher than in their hometowns. Researcher Zhao Shukai from the State Council Development Research Center and Hong Dayong of the Sociology Department of People' University estimate migrants can earn 2,000 yuan annually over and above living expenses and rent.

'Although city life is never as good as in their dreams, most farmers are unwilling to go back to the countryside. In the words of one, 'At first I wasn't accustomed to life in the city. There're too many rules. But when I went back home, I couldn't get used to rural life again either. I'm free but can't get a stable income. Moreover, there's no entertainment except for TV in rural areas.' Dwelling in cities, former farmers have altered their old habits and values. They hope to stay. One says that urban life is rich – karaoke bars, pubs, bowling alleys, concert halls. They can't afford any of these, but they like to see new things and learn. One wouldn't hear the words 'Internet' and 'clone' ever if one always lived in the countryside. City people dress well, especially the girls. Can such know-how be gained in a village? This reflects the psychology of some members of the floating population. Although they live in cities, they know clearly that the city is not their home. The beauty of the city, however, lures them back time and again. They would never move back to the country voluntarily' (*China Today*, February 1999).

In the remaining years of the century, the big challenge is to find jobs for all these restless migrants, particularly in making life more attractive in the countryside (see Box 5.1) so that they will no longer pour into the already overcrowded cities. As will be detailed in Chapter 7, there are estimates, in fact, that the country faces an urban explosion in the next two decades with a massive population shift from rural areas to cities and new townships. During the period from 1991 to 1995, accompanying urban expansion, the labour force devoted to agriculture production dropped from 340 to 310 million, a decline from 59.8 per cent to 52 per cent of total employment (State Statistics Bureau Annual Reports).

According to the 1996 sample census, China had a total rural labour force of 452 million, 50 per cent of the rural population. However, off-farm work has become increasingly important, with many working in business and industry. The percentage of farmers' income earned through agriculture has fallen. In the countryside, 130.28 million people, or 30 per cent of the rural labour force, are now employed by township enterprises. The rest are not necessarily occupied solely by farm work. Over 95 per cent of rural families perform both farm and non-farm work, and some now even consider farming a second job (CASS, op.cit). But the challenge is to find new work for all the idle hands.

> 'By 2000, about 200 million farmers will have to find new jobs outside the agricultural sector. Supposing that 10 million, a generous estimate, can find a new job each year as the country's economy develops, by the turn of the century at least 140 million labourers will remain jobless.' (*Beijing Review*, 18-7-1994).

Bridging the income gap

As noted in the previous chapter, one of the biggest challenges the government faces today is to bridge the widening gap between the prosperous urban areas along the eastern coast, and the vast backward regions of the interior. As the late Deng Xiaoping said on several occasions, and as his successor Jiang Zemin has reaffirmed, socialism does not equal shared poverty. Jiang has stated that: 'It is too embarrassing to see that there will remain several million people short of food and clothing by the end of this century when New China will have been founded for five decades'(Speech to Communist Party Meeting on Poverty Alleviation in Beijing, September 1996).

At a meeting the following year, according to the explanation of Wang Dongjin, Vice-Chairman of the State Commission for Restructuring the Economic System, prior to the introduction of the economic reform process in 1978, there were some differences between urban and rural areas, between different regions and different trades, but the differences were not

Box 5.1 Rural Industry Boom

Township enterprises are run by farmers. They first appeared in a small number of villages and towns in the early 1950s, but, due to lack of money, outdated technology and no access to information, they did not develop much until the family responsibility system was implemented in rural areas in the 1980s. That system quickly increased grain output, saturating the market and forcing farmers to seek other ways to bring in money. At the same time, the number of surplus rural labourers was on the rise. To offset both problems, government at all levels began to support township enterprises through incentives and preferential policies. At the beginning of the reform and opening process in the early 1980s, income increased, but the existing state-owned enterprises were hemmed in by the planned economy and could not meet market demand. Township enterprises appeared at the right time, and although they often made low quality products at first, they found a market in China.

Since then, the expansion of rural industry has created more than 100 million new jobs in recent years to ease some, but only some, of the pressure on rural unemployment and under-employment.. In the most developed areas of the countryside, industry now provides 80 per cent of household income. There have been many success stories reported in the State media. One such case involved the farmers of Wenzhou, in coastal Zhejiang Province, who launched a ground-breaking scheme by pooling their savings to build and run their own town. The construction of Longgang cost 960 Million Yuan, two-thirds of it on housing and the rest on infrastructure and industrial fixed assets. The entire amount was contributed by Wenzhou's residents who each contributed on average 12,800 Yuan. Most were farmers-turned-salesmen/entrepreneurs who had become rich in recent years by running private and co-operative businesses. Longgang emerged from the amalgamation of five former fishing villages that were so poor before 1979 that many residents had to beg elsewhere to survive. When the reforms began many of the fishermen turned their backs on the sea and started family businesses that quickly prospered. The result was inevitable pressure for urbanisation.

But the government of Cangnan County, in which Longgang is situated, did not have any budget for new construction. Instead, it contributed 6,000 Yuan as start-up funds and told everyone who wanted to build a new house that they would also have to contribute to specified amount for public facilities. The idea caught on and a new town was built on wasteland beginning in 1984. It now has a population of about 135,000. Each of the houses on the town's main streets originally had either family-run shops or small businesses on the ground floor with residential accommodation on the upper floors. Some of the businesses (an estimated 800 turning out mainly plastic products, clothing, blankets, carpets and machinery), however, have now outgrown these small beginnings and moved into new factories. Rapid expansion was only possible because of a co-operative shareholding system. The system is practised among families in the same business when each with limited resources could no longer sustain continued growth. They pool funds, equipment and know-how as stocks and share risks and profits. The government does not interfere in the management. The system has proved its efficiency, enabling the local economy to grow by 50 per cent annually (*China Daily*, 18-4-1993).

In Huaxi, a tiny village located on the outskirts of Wuxi in southern Jiangsu Province, Wu Renbao, veteran Party branch secretary, recalled that the tiny village originally had almost no resources to support 1,500 peasants on a plot of cultivated land less than one square kilometre in size. Over a period of three decades, he led the villagers to level the land, plant trees and build irrigation canals to ensure steadily increasing grain yields. But to Wu, the road to real prosperity could only come through establishing industrial and by-product enterprises. The first, a hardware factory which mainly repaired motorboats and agricultural machinery, was actually set up at the height of the cultural revolution, when the establishment of such an enterprise was regarded as 'taking the capitalist road'. To ensure Huaxi wasn't visited by a wrathful group of teenage Red Guards, villagers kept the factory a secret. In the first year, it made profits of more than $6,000, and these soon quadrupled, creating capital for later improvements in living standards as well as knowledge in industrial development. When the political climate changed, Wu seized the chance to develop township enterprises, starting out in 1982 with three small factories manufacturing steel nets, nylon cement bags and pesticide sprayers. By the 1990s, Huaxi had formed its own industrial framework covering metallurgy, chemicals, textiles and building materials, including a steel mill with an annual capacity of 250,000 tons, a 400,000-ton capacity rolling mill and a steel wire plant with an annual capacity of 300,000 tons (*Beijing Review*, 10-5-1993).

Sources: Beijing Review, 10-5-1993
China Daily, 18-4-1993.

that great because of the egalitarian spirit that prevailed under which, as noted above, everyone ate a little 'from the same big rice pot'. Low income, however, was not conducive to creating worker enthusiasm for production. 'There was a vicious cycle of low level productive forces – low income-egalitarianism – low enthusiasm of labourers for production – low level productivity – low level productive forces' (Speech to the Third Senior Policy Forum of Economic Development, Beijing, 27-5-1997).

The introduction of the new system by Deng of 'distribution according to work done' led to a widening income gap. The change, said Wang, 'greatly mobilised the enthusiasm of various social sectors, greatly emancipated and developed social productive forces and promoted prosperity and growth of the national economy. The per capita income of urban and rural residents has increased at an annual average rate of 6.5 per cent and 8.2 per cent respectively. The financial assets of urban and rural residents has increased at a rapid rate, their bank savings hitting 5,000 billion Yuan, which means an annual average increase rate of 33.5 per cent' (ibid.).

China has made great progress; but this has created new problems and contradictions, notably a widening income distribution gap between certain regions and certain trades. The income distribution gap between urban and rural residents was already a reality before the introduction of reforms. But the reforms unfolded first in the rural areas with the introduction of the household responsibility contract system, with remuneration linked to output which fired farmers' enthusiasm and greatly improved farming productivity. Agricultural production increased by a big margin and the transition of rural labourers from farming to non-farming sectors made it possible for the township enterprises to develop apace. The 1978–85 period witnessed fast improvement in the income for farmers (Table 5.1) and corresponding narrowing of the difference in income between urban and rural residents. After 1986, however, the difference in income between urban and rural areas widened again (as shown in Table 5.4).

Given the natural conditions, geographical location, population distribution and many other factors, as noted in Chapter 4 there exists significant differences in economic development and per capita income distribution between east, central and west China. In the 10 years from 1980 to 1990, the difference in living expenditure income between the urban residents in central and west China on the one hand and urban residents in east China on the other widened, with the difference expanding by 19 percentage points in 1980 and 16 percentage points in 1990. From 1990 to 1995, the gap widened further – expanding by three percentage

Table 5.1 Income Increase Of Rural Residents 1978–97 (%)

Period	Annual growth (current price)	Annual growth (actual price)
1978–84	17.6	16.5
1985–88	11.1	4.9
1989–91	4.1	1.9
1992–97	21.7	5.4
1978–97	15.6	8.1

Source: Zhang and Tang (1998).

points in 1990 and nine percentage points in 1995 (Table 5.2). And there has been a similar phenomenon in the incomes of rural residents between the three regions (Table 5.3). The per capita net income for rural residents in east China was 1.7 times that for rural residents in central China and 2.3 times that for rural residents in west China.

The problem has been further exacerbated by differences in income distribution for trades or enterprises. With the sharpening of market competition, the difference in income distribution for diverse trades and enterprises has widened further between those in growth sectors and those in 'sunset' industries. According to the analysis of Vice Minister Wang (see above), 'some trades and enterprises, which hold the dominant position or enjoy special privileges, enjoy obvious advantages in terms of income from business management, and the per capita income for workers in these trades and enterprises stand higher than the social average. The trades referred to are banks, insurance, negotiable securities, tourism, foreign trade, real estate, electric power, posts and telecommunications, air and rail transportation, newspapers and magazines, radio and television broad-

Table 5.2 Comparison of Per Capita Income by Region 1980–95 (in Yuan)

Region	Per Capita Income 1980	Ratio to East	Per Capita Income 1995	Ratio to East
East	477	1.00	4,847	1.00
Central	428	0.90	3,284	0.68
West	338	0.71	3,321	0.69

Source: State Commission for Restructuring the Economic System, 1997, Beijing.

Table 5.3 Per Capita Income of Rural Residents Per Region (in Yuan)

Region	1980	Ratio to East	1995	Ratio to East
East	169	1.00	2,242	1.00
Centre	125	0.74	1,424	0.54
West	127	0.75	1,052	0.43

Source: State Commission for Restructuring the Economic System, 1997, Beijing.

Table 5.4 Annual Living Expenditure Income of Urban/Rural Residents (in Yuan)

	1978	1995
Urban	316	3,893
Rural	134	1,578

Source: State Commission for Restructuring the Economic System, 1997, Beijing.

casting. Some trades or enterprises which have comparatively low income refer to enterprises which belong to sunset industries in economic structural readjustment, trades which are highly dependent on resources being exhausted; trades which can hardly shift to other kinds of production in the face of sharpening market competition, traditionally labour-intensive industries, and enterprises which are burdened by large numbers of retired and overstaffed people or suffer from excessive social burdens'.

Overall, the Chinese economy is booming, directly resulting in an overall improvement of people's living conditions. During the period from 1978 to 1995, per capita GNP index grew threefold, and behind this statistic is a rosy picture of a considerable number of people leading a better life, with a small segment even becoming nouveau riche. This achievement also implies that the population living in abject poverty has decreased by a big margin. China had 250 million people living in abject poverty in 1978, representing 26 per cent of the total population, according to the central government's calculations. It should be noted here, however, that the World Bank considers Beijing's definition of poverty too narrow. It says 350 million people, just under one-third of the population, are below its international poverty standard of $1 per person per day, 5.7 times greater than the Chinese calculation. But, on the basis of the Chinese calculation, the number in dire need had been reduced to half by 1986, when poverty relief was put on the government agenda to become a regular duty of each level of government from top down. The State Council Leading Group Office of Poverty Alleviation and Development was established as a permanent organ planning and co-ordinating the national task.

The following eight years saw a greater achievement of the poverty relief effort, and by 1994, the poverty-stricken population diminished further, according to Chinese statistics, to eighty million. In 1994, the central government drafted the 'National Poverty-Relief Programme' which means a greater effort to help the eighty million people out of poverty in the remainder of the century, resulting in a claim that those in poverty had further shrunk to 65 million by the end of 1995 (Annual Reports of the State Statistics Bureau for the relevant years). Table 5.5 provides a national

Table 5.5 Changes in Distribution of Rural Impoverished Population 1992–7 (in millions)

Year	National	East	Central	West
1992	80.656	18.730	25.085	36.832
1997	49.623	8.026	16.966	24.631
Reduction (millions)	31.034	10.713	8.119	12.202
Reduction (%)	38.5	57.2	32.4	33.1

Source: State Statistics Bureau, Rural Survey 1998, Beijing.

comparison between 1992 and 1997 and a regional breakdown of the reduction in the impoverished population.

Due to uneven development between regions, however, the majority of poverty-stricken people are now highly concentrated in the central and western rural areas where natural conditions are harsh for living and production. Table 5.6 shows the per capita income of six sample areas to illustrate this point. The first two are prosperous cities in the east; the next two are provinces in the central area which have begun a major catch-up effort, while the last two are typical underdeveloped areas in the far west of the country. The contrast between the rich and poor parts of the country as regards past economic growth and future potential is encapsulated in Box 5.2.

A government survey in mid-1998 seemed to indicate that rather than improving, rural incomes and spending were falling more steeply than expected in some areas. A survey in Hunan, Henan and Sichuan provinces found that lower state grain prices had cut per capita incomes of Henan peasants by 62 yuan, a significant reduction equivalent to almost a month's income in the area. A three-year low in the price of pigs had also damaged incomes. The survey found that the income of Hunan pig farmers would be reduced by 5.4 billion Yuan. With 10 per cent fewer peasants finding work in towns, their remittances were also falling. The survey was reported by the People's Daily, which expressed fears the tax burden was not being adjusted. In many parts of the countryside peasants have to pay taxes for butchering animals or for growing 'special products' as well as heavy fees for education, water projects and electricity, it noted (*People's Daily*, 10-9-1998).

Assuming that about five million people are helped to escape from poverty each year, as has been the case in the past few years, even on official data there will still be over forty million remaining untouched by the end of this century, indicating failure of the government's poverty elimination programme. An anti-poverty workshop in Beijing in April 1999 actually expressed this very fear. Some of the officials who attended the one-day meeting said at least half of China's poor still lived in 'abject poverty',

Table 5.6 Sample Per Capita GDP for Selected Cities/Provinces for 1994 (in Yuan)

Shanghai	15,024
Beijing	10.265
Hubei	3,341
Hunan	2,475
Gansu	1,925
Guizhou	1,553

Source: China Statistical Almanac 1996, Beijing.

lacking even the basic resources to survive. And Zhang Lei, deputy director of the State Council's Leading Group Office on Poverty Alleviation and Development, admitted time was running out to meet the target.

Other speakers said women accounted for more than half of the poverty-stricken population and more than 92 per cent of the poor lived in central and western provinces. 'More women are mired in poverty than men and they find it more difficult to shake off the shackles of destitution,' said Shen Shuji, vice-chairwoman of the All-China Women's Federation. Zhou Qijiang, an agriculture technology director, told the workshop: 'Women themselves cannot be solely responsible for improving their lot. Governmental and non-governmental assistance is desperately needed.' The high level of illiteracy among women in rural areas – 25 million women between the ages of 15–40 – had prevented many from taking part in, and therefore enjoying the benefits of, economic reforms, he said. Some areas in central and western provinces were so poor that even basic living conditions were lacking. There were more than 20 million people in 592 counties who had to fight for their lives every day because of a lack of water, he said. He admitted that due to dire conditions in these provinces, 10 per cent of families who had received help to shake off poverty risked renewed destitution when natural calamities struck (*China Daily*, 8-4-1999).

Changing the direction of poverty relief

Should the government let the whole nation greet the new millennium with these people still without enough to eat or wear? This was the key question posed when the CPC Central Committee sponsored a meeting on poverty alleviation in September 1996, at which Jiang Zemin reminded participants of the long-set national goal of per capita GNP at the turn of the century at four times the level of 1980. If China still had a great number of people suffering from inadequate food and clothing, and its income and regional disparity kept widening by that time, realisation of the national goal would be out of the question and China's modernisation drive would be retarded as a result, he stressed.

Several measures were highlighted to speed up the poverty alleviation efforts, which included a strategic shift from mere relief to economic development – providing relief funds or materials being a traditional way aiming to solve poor people's urgent need, but having little to do with their complete escaping poverty. Instead, the conference decided the emphasis would be put on helping the rural poor gain the ability of self-accumulation and self-development through priority being given to planting, breeding and processing industries based on farm and sideline products. This differs from the common practice in the past when poverty relief funds were used to open large industrial programmes in poor rural areas, which mostly ended up operating at a loss or closing down due to poor transportation and

---

Box 5.2 A Tale of Two Provinces

Rural township enterprises in South China's Guangdong Province enjoyed bumper profits in 1997. Gross output value rose 20 per cent from 1996 to 660 billion Yuan and industrial output value will increase by 23 per cent to 530 billion Yuan. Industrial added value reached 130 billion Yuan, up 18 per cent, while exports are expected to be valued at 132.8 billion Yuan, up 25 per cent. The province's township enterprise administrator, Lin Jianrong attributed the prosperity the success in soliciting foreign capital and its export-oriented economy. The province boasts about 30,000 export-oriented enterprises, including more than 2,000 foreign trade enterprises and more than 25,000 foreign-funded enterprises.

But while glittering cities have sprung up on the coast in the past two decades, life in the high mountain village of Bapai, south-western Guangxi Province, Guangdong's neighbour, has hardly changed. The rocky terrain the locals call farmland has long yielded meagre crops. Farmer Wu Tinghe said he had to borrow grain every year, as the annual corn harvest his family grew on its scattered plots – totalling a quarter of a hectare – was only enough to feed them for nine months. His roof, like all in Bapai, is made of straw, and there is no steady water supply, let alone electricity. The village's main link with the outside world, a remote road passable only by four-wheel drive vehicles, is an hour's hike away. Mr Wu, aged 34, feels he has no future in the village. Given the chance to leave, he says: 'Of course I would. There is nothing I can do here.' He is not alone. When the World Bank began looking into how to stamp out poverty in the area, the first thing farmers asked for was a chance to work elsewhere, said senior official Alan Piazza.

The bank said helping some people find jobs in richer areas of China was one of the easiest, most cost-effective ways to boost the prospects of Bapai and similar upland villages. The resulting labour mobility scheme, a key component of the bank's US$486.4 million Southwest Poverty Reduction Project, hinges on the yawning gap between China's urban and rural wages and migrant workers' tendency to send earnings back home. The average migrant working in the city sends home 2,000 Yuan a year. The average annual income in Bapai is 200 Yuan. The exodus of a few mouths to feed does little harm to poverty-hit villages. Of the 870,000 people in Guangxi covered by the project, about 400,000 are surplus labour, said Feng Qiang, vice-director of the State Council Leading Group Office for Poverty Alleviation and Development. One reason why the World Bank invested in labour mobility was because little could be done to develop upland villages, Mr Piazza said. Such areas have never been fertile and were only settled out of desperation. The scheme has set up a network of employment offices, connecting villagers with distant employers in search of workers. It aims to help 343,000 poor people from upland areas find work by 2000.

Source: Author interviews.

technology. Improving poor areas' ecological environment and production conditions was also considered a must. Most of the poor people live in China's plateau, mountainous and desert areas suffering from harsh natural conditions. Ignoring these environmental problems would make it hard to root out local poverty.

The emphasis, the meeting agreed, would be on technical promotion and training. Efforts in this regard have already proved effective. For example, after being trained to employ mulching in planting corns, farmers in some areas of high plateau and cold weather doubled and even tripled their per unit yield and increased the annual income by 200 to 300 Yuan thus successfully solving the food problem. The experiment in Dabie Mountain in Xinyang, Henan Province is an example worth mentioning. By providing technical training to two million poverty-stricken farmers in the area for some years, the local poverty relief project made these people experts in growing tea, peanuts, fruits and breeding fish and poultry. They have established an agricultural business network called 'company plus farm household' which links 1,196 small firms and covers 1.15 million farmers. By so doing, about 1.62 million people bid farewell to poverty (*Beijing Review*, 26-10-1996).

Then, there is the 'Glorious Cause' project, initiated by the All-China Federation of Industry and Commerce in 1994, to encourage private business people to invest in poor areas to help local people get out of poverty. One example is tobacco growing and cigarette manufacturing, which used to account for up to 70 per cent of Yunnan Province's revenue. However, the biggest tobacco production base in China has witnessed a fall both in production and sales volume in recent years due to tightened government controls on tobacco and cigarette production, resulting in the average annual income in the province falling by 150 Yuan. The provincial government chose biological farming, tourism and minerals as the new pillar industries to adapt to the new situation, especially as most of the poverty stricken areas were rich in minerals, biological and tourism resources. Yunnan Green, a biological project limited company, located near Chenghai Lake in Yongsheng county, uses natural products from the lake to produce medicinal products and currently employs more than 300 poor local residents. 'The company is a big help in our poverty relief work,' said one local official (*China Daily*, 27-4-1999).

Another policy reform is to emphasise giving substantial assistance to poor villages, households and individuals – especially women (Box 5.3) – instead of the whole country. In the past, poverty relief used to target whole counties, and whether a county was considered poor or not was determined by its per capita income. However, some county governments used the poverty relief fund to build roads, overhaul county halls, or pursue industrial programmes, while poor individuals remained helpless. This government meeting required a demographic survey to be conducted in the poor rural areas so as to exactly spot the poor villages and households, based on which future poverty-relief measures will be carried out. To guarantee a success of the anti-poverty campaign, the party meeting decided that party and government heads of provincial and county level be responsible for the area's poverty alleviation. Success or failure of the tasks would be entered in their merit record. Immediately after the meeting, many provinces and those poor economically in particular saw investigation groups heading for poor areas led invariably by the first party secretaries or governors (ibid.).

Government investment in poverty alleviation from central revenues during the 1990s amounted to 10.8 billion Yuan annually up to 1996, including 5.5 billion Yuan in poverty relief loans. Starting in 1997, the state began allocating an additional 1.5 billion Yuan a year to build country roads, improving farmland and water drinking system and technical training in poor areas. In addition, another three billion Yuan in loans were to be added to support those profitable projects in the farming and livestock-raising sectors. The State Council decreed that the State-owned commercial banks should provide a certain proportion for poverty alleviation each year. The central government also asked the provincial governments to allocate a sum equal to 30 to 50 per cent of the central government's input to support the campaign according to their varied fiscal conditions. Richer provinces have already begun helping poorer ones under this programme (e.g. Guangdong helps Guanxi, Zhejiang-Ningxia and Jiangsu-Shaanxi). In each pairing, the rich one invests money and technology in projects located in the poor province making full use of local natural resources and labour.

The contribution of township enterprises

Mention has already been made in Box 5.2 of township enterprises, and it is important to consider in more detail the key role they are playing, and will continue to pay, in raising rural living standards. In the 1930s, sociologist Fei Xiaotong wrote a small book entitled *Peasant Life In China*, in which he suggested that running industry in backward rural areas might contribute to national economic development. In spite of his hopes, however, no genuine rural industry developed in the ensuing decades, until the Dengist reforms in the late 1970s provided the necessary impetus. However, the much-maligned 'Great Leap Forward' in the 1950s, when millions of farmers neglected their fields in order to build and tend backyard steel furnaces, may have contributed some important groundwork. Western analysts generally see the Maoist experiment as a ghastly failure, which contributed to a famine that cost millions of lives, and produced very little decent steel. But there is a Chinese counter-argument to this: namely, that while the steel produced in most cases may have been of

Contrasting Housing

Plate 1 Hong Kong's H Blocks

Plate 2 Private Housing

Dramatic Changes: Guangzhou

Plate 3 1980

Plate 4 Same View in 1995

Plate 5 Zhou Le Tain Commune Era

Plate 6 Mancheng County –
Cooperative

Plate 7 Landmark Towers, Beijing

Plate 8 Central Hong Kong

Plate 9 Oriental Pearl Tower, Shanghai

Plate 10 Shenzhen

Slum Clearance

Plate 11

Plate 12

Plate 13 Kitchen, Mancheng County. Hebei Province

Plate 14 Living Room, Mancheng County. Hebei Province

Plate 15 Airport

Plate 16 Sun Dong An Plaza

Plate 17

Plate 18

Rural Contrasts

Plate 19 New Road to Great Wall

Plate 20 Rural Quarry

Plate 21 High Street Chain Store

Plate 22 Streetmarket, Fruit Sellers

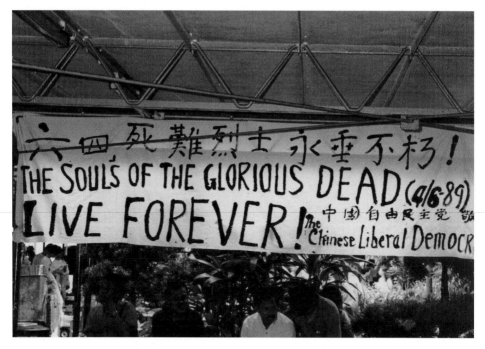

Plate 23 Tiananmen Protest, Hong Kong

Plate 24 Panda, Shangai Zoo

Plate 25 Rural Waste: Hebei

Plate 26 Traffic Congestion

Plate 27

Plate 28

Industry – Baoshan Steelworks

Plate 29

Industrial Pollution – Huang Pu

Plate 30

Industrial Pollution – Huang Pu

Plate 31

Plate 32

poor quality, the experience did, for the first time, introduce the peasantry to the rudiments of engineering and industrial production which would stand them in good stead in later years.

Whatever the truth may be, the fact is that township (formerly communal) enterprises have become the mainstay of the rural economy. Their value-added output in 1996 reached 1,700 billion Yuan, accounting for 60 per cent of rural added value output and 30 per cent of the country's GDP (*Beijing Review*, 17-11-1997). In the early 1980s, the government encouraged their development by setting low tax rates and exempting newcomers from any tax for the first three years. The special tax treatment was only abandoned in 1994, when a unified tax system was adopted for all enterprises. Cheap credit was also made available throughout the 1980s from the four specialised State banks. And although the preferential treatment has now generally been abandoned, it continues for enterprises located in the backward central and western areas.

Township enterprises have admittedly taking up some of the unemployment slack in the countryside, as discussed earlier. But it is now apparent that they have reached a plateau and need to change direction. Jiang Yongtao, Director of the Agriculture Ministry's Township Enterprises Management Bureau, for example, told a symposium in Beijing that the township firms had grown by 17.3 per cent in 1998, contributing about three percentage points to the country's 7.8 per cent growth. However, their reform and development had entered a critical stage. Their exports had only edged up by 2.5 per cent in 1998 and more than 15 per cent of businesses were running at a loss as a result of the sluggish market and the impact of the Asian financial crisis, Jiang said. In the face of the difficulties, township firms should develop more in high-tech and environmental friendly industries to find their way out, upgrading sub-standard equipment and training or employing more qualified people (Xinhua, 22-4-1999). But this will also need substantial investment by the national and local governments in raising the educational infrastructure.

Although generally optimistic about the sector, Chen Jianguang, a senior official in the Township Enterprise Department of the Agriculture Ministry (author interview, 12-8-1997), also identified some shortcomings. 'So far, few large companies have managed to emerge. Most continue to be small, poorly-equipped firms, little different from the village workshops of several decades or even centuries ago. Typically, they comprise six or seven workers engaged in manual labour. The machines, if they have any, are old and usually second-hand equipment bought from state-owned enterprises. There are even some firms that are more like museums of equipment made in the nineteenth century.' In addition, the township enterprises have been censured for their contribution to a polluted environment. In 1996, the State media was full of reports about a government crackdown on notorious polluters, including some 5,000 small paper mills, tanneries and

Box 5.3 Targeting Women For Aid

For many women living in poor rural areas, the main and only concern is to manage the next meal enough for all the family. Luo Guiying, a middle-aged woman living in Gaopao Village in Guizhou Province, is typical. With three children and a tiny 0.2 hectare piece of farmland, the family did not have enough to eat by relying upon poor land with its humble yield. Luo and her husband wove bamboo baskets night and day, but the earnings were too little to entirely solve their food problem. As a wife and mother for over 10 years, Luo was always the last to sit at the dinner table. Consequently, she was physically weak through malnutrition and stomach ache. Her bad luck came to an end in 1995 when she acquired a small loan of 2,000 Yuan. She spent all the money on buying a small number of piglets and sold them for a good profit on the market several months later. After returning the loan, she still had enough to maintain the pig raising business. For the first time, life had become manageable, for Luo, who said with delight: 'Now my husband and mother-in-law smile at me often.' (author research May 1998)

The loan for the piglets came from a poverty-alleviation project called the 'Programme of Happiness.' Luo is one of 10,000 rural mothers who had benefited from the programme by early 1997. Initiated in early 1995 by three organisations – The China Population Welfare Foundation, the China National Family Planning Association and the Chinese Population Gazette, the charity programme was not designed to target all the people in poverty, but only poor mothers, estimated to total about one million. Being consigned to various duties at the same time such as reproduction, bread earning, preparing meals for husband, children and even parents-in-law, these women were the last to enjoy life. They have been placed in an even more inferior situation than male adults, since most are semi-illiterate cut off from information beyond their villages that would enable them to enter the mainstream of life. The Programme of Happiness has sought a successful way to help the poor mothers through small loans ranging from 1,000 to 5,000 Yuan. This is enough for them to run a profitable household business such as raising oxen, sheep, planting fruit, tree, or make bamboo ware and embroidery. For example, nearly every farmhouse in some Guizhou Province rural areas are good at making bean curd. By providing just a 500 Yuan loan for a poor mother can help her open a small business of her own. Sometimes, programme staff will lend her the necessary materials such as oxen, sheep and feed. The loan may be repaid in one or two years, and the money she will pay off will immediately be given to the next eligible woman. This practice operating in a village or community creates pressure on the poor mother to pay off her loan on time, since her neighbours may be impatiently waiting.

The Chinese National Family Planning Association, a national organisation of 1.02 million local bodies and 83 million staff, has got involved because its traditional function has been declining with the general acceptance of birth control around the country. The staff's good information about every household and friendly relationship with various government departments concerned make them a most efficient and convenient tool to carry out the task in the vast rural areas. The Programme of Happiness has become a real part of the women's liberation movement in its implementation. Its slogans call for wiping out poverty, illiteracy and disease. After the poor mothers qualified for a loan are selected, they must attend a special school which teaches them basic reading and writing and the necessary production skills. Their school marks will determine if they eventually get a loan. Now, almost every village where the programme operates has established a 'mother's school'. Pilot work on the programme first started in four counties: Puding in Guizhou Province, Lixian in Gansu Province, Qianshan in Anhui Province and Dali in Shaanxi Province. The organising committee put in 100,000 Yuan for each, which was doubled by a matching donation by the county government. About 300 poor mothers in the four counties benefited and by now more than 70 per cent have returned the loan. The programme was extended to 15 counties in 1996 and 40 in 1997. 'Traditionally, a rural women is a humble figure in the family, not seriously regarded as a major bread earner despite her day and night labour. The programme has dramatically changed attitudes. When some husbands travelling far away from their village to seek seasonal jobs heard the surprising news that their wives had got a loan and were starting to run a household business, they couldn't wait to rush home to provide help. Rural women used to be a silent group, without a big say in family or public affairs. The programme encourages better educated women with less children by giving them priority for loans. Consequently, these women have become eloquent orators in their villages often persuading others to read more while not stubbornly giving birth to too many children.' (*Beijing Review,* 24-3-1997).

Sources: Author research.
Beijing Review, 24-3-1997.

dye factories along the seriously contaminated Huaihe River, which were shut down by the authorities. Also to be tackled is the problem that the more such rural factories that are set up, the more land is taken out of agricultural production.

Nevertheless, the government wants to see the township enterprises, located in rural areas and run by the farmers themselves, become the leading force in agricultural industrialisation. Some pilot projects of this type follow a model of 'company plus households', which means the enterprise links a number of households to handle the production, technical support and sale of products. They also want to see as many of these enterprises as possible forging some sort of co-operative link with firms in the more developed eastern areas, with the latter providing assistance in finance and technology where needed. Local governments have put the development of township enterprise high on their agenda. Gansu Province has listed them as its top development priority. To make the most of the resources in the west and the technology in the east coastal region, pilot projects were launched in 1995 to facilitate the growth of townships in the western region and this has called for a total investment of 75 billion Yuan, 40 billion Yuan injected from the East, in more than 40,000 co-operative projects.

Moving development inland

As government incentives for foreign direct investment are being phased out on the coast – where they are considered no longer necessary to attract the overseas capital that has achieved such spectacular success in developing the east China economy – so they are being stepped up in the interior. And the further inland one goes, the more generous they become. These incentives include tax breaks and exemptions, transport subsidies, opportunities for BOT (build-operate-transfer) deals in basic infrastructure construction, and the chance to buy shares in profitable local enterprises, sometimes with a controlling interest. Foreign-funded projects are also being tempted with priority in land-use rights allocation – an important consideration given that land rights can be a real minefield for any investment – with payments being much lower than those now prevailing on the coast. The information in this section, it should be noted, comes from interviews conducted by one of the authors in Beijing during 1997 and 1998 with officials in the Ministry of Agricultural, Ministry of Foreign Trade and Economic Cooperation and the State Planning Commission.

In August 1995, the State Council granted inland provinces the right to approve overseas-funded manufacturing projects up to a value of $30 million without further reference to the central government, three times higher than the previous ceiling. Foreign businessmen, by and large, have been reluctant to move too far from the coast because of bad publicity about the lack of infrastructure in the interior. And it is true that until recently, the further one moved inland, the more difficult it began to make a long distance telephone call or send a fax; the roads were bad and the railway lines inadequate to handle the efficient transport of goods; power blackouts and brownouts were a constant headache; living conditions for executives were also relatively poor. But that situation is changing. New highways are linking up the various provincial capitals and being integrated into the national expressway network at a rapid pace. New railway lines are being built, typified by the new line linking Beijing with Hong Kong, which passes through many of the chronic poverty-stricken areas en route, and the 'Asia-Europe Continental Bridge' line from the coast in Northeast China, which exits the country through Xinjiang, and continues on to Rotterdam.

The laying of one million kilometres of optical fibre cables, along with 130,000 kilometres of microwave lines, plus 19 satellite ground stations for telecommunications purposes have revolutionised rural communications. The central government says that between 1996 and 2000, as much as 60 per cent of the foreign preferential loans it received would be channelled into upgrading the basic facilities of the central and western regions. In future, when seeking soft loans from foreign governments, the government also planned to ask that these be made available not just to environmental-protection projects as at present, but also the agricultural and industrial sectors.

To upgrade rail transportation, a weak link in moving goods and people around the vast hinterland, the Ninth Five-Year (1996–2000) Plan includes pushing ahead with construction of a new railway line linking Nanning in Guangxi Zhuang Autonomous Region in the far south on the Vietnamese border and Kunming, capital of Yunnan Province, abutting Myanmar (Burma) as well as building the 1,000 kilometre multiple-tracked line between Guiyang in Guizhou and Zhuzhou in central Hunan Province. At the same time, the line between Guiyang and Kunming will be upgraded. Guizhou, meanwhile, is planning to build its first locally-operated railway – part of the central government's programme to end State monopoly of railway construction – to accelerate exploitation of its rich mineral resources. The railway, from the city of Liupanshui to Baiguo, will provide the missing link between the Guiyang-Kunming and Nanning-Kunming Lines, will be an important step in giving the landlocked south-western region a through link to the ports along the Eastern coast. The 121-km Luipanshui-Baiguo Railway will cost 2.82 billion Yuan and is designed to transport 18 million tons of goods annually. Luipanshui, together with the city of Panzhihua in neighbouring Sichuan Province on the upper reaches of the Yangtze River, is one of the most resources-rich areas in China. Coal reserves in Luipanshui and surrounding areas exceed 50 billion tons, equal to the total coal reserves in the nine provinces south of the Yangtze. A long railway opening up 'middle China' is the 1,000 km line linking the important industrial and transportation hub city of Xian (famous for its terracotta warriors) with Nanjing, to give the former improved access, via the Yangtze, to the sea. In addition, work has begun on another part of a key railway line in Xinjiang Uygur Autonomous Region, in the far Northwest. The line eventually will stretch 1,470 kilometres across southern Xinjiang from the eastern city of Turpan to Kashi in the far west.

Box 5.4 Ningxia Catching Up

Development of the Ningxia Hui Autonomous Region, was slow under the former paternalistic central planning system. But, travelling there now, one can recognise a building momentum which heralds an economic take-off, similar to that which has occurred in China's coastal eastern areas. Ningxia, known for its small size, remoteness and lack of advertising, is quietly moving into the front-line of the efforts of China's landlocked west to eradicate poverty and catch up with the prosperous east. Newly-unleashed market forces and profit motives are now shaping the development of the region, and a quickening pace in deregulation makes the region an exciting place for investment. Experts in Beijing studying the possibility of narrowing living standards between people in the country's east and west predict that Ningxia, rich in agricultural and energy resources, is likely to eradicate poverty and enter an economic fast lane ahead of other western provinces and autonomous regions. The per capita production of electricity and per capita coal reserves in the region rank first amongst all of China's provinces, autonomous regions and municipalities. The region also boasts a per capita area of irrigated land that ranks it second nation-wide, and a per capita production of grain ranking it first in the Northwest. The Yellow River winds through Ningxia, nourishing the fertile 17,000-square-kilometre Yinchuan Plain in the region's northern part.

Mao Rubai, the local Party Secretary, vows to break the region's development inertia by unleashing people's creativity in ensuring a GDP (gross domestic product) growth higher than the national average. 'The Hui are the largest Muslim ethnic group in China, but their flair and pioneer spirit was restrained by the command economic regime and inward-oriented policies for decades. Of the region's population of 5.3 million, one-third are Hui people. Among the others, most are immigrants from other parts of the country. This gives us a firm base for innovative thinking,' he said. His goals are to:

- Double the investment amount for fixed assets for the next five years.
- Achieve a GDP growth of 10 per cent, two percentage points higher than the national average, for the next 12 years.
- Introduce a strategy shift from caring for southern poverty-ridden areas to promoting the relatively more prosperous cities and counties to pursue fast economic growth.
- Foster the industries in the fields of petrochemicals, metallurgy, machinery, building materials, medicines and agricultural product processing to develop these industries into economic pillars.

Source: Author research, September 1998.

The link from Turpan to Korla was opened in 1984, and plays a vital role in the exploitation of vast petroleum and gas reserves in the inhospitable Tarim Basin. Now, work is underway on the remaining 975 kilometre section from Korla to Kashi.

With the infrastructure gradually being put in place, the central and local governments are stepping up efforts to lure more foreign investment deep into the interior. Domestic enterprises inland with a chance to co-operate with foreign investors are now eligible for government loans to help them become more attractive to their potential partner. For foreign-invested manufacturing operations in the central and western areas, the Ministry of Foreign Trade and Economic Cooperation (MOFTEC) says it will be more flexible in the export requirement (most projects in the coastal areas have been required to export all or most of their output, but this is becoming less stringent as China's foreign exchange reserves have expanded).

Wang Liaoping, deputy director of MOFTEC's foreign investment administration, explained: 'We will not impose export quotas on companies if they remain self-sufficient in foreign exchange supply (i.e. what they have to import, such as raw materials and parts, is at least balanced by what they sell abroad).' He conceded that given the long distances to the coast, it would be inconvenient for inland companies to be forced to export most of their output and would also serve to push up their production costs.

In addition to these incentives, the inland areas are looking more attractive as the coast becomes more expensive. Foreign firms have been flooding in by the thousands each year, bidding up land and labour costs, and also making the Chinese authorities much more choosy about whom they do business with in the more advanced areas. All this activity will certainly help the poorer interior regions improve their prospects for economic growth. But with the coastal regions continuing to rush forward, it is still not yet clear whether the government can achieve its goal of narrowing the gap between them and the interior. This is likely to take many years to achieve, if ever. But this begs the question whether the more backward regions are willing to wait. Signs of unrest, to be considered in more detail in the next chapter on ethnic minorities, suggest patience is wearing thin.

CHAPTER 6

The Ethnic Minorities Equation

The concept of being Chinese is not based on 'race', but is really a cultural concept. To speak and behave like a Chinese – in short, to accept the Chinese system of cultural values – is to be Chinese. The Chinese refer to themselves as Han or sons of Han (as in Han Dynasty, a period of great historical significance when China was first united). Throughout history, small ethnic groups that came into contact with the Han Chinese have adopted Chinese culture and have been absorbed into the mainstream. This process continues, although there are now legal guarantees designed to protect the rights and culture of minority nationalities. In that light, this chapter will consider:

- Defining a minority
- Stimulating economic development
- Concerns over Xinjiang
- Tibet: a running sore

Defining a minority

Traditionally, the definition of a minority nationality in China is a group of people who speak a common language, occupy a common area, and share a common sense of social values. They see themselves as non-Chinese (i.e. not belonging to the majority Han Chinese population). In 1978 the central government recognised 55 minority nationalities – Zhuang, Hui, Uygur, Yi, Miao, Manchu, Tibetan, Mongolian, Tujia, Bouyei, Korean, Dong, Yao, Bai, Hani, Kazak, Dai, Li, Lisu, She, Lahu, Va, Shui, Dongxiang, Naxi, Tu, Kirgiz, Qiang, Daur, Mulam, Gelo, Xibe, Jingpo, Salar, Blang, Maonan, Tajik, Pumi, Nu, Achang, Ewenki, Jino, Ozbek, Jing, Deang, Yugur, Bonan, Moinba, Drung, Oroqen, Tatar, Russian, Gaoshan, Hezhen, and Lhoba.

According to the 1995 sample survey on one per cent of China's population, there were 1,099.32 million Han people (an increase of 56.84 million since the Fourth National Population Census of 1990), accounting for 91.02 per cent of China's total population. The other 55 ethnic groups represent 108.46 million people (an increase of 17.26 million since the Fourth National Population Census), or 8.98 per cent of the total.. The largest are the Zhuang, with 15.556 million people [see Table 6.1], while the Lhoba, the smallest, has only 2,322 people.

The unique customs and habits of the minorities have developed in the process of their long history and influenced by their peculiar environment, social and economic conditions (Ma, 1994). They also have their own religious preferences. The Hui, Uygur, Kazak, Kirgiz, Tatar, Ozbek, Tajik, Dongxiang, Salar, and Bonan follow Islam; Tibetans, Mongolians, Lhobas, Moinbas, Tus and Yugurs are Lamaists. Dai, Blang, and Deang people believe in the Hinayana (Lesser Vehicle) Buddhism. A considerable number of the Miao, Yao and Yi people believe in Catholicism and Protestantism.

According to one writer:

'Many people imagine China is a kind of colourful folk dance group, town and country brightened by the presence of small communities in traditional costume living in a distinct way of life. Life is all leather-booted Mongolian herdsmen and coy Tibetan girls living harmoniously bound together in common purpose by love of the party. This is a romantic and propagandist view' (Lowe, 1986, p.43).

In some respects, however, reality is beginning to reflect propaganda as the Chinese authorities realise the tourist value of encouraging the ethnic groups to cling to some of their traditional customs, dress and way of life. Many of the groups have been integrated into the late twentieth century mainstream of national life, but not all. In Tibet's Mutuo County, on the lower reaches of the Yarlung Zangbo River, for example, there are settlements of the Menba and Lhoba minorities still inaccessible by highway due to a barrier of ice, snow and swift river currents. The main means of transit are chain cableways, cane-woven bridges and ropeways, while slash-and-burn cultivation and hunting by bows and arrows are still the major means of providing food. Tying knots to record events, woodcutting to calculate and barter goods also still remain (*Beijing Review*, 30-3-1998).

Although the minority nationalities represent a comparatively small proportion of the total population, they have a geopolitical and geostrategic importance far beyond their numbers because of the territories they occupy (see Lattimore 1940 for detailed discussion). Most live along China's sparsely populated frontiers and have cultural relationships with minority groups in neighbouring countries, such as Kazakhstan, Kyrgyzstan, Russia, North Korea, Mongolia, Thailand, and Myanmar (Liao, 1991). Should any elements within these groups became hostile toward the central government – and this certainly exists to some extent in the cases of Xinjiang and Tibet – it could affect China's national security.

In part, the guarantees protecting the minority nationalities are expressed in the structure of China's administrative system (Wang, 1992, pp.164–6). In addition to the 22 provinces, there are five autonomous regions, based on the location of five of the larger and more important minority nationalities. These are the Zhuang occupying the Guangxi Zhuang Autonomous Region on the Vietnamese border; the Hui, or Muslims, a religious group of more than four million occupying the Ningxia Hui Autonomous Region close to Mongolia; the Uygurs, a Turkic group of more than 7 million in the Xinjiang Uygur Autonomous Region bordering on what was formerly Soviet Central Asia; the Tibetans, or Zang, a group of 2.2 million who live in the Tibet Autonomous Region and Qinghai Province, an area of high plateaux and mountains bordering India; and the Mongols, a group of nearly 5 million occupying the Inner Mongolian Autonomous Region between Mongolia and northern China.

There are also smaller units such as autonomous prefectures, leagues, and banners where smaller minority groups are clustered. This administrative system is designed to give the minorities political equality with the Han and to help them maintain their distinctive identities. Linguistically, of the minority nationalities, the Hui, Manchu and She use the same Han language (Putonghua, or the Mandarin dialect spoken in Beijing). Before 1949, only 21 of the minority nationalities had their own written languages, including the Hui, Manchu and She, which used the Chinese script.

During the civil war, the Communists made great efforts to win over the minorities. Cadres sent into minority regions would concentrate first on much-needed local projects such as swamp drainage or small irrigation

Table 6.1 Main Ethnic Groupings

Zhuang	15.5m
Manchu	9.9m
Hui	8.6m
Miao	7.4m
Uygurs	7.2m
Yi	6.6m
Tujia	5.7m
Mongols	4.8m
Tibetans in Tibet	2.3m
Tibetans elsewhere	2.3m

Source: 1995 Sample Census, Beijing.

works while they learnt local customs and were able to identify ways to preach the message of class exploitation. 'As they gained knowledge of local society, the cadres focused their efforts on truly exploited classes, such as the despised blacksmith caste in Tibet'(Spence, 1990, p.556). Unlike the former Soviet Union, which accepted separation of nationalities at least in principle, China was always a unitary not a federal state. It does appear that the party did support a policy of federalism, similar to the Soviet Union, between 1921 and 1940, but 'the war forced nationalities together so that by 1949 there was no need for a federal state' (Brugger, 1977, p.135).

Although separation was not permitted, the early policy was to interfere as little as possible. In particular, religion was to be tolerated, since the new rulers had no desire to create martyrs, and also considered it pointless to destroy religion unless one at the same time destroyed its class basis (Mosely, 1966, pp.113–4). Because of this cautious approach, slavery could still persist among the Yi minority for several years of communist rule (Brugger, op.cit., p136) and monastic serfdom among Tibetans – at least until the crushing of the 1959 revolt.

After 1949, the government set up departments to help create and standardise written languages for 10 minority nationalities including the Zhuang, Bouyei, Miao, Dong, Hani and Li. The Chinese Constitution specifies that all ethnic groups have the freedom to use and develop their own spoken and written languages. *The Law on National Regional Autonomy* stipulates that in performing their functions, the organs of self-government of every ethnic autonomous area should employ the spoken and written language or languages in common use in the locality The Uygur, Kazak, Jingpo, Lahu and Dai have also been given help to have their written languages reformed. At the same time, Putonghua is being promoted as the official spoken language of the country and all minority peoples are urged to learn it.

The regional autonomous areas enjoy extensive self-government rights including independent use of local revenue, and independently arranging and managing construction, education, science, culture, public health and other local undertakings. Officials in Beijing also say the central government has greatly assisted in the training of minority cadres and technicians through the establishment of institutes and cadre schools for national minorities to supplement regular colleges and universities. It has, in addition, supplied the national minority autonomous areas with large quantities of financial aid and material resources in order to promote their economic and cultural development.

One other interesting aspect of the government's approach to the minorities in regard to their involvement in the national birth control policy, from which they have largely been exempt while Han couples, particularly in the urban areas, have been restricted to a single child. The size and growth of the minorities have long been a top concern among China's policy makers, population planning officials, and demographers. The 1990 census placed the population of ethnic minorities at 91.2 million. Although this is only nine per cent of the total population, minorities had an increase by 36 per cent from the 1982 census. The Han majority grew only by 11 per cent over the same time period, less than one third of the rate of increase among the minorities. This has made the question of whether some ethnic minorities should continue to be exempt from the nation's comprehensive measures for curbing fertility a topic of heated debate.

When China's population planning effort was intensified in the 1970s, all minorities were exempt as already mentioned. This action recognised the relatively high mortality and comparatively low level of economic development among minority groups. Gradually, however, fertility limitation was promoted in areas with a heavy concentration of minority populations in the late 1980s, such as Inner Mongolia and Xinjiang. These moves were prompted by the 1982 census results that reported a minority population increase of 68 per cent since the 1964 census. By the time of the 1990 census returns, fertility control was established in all areas of concentration other than Tibet. The measures currently in force in different localities stipulate that the majority of the ethnic minorities can have two children, but that nomads and peasants in specific minority areas can have three children. Only under certain very special circumstances can minorities have four children. The adoption in 1981 of *Guidelines for Restoring or Amending Ethnic Minority Status* opened the way for many to claim or reclaim minority status which swelled the ranks of many ethnic populations. The issue has not been resolved. Because of the concern for political stability, social tranquillity, and national unity, it is highly unlikely that the current policy of allowing more than one birth among ethnic minorities will be changed, but it does mean that the non-Han population is likely to increase for the foreseeable future. This has important socio-political and geopolitical implications that will become clearer in the course of this chapter.

Stimulating economic development

At present, because of various historical, geographical and other factors, the minority nationality areas are less economically developed than the Han areas. Over the last three decades, the government has striven to create policies and measures, including the provision of manpower, financial and technical support, to help overcome this deficiency, culminating in a decision by the State Council in late 1997 to grant them a preferential policy to the help speed up economic growth (*China Daily*, 15-11-1997). The policy included extending low-interest loans, tax breaks and special subsidies to promote ethnic trade and ethnic necessities production enterprises. Each year, the People's Bank allocates 100 million Yuan in low interest loans to set up trade networks in ethnic areas and to innovate technology for designated ethnic necessities production firms, compared with an annual 40 million Yuan ($4.8 million) earmarked in the Eighth Five-Year Plan Period (1991–95).

According to Wen Jing, vice-director of the joint conference and vice-minister of the State Ethnic Affairs Commission, the new policies dictate that most interest balances will be supplied by central finance and a small part by local finance, ensuring that the designated recipients will really benefit. 'We want to explore a new way for the country to serve the production and lives of the people in the ethnic areas in a socialist market economy,' he said in an interview.

Much of the effort is going into the Northwest, where Gansu and Xinjiang, occupying one-sixth of the entire Chinese territory and once the bustling distribution centres on the ancient Silk Road between East and West, are witnessing an economic revival. Gansu Province is an ethnic tapestry of forty-four different nationalities, some of whom are coming down from their remote mountainous regions to help speed the area's economic growth. Linxia, a compact settlement of the Hui ethnic group, for example, used to be a remote and economically depressed region. But now one in every five local residents is engaged in transportation or processing businesses. Tea and timber from the southern part of the country are being sold in the Linxia Hui Autonomous County, and more than 20,000 individual or collective processing enterprises have been established with products sold to coastal regions and Hong Kong. Hui business people from Linxia can be found peddling in almost every large coastal city in the Southeast. Some Linxia farmers have set up joint ventures at Tibet's border markets with businessmen from neighbouring countries. Long-distance transportation teams consisting of Hui, Tibetan, Dongxiang and Shala ethnic groups frequently travel the routes linking Qinghai and Tibet. They transport local products, daily necessities and fashionable clothes from the coastal regions to Tibet, and bring back Tibetan-made artwork and medicinal herbs.

Table 6.2 details the official picture of development, both economic and social, for minority autonomous areas. The figures are certainly impressive, but of course one would need to see comparable figures for non-minority areas, and Chapter 4 has already shown that, notwithstanding great strides in such areas, the largely Han coastal regions are outstripping the inland minority regions on most indicators.

Within the minority areas, Xinjiang is benefiting from its fresh role as China's bridgehead to Central Asia and Europe. The entire Northwest prospered for around 10 centuries as the main trading route between China and the Middle East and Europe, its place in Western history eventually assured by the travels of Marco Polo. But the road fell into disuse in the

Table 6.2 Economic and Social Development of Minority Autonomous Areas: Selected Indices, 1978–97

Index	1978 Absolute Figure	1997 Absolute Figure	1978–97 Annual Growth Rate
Gross Indl. and Agri. Output Value (100m Yuan)	367.7	8,412.1	11.82
Total Agri. Output Value (100m Yuan)	155.6	3,175.1	7.45
Total Indl. Output Value (100m Yuan)	212.1	5,237.0	13.99
Cultivated Area (10,000 hectares)	1,640	2,210	1.58
Total Grain Output (10,000 tons)	3,124	6,963	4.31
Stock of Domestic Animals (10,000)	3,807	5,637	2.09
Stock of Pigs (10,000)	3,260	7,518	4.50
Steel Output (10,000 tons)	128.5	664.0	9.03
Coal Output (10,000 tons)	6,081	19,038	6.19
Crude Oil Output (10,000 tons)	578	2,003	6.67
Railway (10,000 km)	0.9	1.8	3.72
Highway (10,000 km)	20.8	35.4	2.84
Retail Sales of Consumer Goods (100m yuan)	150.8	1,765	13.82
Medical Workers (10,000)	27.94	47.58	2.84
Eth. Min. College Students Nationally (10,000)	3.6	21.7	9.92
Eth. Min. College Teachers Nationally (10,000)	0.6	5	11.81
Min. Language Books (10,000)	3,179	4,999	2.41

Source: *Beijing Review*, October 5–11, 1998, p. 17

thirteenth century as a result of frequent destructive wars and the opening up of maritime routes in the south. Eventually migrant sand dunes devoured both the soil and the prosperity of a vast area extending over Shaanxi, Ningxia, Gansu, Qinghai and Xinjiang. When the market-oriented economic reforms were introduced from the late 1970s onwards, the area fell even further behind the rest of the country. That has now changed, helped by a realisation that the region is a treasure house of mineral wealth. Three of China's four largest coal fields are in this area, as well as four of the most important oil fields. Some 140 kinds of mineral ores have been detected along with large reserves of bauxite for processing into aluminium, and gold.

The Qaidam Basin in the middle of Qinghai Province, home to a large Tibetan population, for example, is described by local officials as the province's 'treasure bowl', containing proven oil reserves of 200 million tons, as well as 4.5 billion tons of mostly high-quality coal with low ash and sulphur content. Under the Kunlun and Qilian mountains are large proven caches of iron, manganese, chromium, vanadium, copper, lead, zinc, nickel, tin, molybdenum, antimony, mercury, gold, silver, platinum, beryllium and selenium. The iron reserves are estimated at 2.2 billion tons, and the province claims the country's largest lead and zinc mines, and is a primary producer of asbestos. The Hui people in the Ningxia Hui Autonomous Region, meanwhile, are sitting on large proven reserves of oil and natural gas, along with mineral resources such as copper, iron, silver, gold, aluminium and nickel.

The growing prosperity of Xinjiang is being built on the back of developments in the vast and inhospitable Tarim Basin, where experts reckon there are reserves of up to 100 billion barrels of oil and 8,300 billion cubic metres of natural gas. The Ministry of Chemistry is developing a large petrochemical industrial base in two stages. The first, already underway, involves establishing facilities to produce basic chemical raw materials and fertiliser; the second calls for the establishment of fine chemical and rubber production. But Xinjiang has really come into its own with completion of a double-tracked railway line between the regional capital Urumqi and the Alataw Pass, completing the Eurasian Transport Corridor which enables goods and people to be moved directly from Lianyungang on the Yellow Sea to Western European terminating at Rotterdam. It was only thirty years ago that the first railway link to Xinjiang was established.

The 'Euro-Asia Land bridge' is being further complemented by construction of eight all-weather highways across the various borders. The latest is a 2,700-km link from Urumqi to Kazakhstan and Pakistan. A separate 1,622 km line to Lanzhou, capital of Gansu Province, has now been double-tracked to allow that remote province better access to the outside world for its minerals and agricultural products. In addition, a 522 km highway across the Taklamakan desert from Urumqi to Haitian in Southeast Xinjiang will help promote oil exploration and development in the Tarim Basin.

These areas are among those included in a radical proposal by a senior economic researcher with the Chinese Academy of Social Science for the establishment of three cross-border special economic zones to ginger up the central and western regions. The proposal by Di Kui covers three trans-national corridors running through zones on the Sino-Russian, Sino-Myanmar and Sino-Kazakhstan borders: the bridge being constructed between Russia and China's Northwestern Heihe City; the road connecting Yunnan Province with Myanmar, leading finally to the Indian Ocean; and the new Euro-Asia Continental Bridge.

'The lack of external trade channels is a major hindrance to the take-off of China's vast central and western areas, and the three economic zones would be the best way to maximise the potential of the links,' he says, pointing out that much cross-border economic co-operation including trade, investment, technological exchange and financial co-operation is already taking place in the three areas, despite the absence of official action. However, due to their small, scattered and unorganised nature, the existing cross-border co-operation is too weak to spark the macro-economy in the regions concerned. 'Nevertheless, they are a precursor for higher-level cross-border economic zones which, embracing organised management and preferential policies, will give a huge impetus to the central and western area's economy.' Among the three trans-border free economic zones he proposes, Di said the one bordering Myanmar is the most mature, and the easiest to develop, with people on the two sides closely linked by blood and custom – an argument that would also apply to the north-western zone on the China-Kazakhstan border (*People's Daily*, 12-9-1997).

Concerns over Xinjiang

The central government likes to present a picture of 1.2 billion happy, smiling people living in peace and harmony under the benefice of the Communist Party. But there are undercurrents in certain border regions populated by key ethnic minorities that suggest this idealistic picture is somewhat distorted. Tibet and Xinjiang are two areas in particular where problems have arisen which have spilled over into the international arena and become a source of dispute between China and foreign governments and organisations regarding its human rights record.

Amnesty International, in a report released in April 1999 to coincide with the annual meeting of the United Nations Commission on Human rights in Geneva, detailed an '*appalling*' rights record in the region, citing 'extra-judicial killings, torture, executions and arbitrary detentions largely targeted at the Muslim Uygur ethnic majority'. It said Xinjiang was the only region of China where political prisoners were known to have been executed in recent years, citing 210 death sentences and 190 executions, mostly of Uygurs convicted of subversive or terrorist acts after 'unfair and often summary trials'. The report also cited the cases of around 200 political prisoners arrested during the 1990s and believed to be still detained or in prison, with arbitrary arrests continuing. Political trials were a formality. Prisoners were often denied access to lawyers and sentenced at degrading mass rallies. Amnesty said the violence had increased in recent years in proportion to the degree of repression and the erosion of the Uygurs' economic, social and cultural rights. The report also pointed to a pattern of discrimination against Uygurs in top jobs, schooling and access to education and health care. However, China's Foreign Ministry spokesman Sun Yuxi responded that 'the Communist Party's ethnic policy in Xinjiang is well-implemented. There may be some problems because China is a big country, but we are striving towards democracy and the rule of law' (Agence France Press, 20-4-1999).

China has held sway over the Xinjiang region for centuries – although it was only brought under full control during the reign of Qing Emperor Qianlong in the eighteenth century (Spence, p.97) – but never assimilated the indigenous Uygurs, who are a Turkic people with close affinity to ethnic groups in neighbouring Afghanistan, Pakistan, Kazakhstan, Kyrgyzstan and Tajikistan. They have a long, proud tradition, claiming to be the only people to have defeated Alexander the Great. For a long time, Xinjiang was a dumping ground for political undesirables banished from court. During the first half of this century, it became the centre of intrigue between Russian Communists and a fragmented China. From the early 1930s, when China was still riven by the rule of regional warlords, the Russian economic hold on Xinjiang increased rapidly, bolstered by oil concessions, joint ventures and economic loans (Fleming, 1936). After 1940, when the war with Germany occupied most of the Soviet Union's attention, the Chinese Nationalist government reasserted itself although following the signing of a treaty of friendship and alliance with Nationalist leader Chiang Kaishek in 1945, Russian influence again became strong (Han Suyin, 1972, p.561). With Russian help, Uygurs established a short-lived East Turkestan Republic in 1944, but it collapsed after the Chinese Communist victory in 1949, and Xinjiang was reincorporated into China as an autonomous region six years later.

For many years, the borders of Xinjiang were tightly sealed. But in recent years, the region has become a crossroads again – of trade and contraband, but more importantly of ideas. The independence of neighbouring Muslim republics has been a powerful example to local Uygurs, especially of the younger generation, because of religious and linguistic affinities.

A double-edged effect has emerged from Beijing's introduction of a more liberal religious policy after the repression of the Cultural Revolution. Hundreds of mosques reopened, new Islamic colleges were formed, classes in the Koran became popular and contacts were renewed with religious organisations in West Asia. There has been a rediscovery of Islam, not just as a religion but as a source of cultural and ethnic identity. There have been settlements of Muslims in China since the Tang Dynasty (618–907), both at the termini of the central Asian trade routes in Gansu and Shaanxi, and in certain Southeast coastal towns in Fujian and Guangdong frequented by Arab traders. Intermarriage with Chinese families created the Hui.

The authorities have responded to growing nationalism by cracking down on unregistered places of worship and screening preachers for their political views. The Chinese government, however, faces a virtual no-win situation. If it adopts a more tolerant approach to religion, it awakens the Uygurs to the religious-nationalist sentiments sweeping Central Asia. But a fresh clampdown would not only further alienate the locals but also disturb ties with Muslim countries. But while the central government may insist that the unrest is a manifestation of Islamic fundamentalism [see Box 6.3],

Box 6.1 Conflict in Xinjiang

The central government blames Islamic militancy from abroad for recent unrest in Xinjiang. The Afghan war in particular had a radicalising effect, and arms from the conflict reportedly were smuggled into Xinjiang. The low-key conflict has been simmering in Xinjiang for some time and follows a long history of Muslim uprisings going back to the eighteenth century (Cotterell, 1995, p.225; Spence, op cit., p.97, pp.169–171,189–90; and Wang, op cit., p.166). The State media tends to present incidents as the acts of a small hooligan element, while a self-styled Uygur independence movement based abroad claim a broader base of support for violence to break the Han domination of the region. In 1996, terrorists bombed an army car in Urumqi and also assassinated Akenmu Sidike, a vice-chairman of the Xinjiang People's Political Consultative Conference. Bombs have been set along the region's principal rail lines. In 1997, eight Muslims were executed for bus bombings in Urumqi, that killed nine people.

Another serious incident took place in the city of Yining in February 1997, when police tried to arrest two 'suspected criminals'. Bystanders intervened, and soon there was a thousand-strong mob. It went on a rampage, torching cars, looting Chinese stalls, burning flags and shouting pro-independence slogans. The death estimate ranged from nine to 90. An alternative account claimed police had entered a mosque during a service and tried to arrest two Uygur religious students. When worshippers refused to surrender the pair, a fight broke out and two people were killed by police gunfire. Protests rapidly escalated and, by some accounts, spread to Urumqi and the cities of Kuqa and Hotan. This was the worst ethnic violence in Xinjiang since 1990, when an armed uprising in the town of Baren, near Kashgar, was suppressed, with an official death toll of 22. But while that incident hardly caused a ripple, the Yining troubles resounded in the Muslim world. In Istanbul, Turkey, Uygurs burned Chinese flags outside Beijing's consulate. And Saudi Arabia urged Western human-rights groups to pay more attention to Chinese violations of the religious freedoms of Muslims in Xinjiang.

In April 1998, police and independence fighters fought a gun battle in which at least three died in Yili. Three Uygurs were executed in May after being found guilty of murdering three Chinese peasants as part of a rebel strategy to sow terror among Chinese settlers. In July, two weeks after President Jiang Zemin visited the province, to warn local officials the struggle against 'separatism' was a long-term one, several 'bombs' exploded in the oasis town of Khotan, although sources insisted they were only detonators causing little damage and no casualties. A few days later, a bomb went off in Korla, on the northern edge of the Taklamakan desert. Some local sources said the bomb makers set off the device by mistake and killed themselves, but a local official insisted it was a 'cooking gas explosion' caused by a careless resident (*South China Morning Post*, 4-8-1998).

Increasingly, however, the security forces are admitting that the pro-independence movement in Xinjiang had escalated in some cities into an 'armed struggle' due to an influx of firearms into the western parts region. Clashes involving heavy firearms sometimes occurred when police officers tried to take possession of arms caches, or when police tried to disperse unauthorised separatist gatherings. Some months after the events, the state media admitted three policemen died during ferocious clashes in April and June. The official Press Digest urged Chinese to 'learn from and salute the three heroes'. The paper called the trio '*martyrs*' and said they sacrificed their lives to safeguard 'stability and prosperity in the western frontier of the motherland' (*South China Morning Post*, 15-8-1998).

The crackdown on 'separatism' in Xinjiang, escalated in early 1999, with the official announcement of at least 21 executions for those accused of involvement in 'counter-revolutionary rebellion', and confirmation of the arrest in 1998 of several hundred Uygurs involved in eight armed clashes with police near the Kazakhstan border (*South China Morning Post*, 2-3-1999, Agence France Presse, 9-2-1999, *Xinjiang Legal Daily*, 1-2-1999). Xinjiang is an area where instability is seen as highly dangerous to national security, hence there are an estimated 12 army divisions, six air bases and most of its nuclear ballistic arsenal posted to protect a long and vulnerable border. One source of Uygur resentment is that the region has for many years been the site of Chinese nuclear testing programme, provoking concern that the fallout from these tests has caused health problems among the local population. The government believes that economic development is the best antidote to nationalism. The PRC is reported to have increased funding to the country's western areas, including Xinjiang, with money specially designated for local industry and infrastructure projects. 'Each year, the autonomous region receives more than 6.5 billion Yuan in central government subsidies. Over the past five years, Xinjiang has attracted 4.7 billion Yuan from other areas of the country' (Xinhua News Agency, 8-3-1998). But, this has been a two-edged sword, since it has stimulated migration of Han Chinese from the more crowded parts of the country. Since 1949, the Chinese Han population in Xinjiang has grown from about 300,000 to an estimated six million. Officially, the Uygurs are said to comprise 49 per cent of Xinjiang's population, and the Han 40 per cent – although some Western media claim the latter figure should be over 50 per cent. The Chinese government says 62 per cent of the population are from 'ethnic minorities' (hence, not just Uygurs; politically, 65 per cent of the deputies to the Ninth National People's Congress are from these minorities, as well as 53 per cent of the regional leaders (*China Daily*, 13-3-1998).

The Han often take better jobs from the less-educated and linguistically disadvantaged Uygurs, especially in the booming oil industry. Chinese tend to settle in the cities, while the Uygurs remain in backward rural areas exacerbating economic disparities. In response to allegations contained in the US State department's annual report on the global human rights situation, the Information Office of the State Council in March 1998 conceded that the Han-Uygur population breakdown was around 75:25 in the regional capital Urumqi, but stressed that this figure had remained virtually unchanged for the past thirty years and, hence, was due to 'historical reasons'. It insisted that Urumqi was a special case which bore no relationship to the situation in the rest of the region. The economic disparities, however, are conceded – minority per-capita income in Xinjiang being 15 times less than in southern or eastern China (*Annual Statistical Report of the State Statistics Bureau*, 1996).

Sources: Agence France Presse, 9-2-1999.
Annual Statistical Report of the State Statistics Bureau, 1996, Beijing.
China Daily, 13-3-1998.
Cotterell, A. (1995) *China. A History*, London: Pimlico (Random House).
South China Morning Post, 4-8-1998, 15-8-1998 and 2-3-1999.
Spence, J. (1990), *The Search For Modern China*, London: Hutchinson.
Wang, C.F. (1992), *Contemporary Chinese Politics, An Introduction*, New Jersey: Prentice Hall, Fourth Edition.
Xinhua News Agency, 8-3-1998.
Xinjiang Legal Daily, 1-2-1999.

hence something being manipulated from outside the country, it can also be presented as the despairing reaction of an ethnic minority to avoid being swamped and losing their land and their prosperity to outsiders.

One interpretation of the problem was offered by Abdul'Ahat Abudrixit, Xinjiang government chairman and a Uygur, at a press conference staged while he was attending a session of the Ninth National People's Congress in Beijing in March 1998. He denied that uneven distribution of resources and money was the cause of the separatist unrest. 'Separatism has its roots in history. [The separatists] ultimate goal is independence. In some cases, economic problems were used by separatists to prompt social discontent. Of course, we should develop the economy and improve people's livelihoods, which will help curb separatism. But no matter how we improve the economy, separatists will not stop their activities.' Separatist groups based in foreign countries were instigating discontent and anger against China in Xinjiang, but the activities were not necessarily sponsored by the governments of the countries where the groups resided, he stressed. Therefore, these countries should not be accused of trying to split China (author's notes).

The main centre for opposition abroad is Almaty in Kazakhstan, where Yusupbek Mukhlisi, who fled to the Soviet Union in 1960 and who is now in his late seventies, heads the 'United National Revolutionary Front of East Turkestan'. Until early 1997, the movement had advocated peaceful resistance to what it calls China's colonial rule. But in March of that year, Mukhlisi and two other Kazakhstan-based Uygur groups issued a common declaration, saying they were 'taking up arms to fight against Chinese oppression' after the executions already described. The three groups claim that since then, over 60,000 alleged Uygur separatists have been arrested by the Chinese and sent to labour camps. They say over 500 of them have died during internment or under interrogation. Mukhlisi says the Uygurs must now fight for survival, or face eventual extermination by the Chinese government. All means are legitimate, he says, against policies aimed at making the Uygurs a minority on their own territory and quashing all resistance to Beijing's rule. Apart from the inflow of Han migrants, there is also concern about the strict enforcement of family planning. To the agriculturalist Uygurs, who see large families as both a source of pride and economic necessity, this is tantamount to cultural genocide.

Despite the rhetoric, it is difficult to see the Xinjiang situation as more than a minor irritant to the central government at this stage. As Cook and Li have observed, Western observers often emphasise the role of minorities in the potential break-up of China, '[b]ut although ethnicity is certainly a factor to be recognised , it does not follow that minority dissent will lead to regional disintegration' (Cook and Li, 1996, p,207). They note that there are scholars such as Breslin or Ferdinand for example who believe that, despite the occasional ripples of unrest, the ethnic minorities are unlikely to pose the same sort of threat to the centre as occurred in the former Soviet Union. The PRC situation is dissimilar to that of the former Soviet Union, 'for China has an historical depth of continuities, greater economic progress and a relative lack of political and economically viable nationalisms to foment disintegration' (ibid., p.208).

Tibet: a running sore

The closest one might come to the Soviet situation is in Tibet, which remains a continuous irritant in China's relations with the West, and a source of much anti-Chinese propaganda. There are some who believe the conflict over the political status of Tibet vis-à-vis China has reached a critical juncture in its long history. The exiled Dalai Lama now finds himself standing on the sidelines seemingly unable to impede or reverse changes in his country that he obviously deplores. The question is whether the frustration engendered by this impotence has seriously heightened the danger of violence in the region.

As Goldstein (1998) observes:

Box 6.2 Religious Overtones

Apart from economic issues, problems such as that now emerging in Xinjiang have religious overtones which cannot be ignored. And the same is true in Tibet, which will be discussed in the next section of this chapter. In the first instance, it is Islam that stokes the fires of local feeling, while in Tibet it is Buddhism. In both cases, elements in the two areas, as well as human rights activists in the United States and Europe, claim that the 'atheistic' communist authorities are determined to eradicate all religion on the grounds that it is nothing more than feudal superstition and stands in the way of China's advancement to become a modern state.

But the central government is vehement in its denials that this is the case. The Head of the State Council's Bureau of Religious Affairs, Ye Xiaowen, is adamant that because of government policy, various religions are alive and well and are going through what many believers call a '*golden period*' (Xinhua News Agency, 13-10-1997). He rattles off the facts and figures to back this up: Taoism Islam, and Christianity have 85,000 places of worship nation-wide and some 3,000 religious groups; there are 10 million Christians, compared with only 700,000 in 1949; in Tibet, there are over 1,700 places of worship and 46,000 monks and nuns living in lamaseries and monasteries; in Xinjiang, there are 23,000 mosques that are home to approximately 30,000 religious officials, and since the early 1980s, more than 40,000 people have made the pilgrimage to Mecca; in Tibet, sutra halls and statues of Buddha can be found in almost every Buddhist's house and prayer flags are a common sight. Each year Lhasa, Tibet's capital, has a million pilgrims.

Nevertheless, Ye says, 'some religious organisations have appeared in China since 1980s engaging in illegal activities under the pretext of carrying out religion, and although there are only a handful of people, they have done considerable harm.' This is attributed to the fact that China is still at a primary stage of socialism when there are remnants of feudalism. They may mislead people when the country is undergoing great social changes and is opening to all kinds of intellectual and cultural influences. 'The heads of these organisations are mostly pleasure seekers with no jobs', he added. 'They either distort religious doctrine, deceiving people and getting them to resist the law or cheat people out of their money and get them together for sexually promiscuous activities. No country in the world can tolerate criminal activities under the guise of religion, and China will not. We have cracked down on some of these religious groups because of its obligation to protect the people's interests and safeguard the dignity of the law and that this is to better protect religious freedom and normal religious activities.'

Source: Xinhua News Agency, 13-10-1997.

'As a classic nationalistic dispute, the Tibet question pits the right of a people, Tibetans, to self-determination and independence against the right of a multi-ethnic state, the Peoples Republic of China, to maintain what it sees as its historical territorial integrity. Such disputes are difficult to resolve because there is no clear international consensus about the respective rights of nationalities and states' (p.83)

In July 1995, for example, the US Senate passed a law which openly stated that Tibet was a sovereign state under [Chinese] occupation, that the real representative of Tibet was the Dalai Lama and his government-in-exile, and that 'the Tibetan people should have the right to self-determination because it had been approved by conclusive evidence that their human rights had been seriously treaded on under the control of the Chinese.' Yet, it is interesting to note that in the period from the collapse of the Qing Dynasty in 1911 to the 'peaceful liberation' of Tibet in 1951, when the area took advantage of Chinese weakness to operate as a de facto independent state, Western countries including the United States and Britain refused to recognise this independence. It also flies in the face of the State Department's 1994 report on Tibet which 'unambiguously reassured China that the United States accepts Chinese sovereignty over Tibet ... .and that this policy is consistent with the view of the international community, including all of China's neighbours' (Goldstein, op.cit., p.93).

Predictably, the Senate action was ridiculed in Beijing, where government spokesmen and the official media launched into a familiar tirade against 'Dalai separatists wanting to break up the motherland', along with the oft-repeated statement that Tibet has belonged to China since 'ancient times'. In complete contrast, the Tibetan government-in-exile and the Dalai Lama have consistently held that Tibet has been under illegal Chinese occupation since China invaded the independent state in 1949/50. The People's Republic of China insists that its relation with Tibet is a purely internal affair, because Tibet is and has for centuries been an integral part of China. The question of Tibet's status is essentially a legal question, albeit one of immediate political relevance. The Chinese case, in which the key works in this regard are *Discussion of the Historical Status of Tibet* by Wang Gui (1997) and *The International Relation and the Tibet Issue* by Zhang Zhirong (1995), can be summarised as follows:

Before the reunification of Tibet, some parts of the area had established close relations with the Han people and other national minorities in west and north-west China. During the first half of the seventh century, Songtsan Ganpo unified the Tibetan tribes on the Qinghai-Tibet Plateau and founded the Tubo Regime and had frequent exchanges with the court of the Tang Dynasty. The two marriages of Songtsan Ganpo and Princess Wencheng, and Tride Tsutsan and Princess Jincheng symbolised the close relations in politics, economy and culture between the Han and Tibetan peoples.

In the middle of the ninth century, the former unified Tibetan Regime collapsed and broke up into many local forces, some of which submitted to the central government of China after the founding of the Song Dynasty (960–1279). In the thirteenth century, during the process of the unprecedented reunification of the many nationalities within the Chinese territory by the Mongols, Tibet was formally embraced into the domain of China. Emperor Shizu of the Yuan Dynasty (1271–1368) empowered the Shakya Regime to handle the local affairs in Tibet under the administration of the central government of Yuan and also set up many administrative systems over Tibet.

The Mongolian, Han, Tibetan and other nationalities formed a political coalition with common prosperity in their economies and cultures. The government of the Ming Dynasty (1368–1644) continued the various systems of the previous dynasty to govern the local affairs in Tibet and conferred the eight leaders of both politics and religion as Fawang or Wang, that is, Dharma or religious king, of local Tibet. The connection of the Tibetan nationality with other nationalities experienced thorough improvement along with the frequent economic and cultural exchanges between Tibet and the central area through trade of tea and horses, tribute to and grants from the emperor.

In the early reign of the Qing Dynasty (1644–1911), the central government claimed the right to approve the appointments of the two top religious leaders in Tibet – namely the Dalai Lama and the Panchen Erdeni [Lama], a practice which has continued to the present day. However, as the West began its attempt to break up China during the late Qing Dynasty in the nineteenth century, it began to promote the concept of 'independent sovereignty" and 'suzerainty' of Tibet. In this, Britain was for a long while the chief villain, due to its control over neighbouring India, which led at one time in the early years of this century to a British invasion of Tibet and brief occupation of Lhasa in 1904. Later on, it was the United States which assumed this mantle, with the CIA being repeatedly accused of helping to foment rebellion by the small band of Tibetan separatists (see Clark, 1955, who gives some credence to this allegation from the US side).

The alternative view of history provided by the Tibetan government-in-exile (extracts taken from its Internet website) can be summarised thus:

Although the history of the Tibetan state started in 127 BC with the establishment of the Yarlung Dynasty, the country as we now know it was first unified in the seventh century CE under King Songtsan Gampo and his successors. Tibet was one of the mightiest powers of Asia for the three centuries that followed, as a pillar inscription at the foot of the Potala Palace in Lhasa and Chinese Tang histories of the period confirm. A formal peace treaty concluded between China and Tibet in 821–3 demarcated the borders between the two countries and ensured that, 'Tibetans shall be happy in Tibet and Chinese shall be happy in China.'

As Genghis Khan's Mongol Empire expanded towards Europe in the West and China in the East in the thirteenth century, Tibetan leaders of the powerful Sakya school of Tibetan Buddhism concluded an agreement with Mongol rulers in order to avoid the conquest of Tibet. The Tibetan lama promised a religious relationship which became so important that when, decades later, Kublai Khan conquered China and established the Yuan Dynasty (1279–1368), he invited the Sakya Lama to become the Imperial Preceptor and supreme pontiff of his empire. The relationship that developed and continued to exist into the twentieth century between the Mongols and the Tibetans was a reflection of the close racial, cultural and especially religious affinity between the two Central Asian peoples. The Mongol Empire was a world empire and, whatever the relationship between its rulers and the Tibetans, the Mongols never integrated the administration of Tibet and China or appended Tibet to China in any manner. Tibet broke political ties with the Yuan emperor in 1350, before China regained its independence from the Mongols. It developed no ties with the Chinese Ming Dynasty (1386–1644). On the other hand, the Dalai Lama, who established his sovereign rule over Tibet with the help of a Mongol patron in 1642, did develop close religious ties with the Manchu emperors, who conquered China and established the Qing dynasty (1644–1911).

The Fifth Dalai Lama agreed to become the spiritual guide of the Manchu emperor, and accepted patronage and protection in exchange. This '*priest–patron*' relationship (known in Tibetan as *Choe–Yoen*), which the Dalai Lama also maintained with some Mongol princes and Tibetan nobles, was the only formal tie that existed between the Tibetans and the Manchus during the Qing dynasty. It did not, in itself affect Tibet's independence. On the political level, some powerful Manchu emperors succeeded in exerting a degree of influence over Tibet. Thus, between 1720 and 1792, Emperors Kangxi, Yong Zhen and Qianlong sent imperial troops to Tibet four times to protect the Dalai Lama and the Tibetan people from foreign invasions by Mongols and Nepalese Gurkhas, or from internal unrest. These expeditions provided the Emperor with the means for establishing influence in Tibet. He sent representatives to the Tibetan capital, Lhasa, some of whom successfully exercised their influence, in his name, over the Tibetan Government, particularly with respect to the conduct of foreign relations. At the height of Manchu power, the situation was not unlike that which can exist between a superpower and a satellite or protectorate, and therefore one which, though politically significant, did not extinguish the independent existence of the weaker state.

Tibet was never incorporated into the Manchu empire much less China, and it continued to conduct its relations with neighbouring states largely on its own. Manchu influence did not last long. It was entirely ineffective by the time the British briefly invaded Lhasa (Bell 1924; Fleming, 1961; Landon, 1905; Younghusband, 1910), and concluded a bilateral treaty with

Tibet, the Lhasa Convention, in 1904. Despite this loss of influence, the imperial government in Peking continued to claim some authority over Tibet, particularly with respect to its international relations, an authority which the British imperial government termed 'suzerainty' in its dealings with Peking and St. Petersburg. Imperial Chinese armies tried to reassert actual influence in 1910 by invading the country and occupying Lhasa. Following the 1911 revolution in China and the overthrow of the Manchu empire, the troops surrendered to the Tibetan army and were repatriated under a Sino-Tibetan peace accord. The Dalai Lama reasserted Tibet's full independence internally, by issuing a proclamation, and externally, in communications to foreign rulers and in a treaty with Mongolia (Bell, op.cit.).

Tibet's status following the expulsion of Manchu troops is not subject to serious dispute. Whatever ties existed between the Dalai Lamas and the Manchu emperors of the Qing Dynasty were extinguished with the fall of that empire and dynasty. Sir Charles Bell, a member of the Indian Civil Service, later a diplomat who had more than two decades of close association with Tibet in the early part of this century and was an intimate of the 13th Dalai Lama and his key officials, states that by the late nineteenth century Chinese influence in Tibet was purely nominal, but was actually briefly strengthened by the British invasion and subsequent withdrawal, which created a vacuum the Chinese were only too happy to fill, and by the treaties which Britain then negotiated which accepted Chinese suzerainty. The Chinese were further assisted when, after their military invasion 1910 the 13th Dalai Lama, fleeing to India as his successor was to do five decades later, sought in vain for British support to oust the invaders – Britain deciding its relations with China were more important (Bell, op.cit, chapter 11).

The collapse of the Qing Dynasty led to the repatriation of the imperial troops from Tibet, and from 1911 to 1950, Tibetans successfully avoided undue foreign influence and behaved, in every respect as a fully independent state. The Chinese waged a border war with Tibet while formally urging Tibet to 'join' the Chinese Republic, claiming that Tibet already was one of China's 'five races'. This, the Tibetans firmly rejected. In an effort to reduce Sino-Tibetan tensions, the British convened a tripartite conference in Simla in 1913 where the three states met on equal terms. As the British delegate reminded his Chinese counterpart, Tibet entered the conference as 'an independent nation recognising no allegiance to China':

'... with regard to the Chinese claim to sovereignty or suzerainty, there is no doubt that [the Tibetans] desire to be free of Chinese control in their political affairs. They are a homogenous people and, though they are akin to the Chinese, the relationship is no closer than that between Frenchmen and Italians' (Bell, p.217).

This, however, does not seem to be how either the British or American governments eventually came to see it. In 1943, when Britain, China and the United States were discussing their wartime relations, the British Embassy in Washington acknowledged 'formal Chinese suzerainty' in Tibet, but also hoped to secure for the Lhasa government 'full enjoyment of local autonomy'. The State Department replied:

'The Government of the United States has borne in mind the fact that the Chinese Government has long claimed suzerainty over Tibet and that the Chinese constitution lists Tibet among areas constituting the territory of the Republic of China. *This Government has at no time raised a question regarding either of the claims* (authors' emphasis)' (Snow, 1963, p.589).

The situation remained somewhat murky on the ground, however, with Tibet able to exercise a great deal of independence in its affairs, given Chinese preoccupation with the Japanese invasion of the mainland and the prolonged civil war. But when the PRC was founded on October 1, 1949, the central government decided to send the PLA troops to Tibet. To this day, the PRC describes this as a 'peaceful liberation' of Tibet which freed the Tibetan people from the misery of centuries-old feudal serfdom, in which the majority were virtual slaves to a small ruling elite, including the Dalai Lama – as well as saving them from (imaginary) British and American invaders. Following some fighting between Tibetan elements and the advancing People's Liberation Army, a Tibetan delegation arrived in Beijing in October 1950 to negotiate a 17-point 'Agreement on Peaceful Liberation of Tibet Between the Central People's Government and Tibet Local Government' which was signed on May 23rd, 1951, in Beijing.

Prior to the signing, the Tibetans did appeal to the outside world for help to hold the Chinese Communists at bay, but without success. The Americans deferred to the British, because of their previous influence in the area, while the British deferred in turn to newly-independent India as the arbiter of Tibet's fate. The Indian government, not wishing to start off on the wrong foot with the newly-emerging Communist power on the other side of the Himalayas did nothing (eventually compounding this by accepting, in a 1954 agreement regularising relations with Beijing, Chinese 'sovereignty' rather than mere 'suzerainty' over Tibet). When this became clear, the Gaxag government in Lhasa decided there was no alternative but to sign the 17-point agreement, seemingly hoping this would assuage Chinese expansionism and allow Tibet to maintain a wide degree of autonomy.

All previous Chinese rulers seem to have been content to exercise territorial claims over Tibet through a symbolic presence there. But the Communists had different ideas, seeing their actions as part of the nation-building process:

'Many writings on Tibet stress the predatory nature of the Chinese annexation ... sometimes arguing that Chinese actions were motivated by a desire to acquire Tibet's natural resources and by a policy of Lebensraum. I think this is a misrepresentation of the Sino-Tibetan conflict. Chinese policies must be seen within the context of the emergence of Chinese nationalism; the Chinese communists and the Guomindang were passionately nationalistic and believed that the territorial limits of modern China lay in the foothills of the Himalayas' (Tsering Shakya, 1999, p.92).

Despite some initial horror in Lhasa at the terms agreed by the Tibetan delegation to Beijing, the agreement seems to have eventually been accepted by the Dalai Lama. It is true that he later repudiated it from Indian exile in 1960, claiming it had been signed under duress – but this hardly explains why the Tibetans had not made any protest for nearly 10 years.

The 1950s represented a period of uneasy truce. One should give credit to the Chinese for recognising the need to go slow and exempt Tibet from most of the communist-inspired reforms taking place in the rest of the country. Even so, there does not seem to be much evidence that they had managed the win the hearts and minds of the Tibetans – sullen tolerance, rather than open-hearted acceptance being the operative word for the local reaction to Chinese rule. All this changed in 1959, with the outbreak of revolt, the Dalai Lama fleeing to India, and the Chinese assuming full control to launch what is officially known as the start of 'Democratic Reform'.

According to Tsering Shakya, the seeds of this were planted at the time of the signing of the 17-point agreement:

'For the Tibetans, the Agreement promised autonomy and that the 'existing status of the Dalai Lama would not be altered'. They thought autonomy meant independence in all but name [in Tibetan the term was translated to mean self-rule]. But, for the Chinese, autonomy meant that the Tibetans had accepted Beijing as the ultimate authority. [But] for the Tibetans ultimate authority always resided with the Dalai Lama. Each party saw what it wanted in the Agreement and it was in many ways doomed from the start' (ibid., p.209).

The Chinese have always claimed the 1959 revolt was instigated by a handful of Tibet's nobles anxious to preserve their power under the old feudal system that the Communists were anxious to eradicate. The local government, the Gaxag, was accused of playing a key role in organising the revolt. In fact, there is considerable evidence to suggest it was a popular uprising, motivated by fear for the safety of the Dalai Lama and anger at the erosion of his power. The Gaxag, indeed the nobility in general, actively sought to halt the rebellion to appease the Chinese. 'The revolt was essentially in defence of the value system of ordinary men and women, to which the Dalai Lama was central' [ibid., p.210).

Despite much hand-wringing in the West, no-one was willing to back the Tibetans in their struggle against Chinese rule. As a result, Tibet eventually disappeared from the headlines, only to regain them when riots in Lhasa in 1987 and again the following year provided a fresh opportunity for allegations that China was not respecting human rights in Tibet – a situation that has largely continued into the late 1990s. The main allegations are that there is accelerating Han population transfer into Tibet which has reduced the Tibetan people to a minority in their own land. Today, claims the government-in-exile, 'there are over 7.5 million non-Tibetan settlers in Tibet including Chinese and Hui Muslims, compared to six million Tibetans.'

'As the Chinese control over all spheres of economic, social and political life is tightened, the Tibetan people are further and further marginalised. Tibet, once a peaceful buffer state between China and India, has been transformed into a vast military base, holding between 300,000 and 500,000 troops and one-quarter of China's 350-missile strong nuclear force.' (Briefing on the Internet site of the Tibetan Government-In-Exile). The population transfer is rebutted by the Beijing government, which says the only Han Chinese living in Tibet are specialists who have gone there voluntarily to help in the region's development. The Han, it maintains, make up less than five per cent of the population and many of the people are there for only a few years before returning home.

The State media carries a steady diet of stories showing the immense benefits that the Tibetan population has obtained through the benefice of the central government, in raised living standards, considerably improved health standards and life expectancy, and in the elimination of illiteracy – contrasting this with the medieval conditions prevailing before 'liberation', reminding the world that the vast majority of Tibetans under the old system were feudal serfs or slaves, and that the biggest serf and slave owner of all as the present Dalai Lama. The fullest account in English of the Chinese position is contained in the document *New Progress in Human Rights in the Tibet Autonomous Region* published by the Information Office of the State Council (*Beijing Review*, 9-3-1998).

Surveying the past three decades, Chinese officialdom likes to cite many achievements in bringing Tibet out of feudalism and into the modern era, and in raising the living standards of its people. These can be summed up as follows:

• **Population.** In 1959, the Tibetan government's census recorded a population of 900,000 – giving a lie, says Beijing, to claims by Western human rights activists and some Tibetan exiles that more than a million

Box 6.3 Tibetan Culture: Crushed Or Conserved?

Following a fact-finding trip to Tibet, American congressman Frank Wolf made a speech in which he strongly attacked the Chinese government for pursuing a policy of 'cultural genocide" in Tibet. He also alleged that Tibet was being 'swallowed up" by an influx of Han Chinese immigrants and that the Tibetans had no freedom of religious beliefs. In its annual reports on the state of human rights around the world, the US Department of State invariably makes similar accusations, as does the exiled 14th Dalai Lama. The Chinese Government, meanwhile, repeatedly insists that life has never been better for the Tibetans, and that the Communist Party has gone out of its way to preserve the best features of Tibetan traditional culture.

In September 1997, the Chinese Foreign Ministry invited 10 Beijing-based correspondents from media in Britain, Hong Kong, Singapore and the United States to spend two weeks in Tibet to discover who was right on the issue. Chew Juai Fong, special correspondent of the Singapore newspaper Lianhe Zaobao was one of the group and the following are a summary of his observations:

'The 14th Dalai Lama's New Palace, also known as the Summer Palace, was built in 1956 with the aid of the Central Committee of the Communist Party of China (CPC) and the central government. It is situated in a big garden built in the eighteenth century. The garden is locally called Norbu Lingka, which means Treasure Garden in Tibetan. The Shoton, or Sour Milk Drinking, Festival is celebrated in summer each year. In the past, whenever the occasion occurred, Tibetan artists were required to stage performances to entertain the Dalai Lama. Although the 14th Dalai Lama has been out of Tibet for 38 years, the local Tibetans still freely continue their tradition of performing for him. The only thing different is that the Dalai Lama is not on the rostrum of the New Palace, and Norbulingka is no longer his own 'imperial garden". 'Norbu Lingka was crowded on September 2 when the group arrived there in the morning. That day was a day off for Tibetans. Old and young, they poured into the Norbulingka, off-limits to common Tibetans in years past, to watch the Tibetan opera. On the second floor, we were surprised to see some Tibetans doing full-length body bows before a bed and a chair while quietly chanting. They were doing this as if no other people were there. The official in our company said they were where the 14th Dalai Lama used to rest and expound Buddhist sutras. In the main hall is a properly furnished gilded throne which is covered with hada (a long white silk scarf Tibetans give in greetings). In front of it are piles of small-value money notes. They were donated by devotees after worshipping.

The Chinese government practically divides the role of the 14th Dalai Lama into two: Religiously, he is a Living Buddha, and politically, he is the separatist Lhamo Doinzhub (original name of the 14th Dalai Lama). Tibetans can freely worship the Dalai Lama, but must stay away from Lhamo Doinzhub. I heard that many Tibetans enshrine the statue or picture of the 14th Dalai Lama in their homes. So, while interviewing Deputy Mayor Zholmagyai of Lhasa, I curiously raised the question of whether Tibetans are allowed to do so and whether it is an offence against the law. 'It is not regarded as illegal if someone hangs the photo of the 14th Dalai Lama at home for worshipping," said Zholmagyai frankly, 'And the public security organs won't deal with it.'

The religious role of the 14th Dalai Lama remains important,' said Phurbu Qoinpe, a young lama acting as our guide during our visit to the famous Jokhang Monastery in Lhasa. He told us, 'To monks here, many first entered into monkhood out of adoration of the Dalai Lama.' It is true. The leaving of the 14th Dalai Lama left the Potala Palace unoccupied. But it is still a place devotees and lay-people love to go. People, worshipping or visiting, come and go in an endless stream. The Chinese central government spent over 53 million yuan on repairing the palace during 1988–94, conscientiously preserving this historical monument which represented the temporal and religious administration in the past.'

Source: Chew Juai Fong, 1997, reprinted in *China's Tibet*, February 1998, p.16.

people were killed in the region's 'peaceful liberation'. Thanks to major advances in public health, the average life expectancy of Tibetans has almost doubled (36 to 65 years) and the population of Tibetans in the autonomous region has risen to almost 2.5 million. This is in marked contrast to the period from the Tang dynasty to 1950 when the population had sharply declined, partly due to the fact that 25 per cent of the population were celibate monks and nuns.

- **Religion and culture.** Although the monasteries, the nobility and the local government of Tibet had collaborated under the rule of Tibetan Buddhist doctrines to reduce the broad masses of slaves and serfs into the state bordering on incarceration, says Beijing, there is total freedom of religion, witnessed by the fact that that there are today 460,000 monks and nuns. Admittedly, during the chaotic 'Cultural Revolution" (1966–76), many monasteries and sites sacred to Tibetan Buddhism were desecrated, but that same thing happened all over China.

In his 1962 autobiography, three years after he fled to India after the abortive Lhasa rebellion, the Dalai Lama wrote that tens of thousands of his people had been killed, not only in military actions but individually and deliberately. They had been killed, without trial, on suspicion of opposing communism or for hoarding money or simply because of their position, for no reason at all, but mainly and fundamentally they had been killed because they would not renounce their religion. He claimed the Chinese were torturing and killing monks and suppressing the religious beliefs of Tibetans, but at the time these allegations were made, the British writers Stuart and Roma Gelder, on an extended visit to Tibet, saw an estimated 30,000 people attending the anniversary celebrations of the founding the Drepung Monastery in Lhasa, placing their votive butter lamps before altars, while 700 monks chanted their sutras, and Tibetan religious life seemed as unconstrained as ever (Gelder, 1964, p.52). Box 6.3 deals with a more recent visitor's observations in this regard.

In the past 20 years or so, the central government has earmarked hundreds of million Yuan for the renovation of monasteries and religious activity centres in Tibet. By 1997, close to 1,800 monasteries and religious activity centres had been renovated, including the Potala Palace and the Samye, Gandain, Tashilhungpo and Palkor monasteries, which are designated as cultural relics for special protection. Customs and habits associated with religion in wedding or funeral ceremonies are fully respected. Some 200 kinds of Tibetan classic works totalling more than one million volumes have been published. Following the creation of the Tibetan Buddhist College in 1983, the China Tibetan Language Senior Buddhist Institute was launched in Beijing, where more than fifty Living Buddhas and Geshes (Buddhist Doctors of Divinity) have taken advanced refresher courses in recent years.. Close to 500 students, under the guidance of noted Living Buddhas and scholars, study Buddhist sutras and classics, and history on religion. The Tibetan Tripitaka: Gangyur, created in the thirteenth century, has been reprinted for recitation in various monasteries in the Tibetan areas.

- **Education**. In 1950, Tibet had old-style official and private schools attended by some 2,000 monks and the children of the nobility. Between 1950 and 1990, the central government earmarked 1.1 billion yuan to fund Tibetan education. During this period, some 40,000 children graduated from high schools and polytechnic secondary schools, and 17,000 graduated from colleges and universities. In 1990, there were 157,000 primary school students, 21,300 middle school students and 5,000 high school and vocational school students; the number of the illiterates and semi-illiterates dropped from 95 per cent to 44 per cent. There are four universities and colleges, 15 polytechnic secondary schools, 63 middle schools, and 2,474 primary schools.
- **Language**. In order to improve the educational level of all Tibetans, Tibetan language schools have been set up in China's hinterland. Each year, a large group of people are selected to study in these primary, middle and high schools. In the Tibet Autonomous Region, both Tibetan and Han Chinese are taught in school. In the primary schools, students study mainly Tibetan, but there are also schools which lay emphasis on

both Tibetan and Han Chinese. In the middle schools, students study mainly Han Chinese, but are also taught some lessons in Tibetan. In universities and colleges, many lessons are taught in Han Chinese, because the Tibetan language lacks natural science terms.

- **Infrastructure**. Over the past forty years, Beijing invested about 20 billion yuan to undertake infrastructural construction in Tibet. At present, it gives an annual allocation of one billion Yuan to the autonomous region, the highest figure in China in terms of the per-capita share. Before the peaceful liberation of Tibet in 1951, no highway in its true sense was available in Tibet. The 14th Dalai Lama had a car which was a gift from the British. It was dismantled and transported on the back of beasts to Lhasa after the liberation. Now, however, there are 22,500 km of highways, with the road network centred around Lhasa, leading to a 16-fold increase in cargo transported by road since 1965 – when much of the goods still had to be carried on the backs of animals or people over rough tracks. Before 1951, no farm machinery and chemical fertilisers were used. Now, tractors routinely plough the fields. In the farming and pastoral areas, large-scale farmland and grasslands construction have been carried out. After 1980, farmers were freed from the requirements of [state] centralised purchases and any agricultural taxes.

- **Economic Development**. Since 1992, the Tibetan economy has increased rapidly. In 1997, its GDP amounted to about 7.35 billion Yuan, an increase of 96.6 per cent since 1991 at constant prices. Since 1987, the region has reaped bumper harvests every year, total grain output in 1997 reaching a record 820,000 tons, 41.4 per cent higher than 1991. Pockets of poverty still exist, but the goal was a comfortable living standard for the vast majority of people by 2000. The average annual per capita income of urban residents used for living expenses rose 2.4 times between 1991 and 1997 to 5,130, while farmers and herdsmen have witnessed a 50 per cent increase to 1,040 Yuan. For the celebration of the thirtieth anniversary of the founding of the autonomous region in 1994, Beijing mobilised the whole country to aid 62 projects related to economic development at a total estimated cost of 2.38 billion Yuan. By 1996, fifty-six projects had been completed with investment consumed surpassing the budget by 3.6 billion Yuan.

In sum, China believes it can be proud of its record in Tibet, and sees no reason why outsiders should criticise its exercise of authority over what it considers an inalienable part of the motherland. At the same time, a 'carrot-and-stick' approach is clearly evident. For example, a senior Tibetan leader in charge of religious affairs, Nimaciren, described as being a party member for 17 years, told one newspaper interviewer that 'a degree of toughness is needed to keep Tibet stable and under control'. He said the process of 'straightening out' monasteries, begun in 1998, would continue and the Government would step up its efforts to spread atheism among cadres. The report quoted him as saying 'Toughness is needed in this case since unstable elements have threatened our safety and tried to upset economic construction. If the Government can control one lama, it can control one temple; if it can control one temple, it can control the public of that region, so it is important to make sure that temples are submissive to the Government'. Despite international criticism of religious oppression, Nimaciren insisted the Government respected religious worship, but 'religious activities must not violate state security and splittist activities will be dealt with harshly' (*South China Morning Post*, 24-6-1999).

It is because of the statements like this, and despite being bombarded with statistics such as those quoted above, that cause many, especially those active in international human rights organisations, to remain sceptical of Chinese goodwill in Tibet. There seems little hope of any meeting of the minds on this issue, so that the Tibet saga is likely to run and run and run for many years to come.

One suspects that this is partly true because of a sense in the West of Tibet epitomising 'Shangri-la' or 'Paradise Lost', something that should not be sullied by the intrusion of big power politics (Bishop, 1989; for examples of the emotional and anti-Chinese approach to Tibet see Harrer, 1953 and 1988, and Wilby, 1988). This is demonstrated in the 1980s and 1990s by a revival in interest in the James Hilton 1934 novel *Lost Horizon*, with fresh editions and a spate of 'Shangri-La revisited' books by various authors. Some Western propagandists, drawing on the recollections of certain highly-placed exiled Tibetans, continue to write of the old Tibet (destroyed by China) as a land where lamas, farmers and nomads lived in Utopian harmony under the guidance of an almost wholly benevolent clergy. The Chinese, however, paint a picture of the vast majority of the people living in abject conditions and virtual slavery, prone to disease and early death. This is certainly borne out by one English visitor, Perceval Landon, the London Times correspondent accompanying the 1904 Younghusband expedition to Lhasa, who found a country in which Buddhism bore no longer the faintest resemblance to the plain austere creed preached by Gautama Buddha. 'Tibetan religion was a system of devil worship and the monkish communities spared no effort to establish their predominance more firmly every year by fostering the slavish terror which is the whole attitude to religion of the ignorant classes of the land' (Landon, 1905, quoted in Gelder, op.cit. p.51).

There is a great deal of misinformed foreign comment about Tibet, so that one can see why the Chinese react so strongly to criticism. One perfect example involves Western newspaper reports soon after the Chinese Communist troops entered Tibet to 'liberate' it, stating that the soldiers were followed by millions of starving Chinese civilians streaming after them carrying only empty rice bowls and chopsticks who then proceeded to eat the Tibetans out of house and home until there was famine in the land. Such stories showed remarkable ignorance of Tibet's geography – its high altitude and severe climate making it impossible to grow rice. There have been others since, perhaps part of a Western political disinformation programme, which have not stood up to even the most cursory investigation.

Given China's obsession with national security and the integrity of its historical borders, one can see why Beijing reacts instantly to any challenge to its authority in Tibet, and will go on doing everything in its power to ensure the region is closely integrated into the mainland Han mainstream. The State Council document previously cited sums up the Chinese feeling in the face of all the international criticism:

> 'People of all ethnic groups in Tibet are constructing the new Tibet with one heart and one mind. But since Tibet's economic and social development, which started at a very low level, is hampered by unfavourable natural conditions such as exceptional elevation, frigid weather and lack of oxygen, Tibet remains economically and socially underdeveloped. As a result, the human rights enjoyed by the Tibetan people have to be further improved. But the Central Government and Tibet's local governments at all levels will continue to make painstaking efforts to promote Tibet's economic and social development, consistently improve the people's lives and further promote the progress of human rights in Tibet.'

It seems clear that China believes that its policy of rapidly modernising Tibet is bound to solidify its position there regardless of what the exiled Dalai Lama or nationalistic Tibetans might think or do. Behind this can be detected the hope that a new generation of Tibetans is emerging who will be less influenced by old religious beliefs and, looking at what has been achieved in recent years, consider that being part of China is in their best interests. In the absence of any credible international action (e.g. sanctions) that could be undertaken to force China to change its tack on Tibet, this approach has every chance of success.

CHAPTER 7

Urban Stresses

China faces an urban explosion over the next two decades, with a massive population shift from rural areas to cities and new townships. The Chinese Academy of Social Sciences (CASS) forecasts that by the year 2010, the urban population will grow to 50 per cent. In the early 1990s, it was 27.6 per cent, and in the early 1980s, just under 20 per cent, according to official data. These startling figures suggest that China, which has hitherto been predominantly an agrarian society, is undergoing a profound social revolution. The urban expansion has tremendous implications in terms of urban infrastructure construction, maintenance of law and order, provision of welfare services, and job creation. The environmental impact of this rapid urbanisation will be dealt with in Chapter 9; this chapter will focus on the pressures towards social polarisation and disintegration, the issue of absorption of China's huge rural labour surplus and the impact of 'Westernisation' on urban society.

The sections are:

- People on the move: the rapid pace of urbanisation
- Transformation of the built environment: the concretisation of the earth
- Social, economic and political issues
- The costs of change: the changing sense of place

People on the move: the rapid pace of urbanisation

The definition of China's urban population is complex, and generally different from that of the West. The main issues have been the extent to which surrounding agricultural populations should be included within the urban realm, and to what extent towns (*zhen*) should be reclassified as cities (*shi*), an administrative procedure that is much to the advantage of the reclassified local government via increased state support and opportunity to raise local taxation. Past studies have grappled well with this complexity, and with a lack of data, but it is only in the 1990s, with the results from the census of 1990 being published, that Chinese data has been gathered and presented in a sufficiently meaningful and consistent manner to permit accurate analysis of urbanisation since the founding of the PRC. The Maoist period especially, was often interpreted as a period of 'anti-urbanism', but this viewpoint is now generally rejected as oversimplified (Kirkby, 1985). The variable nature of urban policy in that period is now more generally accepted. Kam Wing Chan's book (1994) can now be regarded as the modern definitive work, and he has utilised official sources which 'retrodict' back to the Maoist era, from the 1990 results.

Chan argues that the Maoist system generally sought to maximise industrialisation while simultaneously keeping down the costs of urbanisation, via 'suppression of the expansion of urban services and personal consumption, intensification of use of urban facilities and housing, and adoption of a capital-intensive approach to industrial development' (ibid., p.92). Controls on rural-urban migration became more and more tight in the 1960s and 1970s which 'reinforced the wall between town and country' (ibid., p.92). By the beginning of the Dengist period, China had become 'under-urbanised' in contrast with the 'over-urbanisation' of other Third World countries. Although not anti-urban, the policies had kept a tight lid on urban expansion. What has happened since is that the lid has come off – with considerable force!

The low level of urbanisation in the 1970s was often appreciated by many experts outside China; those who witnessed the appalling poverty and squalor of the cities of South Asia or Latin America. For the people actually living in Maoist cities, however, especially during the Cultural Revolution, life was rather spartan and exacting. Cities were 'producer cities' in the main, and certainly not the centres of conspicuous consumption found overseas. Housing was cheap but generally shoddy, and food supplies were adequate but never exciting; ditto for clothing and footwear. There was no night life, except occasionally for a few party members or foreigners, and radios and bicycles were the dominant consumer goods. China's cities had become worthy but dull, and the Open Door Policy brought a growing awareness of the contrasts with other Asian cities, never mind those of North America or Europe.

There seems to be a close link, indeed a logarithmic relationship, between urbanisation and GNP levels per capita for the West Pacific Rim in general (Cook, 1993). Whether economic growth prompts urbanisation or whether urbanisation prompts economic growth are probably questions impossible to answer; what can be said, however, is that the two are inextricably intertwined, and the Dengist period brought economic growth largely through an urbanisation strategy. This is notwithstanding the

149

changes to the Rural Responsibility System noted in previous chapters, and the consequent development of TVEs (township and village enterprises) which it also encouraged.

For example, China introduced the Special Economic Zones (SEZs) in 1980, and although these began as small villages or towns, they are now large urban entities, with Shenzhen's population, for example, now being at least two million and possibly three million. 14 coastal cities were opened up in 1984, and as Chapter 4 noted, similar policies have been introduced in the 1990s for border cities and inland provincial capitals. The Chinese authorities, in common with many urbanists, believe that there is a Law of Urbanisation relative to industrialisation, and that China is still under-urbanised, by at least 22 per cent (Yan Mingfu, 1995, p.4). In terms of the current scale of urbanisation, official figures suggest that the total urban population for year-end 1994 was 28.6 per cent of the total population in China (China Statistical Yearbook, 1995, p.59). This compared with 26.4 per cent in 1990, 23.7 per cent in 1985 and 19.4 per cent in 1980, soon after the reforms were begun. People are flooding into the urban areas, and apart from those who appear in the official statistics, there are also many more of the 'floating population' of transients to contend with – up to 130 million of these according to some estimates.

By 1994, the State Statistical Bureau recognised 622 'cities' throughout the country, 51 in Guangdong Province alone, followed by 46 in Shandong Province, and 39 in Jiangsu Province. In 1993, 32 of these cities were 'million' cities, playing a key role in economic growth not just at the local level, but also at the regional level, and, in some cases such as Beijing or Shanghai, the national or even international one. Yan Mingfu, then Vice-Minister of Civil Affairs suggested that 'Shanghai, Beijing, Guangzhou and Tianjin all have the possibility to be developed into internationalised metropolises' (Yan Mingfu, 1995, p.6). In addition, of course, the return of Hong Kong in 1997 added another key, global, player to this potentially strong urban line-up. Given the role of global cities within the global economy, and in globalisation in general, it will be crucial for such cities to have a truly global presence. More generally, the official expectation is that by 2000 the urbanisation level will reach 34 per cent nationally, with 724 cities, and by 2010 between 42–5 per cent, with 1003 cities (ibid., p.5).

Kam Wing Chan, however, projects two scenarios of 4 per cent and 5 per cent annual growth, respectively (Chan, 1994, pp.152–3). On his data, therefore, urbanisation in 2000 could reach either 35.6 per cent or 39.2 per cent, and 48.2 per cent or 58.3 per cent in 2010. The numbers involved would be enormous, at up to 838.4 million people in 2010 in a 'worst case' situation. If these predictions are accurate, then, as he declares:

'What is going to happen in China in the coming two decades is thus truly momentous – the urban percentage will almost double and the size of the urban population added [our emphasis] will be about that of the current US urban population' (Kam Wing Chan, 1994, p.153)

Recent data suggests these estimates to be accurate, and as noted above, CASS now accepts a 50 per cent level possible for 2010. Also, given that Chongqing was declared in 1997 as the fourth municipality to be run directly by central government (along with Beijing , Tianjin and Shanghai), with its inclusive population expanded to 30 million, the national urbanisation level will be further inflated. The implications of these changes to China's fabric are profound, and it is to some of these that we now turn.

Transformation of the built environment: the concretisation of the earth

Previous research by Cook has focused on urban pressures in the West Pacific Rim in general, and in China in particular (Cook 1993, 1995, 2000; Cook and Li, 1994a). The dramatic transformation of the built environment, especially in China's large cities, he has described as 'the concretisation of the earth'. Dwarfing even the previous fast-building era of the 1950s, the new constructions in Beijing, in Pudong (Shanghai), in Shenzhen and Guangzhou, and other large cities of China, offer dramatic evidence of the exciting changes to China's urban scene. Fuelled in large part by foreign investment (see Cook and Wang, 1998, for further details of the dramatic increase in FDI during the reform era), and also by the lending of China's state banks, a tremendous investment is being made in new high rise and mega-scale office blocks, hotels, trade centres, shopping centres, and residential blocks of flats, as well as related port facilities, airports, freeways and, albeit less frequently, mass transit transportation systems. Cities reverberate to the sound of piledrivers, and the dust from the sinking of new foundations (perhaps especially the fine dust of Beijing) is everywhere:

'The conversion of raw material resources into the gleaming concrete, steel and plate glass spires of modernity is on a huge scale, sucking up a high proportion of China's financial resources as well as the international finance required to oil the wheels of the potentially lucrative property markets underpinning these developments' (Cook, 2000).

Shanghai is one of the key locations for this process to unfold. Its expansion was relatively restricted in the 1980s but the plans for the expansion of Pudong especially (see Box 7.1) have played a major role in the massive newbuild not just in Pudong but also elsewhere in the city. By mid-1997, the city was estimated to have a population of 13 million plus 3 million migrants, and its economy had grown by 14 per cent per year since the early

1990s. Not only that, but the traditional base of the economy – heavy industry – is also being transformed towards the hi-tech, high value-added direction, including for instance a US$1 billion investment from Japan's NEC in a microchip plant due to open in 1999 (Jacques, 1997). Cook counted 100 newly completed high-rise buildings on his way back to the airport in 1997, compared to his previous research visit in 1992. This is a figure which is only those visible from the road, and compares with the 168 claimed within Pudong alone (see Box 7.1). In Shanghai, therefore, as well as in many other cities of China, the concretisation of the earth proceeds at full speed.

Notwithstanding the exciting aspects of this urban transformation, as Cook has noted in his previous papers, there is a potentially high price to be paid, within the city itself, the nation and the international community, as this relentless concrete juggernaut rolls on. For example, many low level localities are overwhelmed by these high rise developments, whether in Beijing, Guangzhou, or other cities. The atmospheric and ancient back street *hutongs* of Beijing are, notwithstanding a few successful attempts at redevelopment *in situ* (dealt with further below in Box 7.4), are being overwhelmed by the inexorable growth of mid-rise or high-rise blocks. In the whole of China, by the mid 1990s it was estimated that over 4000 large-scale blocks of residential quarters, each with a floor space of more than

---

Box 7.1 The Rapidly Changing Map of Pudong

Pudong, on the east of the Huang Pu, which runs through Shanghai, was traditionally 'Shanghai's slum area, infamous for its criminals and triad gangs (Cooke, 1993). By the early 1990s ago it had a population of about one million people, living in mainly mid-rise apartment blocks and working in the traditional shipbuilding, engineering works and factories of the area. Today, the expansion of buildings and employment in Pudong is phenomenal, and it seems like a cross between London Docklands Developments and Hong Kong. A total investment of 40 billion Renmimbi was planned from 1990 to year 1996 (since increased to 70 billion, with perhaps 200 billion being required to year 2000) in commercial, hi-tech, port, science park, residential and other facilities. These new developments, including the striking 'Oriental Pearl' TV tower, the highest in Asia, now dwarf the colonial buildings of the Bund on the other side of the Huang Pu. Not that Shanghai is lacking in other new developments, including a high rise cluster of hotel and commercial buildings west towards the airport, a smaller scale cluster around the huge railway station slightly to the north of the city centre, plus other hotels, retail and commercial projects within the central area itself and even by 1992 there were worries about Pudong becoming 'overbuilt' (Sender, 1992).

It is now estimated that Shanghai as a whole has over one million square metres of vacant office space, and indeed some estimates suggest up to 50 times this figure at the national level (*China Mail*, Jan.-Feb. 1996, p.76). If Shanghai was once the Paris of the East (before World War II), then Pudong is 'La Défense' (Sudjic, 1992), with all the pluses and minuses that such an alternative 'eccentric' location entails, and it is interesting to note recent reports that the local authorities are now encouraging foreign banks, for example, to reoccupy buildings in the partly renovated Bund area, perhaps in part to balance the growth on the east side of the river.

This growth can not easily be balanced, however, for by 1995, the population had grown to 1.4 million people, employed in 4,000 industrial enterprises with 400,000 workers, and by 1997, 168 new buildings, each 24 storeys plus were in construction according to the Pudong New Area Municipal Administrative Committee. Over 50 per cent of the funds for this incredible rate of expansion comes from foreign investment. Pudong is one of the hopes of the new China, the 'dragon head' of revitalisation of the entire Yangtze basin. Pudong therefore encourages investment not just from property developers but also transnational manufacturing companies like Volkswagen and Pilkington Glass, in Waigoaqiao Free Trade Zone, Jinqiao Export Processing Zone, and Zhangjiang Hi-Tech Park as well as the property developments in the Lujiazu Finance and Trade Zone.

'What about the Shanghainese? When they lift their heads from their busy work, they will exclaim that the change is too quick. Taxi drivers cannot definitely inform you what a building under construction will be used for because they have just noticed it. Shanghai officials slightly exaggerate Pudong's construction, 'The map will have to be changed once a week otherwise you'll not be able to find your way about" (Xin Zhou, 1997, p.57). Ian Cook has made two research visits to Pudong, in 1992 and 1997. He can vouch for the fact that the pace of change has indeed been amazing, with new high-rise construction at every turn. GDP in Pudong reached RMB 42.1 billion in 1995, 22 per cent up on the previous year. Can the bubble burst is a key question, but at present, despite potential setbacks, this seems unlikely.

Sources: Author research.

Cooke, K. (1993), 'Pudong Development Zone: New Tiger Will Pace the East Bank', *Financial Times*, June 2nd.

Hua Yequan et.al. (eds) (1996) *Guide to Trade and Investment in Shanghai*, Shanghai: Shanghai Scientific and Technological Literature Publishing House.

Sender, H. (1992) Eastern Promise: Hongkong Developers Flock to Shanghai, *Far Eastern Economic Review*, 17th September, p.72.

Sudjic, D. (1992) Birth of the Brave New City, *Guardian*, 2nd December, pp.2–3.

Xin Zhou (1997), 'Shanghai at Night', *China National Day 1997*, Beijing: China Intercontinental Press, pp.52–7.

50,000 square metres, had been built (Zou Deci, 1995, p.29). Cook has previously expressed his concern about this policy of massive newbuild, which to him has uncomfortable echoes of the justification for British inner-city developments of the 1960's, developments which broke up established communities and left a legacy of unpopular high-rise living and the decanting of population to outer suburbs and new towns, as well as, in the longer term, contributing to subsequent inner-city decline. Also, there is a safety concern about this rapid expansion, with safety standards being flouted, as in other Asian countries, and building standards being low. Relatively quickly, many of the new blocks can deteriorate, while internally, quality of fixtures and fittings leaves much to be desired. Also, this concretisation process leaves swathes of quarries in the rural hinterlands, while the expansion of the urban area takes up fertile and productive farmland in the environs of the city itself, as Smil, for example, notes. Sometimes, the urban expansion, as in the case of Shenzhen (see Box 7.2) and other SEZs is within areas which were wholly rural, and the ecological impact is particularly profound.

Box 7.2 The Transformation of Shenzhen

Ian Cook made a research visit to Hong Kong in 1980 and well remembers some of his friends mocking the few warehouses and other features then found in Shenzhen, just declared as a Special Economic Zone (SEZ). Today, Shenzhen is a vibrant modern city of possibly 3,000,000 inhabitants, according to unofficial estimates. This transformation has come about via the economic policy of the Chinese government, the role of local officials, Shenzhen's superb location straddling Hong Kong's 'neck' to the mainland, plus the entrepreneurial skills of the Hong Kong investors and the high work rate of the migrant workers in the city. Shenzhen SEZ allocated nearly 30 billion yuan (approximately £3 billion at the extant rate of exchange) for capital construction between 1980 and 1991, of which 7 billion yuan came from foreign investment. This investment meant that: 'Towards the end of 1991, Shenzhen had completed 9 industrial areas, 8 harbours, 5 entry and exit ports, an airport, a helicopter field, and a municipal highway of 288 kilometres long. In addition, Shenzhen had installed 250,000 program-controlled telephones, offered direct-dialling service with 196 cities outside China and 1,033 cities within China, established water-storage facilities capable of supplying 630,000 tons of water per day, and power generation facilities with an annual supply of over 4 billion kilowatts of electricity' (*Investment in China*, 1993, p. 187). By 1994 alone direct dialling was with 230 overseas countries and regions and 1700 cities in China, while water supply was 2.43 million tons and power supply 8.87 billion kwh (Gao Shangquan and Chi Fulin, 1997, p. 181)

By the end of August 1992, the city had signed 9,200 agreements to utilise foreign investment, with 'a total contract amount of US$8.502 billion and an actual amount of US$ 4.175 billion. During this period, more than 5,000 enterprises with foreign investment were set up, whose industrial output value constituted 70% of the total of Shenzhen municipality' (*Investment in China*, p. 187). When Ian Cook made a brief field visit in 1995, the city was booming, its central area was obviously aiming to replicate Hong Kong (albeit less successfully in terms of the quality of building and environment) and further afield one could enjoy the possibly dubious pleasure of a visit to tourist theme parks, one with a miniaturised sights of the world (e.g. the Eiffel Tower) or an ethnic minorities of China theme. Near to these was the ubiquitous McDonalds. By 1996, it was reported that these and other investments had totalled more than US$9 billion, with annual industrial output being 80 billion Yuan compared to a mere 60 million Yuan in 1979 (Ridding, 1996).

The latter article refers to the possible insecure future for the city, for it is difficult to sustain such impressive progress indefinitely. Ridding notes that problems such as rising costs, crime, corruption, lack of educational and technology infrastructure and lack of skilled staff must be faced. In a recent report, John Gittings has noted that Shenzhen 'has one of the worst records for workplace injuries ... highest number of retail outlets for pirated video compact discs and fake designer label goods. There are also more brothels than anywhere else in China' (Gittings, 1999b). Further, there is now considerable antagonism within China towards the favourable investment climate and other opportunities which the SEZs have had, to the potential detriment of investment elsewhere. The official line was that the return of Hong Kong, the growth of 1000 plus financial and service institutions, and the 10,000 plus foreign-invested and 100 overseas enterprises should enable sustained growth as a regional finance and transportation hub, regional commercial and trade centre, and regional information centre benefiting from its links with Hong Kong and Guangzhou (Shangquan and Fulin, 1997). Now, however, the special tax concessions are to be phased out (Gittings, 1999, op.cit.). The city will have to increasingly move into hi-tech and high value-added activities to deepen the base for further development and production.

Sources: Author research.

Foreign Investment Administration and China Economic and Trade Consultants Corp., Ministry of Foreign Trade and Economic Co-operation (1993), *Investment in China*, Beijing.

Gittings, J. (1999b), 'China's City of Dreams and Extremes', *Guardian*, 5th May.

Ridding, J. (1996), 'China's Fledgling Export Base Takes Off: But Shenzhen Economic Zone Finds the Future Insecure', *Financial Times*, 16th August.

Gao Shangquan and Chi Fulin (eds) (1997), *New Progress in China's Special Economic Zones*, Beijing: Foreign Languages Press.

Social, economic and political issues

A wide range of interrelated social, economic and political issues are associated with the urbanisation process in China. These are dealt with, as in Ian Cook's earlier work, under the following sub-headings, updated and expanded considerably:

a. Pressures towards social polarisation and disintegration;
b. Problems of mass migration, homelessness and labour absorption;
c. Gender issues;
d. Role of urbanisation in modernisation and cultural imperialism.

Summarising each in turn:

a. Pressures towards social polarisation and disintegration

Urbanisation is often associated with widespread social upheaval and divisiveness, with social cleavages based on class, ethnicity, consumption patterns and/or territory. Cities render disparities of wealth, status, housing provision and the like highly visible, and can threaten social cohesion via the manifestation of unequal access to goods, services, wealth, employment opportunities and other features of contemporary urban life. There are growing pressures towards social polarisation in China, reflecting such disparities of wealth and access to material prosperity. These are also combined with the erosion of traditional cultural norms of social cohesiveness (whether emanating from Confucianism, various religions and cultural practices); the development of 'alien' practices such as the allocation mechanisms in property, housing and labour markets which rely on non-traditional procedures; the strong emphasis on individualism and 'privatised' consumption patterns which are socially divisive; and high population densities in urban areas, especially the new estates, which give rise to stress despite the much vaunted examples of the Chinese or family system for example to cope with such pressures.

The authors' experience suggests that intra-urban disparities are on the increase, with beggars found in different urban areas around the country, and poor quality residential accommodation behind sophisticated hotels and office blocks. For example, detached houses in a western design are being sold in exclusive estates in different cities around the country at prices of one, two or even three million Yuan. Although foreign business people are often the main target of many of these estates, local Chinese too are also purchasing them, in a country where the official average wage, even in urban areas, is 7–8000 Yuan. Then there is the related problem of crime, which reports in the West suggest is markedly greater than before. Reflecting this, Amnesty International regularly complains about the overuse of the death penalty in China, with reports of 1000 state executions in 1995–6 for example. Also of related concern is the increase in drug addiction, especially in or via provinces such as Yunnan or Guangxi, while the Chinese Communist Party has also recently campaigned strongly against corruption.

Consumption patterns are markedly different from what they were even a relatively short time ago. Even in the mid-1980s – several years after Deng Xiaoping had launched his great reform program pointing China towards a market economy – personal consumption was still being censured as 'rotten capitalist economic thought', and considered as 'the need of life, but a minor detail in production' which could not create value. In 1999, however, it suddenly became a goal and end-result of social reproduction, and an engine to drive economic growth, with the central government coining the startling slogan, familiar enough in the West: 'Live Now, Pay Later' (*Business Weekly*, 16-5-1999).

In a situation analysis report, a government think tank presented a convincing argument that the times when economic policies were most closely combined with residents' final consumption was the time when the economy grew most rapidly in the past two decades. It calculated that personal consumption in China in the late 1990s accounted for about 81 per cent of final consumption, and over the previous two decades had contributed some 60 per cent of economic growth (Macro-Economic Research Institute under the State Planning Commission, 1998). The government and commercial banks now want the public to embark on a brave new lifestyle based on credit consumption. The designated areas include housing, cars and information-related technologies. Credit cards, department store discount cards and instalment plans have proliferated, but the results so far have been mixed.

China has initiated housing and car mortgage schemes, but the loan scale and coverage are limited. A traditional preference for saving, based on centuries of desperate financial insecurity for the vast majority of the population, has also prevented expansion of credit services until now. Residents of major cities like Beijing, Shanghai and Guangzhou, however, appear ready to shuck off old habits of caution. In Beijing, one survey found the found 70 per cent of respondents to its survey in January were ready to withdraw the 'bulk' of their savings from banks and spend it on buying property, cars and durable goods such as air conditioners and refrigerators, as well as travel. According to the survey, nearly 62 per cent of the respondents planned to invest their bank deposits in their children's education, as well as buying bonds and securities. Some even intended to start up their own company with the money they saved. The corresponding figure in 1998 was nearly 40 per cent (China Mainland Market Research Company, 1999).

'All these figures put together mean one thing', said Zhou Jiang, general manager of the research company involved. 'Beijingers today have a stronger sense of consumption and investment. Instead of the old mentality of depositing money for interest, they have veered gradually to a more active way of investment and spending.' Gu Ali, the company's deputy general manager added: 'Banks have become a temporary place for money before consumption and investment activities, especially after the government repeatedly slashed interest rates.' (Interviews, 28-5-1999)

However, despite such trends, few people outside the business community yet have a credit card, and many of these are really only deposit cards whereby users deposit an agreed amount with the card company and can then spend up to that limit. Another limitation before was the paucity of shopping and food outlets willing to accept a card, but this is now changing. The mainstream of the credit business currently focuses on housing and cars, albeit on a limited scale. Shanghai is in the forefront of housing loans. Individual housing loans granted by the city's commercial banks rose nearly 3.2 billion Yuan in the first quarter of this year, bringing the total so far to 19.3 billion Yuan, according to the Shanghai branch of the People's Bank of China. For car loans, meanwhile, Beijing was the main activity centre. China Construction Bank, the country's first commercial bank to provide this service in October 1998, reported granting loans worth 370 million Yuan in the first six months.

Although the overall living standard of Chinese people has improved significantly in the past two decades, there remain many families unable to afford most home electrical appliances. The market situation also makes credit consumption in this sector all the more necessary, given that most consumption-oriented industrial products face a supply glut. By the end of April 1999, 17 department stores had introduced individual credit consumption plans for products ranging from computers and sporting goods to musical instruments. For example, the Parkson Shopping Mall, in cooperation with Beijing Merchants Bank, offers credit schemes with all commodities worth more than 3,000 Yuan and built to last more than two years. However, Zhang Chengqiang, an official with the North Star Shopping Center in Beijing, said the credit business remained sluggish for anything other than the purchase of computers. 'Bureaucratic procedures that forces applicants to undergo strict, time-consuming personal credit evaluations, as well as unappealing interest rates, have hampered expansion', he complained (Interview, 17-5-1999).

A government research organisation picked out three characteristics of residents' consumption psychology that could affect the consumer revolution. Firstly, their future income is expected to decline due to a slowdown in personal income growth and intense unemployment pressure; secondly, the simultaneous reform of the medical and old-age insurance, housing and education systems will create some growth in consumption but in limited sectors; and thirdly, a sense of uncertainty about the future will have a negative impact on consumption (State Information Center 1999).

Public opinion has not entirely kept pace with rapid economic growth. The rule of 'eating May's grain in April' still has to battle with the Chinese tradition of 'keeping expenditures within the limit of income' and that 'relaxation comes from being without debt'. Up to mid-1999, only 5 per cent of China's urban citizens have taken out bank loans. One report said 38 per cent of surveyed residents preferred to buy houses with their own savings instead of borrowing money from banks; 30 per cent chose to borrow money from relatives; 17 per cent gave up on loans they had been offered due to the complicated procedures, while 4 per cent were deterred due to not wanting others to know details of their individual income (China Social Investment Affair Office). As an illustration of attitudes, an anecdote tells of two old ladies, one Chinese and one American, who meet on their arrival in heaven. The Chinese lady says: 'I have taken great pains to save money for the whole of my life and finally bought a house and lived in it for a day, yesterday.' The American lady responds: 'I have taken great pains throughout my life and at last I returned all the loans on my house'!

In 1998, the self-reported average family income was 10,400 Yuan a year, a 74.5 per cent increase over the 5,960 Yuan reported in the first survey in 1994. Significantly, the average Chinese family reported they needed 9,010 Yuan per year to meet their basic needs, leaving almost 1,400 Yuan to spend or save as they pleased. Urban families said they made an average of 14,000 Yuan per year and had disposable income of about 2,500 Yuan

Families in the southern economic hothouse of Guangzhou, however, reported incomes twice as high as the urban average, but said their incomes still fell short of their needs by 30 per cent. Household spending on food, including eating out, took the biggest chunk out of a Chinese family's income. The average family spent 368 Yuan per month on food, up 92 per cent from 1994. Savings took the next biggest chunk at 185 Yuan per month, up 87 per cent. Monthly expenditures for medical expenses averaged 44 Yuan per month, more than double the 1994 amount, while insurance took only an average of 11 Yuan per month.

Despite their modest incomes by world standards, Chinese families report they have quite a bit of money put aside for a rainy day – on average 8,600 Yuan. Urban Chinese say they have 13,400 Yuan saved. Residents of the capital city, Beijing, appear to have the most cash under their mattresses – about 23,700 Yuan per family, according to their own accounting.

The differences in financial security between the developing regions of the country and the more affluent eastern part of China are apparent from the self-reported savings data. Families in developed provinces report savings of 14,500, Yuan, more than three-and-a-half times the 4,000 Yuan reported by families in developing provinces (Gallup Organisation, 1998).

Contrasting with the early 1980s, many Chinese households now own major consumer durables, and rising income will encourage further purchases in the near future. The 1998 Gallup survey found that nine-tenths of Chinese households already possessed televisions, and even rural TV ownership was getting close to the national average. Ownership of colour televisions, for the first time, surpassed that of black and white televisions. Most families now own a radio, tape recorder, stove or cooking range, bicycles, electric fans, a steam iron and washing machine. One in every four Chinese households owns a refrigerator and telephone, but only a small proportion of Chinese households owns high-end goods such as pagers (15 per cent), motorcycles (14 per cent), video cassette recorders (12 per cent), air-conditioners (6 per cent) and mobile phones (4 per cent).

The survey found colour television sets and refrigerators topped the list of leading items for future purchase (including replacement of products currently owned). A new colour television set was planned by 34 per cent of Chinese households, and 28 per cent intend to buy a refrigerator. Among the largest discrepancies between short-term and long-term purchase intentions were between those for cars, computers and mobile phones. Only one per cent hoped to purchase a car within the next two years, but 11 per cent held this out as a longer-term objective. Four per cent planned to purchase a computer in the near future, but 16 per cent hoped to in the long-term. Although only three per cent said they intended to purchase a mobile phone within the next two years, five times as many cited this as a product they would eventually own.

b. Problems of mass migration, homelessness and labour absorption

The population numbers involved, partly the result of migration to the new 'Meccas' of China's large, medium and small cities, impose tremendous pressures on the urban infrastructure, especially on mass housing provision. Housing will be considered in the next chapter, but we suggest that much of the new mass housing poses long-term problems of upkeep and maintenance, lack of facilities for social integration, lack of defensible space and inflexibility of unit size for changing family circumstances, replicating some of the worst features of mass housing provision provided for Western cities in the 1960s and 1970s. Quality will be a key word in long-term housing provision, but in the short-term at least, quantity becomes the watchword.

Then there is the problem of those without housing accommodation at all. Estimates have appeared regularly in the 1990s of the floating population (*liudong renkou*) or 'rootless' people in specific cities, or nationally. The publicised figures have increased markedly throughout the decade. In 1992, for instance, 1.2 million of these were reported in the *China Daily* to live in Beijing and up to sixty million nationally. This data is largely from the late 1980s, however, and Chan cites 1.3 million for Beijing alone, from a 1988 data source, and a possible total of seventy million for

1989 (Chan, 1994, op.cit., pp.45–6). It is known that an austerity programme in the late 1980s, coupled with the related upheaval of Tiananmen caused a reduction of numbers in 1989–91 and a resurgence from 1992 onwards (ibid.). By year end 1993 national estimates were of 100 million floating population, or up to 120 million, and it is probable that this number is, in the late 1990s, 130 million. Within Beijing alone a census of the floating population produced a figure of 2.9 million in November 1994. Given that Shanghai is reckoned to have a similar number, it is reasonable to assume that the large cities at least attract 3–4 million floating population each.

The recent migrants at least are most visible in and around the railway stations and tourist areas, but periodic crackdowns ensure that they are forced away from these locations. As the 'restructuring' process operates in the rural areas (Kirkby, 1994), and as urban-rural disparities continue to increase (see chapters 4 and 5) then the flood of migrants is likely to increase even further unless measures are taken to restrict movement and/or to offer greater opportunities in their home location. Further, there is already evidence of considerable prejudice and discrimination against these migrants by the indigenous population, and their situation, as with many other migrants around the world is often rather parlous. For example, of arrests in the late 1980s, in five major cities, 33–77 per cent were of floating population, as opposed to only a few per cent in the late 1970s (Chan, op. cit., p.132). The famous Silk Market off Juanguomenwai Dajie in Beijing was threatened with closure in early 1998, in part due to the fact that most stallholders or workers were now floating population, the original Beijing owners having made their money and sold out or leased the stalls. At the time of writing, it seems it will, in the near future, be closed. 'These out-of-towners are no better than animals' is an extreme, but nonetheless indicative view of these outsiders, cited by Solinger who reviews a range of the problems which the floating population faces in their move to the city (1995).

The floating population is not just from rural areas; some move up the urban hierarchy to the larger cities. Nonetheless, the labour absorption problem in China, where upwards of 100 million became surplus to agricultural requirements in the changes of the 1980's, is enormous. Most have been employed in China's townships as well as its cities:

'During 1979–89 the newly employed in China's cities and towns ran into 85.071 million, 30% of which in units of collective ownership and 8% working on their own ... In 1990 another four million people got jobs in the cities and towns ... The development of township industries in the rural areas has opened up new outlets for the rural surplus labour ... The output value of the country's township industries increased 12.5% in 1990, outstripping by far the 7.6%

industrial growth speed of the country and playing a positive role in absorbing the surplus rural work force. However, the managerial level of some enterprises in certain cities and towns is still very low, and there is a waste of labor power due to overstaff. Besides, with the rising of productivity in agriculture, there will be more and more surplus labor in the countryside. These problems are yet to be solved' (Shi Min, 1991, p.80).

When this is added to the impact of reform of the SOEs discussed in chapter 2, it is extremely difficult to see how the current absorption of labour into basic lo-tech production and services can continue indefinitely, given that the main drive of capitalistic development is labour shedding, allied to moves to hi-tech activities. As Ian Cook has noted (2000), there is some medium term relief likely as service industries develop further, but in the longer term heavy investment will be required in education and training, as is the case in other countries in both East and West.

c. Gender issues

In developing their revolutionary ideology, the CPC paid considerable attention to the appalling situation of women in Chinese society. This attention was less than that paid to the class struggle, however, and the situation of women was viewed as a product of feudalism; once the latter was overthrown then the problem would largely disappear. Blecher suggests that despite campaigns via the Women's Association against foot-binding and wife-beating, the CPC did not promote the scale and depth of consciousness-raising and mass mobilisation that it employed in other campaigns, this being an indication not only of a lower priority for women's issue but also of the concern not to alienate male supporters and hence split the broad base of party support (Blecher, 1986, p.152). Nevertheless, the first major piece of legislation after the establishment of the PRC was the promulgation of the Marriage Law in 1950. This introduced a whole swathe of measures to improve women's rights, including, for example, rights to own and manage family property, free choice of occupation, divorce by mutual consent or on court decree if grounds were warranted, and such practices as bigamy, child betrothal, exaction of money or gifts via marriage, and infanticide were outlawed (ibid.).

This Law (updated in the 1980 Marriage Law) improved women's lives considerably, and the PRC's legislation was hailed as an exemplar for many other countries. In the 1950s, female education expanded, many employment opportunities were provided, and so, for example, by the early 1980s, some areas such as medicine and engineering, previously male dominated, had been fully opened up. There were limits to these changes, however: the expansion of female education did not end the imbalance between males and females as Rai, for example, shows (1995). Likewise, controversies such as *The Dying Rooms*, or *Return to the Dying Rooms*, shown on Western television in the 1990s, and focusing on the plight of orphans, especially female orphans, or the related concern by Jonathan Mirsky and Human Rights organisations to publicise female infanticide in China have brought issues of gender inequalities forcibly to the fore of western consciousness.

In China itself, Croll suggests that her interviews indicate that, shocked by the reappearance of female infanticide, there is now more openness concerning the contrast between the *rhetoric* of equality and the women's actual *experience* since the Revolution (Croll, 1995). The contradiction between these has become more obvious as the Four Modernizations have proceeded, with the 'economic question' becoming the touchstone by which progress should be judged, rather than social transformation (Rai, 1995, op.cit.). Chinese women are now faced by such concerns as the pressures of Western-style advertising with its inbuilt gender bias, exploitation in sweat shop conditions (a recent Trade Union survey found that 'women are harassed, hired and fired at will, have no legal contracts, do not receive equal pay and that companies pay no attention to labour protection regulations' (Croll, 1995, op.cit., pp.13–14)), decollectivisation of agriculture which encourages exploitation as cheap labour and increases domestic chores, the feminisation of agriculture in which the males are more likely to form the floating population discussed above, a state which does not prioritise their concerns, while to complexify the picture are the potential liberating effects of the new employment opportunities.

Table 7.1, adapted from an article by Riley (1996) summarises the situation in the mid-1990s, relative to several other countries, as touchstones, and helps to put the various arguments in perspective. Relative to India, for example, China has made considerable progress on such issues as representation, maternal mortality rate, longevity and literacy. Relative to Thailand, the picture is more variable, China performing well on representation but not on education or literacy, while China has not done as well as South Korea on many variables, except once again representation. As regards the United States the comparison is once again mixed, and it is as regards Sweden that most progress has to be made. Thus, as the Table shows, Sweden has 34 per cent females in parliament, and 35 per cent in ministry-level positions (still not 50, or 51 per cent of course, but one would be hard put to find a better percentage elsewhere), compared to China's 21 per cent and 6 per cent respectively.

Riley herself feels that China still has considerable effort to expend before the issues of 'missing girls' and 'lost opportunities' for women can be redressed, and this was largely confirmed in the controversies surrounding the United Nations Fourth World Conference on Women,

Table 7.1 Women's Situation in Comparative Perspective

Indicator	China	South Korea	India	Thailand	Sweden	U.S.
% females in labour force (age 15+)	90*	47	23	76	61	56
% female literate (age 15+)	68	95	34	91	n.a.	99
% male literate (age 15+)	87	99	62	86	n.a.	99
Females as % of males in post-secondary schools	52	60	51	111	n.a.	124
% females in 'parliament'	21	1	7	4	34	10
% females in ministry positions	6	4	6	0	35	15
% married women contracepting	70	79	41	66	78	71
Maternal mortality rate**	95	26	460	50	5	8
Female life expectancy	72	75	60	72	80	79
Male life expectancy	69	67	60	67	75	72
Sex ratio at birth	113.8	113.1	n.a.	105.5	105.3	105.0

Source: Riley, N.E. (1996), 'China's 'Missing Girls': Prospects and Policy', *Population Today*, February, p.5. Data taken from 1995 sources [but Riley does not clarify whether the data is all 1995], except for * which is from a 1992 source. **Maternal mortality rate is maternal deaths per 100,000 births.

held in Beijing in September 1995. The Chinese authorities dealt in a heavy-handed manner with the NGO delegates, whom they regarded as being activists and potential 'undesirables', hence they were located in Huairou, 30 miles from the main conference in Beijing. Not only were these delegates upset about the location, there were numerous complaints concerning policing of the NGO Forum; alternatively on the Chinese side there were concerns about what they regarded as unwarranted attacks upon China's human rights records. At one stage, Hillary Clinton's involvement in the main conference was under threat (a potential blow to China's prestige), but eventually the ruffled feathers were smoothed sufficiently to persuade her to, after all, attend. Since then, as pointed out elsewhere (Cook, 2000, op.cit.), the vice-director of the All China Women's Federation, Liu Yingjiang, has claimed that the Conference was a great success and 'had propelled developments in women's causes all over the country' (Liu Yingjiang, 1996). Time will tell whether such a claim is substantiated via improvements in the conditions of women summarised here. Unless the patriarchal nature of the traditional family system is confronted, however, as Rai has noted, it is highly unlikely that substantive transformation will occur (Rai, 1995, op.cit., pp.192–3).

In part, the situation of women is affected by, and also affects changing family structures, and attitudes. Drastic changes have taken place in the Chinese family. The traditional family home where four generations usually lived under one roof has virtually disappeared in urban areas, where modern housing, mainly small apartments – until recently supplied with a job (see Chapter 8) – makes such a lifestyle almost impossible. The nuclear family of husband and wife and the state-stipulated one child is now the norm. As part of the post-liberation economic rehabilitation and development, there was a nation-wide upsurge of women stepping out of the homes to take part in social production. By 1957, various government studies found around 70 per cent of rural women were engaged in agricultural work, and the number of urban women workers reached 3.28 million, a 5.5-fold increase over 1949. By 1992, some 44 per cent of the work force were women. In urban areas, an estimated fifty-six million were in employment. But as noted previously, this must now be set against the increasing difficulty women are now experiencing in finding work, and the continued problem of unequal pay with men.

In new China, the share of women's earnings in total family income by the mid-1990s had risen to 40 per cent, and in some rural areas was as high as 70 per cent. As they have become more economically independent, Chinese women have gained more management and decision-making powers in principal family and economic matters. This has given rise to changes in attitude towards marriage and sex. In big cities like Beijing, at least, one of the most profound changes is the surge in divorce, almost a quarter of all marriages ending in this way, double the rate seen at the start of the 1990s. The national divorce rate has now crept over 10 per cent, still far behind many Western countries, but still a remarkable increase in a short time.

For women in Beijing at least, the growing divorce rate is a reflection of a new social and economic freedom and of damaging effects from what many Beijing residents say is the remarkable increase in adulterous affairs. More than 70 per cent of divorces are now initiated by women, and the most common reason given is that the husband has had an affair. 'Only a few years ago, people would let a temple be destroyed before they would let a marriage fail,' says Pi Xiaoming, a leading divorce lawyer whose work at the East Beijing Women's Federation used to involve applying intense pressure on couples not to divorce. 'We did everything possible to keep people from separating,' she recalls. 'If there was a one per cent chance of saving the marriage, we'd expend all our effort to overcome the 99 per cent of difficulty. Now divorce is an acceptable alternative to an unhappy marriage, and a legal separation that once took years to win approval can now be processed in three days if both sides agree.'

Many female grievances relate to sex. 'Before, marriage was stable, but the quality was very low,' according to Wang Xiangjuan, who listens to hundreds of complaints each month on the women's hot line in Beijing. 'It was something you did, and didn't think about. Now people have high expectations from marriage.' Most women traditionally had sex only for the purpose of bearing children. But China's one-child policy has made urban women at least freer to pursue careers and seek greater sexual satisfaction outside the marriage if necessary, she said (Interviews, 15-12-1998). However, as with other topics dealt with in this book, there are contradictions here also, for more and more Chinese families are seeking a Western-style white wedding, with adverts (in English) which include: 'May the love we've discovered as husband and wife, grow richer and deeper each day of our life' (Vivi catalogue cited in Gittings, 1999a)!

d. Role of urbanisation in modernisation and cultural imperialism

The role of urbanisation in processes of modernisation and cultural imperialism is also of importance in determining the type of development which will become dominant in China. Processes of global transformation operate through and from cities, escalating and concentrating the pace of change via the complex hi-tech interactions and linkages which annihilate old spaces and structures and continually create the new structures, images, icons and products of modernity and postmodernity. And so, at the mundane level:

> 'Wheat replaces rice and corn as a major staple of Third World Cities and radio, television, cinema and pop music supplant the traditional entertainments of oral history, theatre and folk music' (Armstrong and McGee, 1985, p.5).

While at a more dramatic level:

> 'Cities are, stated simply, the crucial elements in accumulation at all levels, regional, national and international, providing both the institutional framework and the *locus operandi* for transnationals, local oligopoly capital and the modernizing national state ... cities also play the role of diffusers of the lifestyles, customs, tastes, fashions and consumer habits of modern industrial society ... we see Third World urban systems not only as theatres of accumulation, but also as centres from which are diffused the culture and values of westernization' (ibid., p.41).

This is evident in a number of ways. For example, there are the highly visible multi-storey international hotels and business centres in cities such as Guangzhou and Shanghai, often situated off increasingly sophisticated ring roads and expressways which count BMWs, Nissans, Mercedes plus joint venture Audis and Jeeps among their traffic; Kentucky Fried Chicken, Pizza Hut and McDonalds take aways; huge satellite dishes which pick up CNN, Star TV and other channels (although some government restrictions on satellite television were introduced in 1993); department stores which offer a growing range of goods as well as, in the example of Yaoshan (Japanese retailers) and Hong Kong retailers, foreign ownership, while the Friendship Stores seem to offer more choice than ever before. Then there are the karaoke bars, laser discos, and bright lights (especially the further south one travels) of the international city.

In any rapidly changing society it is often the children who are most affected, and certainly this is the case in China. With grandparents no longer living under the same roof, and, often, no longer even residing in the same city due to increased job-related family mobility, care of the family offspring in the early stages of life has now become society's responsibility, either through state, enterprise or privately-run day-care centres and kindergartens. This has created a long-running national debate over who is responsible for character development in the crucial formative years. When something goes wrong, as is increasingly the case through rising levels of juvenile delinquency, parents and teachers exchange mutual recrimination over this issue.

Under the rigidly-enforced 'one child' birth control policy, first introduced in 1979 to curb the mainland's runaway population growth, modern parents, aware the first child will be the only one, are alleged to have become over-protective, as well as pandering to their offspring's every whim. A whole generation is said to be growing up in China living in a cocoon, cut off from the harsher realities of life and increasingly unable to cope with unexpected difficulties. They are also said to be more self-centred and selfish – hence the pejorative nickname 'little emperors'. Health experts, meanwhile, fret over the weight problems of the young – obese children are a common sight in primary school playgrounds – brought on by a richer diet, especially the fast food revolution that has put a McDonald's and a Kentucky Fried Chicken outlet within easy reach of every city resident.

Today's youngsters are enjoying the most privileged upbringing of any generation in China's history. Their ability to command attention and wheedle gifts from doting parents and grandparents brings smiles to the faces of businessmen catering to this growing sector of the market. According to one newspaper survey of first year college students, a quarter were receiving almost 1,100 Yuan, double the average urban wage, as spending money each month (*People's Daily*, 11-8-1998). Another survey claimed that 90 per cent of secondary school students had never cooked a meal, and half had never made a bed (*Guangming Daily*, 13-5-1996).

Lu Qin, who runs an advice column for the newspaper *China Children's Daily*, explained that many parents whose children are now primary or junior middle school students were deprived of schooling themselves during the Cultural Revolution (see Chapter 1), when the education system was virtually closed down and the bands of red guards roamed the country on rampages of destruction, or were sent to live in remote rural areas to 'learn from the peasants'. Hence, they hope their offspring will have a brighter future and make up for their own loss. 'Some parents satisfy every material desire of their children, and only demand one thing in return: good marks and acceptance by a key school that can virtually guarantee a good job at the end of the road' (Interview, 15-11-1998).

With nine-year compulsory education virtually ensured for most children, or at least those in developed areas, the emphasis in the mainland education system is now on improving quality to cope with youth-related social problems. There is a determined move away from rote-learning, a hangover from the Maoist days, to make subjects more interesting. In Beijing, for example, an experiment is underway where at least a third of classroom time must be allocated for student participation, either in debate or research. In some of the major cities, exams determining secondary school places are being cancelled. The primary curriculum has been slashed and simplified and homework reduced, all with the purpose of making schooling more relevant and to harness the creativity of the next generation. Shanghai is experimenting with combining primary and lower secondary schools to allow more time for individual development, especially in enabling slow learners to catch up.

Academic life is balanced by education in practical life skills. In primary schools children learn the basic skills such is how to sew buttons, cook their lunches, gardening and room cleaning. Extra-curricula activities are expanding and becoming more interesting. Communication skills are built up through drama clubs, recitals, speeches and debates. Every year class teachers visit the home of each of their pupils in order to work closely with the parents so that the home becomes an extension of the classroom.

Such processes of transformation still have some way to go but the pace of change is dramatic. For example, Ian Cook's first visit to Guangzhou in 1980 involved a stay at the Bai Yun hotel which then overlooked green fields, albeit within the urban setting; now it overlooks a busy dual carriageway and high class international hotels. Likewise, Beijing has changed dramatically in the last few years, with many new department stores in Jianguomenwai, Xidan and the Lufthansa Centre for example, a proliferation of private sector residential developments around the city, the newly opened Beijing West Railway Station and an increasing pace of movement in the city. Nor does this pace seem set to change: the targets for 1996 alone included a 20 per cent increase in retail sales, a 10.6 per cent increase in fixed-assets investment, and foreign investment of US$1.2 billion (*Business Beijing*, 1996; Cao Min, 1996). By the beginning of 1999, it was estimated that Beijing alone contained 5000 building sites, and coupled with the preparations for the 50th anniversary of the PRC, in the summer of 1999 the entire city seemed like one giant construction site!

Many of these changes appear to the outside observer to be westernisation, but it is not just 'Westernisation': it is also '*Japanisation*' due to the regional influence of Japan, '*Tokyoisation*' given the local influence of Tokyo itself (Hanes, 1993) and so on down the urban hierarchy, with Hong Kong being such a key player in the urban structure of South China, and increasingly further afield. Hong Kong as a model is discussed in Box 7.3. As Cook has suggested elsewhere, such dominance is not just economic, it is also social and cultural in that new products, ideas, exemplars cascade down the urban hierarchy and hence into the countryside. Rural-urban migration, for example, is due to more than the attraction of the bright lights of the city or the push of rural poverty and tradition, but also to the cultural dominance of the urban in which material goods, materialist lifestyles, and the positive features of city life overwhelm the presumed dreariness and drudgery of the rural alternative.

Box 7.3 Hong Kong as the Urban Model

Hong Kong (HK) provides a seductive model for urban development in China. At first this was seen in South China, where it has been a major source of investment and expertise since the late 1980s. HK investment is 60 per cent of total foreign direct investment to date, around US$132 billion to early 1998, in real estate, finance, trade, manufacturing and other activities (*Beijing Review*, March 9-15, 1998). It is spreading to the Yangtze, some inland provinces and SW China, as well as Beijing. HK is now the leading source of investment in Pudong, for example, while its New World Capital Construction invested HK$23 billion in inland areas in 1997, and HK$ 2 billion in old downtown areas in Tianjin in 1998 (ibid.).

In planning terms, HK is a well planned and managed urban entity, with high density, high-rise development, especially in the new towns of the New Territories. Its housebuilding programme has been particularly impressive, and has been at an amazing scale. Attempts have been made to provide green spaces and urban parks, for example, by roofing over expressways between blocks of flats, and the quality of construction has improved markedly in recent decades. Investment in the Mass Transit Railway (MTR) has paid off handsomely in terms of journeys made, and reduction of potential pollution, while the Mid-Levels escalator on Hong

---

Kong island is an interesting innovation, along with mirror technology to maximise the impression of space in crowded areas, and these sit well alongside the old ideas such as the trams on Hong Kong island or Star ferries across to Kowloon.

However, not all things about Hong Kong are exemplary. As Johnston amusingly but pertinently puts it, 'If Shanghai's ubiquitous Karaoke bars are, as often maintained, Japanese retaliation for their defeat in the war, then smoked glass and tacky tiling may be Hong Kong entrepreneurs way of cocking a snoot at their countrymen to the north' (Johnston, 1994, p.4)! More seriously, Hong Kong has to cope with an increasing number of environmental problems. Traffic congestion, notwithstanding the MTR, is on the increase, and Hong Kong Environmental Protection Department estimates that 1 million people suffer from traffic noise and 3 million from polluted air. In 15 years from 1980 to 1995 population grew 30 per cent but waste grew 300 per cent and now there is the equivalent of 480 double-decker bus fulls of garbage, plus 25 bus fulls of plastic bags. Waste water problems are also found, with half untreated, threatening rare species in the surrounding waters. The environmental impact of the new Chek Lap Kok airport will also be high, although people in Kowloon will now be able to sleep more soundly via the closure of Kai Tak.

Lin (1997) details the impact of HK on Dongguan, between Hong Kong and Guangzhou. By the end of 1993, nearly 500,000 factory workers had been employed via HK investment of US$400 million into export-processing industry, building on the 650,000 relatives of Dongguan people living there, plus 180,000 overseas. The previously agricultural area has been transformed, with huge investment also in infrastructure including expressways, phone systems and housing. Many female migrant workers have been attracted to the area, and Lin describes the harassment and assault which these women face. HK money, allied to global forces has 'effectively drawn the young and cheap labour from the interior of China into the theatre of mass production and global capitalism' (ibid., p.259). Social changes have been great – locals now watch HK TV, play video games, sing HK karaoke and watch smuggled videos, drink Pepsi or Coca Cola, use Colgate toothpaste, wear Nike trainers and have translated many HK words, including transla-tions of English, into local dialect, such as 'sari' (salad), 'pisabing' (pizza). A hybrid culture is emerging, light years away from that of the past.

Sources: Author research.

Johnston, T. (1994) 'Disappearing Shanghai', *Britain-China*, No.54, pp.4–5.

Lin, G.C.S. (1997), 'Intrusion of Global Forces and Transformation of a Local Chinese Economy: The Experience of Dongguan', Chapter 16 in Watters, R.F. and McGee, T.G. (eds), *New Geographies of the Pacific Rim*, London: Hurst & Co.

The costs of change: the changing sense of place

In the face of this relentless onslaught of change there is a small but significant return to the past, a 'back to the future' tendency, in order perhaps to fulfil psychological needs to localise identity in the face of the 'global forces' to which Lin refers (1997). As Cook has previously noted, China has a rich and varied tradition of urbanisation on which to fall back for succour and ideas for alternative futures (Wheatley, 1971), and had a considerable influence on the urban form of South East Asia in particular. The traveller Marco Polo was so struck by the scale and splendour of Chinese cities that on his return to Europe he allegedly acquired the derisory nickname of 'Il Milione' after his account of his travels, with his compatriots believing him to be guilty of gross hyberbole! However, the drive for modernisation can ignore the past, seeking to provide new ideas and new concepts rather than perpetuate the old, which can be stereotyped as reactionary and backward. We feel, for example, that there is a great need to preserve the hutongs of Beijing (see Box 7.4), and many Chinese would agree with us. Others, however, would see this as the unnecessary perpetuation of past forms and lifestyles inappropriate to the new China.

Box 7.4 Preserving the Hutongs of Beijing

'If the city of Beijing is comparable to a museum, then the streets and Hutongs are exhibition rooms. Through the show-windows, you can see the changes of the streets and Hutongs, and furthermore, you can find the traces of changings in the past thousands of years' (Hu et.al. (eds), 1995, p.165). Strictly speaking, 'hutong' is Beijingese for 'lane', while 'siheyuan' refers to the quadrangle residence found along these, but over time the use has broadened to encompass the whole area of ancient low-rise housing within the narrow lanes of old Beijing. Hutongs were first formed 700 years ago in Dadu, the city's name during the Yuan dynasty, when they were 'Hong Tong' in local dialect, meaning 'water well', essential for building. There were 29 of these lanes at this time, each on a grid-iron pattern, N–S or E–W, with a width less than 9.24 metres (there were also Xiao Jie up to 18 metres, then Dajie up to 36 metres). The Ming rebuilt the city after their conquest and the number of hutongs soared to 459, in a similar pattern, plus 711 Xiao Jie which became undifferentiated from hutongs. The lanes had one-storey houses only, being deliberately dwarfed by the Imperial City and other public buildings such as the Drum Tower. By the 1940s the total number of passages reached 3,200 and nearly double that after the revolution, when the city walls were removed (many reportedly wept over this destruction) and the city expanded (all details from Zhang et.al. (eds), 1993). To the outsider, these narrow lanes can seem dark and forbidding, but once initial reserve is overcome, they form a treasure trove from the past, with their ornate features, their variable scenes of everyday life, and their names which can be after people, functions, shapes, geographical features or concepts such as 'happy', or 'fortune'. They are reminiscent of the narrow cobbled or terraced streets of Britain's past, but with an even greater depth of history, and vitality. They are evocative, and retain a strong presence and identity.

Hutongs are, however, under perennial threat. The planner, developer, or official may seek to decant population into 'better' homes, or to redevelop in a manner more 'appropriate' to central Beijing. The hutongs often lack modern amenities, and access is difficult. Their population densities are high, and living conditions may be less than ideal, at least in physical terms. Car ownership is awkward within these areas. Not, that the hutongs are full of poor people – many of the families living in them are relatively prosperous and have lived there for generations. 'Community' is strong in such areas, but community may not fit the plans for the Beijing of tomorrow, never mind today. The parallels with Britain of the 1960s and 1970s are obvious. Also, some may see the walled compounds as being too introverted, producing self-centred family or other groupings, incapable of meeting the needs of an Open Door policy and of modern society (see Murray, 1999, for examples of such negative views).

Today, it is estimated that four million Beijingers still live in hutongs, and many are under pressure to move out to new homes on the outskirts. Height and building restrictions are in place for old Beijing, and 20 hutongs are appointed historic and cultural protection areas. Nonetheless, the pressure is always there to transform these areas into more modern multi-storey blocks with conventional streets. Preservation is found, with a number of classic examples such as in Liu Li Chang (originally 'the place where glazed tiles are fired') which is a place for antiques and rare books, or in Ju'er Hutong near the Drum Tower. Sometimes, the preservation is highly imaginative, with for example modern buildings of several storeys being built within the ancient walls (Gaubatz 1995; Yang 1995), and may involve the community as in the case of the new Hutong Tours, by pedicab, which caters for tourists and yet provides direct employment for locals and a reason for preservation of these narrow lanes and buildings.

Sources: Author research.

Gaubatz, P.R. (1995) 'Urban Transformation in Post-Mao China' (see refs.).

Hu P. et.al. (eds) (1995), *Historical Photos of Old Beijing*, Beijing: Beijing Publishing House.

Murray, G. (1999), 'Modernising Beijing', *Property Review* (Singapore), January, pp.58–60.

Yang, D. (1995), 'Residences in Beijing: From Siheyuan to Modern Highrise', *China Today*, 14, 7, July, 29–31.

Zhang Z. et.al. (eds) (1993), *Hutongs of Beijing*, Beijing: Beijing Arts and Photography Publishing House.

Within the massive changes to the urban scene, we would argue strongly for preservation and conservation of old structures and concepts, but adapted to the needs of the present and the future. The past can be a source of ideas, even 'enlightenment', as Shen Yahong illustrates in his review of ancient city planning in China (Shen Yahong, 1992). The strengths of ancient practice were its unified nature, its 'macro-concept' of the role of the city as the regional centre of the countryside, and its ecological consciousness. Shen argues that the overemphasis on experience and techniques in recent years led to a neglect of theory and hence, eventually, to stagnation. He develops 'seven historical insights' which include the need to develop 'a theoretical system of modern urban planning with an advanced world level and with Chinese characteristics' (ibid., p.73); to draw on the experience of the 'excellent' ancient traditions and also include ecological theory. The urgent need for the latter is seen in Chapter 9 below. The indigenous tradition must be reinterpreted for the needs of the future. Many parts of China's cities are, to Western eyes at least, dull, dirty, unimaginative and unattractive, with little attempt to preserve and conserve some of the positive legacies of the past in the face of rapid economic development. As Cook suggests: 'The return to ancient traditions would enhance the ambience of the Chinese city via retention and redevelopment of those urban features and forms which are unique to China, enabling China's cities to be *Chinese* cities, rather than just 'cities', and fusing the best of the past and the present.' (Cook, 2000).

The urban stresses throughout China are enormous, as this chapter has shown. The next chapter will consider the housing situation within urban areas, but for now we note that Chinese cities will require considerable initiative and a will to plan more effectively, involving local people wherever possible, in order to create an urban environment which can not only meet the needs of today, but can also meet the ever-pressing needs of tomorrow.

CHAPTER 8

Case Study: Housing

An acid test of good government is the ability to provide citizens with guaranteed means of livelihood, as well as promoting personal health and welfare. One important aspect of this is the provision of decent housing. Following on the previous consideration of a wide range of urban issues, this chapter looks at the Chinese government's efforts to reform the housing sector so as to overcome chronic overcrowding and the existence of ageing, sub-standard accommodation in the major cities.

This will cover:

- The need for housing reform
- Housing reform in practice
- Problems with low-cost housing
- Weakness of the mortgage system
- Problems with malpractice
- Construction quality questioned
- One step forward, two steps back

The need for housing reform

These are illustrated via some snapshots of the housing problem in urban China (Murray, 1993):

- A young man was arrested by police as a suspected 'good-for-nothing' after sleeping several nights in the cavernous Beijing Railway Station. On investigation, he turned out to be an employee of a reputable Sino-American joint venture who found a railway station bench more comfortable than staying at home, where several generations of his family lived in one room and he had so little space it was impossible to sleep in a flat position.

- Zhou Lihong shares a tiny room in a company dormitory with two other women. Her husband, who works for the same firm, lives upstairs. The company offered them part of an old house with no gas, heat or plumbing, but the young couple rejected it, gambling that a better offer would come, even though it was far from certain. Some couples delay marriage rather than face the prospect of several years of married life apart in cramped company dormitories.

- Possession of proper housing is one of the best possible marriage dowries any young man or woman can possess. A 24-year-old female spinner in Beijing, for example, registered with a match-making service with a demand that her intended spouse would have to have his own home. 'If you have a house you have a base. I don't want to be living in a twelve square metre room with the whole family crowded together like pigs,' the woman explained. She was regarded as fairly typical by the officials of the match-making service.

- In some families, three generations still sleep in one room. The stress of this, say experts, can cause psychological and physiological problems. Zhang Guowei, a psychologist, says most of his patients blame their sexual failures on bad housing conditions. One couple who lived in a single room with an ageing father remained childless after four years of marriage, and the husband was convinced lack of privacy was the main problem. They borrowed an apartment for five months and the wife soon became pregnant.

- People live on top of each other with little privacy. Conflicts are common over minor issues – a playful child, a noisy radio. Youngsters also become precocious because they see too much of adult life. A primary school headmistress told the story of a second grade girl who came to her office one day and said her parents often fought with each other in bed at night which kept her awake. The girl was afraid and asked the headmistress to help her persuade her parents to stop fighting. 'What can I say to such a naive little girl,' the teacher asked.

Given such problems, it is hardly surprising that:

> 'A goal of most Chinese these days is to move into new and larger houses. Those inhabiting a single room yearn for a living room or an additional room for their only child. Flatlet-dwellers, some still sharing a kitchen or toilet with their neighbours, have in mind a decent apartment of their own. Single men and women living in dormitories dream of privacy, whether the space be only six square metres' (*China Daily*, 2-8-1996).

Most urban residents suffer housing problems. Beijing city officials say a quarter of the capital's residents lack adequate accommodation. The city's population has grown from two to eleven million since liberation and is

175

expected to reach 14 million by the turn of the century as it sprawls out into the countryside swallowing up former separate villages. Per capita living space has grown from six to eight square metres but that is an illusion because of the large rural areas inside Beijing which tend to inflate the figure (author interview with Beijing Municipal Government official, 15-6-1997).

The housing problems already described should not necessarily be seen as a criticism of the government, or evidence of the failure of communism. A great deal has been done in the past five decades, but, as in so many areas of life, China's sheer numbers dilute the impact. Firstly, the population has more than doubled in that period, from some half billion to nearly 1.3 billion. Secondly, as detailed in the previous chapter, there has been an equally rapid growth of the urban population, especially with migration from rural areas in the 1990s. Hence, there is some justification to the government claim that the problem is not one of lack of construction. In fact, China has been building a yearly average of 100 million sq. m. since 1978, which should have resolved the housing problems of around 22 million families.

According to a Construction Ministry study (Xinhua, 9-12-1996), at least 5.5 million urban families occupied less than 45 square metres of living space. But this number is expected to grow to eight million by the year 2000, as more young people get married and start families, especially as rapid social change, and the new freedom to move around the country with the abandonment of the residential permit system, is breaking up the traditional extended family.

As a result of these and other factors – such as the need to build new towns to create jobs in the interior and prevent a flood of unemployed rural migrants heading for the richer eastern cities – all the construction of recent years has proved to be a mere drop in the ocean. In addition, the issue is complicated by the complexity of the reforms that have been transforming China from a central planned to a market economy. Housing, belatedly, is having to catch up with other areas, with a pressing need for a whole range of radical new policies which take time to formulate and put into action. 'In 1978, there were more than eight million families living in extremely poor conditions. In the 1990s, there are still about the same number. Why? because of an unfair housing distribution policy,' admitted Zhang Zhongjun, director of the Office of Housing System Reform Under the State Council (*China Daily*, 23-5-1997).

Housing distribution became a form of welfare from the 1950s. Employers assigned housing according to post, rank, professional title, length of service, age, family numbers and whether the applicant was male or female (the latter often being rejected purely, it seemed, on gender grounds). Party membership has always ensured a place at the head of the queue. At the same time, tying accommodation to a specific work assignment discouraged workers from job-hopping, and also helped the authorities for many years to enforce a strict residential permit policy, making it hard for residents of one town to more to another without official permission. The attraction for the workers was a nominal rent – city dwellers paying, on average, less than one per cent of their monthly salaries. But, as the rents tended to be only a fraction of the costs in building and maintaining housing, the policy was a massive drain on central government finances which could not continue indefinitely if the economic reforms begun in the late 1970s were to achieve their long-term goals.

Housing reform in practice

Housing reform was initiated by the late Deng Xiaoping in the early 1980s, but actually got underway in 1988 when a few cities began raising rents and selling apartments to tenants to finance construction of more housing. The reforms were not applied nation-wide, many local officials being unwilling to pay the higher rents themselves or losing the power they got from assigning scarce apartments. This slow progress was acknowledged by a conference in late 1991 attended by provincial heads and housing officials nation-wide, which urged all local governments to immediately draw up concrete plans and implement them before the end of 1992. By 1995, rents were required to reach a level where they would at least cover building maintenance, management and depreciation costs, and by the turn of the century, investment costs, interest payments and estate tax as well. Some time in the 21st century, the goal is to have rents also cover land-use charges and insurance fees, by which time it is estimated an ordinary family will be paying a quarter of their income for housing. But the most important element of a 'new housing system compatible with a socialist market economy' is the commercialisation of housing: encouraging an increasing number of families to buy their own home. In the early part of the 1990s, real estate developers most domestic and foreign (although mostly from Hong Kong in the initial stages) rushed in to create a construction boom at the upper end of the market. Some achievements are detailed in Box 8.1.

Despite many achievements, one result of early reforms was a vast oversupply of luxury condominiums and villas which could never hope to find buyers. Many of the overoptimistic developers collapsed when they could not gain any return on their investment. Eventually, the central government stepped in to discourage further expansion, and to encourage heavy investment in mass housing – especially so-called 'Comfort Housing' projects, low cost developments with a minimum of frills, designed for the mass of Chinese with limited income (details shown in Box 8.1 for Guangzhou). Many of these projects have involved razing overcrowded and sub-standard housing in slum districts that were regarded as a blot on the inner city areas of Beijing, Shanghai, Guangzhou, Tianjin and Chongqing in particular.

In June 1996, the Shanghai municipal government announced a package of preferential policies including sharply reduced popery development fees to attract more domestic and foreign investment in the city's rundown areas. Domestic and foreign investors were encouraged to renovate the city's 3.65 million sq.m. of dangerous and shabby housing as part of an effort to completely renovate such areas by the turn of the century. The city government said foreign investors would be exempt from land-use fees, while 13 other charges would be reduced, including administrative fees for housing demolition, residents' relocation and construction licenses. The incentives were sufficient to attract a Singapore consortium and several Hong Kong construction companies to take part in the inner city redevelopment. Until recent years, the average Shanghainese was used to sharing a bathroom and kitchen with at least 10 others. But some 3.7 million people have now been resettled in new housing estates on the edge of the city, while the old central districts, a mass of alleyways and two-storey dwellings in which five or six families were cramped together, are being demolished to make way for redevelopment. But the municipal government estimated that at least 200,000 people in 80,000 to 90,000 households were still living in appalling conditions at the end of 1997. It earmarked 23 old districts containing an estimated 13 million sq.m. of 'poor, dangerous and crude housing' to be demolished and redeveloped by the year 2000, and another 29 million sq.m. of new housing built to meet the city's targets for minimum per capita living space. Further north, Tianjin signed a US$1.2 billion contract with a Hong Kong group for the removal of dangerous houses covering a 42-hectare site in the Heping district. Despite its outstanding economic growth in recent years, Tianjin still contains numerous one-storey houses in need of restoration. The area to be renovated is inhabited by low-income people and is composed of single-storey structures, many of them over 100 years old. The area will transformed into a commercial and trade zone and its residents rehoused elsewhere.

Looking at these developments, Construction Minister Hou Jie took heart that the government's new housing programme was beginning to work, although there was a long way to go. 'Adequate housing for everyone is a basic human right and China has worked hard to supply universal and satisfactory housing. However, due to the rapid increase in the population and many other problems, there is still an imbalance between demand and supply in the housing market. For example, more than four million families are waiting for suitable houses, while on the other hand, more than 50 million square metres of commercial housing lie empty due to lack of buyers. This glut is indicative of limited purchasing power in the country and that more work must be done to cultivate and commercialise the housing market' (*China Daily*, 17-5-1997).

Box 8.1 Some Gains in Building Homes for Sale

Although they have lived in inexpensive public housing for decades, more and more Chinese want to buy their own homes, and with the deepening of housing reform, they now have to. This mindset is especially prevalent in Shenzhen, a showcase for the economic reform and opening-up drive in south China's Guangdong province; where about 82 per cent of residents have opted to buy rather than rent. In contrast, more than 80 per cent residential housing in the nation was not for sale until a few years ago. 'We used to regard living comfortably in public houses at a low rent as one of the great advantages of socialist society,' said one new house buyer. Residents in Shenzhen now enjoy an average of 14.2 sq.m. of living space per head; while the urban dwellers in Hainan further south have more than 15 sq.m. on average – a substantial figure given that the national target by the turn of the century is nine sq.m. per head.

According to Vice-Minister of Construction Ye Rushang, China invested more than 1.1 trillion Yuan into the building of 1.4 billion sq. m. of urban residential housing between 1991 and 1996. In that period, Beijing built more than 38 million sq.m. of new housing, improving the living conditions of 700,000 families, much of that on the outskirts of the city. The municipal government was building ten more housing sites in suburban areas, six of them completed by the end of 1997, according to the Municipal Urban and Rural Construction Committee. In addition, the city has pulled down 2.89 million sq.m. of shabby housing and moved at least 8,500 families from ageing houses. Since 1993, the city has given priority to improving the living conditions of people with special difficulties and has built 1.88 million sq.m. of housing for them. It has seen to it that any whose per capita living space is less than 4 sq.m. can move into new housing by the end of the century.

Meanwhile, the Guangzhou Municipal Government switched its attention to its 'comfortable housing' project in 1998 to provide shelter to those with scarce living space. The city has provided about 39,000 flats to the 26,000 families whose living space is less than five sq.m. per person and those who earn less than the city's average annual income of 13,634 Yuan. Between 1998 and 2000, the city plans to raise about 1.8 billion Yuan each year to construct several blocks consisting of multi-storeys or high-rises, with the floor space of each condominium ranging from 50 to 75 square metres, a spokesman said. Prices will be between 1,900 Yuan and 3,100 Yuan psm. Eighty per cent of the residential buildings in the project will be directly sold, 10 per cent will be covered by bank mortgages to help low wage earners, and the remaining 10 per cent will be set aside for rent

Sources: *China Daily*, 3-9-1997, 27-11-1997 and 11-12-1997.

Box 8.2 Expectations for the Real Estate Industry

The government is placing high hopes on development of a modern real estate industry as one of the pillars of economic growth. The key elements, as outlined by the Minister of Construction Hou Jie in December 1997 are:

1. Economic development goals require the real estate industry to maintain a definite rate of growth. According to the goal set in the Outline of the Ninth Five-Year Plan (1996–2000) for National Economic and Social Development and the Long-Range Objective Through the Year 2010, the annual economic growth rate will be maintained at eight per cent, and the rate of fixed asset investment at 30 per cent. To co-ordinate with this goal, the real estate sector must maintain a rational development level, before it can provide necessary material conditions for economic and social development. At present, the industry accounts for only about two per cent of the gross national product (GNP), but the figure will reach five per cent by 2000. This still compares unfavourably with the 20–30 per cent level in developed countries, leaving much room for growth.

2. According to the state plan, housing construction will maintain an annual growth rate of 15 per cent between 1996 and 2000. By the latter year, the urbanisation level will rise from 28 to 35 per cent. There will be 230 new cities and towns created, while 1.2 billion sq.m. of urban housing and 3 billion sq.m. of rural housing will be built. This is in addition to the 2.9 billion sq.m. of existing houses needing to be transformed, providing a massive market for foreign investment.

3. The speed of urbanisation in China has been accelerated. It is forecast that in year 2000, China's urban population will surpass 400 or even 500 million. The number of cities will increase from the present 622 to 724. The size of the current cities and towns will grow by 30 per cent.

4. By 2000, each urban household will own an apartment with average per-capita living space of nine sq.m., and some 70 per cent of the households would be able to afford 'well-equipped houses'.

5. As part of an effort to boost housing development and reform, the government has begun nation-wide experiments in the provision of commercialised housing – ending the practice of subsidised accommodation coming with a job in the state sector – with publicly funded housing funds, individual home mortgage loans and other financial assistance gradually becoming available.

Nanjing became the first city to totally abolish subsidised housing for workers and staff of state work units in 1997. In an experiment which was supposed to be adopted throughout the country in due course, all new housing built by the government bureaucracies and state enterprises had to be sold not rented out. Staff were able to obtain 70 per cent mortgages over 15 years. All medium and low-income families applying to buy low-cost government houses were entitled to grants covering 40 per cent of the cost. 'However, some work units continued to distribute free housing to staff while forcing other members to buy their homes. In response, Nanjing put forward new provisional regulations which outlaw the former free distribution system. The regulations are intended to protect low-income families who benefit from various loans and subsidies. The regulations stipulate that households living on the dole, whose incomes have fallen below the poverty line or which are registered as being in hardship by the municipal labour unions can be exempt from having to buy their own homes' (*Legal Daily*, 30-7-1997).

Sources: *Legal Daily*, 30-7-1997, Xinhua, 4-12-1997.

Developing this theme, Hou argued that commercialisation of housing was vital to replace the system of subsidised housing provided for workers in the state sector over the past half a century which amounted to many billions of dollars, a crippling financial burden. Unfortunately, he conceded, things had not gone as smoothly as the government expected. 'In the past few years, real estate developers have been encouraged to build flats which, it was supposed, increasingly well off Chinese would buy,' said the minister. 'But, it has become obvious the prices are too high for the market to bear'. In developed countries, mortgages and instalment plans are used to finance housing purchases. These policies are on offer by the Chinese financial sector, but due to stringent loan control, demanding payment plans and high interest rates, loans, although perhaps the correct solution, can probably not be expected to become popular in the short-term.

'Today's high prices are also hindering the maturation of the housing market. In Beijing and Shanghai for example, prices for a single-family dwelling are 3.000–4,000 Yuan per square metre. This contrasts to 1995 statistics which indicated the average price for a house elsewhere in the country is 1,700 Yuan ($204) per square metre. Although this is lower than in Beijing and Shanghai, it is still 28–35 per cent higher than that of 1994, and apparently unacceptable to Chinese consumers. 'Therefore, prices must be reduced,' Hou argued. 'In general, land, construction and installation costs, affiliated civic facilities and various taxes represent an extremely high proportion of a property's list price. Land accounts for about one quarter of the overall cost. Land speculation and profiteering has kept land prices high. Regulation is necessary to reverse this.' (*China Daily*, 2-8-1997).

Problems with low-cost housing

Despite high expectations, some problems have occurred with the high profile 'Comfort Housing' project, where unexpectedly poor sales raised the prospect in 1998 that the government would have to impose restrictions on the programme. Benefiting from a series of preferential policies in terms of bank loans and land use – and available only to families below a certain level of household income which differs according to the local government area involved – the programme had been introduced in 232 cities by the of 1997. But by the middle of that year, 66 per cent of the constructed housing totalling 5.03 million sq.m. of floor space remained unsold (*China Daily*, 1-12-1997).

In Beijing, 660,000 sq.m. of housing were finished in 1997, but only 50,000 sq.m. found immediate buyers. In the Northeast port of Dalian, 40 per cent went unsold for several months, while in Guilin, capital of Guangxi Zhuang Autonomous region in the South, at least 60 per cent of the 130,000 sq.m. of completed homes found no buyers (Ministry of Construction figures). As a result, the Ministry of Construction raised the prospect that the Comfort programme would have to be scaled back. 'Comfort housing should be limited to a suitable scale when the residential housing reform is intensified,' declared Shen Jiazhong, Vice-Director of the ministry's Real Estate Department (author interview, 14-3-1998). The favourable policies and low prices, combined with strong demand, should, in theory, have ensured a sell-out of all the Comfort housing coming onto the market. That this did not happen appears due to problems of affordability and poor quality projects. In view of the profits normally derived from land transfers – which are free in the case of Comfort housing – local governments have been reluctant to allocate prime sites for their construction. Hence, the accommodation tends to be in out-of-way locations, poorly served by public transport. In fact, public utilities and services have always been a problem in such housing areas around the country. Comfort housing projects benefit from preferential bank loans, which are denied in any form for property development companies under a government policy to calm down the overheated real estate market. Some developers, it is alleged, took the opportunity to participate in Comfort projects to obtain bank loans and land, but then diverted both to build ordinary commercial housing.

'In principle, the Comfort Scheme doesn't need the involvement of property developers, since all the costs are provided by governments at various levels, and no profit is supposed to be made,' observed Liu Chan, Division Chief of the Housing Reform Office under the State Council (ibid.). But this is contradicted by the central government's desire to generate as much investment capital as possible for the programme by offering special incentives to foreign real estate developers and builders to lure them away from the luxury end of the market and become involved at a comparatively low cost sector. Because of the low profit margins involved, it promised to buy back the completed homes with a guaranteed rate of return of between 10 to 15 per cent on the original investment. This meant a low rate of risk for developers, with the government also confident that it would not lose money as it would be able to sell off the purchased housing very quickly. Unfortunately, in some cases, even the somewhat modest profit level promised to the developers pushed the house prices beyond the means of those most in need.

A spokesman for the Beijing Construction Committee admitted: 'The poor sales are a disappointment. It seems there is still a distance between the price that ordinary people can accept and the market price despite our efforts to keep costs down. The low penetration rate of mortgage is also something to blame. However it is difficult to lower the price because the development costs are climbing. In order to attract foreign investment to participate in the development of common accommodation, the government has had to set a minimum price. If the price has to be lowered, the government has to subsidise more or the developers have to lower willingly its rate of return, both rather unlikely. All we can do is wait for people's income levels to climb, while trying to develop more funding channels for them to tap' (author interview, 15-2-1998).

The reasons for poor housing sales are complex, as illustrated in Table 8.1, which shows some of the discouragement factors cited by potential buyers. Table 8.2, meanwhile, contains the key suggestions by the same respondents as to what should be done to stimulate market demand.

Table 8.1 Reasons for Housing Remaining Unsold

Ranking order	Main Influencing Factors	Percentage	Unsold Commercial Housing Area
1	Price too high.	81.3	5.782 m sq.m.
2	Location	65.6	4.042
3	Market Demand	58.4	3.256
4	Design	46.4	1.866
5	Facility Equipment	40.4	1.75
6	Property Management	26.1	0.923
7	Engineering Quality	22.1	1 m
8	Company Marketing	13.8	0.455 m
9	Company Management	10.1	0.343 m
10	Others	5.5	0.264 m

Source: State Statistics Bureau and Ministry of Construction (1998), Beijing.

Table 8.2 Expectations and Suggestions for Boosting Home Sales

Ranking Order	Expectations and Suggestions	%
1	Abolish the unreasonable charges	69.5
2	Accelerate the pace of housing reforms	58.7
3	Establish Housing Fund on a full-scale	38.8
4	Improve the related Financing System	37.2
5	Sell at a discount price subsidised by Government	35.9
6	Lower bank loan rate for building commodity housing	34.4
7	Strengthen macro-regulation	27.7
8	Regulate the real estate market	18.4
9	Develop the resale market	12.1
10	Create new laws on real estate operations	11.5
11	Develop and standardise the resale market	3.5
12	Develop and standardise the rental market	2.9
13	Others	2.1

Source: State Statistics Bureau and Ministry of Construction (1998), Beijing.

Weakness of the mortgage system

The real breakthrough for commercial housing is likely to occur only when a mortgage system becomes the norm for property purchases, but that is still far from the case. By the end of 1996, for example, less than 1.6 per cent of urban salary earners had bought a home using a mortgage. In the final quarter of that year, the Tianjin branch of China Transportation Bank, one of those in the forefront of promoting the mortgage concept, received only eighty-one inquiries from would-be home buyers and granted loans in only fifty-five cases with a total of 6.64 million Yuan advanced. In Beijing, the Fengtai Branch of the Construction Bank the earliest to offer the service, extended 96 loans, while its Shenzhen branch approved only 19 mortgages.

'Between 1994 and 1996, housing prices in Hainan [the Southernmost island enjoying a major economic boom] fluctuated between 1,875 and 3,842 Yuan per square metre. The average annual income of an ordinary Hainan worker was in the range of 4,485 to 5,476 Yuan. This indicates that it will take a common family with two working members 10 years to buy a house of 85 square metres using all their savings. Although Hainan has implemented a house mortgage scheme, it has only been carried out on a small scale and with relatively high interest rates.' (China Daily, 26-1-1997).

One of the problems is loans require a 30 per cent deposit, compared to the 5–10 per cent level prevailing in the countries like Britain and the United States, where there are even prospects for 100 per cent loans. This means that a

Beijing resident wanting to buy a modest 60-sq.m., two-bedroom apartment near the Third Ring Road, a highly desirable area, would more than likely have to put down a deposit of around 90,000 Yuan and the remainder covered by a 15-year loan at a monthly repayment rate of 3,433.14 Yuan. Even for the best paid industrial worker, this would amount to about 80 per cent of take-home pay – compared to a level of between 10 and 30 per cent in America and Britain. The 15-year repayment period is actually the most generous. Many banks insist on getting all their money back within five to 10 years, compared to the 25–30 years prevailing in other countries.

Yet another barrier is the guarantee system that banks operate, In order to reduce their risk, they demand that the borrower's employer provides a guarantee backed by physical assets, along with another third party guarantee. This might have worked in the past when a worker was tied to one company for life. But job mobility is now beginning to take hold in China, so that most companies are unwilling to provide such guarantees in case of being left in the lurch. Secondly, with so many firms in the state sector in financial difficulties if not on the verge of bankruptcy – partly due to past policies of lavish welfare support for the work force in lieu of a government system – what value are the guarantees to the bank? There is a further discouragement for the average buyer, in that the bank also requires the deposit of five per cent of the purchase price in a special account for the duration of the loan. But the interest rate on the house purchase savings is currently 0.36 per cent lower than other interest rates, so that it acts as a further deterrent even if the prospective purchaser has this additional money to invest.

According to official estimates, personal loans only account for between five and 10 per cent of the credit being advanced by Chinese financial institutions. Some 70 per cent of the loans go to enterprises, usually state-owned for industrial development, and only about 20 per cent is available for property development (Ministry of Finance figures for 1996). Internationally, the norm is for about one-third of all credit to be advanced for house purchases. Some experts in the real estate industry have calculated that if the banks were able to advance between 30–50 billion Yuan in private credit, all the commercial housing stock could be sold in a relatively short space of time. But this is unlikely to happen. The financial sector remains wary of the property sector pending further evidence of its stability and reliability as an investment target.

Problems with malpractice

Like many other sectors of the Chinese economy, enthusiasm has sometimes run ahead of experience. The sudden vision of large and fast profit attracted many developers who in the West might earn the epithet of 'cowboy operators', although if one wanted to be more generous, 'inexperienced'

Box 8.3 Imaginative Incentives to Buy

Faced with public reluctance, or inability to buy, developers have had to come up with some imaginative schemes to try and get properties off their hands. Nowhere is innovation in home sales more apparent than on Hainan Island, where some developers began promoting forward buying with a 'value guarantee repurchase' agreement. The idea is that the customer pays for a property in full while it is being built, enabling the developer to maintain his cash flow at a crucial time. At the time of handover of the completed house, if its value has not increased the developer agrees to immediate repurchase at a 15 to 20 per cent premium. Another promotion by a handful of developers has overtones of the supermarket – buy one home and get a second one free.

In the provincial capital Haikou, some office developments offered special deals on mortgages. If the purchaser was willing to pay back within five years, the normal 70 per cent mortgage could be increased to 80 per cent through a special deal negotiated with local banks. In addition, the developer will pay half of the remaining 20 per cent deposit.

In the residential sector, Hainan, Shenzhen Special Economic Zone and Shanghai all played on the desire of rural residents to move to the city in search of a better life. In both places, would-be buyers were lured with the offer of an inside track in obtaining a local residential permit – vital for any Chinese wanting to move from one area to another, without it there is no hope of obtaining a 'legal' job at a proper salary nor any chance of receiving social welfare benefits. In Shenzhen, a magnet for job-hungry peasants ready to take any sort of work in the city's booming low-tech manufacturing operations, the districts of Longgang and Baoan sold 3,700 apartments in one four month period by offering residence permits, mortgages and even a license to own a car.

Elsewhere, the Northern port of Tianjin offered a 'rent to purchase conversion' arrangement. A potential buyer and the developer draw up an agreement stipulating the house price, the period for which it will be rented and the date on which the occupant agrees to buy the property. The rent paid is deducted from the final payment. There is also an opt-out clause in which the occupant can simply walk away without buying at the end of the rental period, leaving the developer with some capital in hand and the property that can be then be put up for sale again.

Source: Author research.

might be a word that could readily be used. What tended to happen at the luxury end of the market was that a developer would start putting up building in expectation of quick sales or rentals. This, in fact, was vital because, in many cases, the developer faced immediate cash flow problems. If clients could not be found to show faith in the pretty 'artist's impression' drawings in the glossy brochure, the project could quickly run into trouble. Cities across China throughout the 1990s have been littered with half-completed buildings because developers ran out of money to continue.

At the same time, would-be tenants have been left with lost deposits or even the full price which could not be recovered. In late 1995, for example, the head of the Hong Kong Consumer Council met officials of the central government and the provincial government in Guangdong, over hundreds of complaints it had received from Hong Kong buyers about mainland malpractice. Complaints included developers failing to complete projects on time, poor construction quality due to use of substandard materials and completed properties which turned out to be significantly different from what was advertised. In a number of cases, buyers who had paid the full amount for the purchase of a property then visited Guangdong to discover construction work hadn't even begun.

According to experts in Hong Kong at the time, when a property was being sold there, the developer was required to demonstrate that it had the financial capabilities to complete the property. In China, as long as the company could demonstrate it had completed the foundations, or it had put up 20–25 per cent of the total fee, it was allowed to put the property up for sale. A not untypical case involved the L & D property consultancy from Hong Kong, one of foreign pioneers in China, which got into serious financial trouble when it bought the half-completed Rose Garden villas in Beijing from its developer in 1993 when the latter got into financial difficulties that threatened the project with collapse. Not until too late did it discover that the developer did not possess the proper documentation for the project and there were also design and construction quality problems. Due to the unexpected change in government policy regarding luxury housing, L & D faced severe financial difficulties as banks were unable to provide any loans to complete the project. In July 1999, the project was auctioned off to one of the major creditors.

The main problem that government supervisory organs at central and local level have only begun to tackle certainly relates to properties not matching up to the rosy descriptions in the brochures or the handsome models in the developer's office. According to Liu Gang (author interview, 23-2-1997), a deputy chief of Beijing Municipal Government Administration, the department overseeing the industry, many mainland real estate agents 'put profit first instead of the legitimate rights and interests of consumers and developers. This includes illegal marketing, including false advertising, to mislead buyers.'

Property rights are another minefield. For example, land use rights are the prime concern of villa owners in particular. All the land belongs to the government, and at best, the buyer might get a 70-year lease. Often a land developer will tell a prospective buyer he or she doesn't have land title but only 'village title'. That means that the village which has jurisdiction over the land says the title belongs to the buyer, but they haven't got approval from the authorities in Beijing. As a result, the central government can turn up at any time and declare the property is on land scheduled for factory development or for a new highway, and the buyer has absolutely no comeback when the happy family home is torn down. This problem was particularly prevalent in booming Southern China, especially in Guangdong Province, which eventually established a committee involving construction, commerce and land administration officials from the various important cities within its boundaries to try and establish the extent of abuse and eliminate it.

Worried by the impact of the growing bad image on property sales, the Ministry of Construction in 1996 began undertaking an annual nation-wide inspection of projects to unearth unfair competition in the real estate industry, including fraud in bidding for building contracts and shoddy building practices. In the 1997 inspection, between June and September, inspectors checked 235,200 projects, of which 1,730 finished before 1995 had serious quality problems, and 107,600 violated regulations in some way, especially in building on land not designated for the purpose. There were 2,987 cases of officials taking bribes in connection with construction projects. (*China Daily*, 20/11/97). The ministry said it had received many complaints from residents who moved into new apartments bought on the strength of rosy brochure descriptions only to find them prone to leaks, structural cracks, peeling of wall surfaces from bricks, along with rough decoration, inferior equipment and deficiencies in basic utilities. 'Mostly this is due to poor management in construction, and many of the problems are definitely linked to deliberate malpractice by unscrupulous developers,' according to Zheng Kunsheng, head of one such investigative team (author interview, 19-5-1997).

Construction quality questioned

Malpractice is also evident in the area of construction quality. The remainder of this section draws heavily on research in 1997 and 1998 carried out by the *Real Estate Newspaper*, published by the Ministry of Construction.

In the Qiao Yuan residential area of Wuhan, an 18-storey building with a construction area of 17,000 sq.m., having reached its planned height of 56.6 metres high, was about to be roofed in when it suddenly began to subside in a very uneven manner. After three weeks, it began to tilt at a most alarming angle, before correcting itself and swaying the other way. Within 24 hours the angle of tilt had reached some 24 degrees and the top was off vertical by 2.8 metres. Three days later, its developer, Wuhan No.1 Construction Company, blew up the entire structure sending an investment of tens of millions Yuan up in smoke. Meanwhile, near the Jiaozhou crossroads in West Shanghai, passers-by saw a lot of office and residential buildings going up, but amid all the frenetic activity, the building site of the Jingkou Mansion was silent. Having reached the 14th floor, construction work stopped abruptly. Several days later, the top four floors were demolished. These floors, it transpired, had used cement supplied by Sui Qi Electricity Supply Bureau of nearby Anhui Province, which had one cement manufacturing plant under its wing as a sideline business. The cement turned out to of a dangerously inferior quality and Shanghai Construction Committee stepped in to order the high profile demolition.

The Wuhan and Shanghai incidents are merely the tip of the iceberg, a sign of the growing quality problems facing the Chinese building industry and government regulators trying to bring some order out of the chaos that has emerged with the explosive growth of office, commercial and residential buildings right across the nation. At many worksites, there are big banners declaring 'quality above everything'. But it's mere words and doesn't seem to be practised,' lamented a source in the Ministry of Construction.. Corners are being cut, it seems, and the problem is most acute in the housing sector. According to the source: 'There are many people working hard to try and save money to buy a house. But when they do so, the dreams turn to dust because of numerous quality problems.'

According to a ministry study, housing constructed in the 1950s was reckoned to need serious maintenance and structural repair after some 15 years. Now, there are many buildings which need extensive repairs even before the first tenants move in. 'Some buildings immediately after they are finished have to be condemned as dangerous housing and people cannot be allowed to move in under any circumstances.'

Ministry of Construction officials acknowledge the extent of the problem and stress that everything is being done on the government side to bring the construction and real estate industries under tighter control and regain public confidence – vital of the housing market is to be developed into an economic mainstay. A nation-wide probe into unfair competition, fraud in bidding for building contracts and shoddy building practices led to new procedures and regulations for supervision and management of enterprises by both local and central government. As part of the efforts to promote construction quality, the ministry disseminated nation-wide information about procedures used in building high quality housing projects and to implement a construction inspection system in all China's major cities. Programmes are also underway to upgrade the skills of the country's thirty million building workers through education in operation, safety and quality.

Box 8.4 Seven Factors in Quality Problems

1. According to government statistics, 40.1 per cent of the quality problems were caused by **design deficiencies**. Some analysts suggest that many building designers are irresponsible. It is claimed there are many underground architects who don't have the right professional qualifications. Many have emerged because of the rapid development of the industry. They are very quick at drawing and their costs are very low. So the developers use them because they can save money. Some students after the first or second year of study start 'putting on their stage costumes' – as the Chinese saying goes – often in collusion with their teachers. One example involved two schoolteachers who were moonlighting. In order to establish their bona fides, however, they had to forge the signature of the head of a design institute as well as the institute's stamp. They then began the rounds of the real estate industry seeking customers. One construction company won a contract to construct a building according to their design, and then sub-contracted the work to a private contractor. Before it was finished, however, it collapsed. The teachers are now serving long prison terms.

2. **Poor quality materials**. There are, for example, many problems with bricks, steel and cement. There are 12,000 brick factories around the country, but only about 50 which have a guaranteed record of producing quality goods. In China, 500 billion bricks are produced each year. Only 50 per cent are reckoned to be qualified for use. But, of course, the other half are also used in projects and after a few years they become like powder and start cracking. Poor quality cement, steel and aluminium alloy waterproof materials are starting to come into the market. The collective township, street corner or private enterprises products are become the mainstay because they are cheap and thus attractive to builders who have to keep down their costs in order to gain any sort of a profit margin in a very competitive industry.

3. **Developers try to save on materials**. The *Real Estate Newspaper* quoted one sub-contractor from Hebei Province as declaring quite openly: 'Houses are long-line products. A contract once signed is dead. But raw materials are changing in price every day. If we don't save on the materials we will lose money.'

4. In recent years, commodity house construction scale is large so the macro control is lagging badly behind. Developers and builders often use sub-contractors in order to frustrate control. Some unqualified people with no legal status are trying to break into the market with low fees, less labour and low price in general, so they can get the private sub-contract. The sub-contractors sub-contract, so that there are many layers and the

market is in disorder. The *Real Estate Newspaper* cited the case of a woman who had been a persistent failure in business. Eventually, she became the public relations manager of a construction company, but then quit after 12 months to set up her own construction company. Despite having no funding, no staff and no office, she still gave herself a title of general manager. 'Using her charm and big kickbacks, she got 18 construction projects and then sub-contracted them to 31 building companies each of which had to pay her a large management fee. After some years, she became a millionaire.'

5. **Lax supervision** as a quality monitoring system has not yet been adequately formed. According to the newspaper's investigation: 'Normally, when the project is finished, the inspection is just starting. For many projects, it is not easy to detect the problems inside no matter how much experience the inspectors have. And on many occasions, the quality evaluation meeting is not held at the worksite but in KTV [karaoke television] rooms.' In 1994, Shenyang in Northeast China chose 192 construction projects as 'excellent' ones, citing their excellent engineering work etc. But when the news got out, there were so many complaints from the occupants of some of these projects, that a fresh evaluation had to be carried out which resulted in only 66 meeting the required standard.

6. **Poor quality construction workers**. The main force of construction workers are farmers. There is no training; no construction technique; they don't have certificates; there is no skill, only muscle. They walk up the ladders on a building site and start building a high rise without any preparation.

7. **Powerful money creates loopholes**. Commercial houses need a huge investment and need the approval from many different departments, opening the door to corruption. The *Real Estate Newspaper* reported on one city, where a flock of construction companies went to visit the deputy mayor concerning contracts for a 20-floor residential building. 'Each got a task according to how much he was paid,' the newspaper alleged. 'He had a list and then prioritised according to the payment. Construction firms with reputation and strength didn't get any part of the job. If a commercial building project costs 10 million Yuan, its ultimate cost will be 13 million Yuan. The other three million goes to different private pockets. However, 'the wool will still come out of the sheep' (meaning the end users will pay).'. According to incomplete government statistics, in 1994, different inspectorates discovered 101,142 bribery cases of which 64,270 related to real estate. In 1995, the bribery related to real estate was 88.6 per cent of the total.

Sources: Real Estate Newspaper, 1997 and 1998, various editions.

The State Council threatened to 'deal severely' with violations and to 'demolish development zones and buildings constructed without proper approval'. Cities with a population of more than one million will no longer be allowed to expand further. All local authorities were told to abide strictly by the 1989 Urban Planning Act. In particular, the amount of land used for urban construction 'should not exceed limits specified by government-approved plans for 2000'. Cities should make better use of land within existing boundaries and refrain from expanding on to surrounding farmland. All construction projects have to conform to overall development plans, which for cities with populations of more than half a million means that they will have to be approved by the State Council. For cities with smaller populations, plans can be approved by lower-level governments, but only after being checked by the Ministry of Construction, the State Planning Commission and the State Land Administration.

One step forward, two steps back

A government policy document published in 1997 ('*Main Points of Implementation of the 1997 Economic Restructuring*', State Commission for Economic Restructuring), meanwhile, also set the following key goals for the real estate sector in the years ahead:

- 'Accelerating the magnetisation process of housing distribution, gradually abolishing the practice of housing welfare distribution and introducing a new system for the distribution of new houses. In light of the actual conditions of different types of work units, plans need to be formulated to carry out magnetisation of housing distribution step by step, gradually including housing subsidies into monetary wages. Various enterprises and institutions should abolish welfare distribution of new houses and instead implement a policy of selling before leasing.
- Continuing to readjust public housing rents, and steadily promoting sales of public houses. In line with the requirements of the housing reform target as set in the Ninth Five-Year Plan, the public house rental level in various cities in 1997 is raised by two percentage points, calculated in accordance with the average income of workers' families. In light of the actual family conditions, detailed and strict policies for exempting or reducing rents and subsidising low-income residents, families with financial difficulties and retired workers should be formulated. In line with related stipulations, it is necessary to promote sales of public houses and vitalise housing stock assets.
- Adopting effective measures to set the residential market in motion. These measures include liquidating the irrational factors in the price formation of commodity prices, reducing the selling prices of commodity houses, freeing funds occupied by stockpiled commodity housing, so as

to promote the rapid growth of related industries. Actively developing housing finance, opening various forms of housing deposit business and guiding large amounts of social funds to housing consumption.'

'We should expand the proportion of housing credit in bank loans. The credit structure should gradually change from the previous housing construction credit to the simultaneous development of housing construction and consumption credit. The efficient use of housing loans should be continuously enhanced. We should actively open the mortgage loan business for home purchase and introduce standard management. In regard to residents' mortgage loans, we should encourage buying homes by adopting such measures as differentiating different consumer groups, prolonging the loan time limit and increasing the flotation of interest rates. We should a establish policy mortgage loan system and use housing public accumulation funds to provide low-interest loans to house purchasers, so as to enhance personal house purchasing ability.'

In March 1998, the central government took the boldest step of all in finally setting a date for the end of subsidised housing for state employees, the pre-requisite for any programme to create a commercial housing market. But the difficulty of achieving the decisive breakthrough quickly became apparent. By early June, the deadline for achieving the planned reforms was put back, after a number of officials and housing experts began warning that the programme would have to be delayed for at least two years, because making private housing more affordable could wreck the economy.

In March, a government circular revealed a new policy which called for rents to be quadrupled from 1 July in a deliberate attempt to encourage state employees to buy homes in new developments. Rents would eventually rise to 15 per cent of a family's income. Half of the money invested in the city's housing construction has for years come from work units which rent out cheap housing to their members. To encourage quick sales, it also offered new homes at bargain prices if purchased before June 30. Weeks before the deadline expired, however, the Beijing city government announced it would extend the deadline to the end of the year and not raise rents for public housing after the initial June 30 deadline. Other cities quickly followed this lead. While central government officials claimed sales were going well, other sources insisted this wasn't true. Ministries in Beijing, for example, reportedly had sold less than 20 per cent of their stock by late June.

The Housing Reform Office of the Beijing government denied the plans were facing difficulties and insisted the deadline extension was to accommodate a rush of would-be buyers. 'As it is so close to the deadline, people are anxious and worried that they might miss it so we are extending the deadline,' one official said. 'There is no agenda on raising rents. It will be made public together with the housing miniaturisation plan which is still being drafted. It could be ready before the end of the year.' Nevertheless, if the new policy had been immediately implemented, when few can afford to buy the capital's high-priced homes, many experts feared construction could slow so much it would drag down economic growth and derail the central government's entire economic development plan for years to come. There was widespread belief that the Beijing authorities were reluctant to raise rents for fear of enraging laid-off workers and others facing economic hardships.

Conceding the difficulties, State Planning Commission vice-chairman Ma Kai said: 'The current price of housing is too high and fees and taxes are numerous and exorbitant. The structure of the housing market is confusing and difficult to navigate.' The interests of developers, the local government and banks were threatened by making home ownership more affordable, said Mr Ma. He said the problem could be solved by raising rents, curbing or abolishing taxes and fees, and state intervention to force down prices. The cost of renting a flat in Beijing was so low there was little incentive to buy the expensive new housing, he said. This, plus high fees for land, construction and management, resulted in much of the 2.47 million square metres of housing built in the capital in 1997 standing empty (author interview, November 1998).

Gu Yunchang, Secretary-General of the China Real Estate Association, meanwhile, predicted that without government intervention housing prices would not fall to levels which medium and low-income families could afford by themselves. 'The current price for a 60-sq.m. flat is usually more than 10 times the annual income of a typical double-salary family in large and medium cities, mainly due to unreasonable costs incurred during construction'. The cost of commercial housing includes paying for construction, land-use fees, resettlement, construction of public facilities, and administrative fees. The fees for land use and administrative charges usually account for 50 to 60 per cent of the housing cost. Construction costs account for about 20 per cent of the total, while construction of public facilities accounts for 10 to 20 per cent. The reduction of government-related taxes and fees had not led to a significant fall in housing prices so far, he claimed (author interview, November 1998). The central government eliminated forty-eight tax items and fees levied on property developers in 1997 and another ten items in 1998. However, the main administrative charges were not affected. Developers in some medium-sized cities, for example, have to pay more than ninety different fees to administrative departments of local government (author research, 1998).

Workers' fury over the 'unfairness' of the housing system overhaul also seems to have influenced the government decision to go slow on reform. Employees of government ministries with less money to hand out in financial subsidies or other forms of assistance claimed the new system would place them at a distinct disadvantage. One official said employees of the so-called poor ministries were angry that their counterparts in richer ministries would have the chance to buy their state-subsidised homes at a discount. This was set at 1,450 Yuan in Beijing's Dongcheng, Xicheng, Chongwen, Xuanwu, Chaoyang, Haidian, Fengtai and Shijingshan inner city districts, much lower than the market price, which ranges from 4,000 Yuan to more than 10,000 Yuan. Those who had not been living in state-provided houses and had been on a waiting list for years would have to pay market rates under the new system.

'Many cadres who still were not given welfare housing have lodged complaints with Premier Zhu Rongji attacking departmental seniors for their bias in allocating welfare units,' the official said (author interview, November 1998). 'Even those who have benefited from welfare housing complained that their apartments were much smaller than officials of the same rank in other ministries. They argued it was unfair to lure them to buy their tiny apartments while other departmental cadres could enjoy larger space.'

Not every city faced difficulties of the scale experienced by Beijing. The prosperous southern metropolis of Guangzhou, for example, was one of the pioneers of commercialised housing and city officials claimed it had gone well – perhaps because the local government heavily sweetened the deal with subsidies for state employees who buy. It offered a monthly wage supplement of 233 Yuan to a clerk, 420 Yuan to a deputy divisional chief, 467 Yuan to a divisional chief, 513 Yuan to a deputy director, 607 Yuan to a director, 747 Yuan to a vice-mayor, and 933 Yuan to a mayor. The subsidy may change to match inflation, and was expected to cover 80 per cent of the cost of a 3,500 Yuan psm apartment. Yantai in Shandong Province was another city where house sales went well in the initial stages – no doubt helped by the fact that the local government began paying a subsidy equivalent to 35 per cent of monthly salaries into a general housing support fund from 1 January this year.

Nevertheless, by the end of 1998, there were 19.688 million sq.m. of unsold commercial apartments involving 2,375 different developers in the 20 biggest cities (out of a nation-wide total of 50 million sq.m.). A quarter had been on the market for more than two years and had tied up 50 billion Yuan in capital (Ministry of Construction figures given to the authors).

Leading Economist Wu Jinglian argues that the housing construction and real estate industries have to be linked to the realities of economic development. 'From the sellers' point of view, there are many empty houses on the market now, but they aren't willing to bring their prices down to the level that would match potential demand. People cannot afford to buy, but we cannot raise wage levels to a sufficient extent to overcome that problem – especially with so much unemployment. If we are to have a real market economy in China, then the players who make the wrong decisions should bear the results of that decision. Developers should be prepared to shed some fat. In the West, when the economy hits bad times, house prices are adjusted dramatically, and this helps fuel a revival. Yet in our country, the developers are quire prepared to see houses remain unsold for a few years in the hope that demand will somehow miraculously pick up. This is naïve and it's also suicidal. Developers are going out of business almost every day but no-one learns the obvious lesson.' (*China Daily*, 23-3-1999).

The official *Economic Daily,* meanwhile, suggested the market could best be boosted by encouraging rentals while at the same promoting sales of residential property. 'Putting undue emphasis on the sales of residential housing will result in an increase in labour and land costs to the detriment of a developing country like China. Individual house purchasing is currently only suitable for the few people with high incomes. The first choice for most low- and medium-income people should be renting,' it argued.

To solve the problem, it proposed, the state should clearly define property rights and separate land property from house property. In the current housing market, land for construction is obtained from the government on a long-term lease, which in practice is equivalent to sale. The term of the lease usually runs for 50–70 years, and the rent for the use of land during the whole term should be paid in a lump sum. As a result of the inclusion of land cost in housing prices, the rents and sale prices of residential housing have soared well above the average income level in the country.

'From now on, the state should collect rent for the use of state-owned land on a monthly basis after the approval of a property project. When the project is completed, it will be sold at a price which includes the land rent paid during construction. The owner of the property rights will then pay the land rent monthly. As a result, housing rents and prices will drop by a large margin. The price of housing in particular could be reduced to half the current market price.' The article recommended the government buy back land property from developers at a preferential price. 'Real estate developers have paid for the land for the excess supply of newly built residential housing. Therefore, the state should return the sum to developers and reclaim ownership of the land property. As the owner of the land property, the state can adjust the land rent according to the economic development situation. It can thus convert socio-economic progress into an increase in the value of state-owned property and prevent a bubble economy resulting from excessive speculation in landed property.'

Considering all the above, therefore, it seems obvious there is still a long way to go before China will witness the emergence of a rational, modern housing system to meet market needs. In the meantime, millions of urban dwellers will continue to live in crowded, difficult conditions.

CHAPTER 9

Environmental Deterioration: Can the Environment Recover?

Western experts such as Lester Brown, Richard Edmonds and Vaclav Smil and the path-breaking television series *Tears of the Dragon* broadcast by UK's Channel 4 in 1993, have repeatedly pointed to the severity of China's environmental crisis. The Sanxia (Three Gorges) Dam Project has been a particularly potent symbol to many in the outside world of what is seen as China's wilful disregard of environmental quality in the pursuit of economic growth. To the Chinese, such criticism is often viewed as a reflection of outside ignorance as to the true needs of China, coming from Westerners who themselves have, in the main, environmentally costly lifestyles. 'China knows best' is the official refrain. There are, however, many Chinese who have a growing awareness of the environmental threats to their development strategy, there is increasing internal opposition to mega-scale projects, and there are also some environmental success stories among the environmental failures. Environmental education and environmental consciousness have a long way to go in China, however, and this chapter will discuss the limits to which China's environmental deterioration can be checked, and recovery assured. The structure is:

- Conflicting legacies: from harmony to control
- Evidence for the scale of China's environmental problems
- What has already been done: policies and exemplars
- What needs to be done: can the market provide?

Conflicting legacies: from harmony to control

We must be careful not to over-romanticise the environmental legacy of the past, which was periodically a time of flood and famine, but many ancient Chinese traditions were ecologically sound. Daoist concepts for example emphasised the harmony between 'man' and nature. This contrasts with a greater emphasis on 'control' and 'stewardship' from the Judaeo-Christian tradition, for example. The intensive agriculture which developed to support and stimulate the large population of China was often based on good ecological practices – the use of 'nightsoil' for example, and of pigs to recycle human waste – and the minimising of waste, in whatever form. A sixth century CE agricultural encyclopaedia provides instruction for improving soil fertility, preventing erosion and improving yields, and protection from insects (Muldavin, 1997). However, these environmentally positive legacies of the past are offset by the pressures exerted by the Han people as they sought to extend the ecumene, or living area. And so, deforestation began on a large scale more than 2000 years ago in the time of the Qin and then the Han dynasty, leading to 'serious erosion and the Huang River [Huang He] took on its characteristic yellow-brown colour' (Edmonds, 1994a, p.30). More than 1000 years later, similar deforestation took place in the Yangtze area, with the deforestation process accelerating from the time of the Ming, as urban construction took place and agricultural activities expanded in area.

Similarly, as regards desertification, this also has an ancient history, as Han Chinese settlers migrated into Inner Mongolia or further towards the North West, with farmers being continually obliged to move on, for their 'ploughing had loosened the grassland soils exposing the lower sandy layers which drifted under windy conditions' (ibid., p.36). The upgrading of the Great Wall by the Ming, plus intermittent warfare, contributed to destabilisation of the environment in many areas, encouraging desertification further. Desertification is not, of course, solely the product of human action; it also reflects cycles of climatic change. Nevertheless, human activity has contributed markedly to the spread of deserts, in North and North West China in particular.

The modern era brought the more interventionist traditions of the West to China, and Maoism was based partly on the materialist Marxist view that the earth could be controlled via human intervention. Mao, for example, referred to the fable of the foolish old man who moved the mountains, and although he was referring figuratively to the 'mountains' of imperialism and feudalism which could be moved by the masses of the people, there was also an implicit reference to the potential of human action to transform the earth (Mao Zedong, 1971, p.320). Human development would know no bounds once the feudal shackles were broken, and this perspective informed the Great Leap Forward in particular, plus the later Cultural Revolution. Fortunately, in some cases, despite the negative outcomes possible in this interventionist policy, positive environmental change could occur as can be shown via the example of the communes.

The communes were created during the Great Leap Forward in 1958, being based on the different types of co-operatives which preceded them, and were 'total' forms of social organisation which combined political, economic and social control over their area. They were continually modified in size therefore their numbers varied from 23,630 in 1958 to 80,956 in 1963 to 51,478 in 1970 and 54,183 in 1980 (Chao, 1990, p.131). As regards population, the communes contained over 560 million people in 1958, 568 million in 1963 after the famines of the 1959–62 period, up to nearly 700 million in 1970 and just under 811 million in 1980 (ibid., p.131). The 'Eight-Point Charter' was introduced, in which agriculture was intensified via four activities which required more labour – water conservancy, close planting of crops, plant protection from locusts and other threats to crops, plus adequate manuring via the use of 'night soil', green manure and chemical fertiliser – while those activities which needed less labour were better seed selection (of higher yielding strains), mechanisation (usually semi-mechanisation, what we would today term 'intermediate technology'), deep ploughing and better management (Buchanan, 1970).

Of these activities, water conservancy was particularly important, as Mr. Mu the leader of Zhou Lu Tain commune near Guangzhou noted during a research visit in 1980, for example. A '3 pronged' policy developed which involved mainly small projects plus larger ones where feasible, accumulation of water, rather than its diversion, and reliance on people rather than government. In 1965, for example, forty-three million people were engaged in extending the irrigation system, while one of the abiding memories of the research visit to Zhou Lu Tain commune is of the ponds and irrigation ditches which were so important to its production system. Across China there were different types of projects to suit different needs; thus there was an emphasis on drainage and water storage to fully utilise the waterlogged lowlands near Tianjin, deep and shallow artesian wells were dug in the Beijing area as well as the loessland of Shanxi, while irrigation and storage was more important in the dry uplands of Hubei. Also, for example, 85,000 miles of canals were built in the North Huai plain, a great problem area.

In addition to the Eight-point Charter, afforestation was also very important, for China has a very low per cent tree cover – it was 5 per cent compared to an estimated 30 per cent required for adequate climatic and soil regulation. Thus great 'shelter belts' over 1000 km long were constructed in North China against soil erosion, sand and storms. The shelter belt in North Gansu took 700,000 workers to construct. The Northeast. and North China Plain were key locations of this activity, plus the loess region and the lands of the desertified interior. Despite successes, in recent years concerns have been expressed that trees planted often died through subsequent neglect, while the numbers involved were often exaggerated by local officials. In any case these projects were largely superseded by later projects described below. Interestingly, afforestation has an ancient past: Edmonds points out that afforestation was presaged over

2000 years ago in Qin and Han times when a belt of elm trees was planted along the Great Wall, while an even older belt has been found further north in Inner Mongolia (Edmonds, 1994a, op.cit., pp.30–31).

These positive legacies of sound environmental practices during the Maoist era are counterbalanced by the drive to industrialisation of the 1950s and 1960s. This left a negative legacy of industrial pollution from the plants themselves, plus the knock-on effects of industrial growth on the environment in general. Various campaigns of this era also had detrimental effects, especially the 'Four Pests Campaign' of the 1950s against flies, rats, mosquitoes and, more sadly, sparrows, thought to be eating crops or spreading disease. Pots and pans were beaten continuously for days until the sparrows fell dead with exhaustion, and it was only some time later that the beneficial action of sparrows in the ecosystem was realised. Of course other bird species too would die, and even today, partly too because, as the Chinese say, 'the only thing that flies which the Chinese won't eat has metal wings', there is a relative lack of bird species in China. This contrasts strangely with the tradition of old men walking their caged songbirds in the same way that the westerner would walk the dog.

Evidence for the scale of China's environmental problems

Apart from the perennial problem of demographic pressures on food supply, which has once again recently been widely aired and has been dealt with by Geoff Murray in Chapter 5 of his recent book (Brown, 1995; Murray, 1998), several key 'vectors' of relevance to environmental concerns can be identified across China (Map 9.1). These help to 'patch in' some of the complex contrasts within the country. Thus, the population vector runs mainly West to East, peaking at the coast. In contrast the aridity vector runs from South-East to North-West, from the humid sub-tropical conditions of Guangzhou to the arid landscapes of Xinjiang. The altitude vector – more correctly presented as the classic four 'great steps' (Derbyshire, 1990) – runs from the North China Plain around Beijing south westwards towards the Tibetan Plateau and the Himalayas. The acidity vector runs from North to South (with a cluster around Beijing, and a much higher cluster around Chongqing) with the high temperatures of South China helping 'sulphur dioxide convert to acid faster than in most other places in the world with high levels of acid pollution'(Edmonds, 1994b, p.174).

In 1997, Chongqing became designated as China's largest city, with a population of just over thirty million, including surrounding agricultural areas (Wu Fang, 1997). Hopes are high for its long-term prospects. The acid rain problem will have to be resolved, however. The city burns fifteen million tons of coal each year. Encircled by mountains and with little wind or sunshine, the dust in the air gathers above the city to cause frequent acid rain showers. According to Chongqing citizens, the bus signs have to be changed every few years as the words become illegible. Marble buildings retain their shine for only a few months before turning dull and grey. The acid rain not only corrodes buildings but also causes reductions in agricultural output and soil damage, leading an estimated economic loss of 1.6 billion Yuan a year, according to an estimate by the Chongqing Municipal Government. The 'Tears of the Dragon' publication for the TV series shown in January 1993 noted:

'In Chongqing, for example, where the locally mined coal has a very high sulphur content, 820,000 tonnes of sulphur dioxide are emitted into the atmosphere every year. And because the city is sheltered from the wind by the surrounding mountains, most of this sulphur dioxide comes straight back down in rain so acid that it can dissolve steel. In 1990, Chongqing spent US$250,000 just to replace lamp-posts and buses that had been eaten away' (Catton, 1992, p.21).

A large part of the environmental problem is due to the enormous urban expansion of recent years (details in Chapter 7). Ian Cook has explored the fragility of China's environments at the urban level (Cook, 1993, 1995, 2000, op.cit.). As far as Beijing is concerned,

'Since the 1980s, the environment has deteriorated to a deplorable state. Concrete tower blocks erase historic hutongs as industries ooze with the filth and sludge of a fast track modern metropolis. The rivers became ugly and unhygienic. About 10,000 cubic meters of rubbish and 12 tons of industrial sewage per year are dropped into the toxic waterways like so many dead fish. According to *Economic Daily*, 80 per cent of rivers in Beijing were polluted in 1998' (Bei Jingshi, 1999; p.22).

The concept of 'ecological footprints' has been developed to measure the ecological impact of, especially, urban development (Rees, 1992). Cook has amended this to '*ecological tramplings*' for cities have such a negative impact upon their surrounding ecosystems at the local, regional, national and even global scales (Cook, op.cit, 1993). Thus, at the local level, many if not most of China's large cities suffer from some form of environmental pollution, whether from traffic noise, vehicle exhaust fumes, industrial atmospheric pollution, the degradation of valuable agricultural land surrounding these centres, or the problems of sewerage and waste disposal. The authors' research and fieldwork visits have highlighted such environmental issues as atmospheric pollution in Beijing (where the legendary 'Beijing Throat', is a local hazard from the combination of fine loess dust and vehicle exhaust pollution, so problematic that staff of the British embassy have their residences above the eighth floor of their high rise blocks!), watercourse pollution in Nanjing and Suzhou Creek in Shanghai, plus severe traffic pollution in Shanghai and Guangzhou, and (in the new

Special Administrative Region (SAR) local concerns over the once 'Fragrant Harbour' of Hong Kong. In addition, colleagues from the Institute of Economic Geography of the Chinese Academy of Sciences have highlighted such issues as high energy consumption and the control of pollution from industrial enterprises in Beijing, given that local government lacks the political power of such enterprises.

Such local issues as these were once regarded as just that – local issues. It is increasingly recognised, however, that local urban issues have a much wider impact due to their severity and scale. At the national level, therefore, it is the urban dwellers who are most responsible for high energy use, food consumption, industrial and traffic pollution, resource depletion and other ecological tramplings as they are encouraged to pursue high levels of consumption, production and exchange. For example, in the key area of water, up to 80 per cent of urban surface water is reckoned to be polluted, mainly by ammonia and nitrogen. Concerns were recently expressed by a local scientist about severe pollution of the Yangtze River, which is threatening the entire basin ecology. 70 per cent of this pollution emanates from Chongqing, which discharges most of its sewage directly into the river without treatment. Further, only 40 per cent of its industrial waste meets national standards. It was only after it became a municipality in 1997, under direct control of Central Government that Chongqing's first waste disposal plant was built (*South China Morning Post*, 7-4-1998). The article actually led to an editorial in this influential newspaper, noting that the Yangtze was vital to the future of China.

The Annual Report of the National Environmental Protection Agency (NEPA, as was; now upgraded to the State Environmental Protection Agency, SEPA), made public on June 7,1997 stated that: 'In 1996, pollution continued to develop in the cities, while also spreading throughout the countryside.' According to the report, respiratory diseases were the joint main cause of death in urban areas, with 0.91 deaths per thousand. The cancer rate was 1.31 deaths per 1,000. The study declared that both respiratory diseases and cancer were attributed partially to environmental pollution. The report admitted that China's air quality has continued to fall well below World Health Organisation standards. More recently, NEPA released the results of the first comparative air quality study in the mainland's 18 largest cities (*South China Morning Post*, 13-1-1998). The data showed that air quality failed to meet even minimal standards in Beijing, Guangzhou, Qingdao, Tianjin and Zhenghzhou, and represented a health risk for infants, the sick and the elderly. Residents of these five cities suffering from 'weaker constitutions' – heart ailments, asthma or other respiratory diseases – would suffer from prolonged exposure to breathing the air. Three cities – Hefei, Shenzhen and Xiamen – were the cleanest of the group. While NEPA had previously classified Beijing as the country's most polluted city, the various local authorities refused to release their own air quality reports, saying that work on air monitoring was still underway and no decision had been taken on when the data might be released. In descending order (best to worst), the rankings of NEPA were:

1. Shenzhen
2. Xiamen
3. Hefei
4. Zhuhai
5. Fuzhou
6. Nanning
7. Dalian
8. Chongqing
9. Wuhan
10. Hangzhou
11. Shanghai
12. Nanjing
13. Shenyang
14. Qingdao
15. Tianjin
16. Guangzhou
17. Zhengzhou
18. Beijing.

The next section will explore further what has been done to tackle the urban aspects of the environmental problem. At the regional level, Cook has developed the basic typology of Table 9.1, based on the work of Zhao Songqiao (1994). Based on a seven-fold subdivision of China, the Table shows that the combination of climatic, biogeographic and human factors lead to specific spatial concentrations of environmental pressures (apart from the unlisted deforestation, which is more of a national problem throughout). It is the ancient heartland of North China for which the list is longest, with periodic drought, being highlighted for example by John Gittings who referred to the 'danger signal' of China's worsening water resources, in which 'The Yellow River is drying up so often that it may become an inland waterway' (Gittings, 1996, p.15). And yet, paradoxically, because of deposition of silt on the bed of the Huang He (Yellow River), which is raising its level ever upwards relative to the Plain, when seasonal conditions are appropriate, 'the danger of a catastrophic flood still exists, and is even increasing' (Zhao, op.cit., p.150).

In other regions, the list may not be as long, but the pressures are nonetheless, severe. Thus Inner Mongolia (Nei Monggol) also suffers from drought and, on the Ordos Plateau, largely via 'ruthless' cultivation in the Qing era, and more recent bad management during the Great Leap Forward and the Cultural Revolution (Zhao, op.cit., p.159). Rats are a problem here, as they are on the Tibetan Plateau and in the pastoral area of the NW.

Table 9.1 Regional Environmental Pressures

Region	Main Environmental Pressures
1. Temperate Humid and Subhumid Northeast China	Water pollution; Soil pollution; Frost.
2. Warm Temperate Humid and Subhumid North China	Water pollution; Soil pollution; Lowering of groundwater table; Drought; Desertification; Floods; Soil erosion (Loess Plateau); Locusts (North China Plain); Salinisation (North China Plain); Tidal waves.
3. Subtropical Humid Central and South China	Air pollution; Frost; Drought; Floods; Soil erosion (Mountains); Leaching (South West); Tidal waves and tsunami.
4. Tropical Humid South China	Typhoons; Frost; Floods; Soil Erosion (Mountains); Leaching; Earthquakes and avalanches (Mountains).
5. Temperate Inner Mongolia Grasslands	Drought; Desertification (Ordos Plateau); Rats.
6. Temperate and Warm Temperate Desert of Northwest China	Drought; Salinisation; Rats (Pastoral Area).
7. Tibetan Plateau	Frost; Hailstorms; Rats.

Soil leaching of nutrients is more associated with sub-tropical or tropical conditions towards the South or South East, while the South East coast is prone to the typhoon season of summer and autumn, especially July to September. Despite the warm conditions in the latter areas, frosts can be a problem, and a threat to the crops of tea, citrus fruits and rubber trees. Salinisation (salt deposits building up at or near the surface of the soil) is an issue which affects up to one-fifth of China's farmland, especially the oases of the Tarim River in the arid Northwest, the middle reaches of the Yellow River, and along the coastal North China Plain where 'the interplay of natural conditions and human impacts also creates a serious salinisation problem' (ibid., p.160). The 'human impacts' are also evident in the various types of water, soil and air pollution which have a particularly serious impact in Northeast China plus subtropical humid Central and South China, especially in the Southwest where, apart from Chongqing referred to above, Guiyang and other urban areas also suffer from acid rain. And finally, there is the intense debate about the Three Gorges project which is briefly summarised below.

Across the country:

'China experiences virtually every type of environmental degradation and the situation is worsening. As a poor and populous country undergoing rapid economic changes China's environment is facing a double threat. On the one hand, problems commonly found in an underdeveloped agricultural society such as soil erosion, deforestation and desertification are becoming increasingly critical; on the other, industrial growth has led to severe pollution' (Edmonds, 1994b, p.156).

Vaclav Smil in his writings is even more alarming and points up the catastrophe to which China is heading (e.g. Smil, 1984; Smil, 1993). Both Edmonds and Smil link environmental issues to that of population growth, but note that it is not just numbers of people that are important, instead it is lifestyles, and also ideology. Muldavin, for example, in his long-term analysis of environmental degradation in Heilongjiang presents a resounding critique of the impact of market forces on the environment (see Box 9.1). To him, the 'communal capital' built up in the Maoist era has been overmined in the Dengist period, and the ensuing environmental deterioration is very much due to the flaws of the market approach.

Across China, environmental problems include:

- Increase in soil degradation: there is a loss of organic matter and fertility due to such factors as triple cropping and rice monoculture combined with poor drainage. This lowers growth potential in paddy fields.
- Problems due to poor agricultural practices, including '*irrational use*' of agricultural chemicals according to SEPA in its report for 1997 (*China Daily*, 4-6-1998); a point repeated in the review of 1998 (Li, 1999, p.14). Up to one-fifth of irrigated crop land – especially in interior marginal lands of Ningxia, Xinjiang and Nei Monggol and the North China Plain – may be salinised.
- Soil erosion and vegetation loss, partly related to lack of forest cover (officially estimated at just under 14 per cent (*China Daily*, 4-6-1998, op.cit.), compared to the thirty per cent need noted above) and farming practices in marginal areas such as on steep slopes for example. These issues are being tackled via a range of measures including tree planting – the 'Three Norths Shelter Project', for instance, is a 200,000 km^2 shelter belt including shrubs and grasslands, not just trees, to halt soil erosion in Shaanxi, desertification in Nei Monggol and protect Beijing – while the 'Obligatory Tree Planting Programme' has from 1981 obliged all Chinese citizens aged 11 and over to plant 3–5 trees each year or do some other afforestation work. Such measures will be assessed in the following section.
- Increased desertification. Of the total area of desertified land, 197,000 km^2, 38 per cent has been desertified in the last century, and another 137,000 are in the category of 'latent desertified lands'. Even more

---

Box 9.1 Environmental Deterioration in Heilongjiang

Long-term research by Joshua Muldavin has focused on 'the great northern granary' of Heilongjiang, where grain production is less than 100 years old, and single-season crop production only is feasible given the hard winters of the province. Muldavin develops a critical analysis which contrasts the favourable Maoist legacy of what he terms 'communal capital' with its recent 'mining' in the Dengist period, and the problems associated with the 'invisible hand' of the market. Due to such factors as intensification of land use and increasing size of herds, the outcomes include:

- rapid decline in overall soil fertility in some counties
- increased rate of organic matter decline in the reform period
- 'Salinization, ground water pollution, and micronutrient deficiencies' (Muldavin, 1997, p.591)
- accelerating sodic alkalinisation and desertification
- short-term production gains but long-term problems of sodic alkalinisation
- increased patriarchal domination of decision-making
- a riskier production environment requiring peasants to 'utilize practices they know undermine long-term sustainability' (Muldavin, 1996, p.300)
- increased disrepair in basic infrastructure of reservoirs, dikes, irrigation canals, and tree planting
- rapid increase in so-called 'natural disasters' at the local level as the protection afforded by tree-breaks, for example, is reduced, although there is also an element of seeking to win resources from State authorities by over-declaring such disasters
- inability to organise previously collective enterprises for, say, building a levee in Hesheng Village, has led to inappropriate yearly labour, the results of which are washed away by annual flooding, leading to demoralisation, eventual impoverishment of the Village and enhanced out-migration

In sum, Muldavin argues that such issues are undermining the legitimacy of the state, especially at the local, rather than central level, with rural unrest spreading in response to the wide range of problems associated with the reforms. He calls for 'locally-based collective action and long-term production strategies [which] must be promoted if the difficult problems of sustainability are to be resolved' (Muldavin, 1997, op.cit. p.607).

Sources: Muldavin, J.S.S. (1996), 'Impact of Reform on Environmental Sustainability in Rural China', *Journal of Contemporary Asia*, 26, 3, pp.289–321.

Muldavin, J.S.S. (1997), 'Environmental Degradation in Heilongjiang: Policy Reform and Agrarian Dynamics in China's New Hybrid Economy', *Annals of the Association of American Geographers*, 87, 4, pp.579–613.

seriously, 90 per cent of grassland 'has been or is being degraded', and the area of degradation is increasing by two million hectares per annum (ibid.).

- Loss of valuable agricultural land, especially in the South-East and other coastal areas – the emphasis on small township enterprises, the creation of development zones and the spread of cities generally is causing a small but significant dent in China's small percentage of agricultural land, usually in the most overcrowded areas where food needs are greatest.

- Increased risk of floods. It is estimated that the average area affected by floods is 68 per cent more than in the 1950s, and dramatic media reports have highlighted floods in the late 1990s. In summer 1998, Vice-Premier Wen Jiabao reported to the CPC Standing Committee on August 26 that 29 of China's provinces, regions and cities had suffered varying degrees of flooding, according to statistics up to Aug. 22. The floods affected 8,150 hectares of land and some 223 million people, with 3,004 killed (1,320 in the Yangtze River area), and 4.97 million houses collapsed. Direct economic losses of the country are 166.6 billion yuan. The worst hit areas were Jiangxi, Hunan, Hubei, Heilongjiang and Jilin provinces (*Beijing Review*, September 14th–twentieth, 1998). At the time of writing, more floods are expected in summer 1999, especially on the Yangtze (Gittings, 1999).

To deal with such problems, China has some mega schemes, including the controversial Three Gorges Dam Project to create a huge dam on the Chang Jiang (Yangtze), with the green light finally being given in 1992 after years of debate. Box 9.2 provides details, but we can note here that the arguments for and against will continue for many years, and if the environmental consequences are as severe as some predict, the outcomes could be calamitous. The dam is very much associated with Li Peng, and an interesting turn in 1999 has been the rise in internal debate concerning the dam. For example, a critical article was published in the February 1999 issue of the Chinese journal *Strategy and Management*, which has close ties with the Government and military, while concerns over corruption, have led to calls for Western consultants to be employed, rather than local consultants, to check safety issues. The writer Dai Qing is a noted opponent – 'an independent thinker with an open, flexible mind who dares to express her opinions' (Topping, 1998, p.xxv). To commemorate the 10th anniversary of the temporary shelving of the project in 1989, she has once again called for a 'free and open debate' plus a halt to foreign funding and support (*South China Morning Post*, 7-4-1999). Not that this is the only mega project – there are also many other such attempts to control nature, including the proposal to divert water from the Yangtze to the Huang He to resolve water shortages in the North.

In addition to these perennial issues of soil and water, there are also modern issues with which to contend. For example, industrial pollution is a

Box 9.2 The Three Gorges Dam Project

The Sanxia (Three Gorges) Dam Project was first suggested by Sun Yat-Sen in the early 1920s. Years later, Mao gave the project his wholehearted support and the 1950s witnessed immense research into the possibilities of holding back 'Wushan's clouds and rain'. The financial cost was deemed too high, however, and it was not until the 1980s that the plan was resurrected. By this time the huge investment in Pudong (see Chapter 7) was under way, and Shanghai was being rapidly developed as the 'dragon head' of the entire Yangtze development project. The dam is regarded by the Chinese authorities as essential to solve the energy shortages of the Shanghai area and the flood danger to the lower Yangtze. It will also quintuple river freight traffic and enable Chongqing's port facilities to grow further and faster, with 10,000 ton vessels being able to sail from Shanghai to Chongqing. This will ease the strain upon the overstretched railway system.

The sheer scale of the project is breathtaking. This is the biggest dam to be built, 2 kilometres long and 188 metres high, creating a lake 603 km (375 miles) long with a water level of 175 metres. The historic first phase was completed in November 1997 with the river being dammed. Electricity will be produced in 2003 and the project completed by 2009. HEP production will be 18 Gigawatts p.a., the equivalent of 18 nuclear power stations or the burning of 100 million tonnes of coal. This will meet 11 per cent of China's total energy needs. Total cost is 90 billion Yuan. At least 1.2 million people (some say 1.9 million) are being relocated, with 103,000 resettled by year end 1997. Ten towns are being flooded, archaeological sites will be inundated, and rare species of flora and fauna adversely affected.

Chinese officials suggest that without the dam, in a major flood similar to those of the past, 'over 600 million hectares of high-yield farmland would be flooded and the lives of some 5 million residents would be in jeopardy' (Hing Qingyu, Yangtze River Water Conservation Committee, in Pang Bo, 1998). Similarly, without its HEP, the equivalent burning of coal would produce 370,000 tonnes of NO_x, two million tonnes of SO_2 and 10,000 tonnes of CO (Zhoa Bian, 1998). The dam will thus reduce the risk of acid rain, 'help curb the global greenhouse effect and thus contribute to environmental protection' (Wei Tingcheng, State Council Three Gorges Construction Committee, cited in Zhoa Bian, op.cit.). Farming incomes in the area affected were half the national average and so the resettlement process is viewed as 'providing ... a historical opportunity to move from poverty to wealth' and the migrants 'will be guaranteed a happy and peaceful life' (Wu Bian, 1997).

In contrast, 'This is the most socially and environmentally destructive infrastructure project in the world today' according to Owen Lammers,

Three Gorges Campaign Manager for the International Rivers Network (cited in Fisher, 1996). The internal critic Dai Qing is similarly scathing (Dai Qing, 1998). And so, for example, the health of millions of people downstream will be endangered by raw sewage or toxic waste pumped into the reservoir or from the 657 inundated factories which will not have been cleaned. Upstream, 500,000 people would be threatened by backwash from the reservoir in the event of a flood, while sedimentation and siltation might not only clog up the reservoir itself, but could also lead to Chongqing's harbour being unusable. The rare white dolphin, giant salamander, and other animals are all under threat from siltation and the reduction in river flow. The weight of the dam could precipitate an earthquake, leading to massive loss of life in the ensuing flood. As for those resettled, 'They are depressed by the economic loss they will suffer and disturbed by the inevitable break-up of the emotional ties they have had with this land' (Wu Ming, 1998).

Sources: now voluminous, but include: Dai Qing (1998), *The River Dragon Has Come! The Three Gorges Dam and the Fate of China's Yangtze River and its People*, (edited by Thibodeau and Williams; tr. Yi Ming), New York: M.E.Sharpe.

Fisher, A. (1996), 'China's Three Gorges Dam: Is the 'Progress' Worth the Ecological Risk?', *Popular Science*, August.

Pang Bo (1998), 'Dam Needed to Prevent Flood', *Chinafrica*, 85, January.

Wu Bian (1997), 'Damming of the Yangtse', *Beijing Review*, 15th December.

Wu Ming (1998), '*Resettlement Problems of the Three Gorges Dam*', www.

Zhou Bian (1998), 'Hydropower to Cut Greenhouse Gases', *Chinafrica*, 85, January.

severe problem, and ranges from contamination of water channels to air and land pollution. Thus, for example, the total volume of waste water reached 41.6 billion tons in 1997, 54.6 per cent from industry but by 1998, this had dropped a little to 39.5 billion tons, 50.9 per cent from industry (Li, 1999, op.cit., p.16). This might reflect a downturn in the economy in 1998, resulting mainly from the Asian Financial Crisis, rather than positive policies. Eight major river basins (systems) – the Yangtze, Yellow River, Pearl River, Huaihe, Haihe, Luanhe, Liaohe (the last three were 'badly polluted') and Songhuajiang – are contaminated, plus a host of lakes, reservoirs, underground and offshore water. Chinese colleagues emphasise the severe pollution problems of Lanzhou, for example, which, as with other industrial cities surrounded by mountains, is particularly affected by industrial atmospheric pollution in the summer months. In addition, the petrochemical industry in Lanzhou has polluted the Huang He (Yellow River) to such an extent that is currently black in that vicinity!

An increasing problem is pollution from the rural township enterprises which were, until recently, subject to little environmental control. Similarly, industry contributes to nearly 80 per cent of air pollution, especially via coal burning, dealt with presently, while increasing vehicular traffic is contributing to a growing smog problem and the release of CO, hydrocarbons and NO_x among others into the atmosphere. Even the magazine, *Business Beijing*, which emphasises business opportunities rather than the negative features of development, carried several critical articles in its February 1999 issue. Among other stories it noted that Premier Zhu Rongji has joked to the Mayor of Beijing that the latter has taken five years off his (Zhu's) life through being unable to control the capital's pollution! Although the authorities are taking considerable steps to reduce pollution – for instance via banning the heavily polluting 'Miandi' (yellow mini-cabs, shaped like small loaves) in Beijing, and are having some successes nationally, the pace of industrialisation usually outstrips their efforts. In addition, there seems to be an increasing import of noxious industries into China, as Taiwan and Hong Kong in particular export their own pollution problems to the less-regulated mainland.

In total, Chinese industry in 1998 produced 13.35 million tons of soot (7.58 million in 1996) and, in 1996, 5.62 million tons of industrial fly ash – but pollution created by the township enterprises remained serious (*Beijing Review*, 22-10-1996 and 12-7-1999). Sulphur dioxide, along with nitrogen dioxide, is the chief cause of acid rain, and by 1998 SO_2 emissions were 20.87 million tons (*Beijing Review*, 12-7-1999, op.cit.), albeit a decline from 23.46 million tons in 1997, of which nearly four-fifths was from industry (*China Daily*, 4-6-1998, op.cit.). Coal burning is a major source of particulates and sulphur dioxide. According to Edmonds (1994a), China's fuel conversion efficiency is low at 28 per cent compared to, say, 40–55 per cent in North America and 60 per cent in Japan. Coal is still a major source of power; in 1991, China used 1.6 billion tonnes, and by 1997, coal consumption was 73.5 per cent of total energy consumption (*China Statistical Yearbook 1998*, p.251). As a result of coal burning and vehicle pollution, the Total Suspended Particle (TSP) index is high across the north of the country, and in addition, global atmospheric tests have revealed that the five cities of Beijing, Shenyang, Xian, Shanghai and Guangzhou were among the 10 cities world-wide with the highest levels of dust pollution. During the 1990s, the areas affected by acid rain spread in coverage from 1.7 million km^2 centred on south-west China to take in an additional 1 million km^2 south of the Yangtze River, the eastern parts of the Qinghai-Tibet Plateau, most areas of the Sichuan Basin, Changsha in Hunan Province, and Ganzhou and Nanchang in Jiangxi Province (*China Daily*, 4-5-1999). In 1998, 'The problem of acid rain remained serious' (Li, 1999, op.cit., p.15).

Less than one per cent of China's 600 plus cities meet state first class air quality standards. It is estimated that coal use will double from 1980–2000, contributing to problems of global warming. A switch to HEP, however, brings other problems, as we have seen above with regards to the Sanxia Dam, and nuclear power is equally problematic. One small ray of hope comes from the development of biogas, with 500,000 family biogas units being constructed annually since the 1980s. This alternative continues the ancient tradition of harmony with nature and perhaps China needs to keep returning to its past for ideas about ecological policy today.

There is also the issue of waste disposal. In 1991 only 29 per cent of the 320 million tons of industrial solid waste was recycled, and the target is 37 per cent by 2000. SEPA showed that the quantity of industrial solid waste was 800 million tons by 1998, of which nearly 10 million tons was 'dangerous waste' (ibid.), and although in 1997 the larger enterprises 'at and above county level' reused 45 per cent of this solid waste, this leaves a massive amount, some of it hazardous, to pollute the land and water courses (*China Daily*, 4-6-1998, op.cit.). Likewise only 'around a quarter of urban sewage will be treated by the year 2000' (Qu Geping, 1992, p.64). 'Night soil' collection is diminishing fast and the pace of economic development means that the content of the average dwellers' dustbin is likely to contain far more non-biodegradable material than 10 years ago, especially in the cities. Only 2.3 per cent of urban refuse is treated and despite building of incinerators, for example, it is once again difficult to keep pace with the problem. Edmonds quotes one prediction that 'China's urban rubbish will have annual growth rates of 8 to 10 per cent between 1980 and 2000' (Edmonds, 1994b, p.170), and by 1997 the total amount of garbage reached 140 million tons (*China Daily*, 4-6-1998, op.cit.). Edmonds also notes that, by 1991 alone, control of solid wastes cost China over 672 million yuan, 11 per cent of the fund spent on pollution control. Increasingly, local authorities rather than central government will be expected to come up with these funds, which they are likely to be unable or unwilling to do.

Finally in this detailing of environmental problems, 'natural' disasters also occur. The Tangshan earthquake of 1978 resulted in severe loss of life, but traditional Chinese earthquake prediction which included study of animal behaviour was reckoned to be effective in earthquake prediction. Whether that is still true remains to be seen and as we have seen, the Sanxia Dam may precipitate an earthquake. Drought is most likely in the North China Plain, North-East or in Sichuan. This is contributed to via human action/ inaction and the process of desertification noted above. Rainfall in the north in June/ August 1997 was down 50–70 per cent on the norm, causing a severe reduction in grain yields (*China Daily*, 4-6-1998). Further, China's biodiversity is under severe threat, with 1000 plant species on the brink of extinction, twenty-eight 'extremely endangered' and seven thought 'likely to be extinct'. 433 breeds of animal are also endangered, according to SEPA (ibid.). Finally, '(I)n 1998, three major calamities took place in succession in the country: flooding in the Yangtze, Songhuajiang and Nenjiang river basins, red tides in offshore waters and sandstorms in Inner Mongolia and Xinjiang' (Li, 1999, p.18). In sum, therefore, this section has demonstrated the huge pressures on China's environment, and the severity of the problems China faces.

Table 9.2 National Environmental Initiatives

Environmental Protection Law (for trial implementation) promulgated in 1979.

Environmental Protection Law (including concept of 'harmonious development') promulgated in 1989.

Other Laws have been promulgated on Water Pollution, Air Pollution, Pollution by Solid Wastes, Land Administration, Protection of Wild Animals etc.; plus more than thirty administrative decrees on a range of pollution measures and environmental protection, and more than 600 local laws on the latter.

National Environmental Protection Agency (NEPA) established as independent quasi-ministerial body in 1984. Became a full ministry in 1998 'to strengthen control over green issues', as the State Environmental Protection Administration (SEPA).

The National Plan for Ecological Environment Construction approved and promulgated by the State Council in 1998.

Nature Reserves first established 1956; massive expansion from 1980s to 136 by end 1998.

China now has (1999) 15 Biosphere Protection Zones.

China joined the World Health Organisation's Global Environmental Monitoring System in 1980.

Agenda 21 White Paper presented in July 1994; includes proposals for Office for the Conservation of Diversity to co-ordinate conservation and research.

Chinese Academy of Sciences have established:

Institute of Applied Ecology in 1954

Commission of Integrated Survey of National Resources (CISNAR) in 1956

Experimental zones for comprehensive agricultural management to cope with problems of drought, salinisation and wind-sand in the North China Plain, Loess Plateau, Manchuria and other areas from the 1960s

Institute of Mountain Hazards and Environment in 1966

Institute of Desert Research in 1978 (forerunner 1959)

Research Center for Eco-Environmental Sciences (RCEES) in 1975; focus amended in 1986

Institute of Remote Sensing Applications in 1980

Center for Sustainable Development Issues Studies in 1990s

Bureau of Co-ordinated Development of Nature and Society in 1990s.

Ecological Society of China established a Speciality Committee on Urban Ecology in 1984.

Sources: Bradbury, I. and Kirkby, R. (1995), 'Prospects for Conservation in China', *Ecos*, 16, 3, 4, pp.64–71.

Chinese Academy of Sciences (1995), Brief Account of the Chinese Academy of Sciences, Beijing.

Edmonds, R.L. (1994a), Patterns of China's Lost Harmony, London: Routledge, Chapter 10, pp.228–260.

Information Office of the State Council (1996), Environmental Protection in China, Beijing.

Li Wen (1999), 'China's Environmental Conditions in 1998', Beijing Review, 12th July, pp.13–18.

Official Briefing (1998), Beijing.

What has already been done: policies and exemplars

In the face of such issues, there is no doubt that the Chinese government has made tremendous strides in recent years in the broad field of environmental policy. Table 9.2 illustrates some of the policy and research initiatives which have been developed since 1949 but especially since the reform era of recent decades. Thus, as the Table shows, an Environmental Protection Law was introduced on a trial implementation basis in 1979 and a fuller, updated law promulgated in 1989. The latter incorporates the concept of *'harmonious development'* (sustainable development) described 'as a cycle in which physical or 'natural rebirth and economic rebirth processes work together' (Liu Tanqi quoted in Edmonds, 1994a, p.232). Many other Laws and administrative decrees have also been passed, and the new SEPA is heavily involved in legislation and co-ordination of initiatives in this area. In 1998, the National Plan for Ecological Environment Construction was issued by the State Council. The principle of 'the polluter pays' is increasingly applied, and there is evidence to suggest that pollution has been considerably reduced in a number of locations, including the cities of Benxi and Baotou for example. Similarly, the prestigious Chinese Academy of Sciences is stimulating multidisciplinary and interdisciplinary research via the creation of the Institutes, Bureau and 'Centers' noted in the Table.

According to Zou Ping, an Associate Research Fellow with the State Council Research Office, the government listed environmental protection as basic national policy for the first time ever in 1983. China then launched its battle against environmental pollution in 1989. However, fund shortages prevented the implementation of a number of badly needed pollution control projects, and thus no major breakthroughs were recorded in harnessing pollution. In 1994, the country introduced Agenda 21 – White Paper on Pollution, the Environment and Development in the 21st Century, which stresses the nation's development strategies.

China's development programme between 1996–2010 features rapid economic growth and continued emphasis on environmental protection. To this end, the Chinese government will strive to control waste water, waste gas, solid waste materials and noise pollution at 1995 levels, and formulate the National Cross-Century Green Project. The goal of the various projects is to amass funding and materials to control pollution in various important areas, including river valleys and areas plagued by environmental problems. According to NEPA (as was), the programme is being implemented in three stages, with the first stage between 1996–2000 focusing on 1,591 projects that will cost 188.8 billion Yuan. The plan features clear-cut proposals for using funds to implement projects.

This total compares with the 150 billion Yuan, for the controversial Three Gorges Project, over a period of 10 years, 15 billion Yuan per year. In contrast, China earmarked 47.6 billion Yuan for environmental protection

213

between 1985–90, a figure representing 0.7 per cent of the nation's total GDP. Respective investments between 1991–3 stood at only 60.3 billion Yuan, 0.73 per cent of total GDP. According to Guo Xiaomin, then deputy director of NEPA's planning department, the figure is still below the 0.85 per cent listed in the state environmental protection plan.

The massive funding for such policies will come, according to Guo, mainly from enterprises and local governments responsible for creating pollution and resulting losses. In addition, China plans to attract $4 billion in foreign investment, domestic funding of 70 billion Yuan, special environmental protection loans from the development bank totalling 5.5 billion Yuan, 1.35 billion Yuan in allocations from central financial departments and 1.9 billion Yuan from local financial departments. The majority of these expenditures will be earmarked for the construction of urban environmental infrastructure.

According to Zou Ping, this monumental programme is regarded as crucial for ensuring China's long-term economic and social development. To him, it shows that China is shouldering responsibilities outlined in international treaties. China is currently passing through a transitory stage from low to medium income levels, a stage at which environmental issues often increase. Therefore, the Chinese people must extend the greatest possible effort to control pollution. Given China's size, solving China's environmental pollution problems equates to reducing global pollution. However, China is in dire need of international cooperation, including technology transfers, international trade and various other forms of assistance needed to solve pollution problems. Foreign investment currently accounts for only 10 per cent of China's total investments in environmental protection. This fact readily indicates the great potential for attracting foreign capital and international assistance. According to other reliable sources, China is actively seeking environmental protection investments far in excess of the aforementioned 188.8 billion Yuan, with projections calling for total funding to reach 450 billion Yuan by the year 2000. Achievement of this ambitious goal will represent not only the highest level of investments in environmental protection since the founding of New China in 1949, but also the largest investment among developing countries.

Examples of positive policies come from around the country. In the Northwest, Qinghai Lake in China's Qinghai province is losing 11 cm a year in water level because of dry weather and biological degradation, according to an international conference held in Beijing in late 1997. Drought and serious soil erosion have caused a major decrease in the flow of the Yellow River, a major source of the lake's water, causing the lake's water level to drop, according to Liu Guanghe, vice-governor of the province. The lake, which lies 3,200 metres above sea level in Qinghai province, is China's largest lake and largest saltwater lake. It is fed by seven rivers. The lake has an average depth of 19 metres and is over 30 metres at the deepest. Liu explained that Qinghai's forest coverage is only 2.59 percent and 330,000 sq. km of land, or 46 per cent of the province's total, suffer from soil erosion. The province has worked out a 15–20 year plan to control soil erosion by planting trees and growing grass and by developing environmentally friendly agriculture and animal husbandry, as well as environmental protection in the areas along the lake (*China Daily*, 21-11-1997).

The Loess Plateau is one of the most seriously water-eroded area in the world and the major source of silt in the Yellow River. Nine tributaries of the Yellow River run through it. An erosion control project there, using World Bank loans, is nearly half through, with 250,000 ha. of water-eroded land treated and 22 million tons of silt dammed. Preliminary assessment by World Bank officials is that the project is helping the affected area to shake off poverty and reduce the silt deposition in the Yellow River (*China Daily*, 22-12-1997). China plans to spend 2.1 billion yuan (253 million US dollars) in eight years on transforming farmland under threat of erosion into steady high-yield fields and on planting trees and grass in the valleys of the nine tributaries. A longer-term plan, currently awaiting approval from the State Council has the target that, by the middle of the next century, more than 80 per cent of soil-erosion areas in the plateau will be rehabilitated, and the amount of silt discharged into the Yellow River will be reduced by 50 per cent. The treatment will focus on a specific area, which is located from Shaanxi's Hekou to Henan's Longmen and covers upstream areas of the Jinghe, Weihe and Luohe rivers. With an abundance of sand and grit, this area discharges 1.4 billion tons of silt into the Yellow River, more than 80 per cent of the total the river receives each year. An amazing 19,097 dams are due to be built in several stages over a fifty-three year period (*Business Weekly*, 6-6-1998).

Box 9.3 and 9.4 give examples of other successes. The first (9.3) gives details of the difficult struggle to preserve that world-wide icon, the Giant Panda. Despite pressures on their habitat it does seem that the line is being held against their extinction. In contrast, 9.4 shows the example of Beijing's endeavours to cope with the growing amount of garbage noted above. These struggles are difficult, however, for it is difficult to keep up with the growing scale of these and other problems noted in the previous section. China's concern to encourage tree-planting for example has been impressive, and the percentage coverage has certainly increased, albeit from what was a very low level. However, local officials, as with other target-setting still have a tendency to exaggerate plantings in order to curry favour with their bosses, while concerns have been expressed about the quality of care provided for the new plantings. Despite the measures taken, as we have seen previously, the problems of desertification and degradation of environmental quality continue to escalate.

The success stories have a downside, therefore, which is the question of change at the local or regional level. Laws can be passed and research can

Box 9.3 Saving Endangered Species: The Giant Panda

Perhaps the supreme global icon for the threat to endangered species (rivalled only by the tiger or whale), and symbol of the Worldwide Fund for Nature (WWF), the Giant Panda now has estimated numbers of only 800–1000 in the wild (compared to estimates of 1200–1400 in the 1970s) and around 100 in zoos and breeding centres. First referred to in the ancient *Classics of the Seas and Mountains* around 2,500 years ago, the Giant Panda briefly became the leading target for white hunters in the twentieth century before becoming the *sine qua non* of any zoo worth its salt. The creature once roamed over an area estimated to be four times that of its present living space, mainly in Sichuan province (plus Gansu and Shaanxi), and has been under continual pressure from human encroachment. It requires huge quantities of bamboo to survive therefore it needs a large territory in which to roam for food , while the female's time in season is extremely short, two to three days only, adding to the pressure for survival.

In the late 1980s the WWF raised £1 million for an urgent set of projects to save the species, and has worked closely with the Chinese Ministry of Forestry to produce a 'Management Plan for the Giant Panda and its Habitat' which established better practice plus 14 new reserves (*'bamboo corridors'*) to allow previously isolated groups of pandas to communicate and interbreed. The biggest panda reserve is in Sichuan at Wolong, which also contains a research laboratory and breeding centre. Research on panda ecology and population dynamics, for example, has been ongoing since 1970, and of the bamboo forests since 1984, while the first successful births in the breeding centre were in 1991, but there was only a 50 per cent survival rate, although this is improving. The emphasis in the reserve is on monitoring, training and raising of environmental awareness among staff, visitors and the local population.

Despite undoubted progress, the reserve is under heavy pressure from local people engaged in their own struggle for survival. 4000 people live in the reserve area itself and many more in surrounding areas. The search for firewood and timber for house-building has led to 'Massive deforestation ... which has resulted in hillsides being stripped of vegetation. Any attempts at re-afforestation have usually failed as trees get washed away. Has resulted in some large floods.' (Chapman, 1993, p.1). Snares are also a problem, snares targeted at other animals but dangerous also to the panda. A stuffed panda is worth US$200,000 in Japan, however, and despite the death penalty some may risk poaching the Giant Panda itself. Management practices in the early 1990s were also poor, with the reserve guards receiving insufficient food and clothing allowances, plus tents, to facilitate treks to catch poachers, while the guards could be disciplined if they reported poaching as they would then be regarded as not having done their job properly for poaching to have occurred! The Chinese were informed of these issues by the WWF representative and replaced the incumbent leader responsible (ibid.).

In 1992, 'The National Conservation Program for the Giant Panda and it's Habitat', received final approval in 1992 from the State Council of China. This is a broad-based ten-year programme in conjunction with the WWF which, aims to integrate environmental conservation with the needs of the people in the three rural provinces where pandas are found. New reserves have been established, and old ones upgraded; and a central office is up and running at the ministry of forestry to oversee the program:

'But, the financial cost is high. For the ten years, the program has a budget of RMB 300 million (US$ 34 million), of which one-fifth will be provided by the Chinese government. The Ministry of Forestry has to secure the remaining funds, and WWF has agreed to help it raise them. WWF has, to date, spent a total of SFR6 million (US$4.3 million) on panda conservation in China', according to the WWF Factsheet from Hong Kong (1998).

Sources: Baron, W.M. and Jhaveri, N. (n.d.), *Wolong: A Haven for Animals*, WWF.
Chapman, S. (1993), *Panda Project*, China, WWF.
Laidler, K. (1987), 'Living Dangerously', *The Guardian*, 27 October.
WWF (1992), *International Country Profile: China*.
WWF (1994), *International Project Programme (Asia/Pacific Programme)*.
WWF (1998), WWF Hong Kong, Factsheet 49.

Box 9.4 Coping With Beijing's Waste

In 1950, the new government decided to remove the capital's rubbish tips that had been steadily accumulating since the nineteenth century. 7,000 labourers, 800 trucks and 30,000 animal-drawn carts were mobilised and in 61 days an estimated 600,000 tons of rubbish were removed from the existing inner city area. This was, however, merely to new sites in what were then the rural outer suburbs. As Beijing grew, the rubbish piles were continually resited further and further out into the new outer suburbs – all the time growing in size. By the mid-1980s, satellite remote sensors established the presence of 4,700 rubbish dumps, each with a minimum diameter of 50 metres, in a giant ring around the city's outskirts. In the 1950s, Beijing generated two million tons of household rubbish a year. Now, it is at least double that, with the much enlarged city generating an estimated 11,000 tons of waste a day. Just over two per cent is processed. The municipal administration has therefore launched an ambitious waste disposal program to treat 60 per cent of waste by the end of the century.

The first step was a 60 hectare landfill site developed with loans from the World Bank at a location 35 kms from the city proper. This was opened in mid-1994, with a daily handling capacity of 2,000 tons. Special trucks pick up the garbage around the city, spray it to kill germs and compress it into a two-metre-high layer for delivery to the site. Waterproof sealant has been applied to the site foundations to prevent toxic liquids leeching out to penetrate the underground water supply. Deep wells have been sunk at regular points nearby so that water samples can be taken constantly to check for contamination. With a projected capacity of nine million cubic meters, at present rates this facility will reach saturation point in 2005, whence an artificial hill 40 metres high will be planted with trees and the site turned into a park. But this is still just a more advanced version of the old method of permanent rubbish dumps around the capital, and Beijing environmental experts acknowledge that it is only a stopgap measure. The future, they say, lies in finding ways to either eliminate the waste or convert it back into something useful.

In March 1995 a small pilot plant opened to convert selected rubbish into organic compound fertiliser through a process of repeated fermentation and magnetic separation. In July 1996, a pioneer furnace burning rubbish was opened using local technology supplied by the Beijing Modern Rubbish Disposal Engineering Co. Using a core sintering technique it aims to create cinders to be used as a light building material. Waste gases are scrubbed to prevent air pollution. The facility has a daily capacity of 500 tons. However, officials admit that it will take some time to train the population to sort their waste into readily treatable categories. For the moment, there is a tendency, as in many other countries, to throw away indiscriminately, regarding waste as someone else's problem not your own.

Zhang Guolin, Director of the Planning and Infrastructure Protection Agency in the Beijing Municipal Government, says the city invested 1.3 billion Yuan in domestic rubbish disposal in the period 1991–5 to render garbage harmless. As a result, the rubbish that met the criterion of 'no air nor water pollution threat' had risen from two per cent in 1993 to 21.2 per cent in 1995. Two major new landfill sites are currently being developed with a DM39 million grant from the German Government and a 236 million Yuan investment by central government. In the next five years, said Zhang, three compost-making factories, four comprehensive recycling centres and two power stations burning rubbish to provide the necessary heat, are due for completion. These will cope with the disposal of 2,100 tons of rubbish a day.

Recycling used to be a way of life during the periods of acute shortage up to the 1980s, but affluence has reduced public concern. With rising costs of collection, most plastics, rubber and glass, for example, is now thrown away to add to the waste problem. As Beijing's population continues to swell (to 12.51 million at end 1995, a level not previously expected before 2010), the city has some way to go to catch up with its waste disposal problem.

Source: Author research and interviews, 1996.

be conducted (much of it producing innovative and uniquely Chinese solutions, for stemming desertification, for example) but the overriding emphasis on economic development threatens to overwhelm the environmental regulations which SEPA and others seek to impose. There is much in-fighting within the Chinese bureaucracy, and, for example, 'there is informed speculation that the Academy's [Chinese Academy of Sciences] reservations about the Three Gorges project on the Yangzi could not resist the vested interests of ministries whose principal concerns are with power generation and flood protection' (Bradbury and Kirkby, 1995, p.69). At the regional or local level, environmental pressures interweave with regional contrasts of wealth and poverty to create a situation in which, often, provincial governments either have the resources but lack the political will to grapple with these environmental issues, or have the political will but lack the financial and other resources to deal with them. And so, 'the much feared luan – chaos – could still emerge as the consequence of more fundamental unrest in Chinese society, where economic boom jars increasingly with social and environmental disorder' (Gittings, 1996, op.cit., p.15).

More research is needed on such concerns. Not that the scenario is necessarily all 'doom and gloom'. Economic development can be environmentally costly to achieve, but once achieved, investment in Research and Development can be made to improve energy conservation, anti-pollution measures and so on. However, it is always difficult, if not impossible, for the research process to keep pace with these development pressures, given that most of the available financial and labour resources focus on economic growth rather than its environmental impact. As motor vehicle use in particular increases, the price to be paid for this may be too high, as it seems to be in the West. Not that Chinese authorities are unaware of these and other issues; in Beijing, for example, the Traffic Management Bureau introduced, on 12th February 1996, drastic measures to cut road traffic by almost half, via restrictions on vehicles (except taxis) of one litre or less, and licence plate restrictions for travel on certain dates (Shen Bin, 1996). Intense lobbying began immediately against these measures so their long-term application is in doubt, but, when combined with 'Beijing Master Plan' objectives to increase the small subway length to 90 km, adding another 10 lines to the current 2 (including the loopline) by 2010, there is at least some evidence of a willingness to tackle these problems. Also, recent measures include the banning of the miandi noted above (*China Monitor Special Report*, 1994; *Business Beijing*, January 1996 and February 1999). Nevertheless, 'The prime objective of the plan [Beijing Master Plan] will be to accelerate Beijing's economic development' (China Monitor Special Report, op.cit., p.12), therefore such measures will only be taken if they are seen to complement, or at least not to undermine, the economic targets which are set.

What needs to be done: can the market provide?

The Office of Renewable Resources of the Ministry of the Interior has stated that the domestic recycling industry suffers from outdated facilities and technology and so can not make the most of the resources on offer. The Ministry now encourages more participation by foreign companies with modern recycling technology, especially in setting up export-oriented processing plants. One of the keys to resolution of the worst of China's environmental issues will, therefore, be foreign investment, and also international co-operation. International pressures will also be important, as with other countries. For example, it is becoming clear that China is exporting pollution. On the plains of land-locked Sichuan province, for instance, construction engineers have started work on the Luohuang power station. When finished, its four giant turbines will produce 1,400 megawatts of electricity to help drive China's fast-growing economy. But, as noted in a *New Scientist* article reproduced in the *South China Morning Post* (21-3-1997), while Chinese officials congratulate themselves on completing another step on the road to becoming Asia's next economic miracle, their Japanese counterparts are looking on with trepidation. China's rapid industrialisation is being accompanied by a tremendous rise in air pollution, which Japanese scientists claim is causing acid rain that could be damaging trees in southern Japan.

Across East Asia, as the article notes, fast economic growth, antiquated industrial plants and a lack of environmental regulations are pushing air pollution to record levels. The region now accounts for more than a third of the world's output of sulphur oxide gases. In China, the north-eastern city of Shenyang alone pours out 200,000 tonnes of sulphur oxide a year, equivalent to a quarter of the emissions of the whole of Japan. The US-based Worldwatch Institute estimates that within a decade, China could overtake the US as the world's largest source of air pollution. The problem, says Kishibe Kasumi of Japan's Environmental Agency, is the high sulphur coal that is China's major energy source. The large amounts of sulphur dioxide produced as the coal burns dissolve in rainwater and fall to the ground as sulphuric acid. Nitrogen Oxides, emitted predominantly by car exhausts, also cause acid rain, but sulphur is the main culprit. Old, inefficient technology means that China must burn 50 million tonnes of coal more than a developed country would have to for the same amount of energy. And 50 million tonnes of typical Chinese coal produces 1.4 million tonnes of SO_2.

In Europe, the agreed Convention on Long-Range Transboundary Air Pollution should ensure that over the next 15 years sulphur pollution from factories and power stations drops to about 10 per cent of 1980 levels. Japan is using this Convention as a model for control of pollution in the region. Japan's Environment Agency set up, in 1993, the Acid Deposition

Monitoring Network, which has recruited scientists and institutions throughout East Asia to gather data on pollution levels and acid rain. Scientists from eight countries, from South Korea to Thailand, are exchanging information and co-ordinating research to discover how acid rain is spreading. Japan is deeply concerned about pollution from China, especially from the rapidly industrialising Northeast. 'The spread of pollutants is complicated, but of course winds travel from China to Japan', Ken'ichi Satake, head of acid deposition research at the National Institute for Environmental Studies stated. 'The problem will be worse in the future as China's use of coal grows.'

Researchers at the Institute are setting up a sophisticated computer model to predict what effect China's future emissions of nitrogen and sulphur oxides will have on Japan. The imminent threat of pollution from China has become a major foreign policy issue for Japan and is seriously affecting the country's relations with its giant neighbour. At first, discussion of acid rain was kept out of the official records. But in June 1993, Japan's foreign minister, Kabun Muto, demanded that China either take measures to prevent pollution or risk losing Japanese aid for building power stations. Japan has developed a carrot-and-stick approach. The threat is that it will withdraw some aid if China fails to clean up its pollution. At the same time, its Green Aid Plan offers incentives and technical help to reduce toxic emissions. The Green Aid Plan was launched in 1991 by MITI to help Asia countries overcome their domestic pollution problems. It has become increasingly focused on China's belching power stations and steel mills. In 1993, MITI set up a study group to investigate air and water pollution in China. One of its earliest projects was an experimental flue gas sulphurisation plant at the Huang Tao power station in Shandong province. Mitsubishi Heavy Industries, the Japanese company that built the plant, has since won contracts for three more. Nonetheless, Chinese industry still has a long way to go. 'The amount of anti-pollution equipment which has been installed so far is insignificant', says one Japanese expert. 'But to protect the environment in the future to the standard attained by advanced countries the Chinese have started to consider compulsory installation of cleaning equipment in power stations.'

In September, 1996, the Chinese Government announced it intended to spend up to 320 billion Yuan in the next five years to cut pollution. It claimed that by November 1996 it had shut down 57,000 dirty factories, mainly paper and chemical plants. China is sensitive to western criticism of its environmental record and claims that it has done more to curb pollution than developed countries did in their early days of industrialisation. This sensitivity might well be a necessary element in ensuring that action matches intentions and rhetoric, and in 1998 a new Plan to control sulphur dioxide pollution was introduced, forbidding new coal mines where the sulphur content was more than 3 per cent, and aiming to gradually close, limit or suspend production in those where the sulphur content exceeds that level (Li, 1999, op.cit., p.15). The State Council has demanded that the 175 prefectures and cities in the new control zones in the worst affected areas in southern and central China draft effective plans for substantial reduction of acid rain and sulphur dioxide emissions by 2010 (*China Daily*, 4-5-1999).

Perhaps economic imperatives and the environment can be reconciled. For example, Hu Angang, an environmental studies expert, points out that the environment constitutes a special property owned by the people. Pollution not only damages the environment, but also leads to a decline in actual GDP. 'Controlling environmental pollution is tantamount to improving environmental quality, and in turn leads to a rise in GDP'. After making an in-depth analysis and evaluation of the positive and negative influences the environment has on economic growth, an official with the Organisation of Economic Cooperation and Development (OECD) noted that appropriate environmental policies yield direct output. 'Decreased costs' and 'increased output' resulting from US environmental policies in 1978, for example, were valued at $2.8 billion. According to French estimates, reduced losses resulting from pollution led to an increase of the nation's GDP by 0.7–0.9 per cent. China refrains from considering the functions of environmental protection measures in terms of GDP, but beneficial results are nonetheless included in related growth figures. Assuming no overall environmental deterioration, China's GDP would rise by 1–2 percentage points, a figure now accepted by SEPA (*China Daily*, 4-5-1999).

Despite this, it seems to be the case throughout China that the economy comes first and the quality of the environment a poor second. Obviously, such a situation is found in other countries; the difference with China, however, is that there is a lack of substantial NGO activity at the grassroots. The legacy of Tiananmen, and the transition to the post-Deng era means that the authorities are extremely wary, to say the least, of political activity which smacks of dissent. Other countries have active Friends of the Earth, Greenpeace and other agencies engaged in raising environmental consciousness. China has very few, and they are largely controlled. Although the Chinese government is itself encouraging environmental education, experience elsewhere suggests that such top-down approaches have their limits. The environment is too important to be left to the state. It remains to be seen, therefore, whether China's environment can be improved via state (and market) activity alone. Despite a wide range of measures, 'China continues to face a grim environmental situation' (bid, p.13). In sum, we concur with Ming Wan who recently concluded that:

> 'with greater determination, better choice of technologies, more foreign assistance, and enhanced public awareness, China could do a better job of addressing its environmental problems despite the tremendous challenge it is facing' (Ming Wan, 1998, p.378).

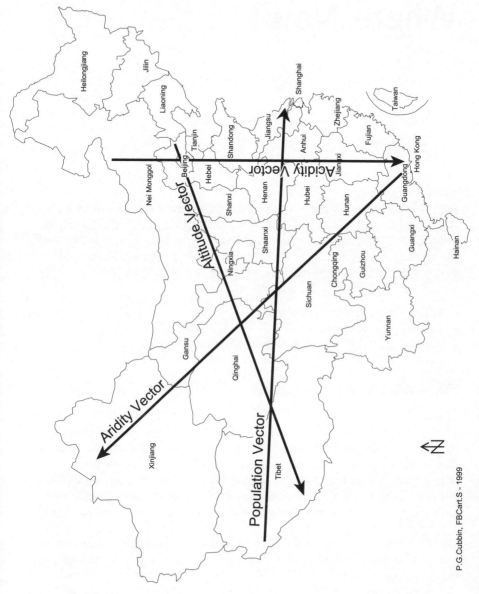

P.G.Cubbin, FBCart.S - 1999

Map 9.1 Key Environmental Vectors

CHAPTER 10

Where Now?

In this final chapter, we have decided to pull together the various elements that have been studied at length in previous chapters via a SWOT analysis, of Strengths, Weaknesses, Opportunities and Threats to China, before using this as the basis for divining the outlines of China's future direction. Given that strengths and opportunities interlink so closely, however, as do weaknesses and threats, the sections are:

• China's strengths and opportunities
• China's weaknesses and threats: internal/ external
• Alternative futures; towards a post-Communist society?

China's strengths and opportunities

Not the least strength of China, both of its people and government, is sheer survivability. Through the revolutions of 1911, 1949 and today, and despite the considerable hardship and suffering that the people have undergone in this welter of constant change, they and the Chinese state have endured. Also, in many ways they have prospered, and China has to date avoided the political break-up and recent economic hardship of the once-proud Soviet Union. In a world where capitalism is now widely regarded as being triumphant and all-powerful, this in itself is no mean feat for a Communist system. If, of course, it is still Communist, and there has been much debate within China and outside as to what type of Communism is now found there. As we have seen in this book, it certainly is what we would call 'Communism with a consumer face'; one in which many millions of people aspire to an ever-increasing level of material prosperity. For example, in the 1990s, Foreign Direct Investment (FDI) poured into the country, helping to underpin the rampant consumerism of China's gold coast, as well as the

224

export-led economic growth which underpins it. China's cities especially are being transformed, as we have described, and impressive new structures are found across the land – but especially in the coastal region, in Shenzhen, Guangzhou, Shanghai, Beijing and other cities.

Despite this rapid transformation, another strength of China is the element of continuity. Based on rich historical traditions, there is a depth to China which can be lacking in other societies. In his previous book, Geoff Murray refers to the legacy of Confucianism, and cites Lucian Pye's observation that 'It could be that no people have ever outdone the Chinese in ascribing model virtues to the state or in deprecating the worth of the individual' (Pye, 1991, cited in Murray, 1998, p.199). What to the Westerner may seem callous indifference to individual human rights, might seem to the Chinese essential to the good of the wider society. However, the CPC may ascribe to itself 'society', and 'the good of society' may be the good of the party rather than the wider mass of the Chinese people. Nonetheless, the CPC does have fifty-eight million members, many of whom do have the wider good of the people at heart if not always in mind.

There is no doubt that, in some ways, the political climate in China is more relaxed than in the Maoist era. Whether Western critics would regard it as true democracy is debatable, but there are undoubted moves towards creating a more democratic system in China that gives an increasing number of people a voice in how the country is run. Elections are now held right down to the village committee level, and there seem to be genuine efforts to provide voters with a choice (e.g. more candidates than there are offices so that the ballot actually means something, even if this still means largely voting on a slate of party-approved names). The National People's Congress, the country's parliament, used to be dismissed in the West as a rubber stamp body with no real power. But if this was the case in the past, it is no longer so. At the first session of the Ninth NPC in March 1998, for example, delegates showed their independence by casting negative ballots, sometimes in significant numbers, on proposals they didn't like or against the election of officials of whom they did not approve. The election of outgoing Prime Minister Li Peng to head the NPC suggests it will have an increasingly large voice in how the country is run,

The same goes for the Chinese People's Political Consultative Conference (CPPCC), the country's top advisory body comprising the 'democratic' (non-communist) political parties and representatives of various professions and intellectual associations (See Table 10.1 for a breakdown of the parties). These democratic parties were founded before the establishment of the People's Republic of China. However, they support the political leadership of the CPC, which has become their historical choice during long years of co-operation and through common struggles. They are independent in organisation, sharing political freedom, organisational independence and legal equality under the Constitution. Relations between the Communist

Party and the democratic parties follow the guideline of 'long-term co-existence and mutual supervision, treating each other with full sincerity and sharing weal or woe'. The democratic parties in China are neither parties out of office nor opposition parties, but parties participating in the discussion and management of state affairs, including participation in state power, decisions on state policies and strategies, discussions about state leadership, management of state affairs, and implementation of state policies, laws and regulations.

Despite the small number of members in these parties, compared to the giant CPC, nonetheless the CPPCC is emerging as a key forum where the issues and complaints from the grassroots can be aired, and acts as an important channel for the Communist leadership to stay in touch with public sentiment across the vast land. The advisory, and the 'supervisory' role of the CPPCC, were enshrined in changes to the constitution in 1993. And, the fact that the CPC top leaders attend sessions of the body to listen and exchange ideas is cited as clear evidence that genuine democracy is beginning to find root in the Chinese political soil.

Table 10.1 Eight Democratic Parties in 1998

Party	Founding Date	Composition	Membership
Revolutionary Committee of Chinese Guomingdang	1948	Guomingdang democrats and other patriots	54,900
China Democratic League	1941	Mid-high-level intellectuals	131,313
China Democratic National Construction Association	1945	Experts in economic fields	71,390
China Association for Promoting Democracy	1945	Intellectuals in education, culture, publishing and science & other professional sectors	66,954
Peasants' and Workers' Democratic Party	1930	Mid-level intellectuals in Public health, science, Culture and education	67,071
China Zhi Gong Dang	1925	Returned overseas Chinese and their relatives + experts with overseas relations	16,000
Jiu San Society	1946	Intellectuals in science, technology, education, Culture	70,576
Taiwan Democratic Self-Government League	1947	Taiwan patriots	1,400

Source: China People's Political Consultative Committee, Beijing.

If China *was* an autocratic 'police state', as many Western commentators have suggested over the past five decades, it seems less so now. The rule of law, although still somewhat weak, is being to permeate many aspects of life. Those facing criminal charges not only have the right to a defence lawyer of their own choosing, but the latter is permitted to participate in court hearings in a way unknown until a few years ago. Citizens who go to court to seek compensation for a civil wrong have a reasonable chance of winning, even if the state is the defendant.

This point is made strongly by Chief Justice Luo Haocai, vice-president of the Supreme People's Court, as well as chairman of the China Zhi Gong Dang Party and CPPCC vice-chairman. He participated actively in drafting the Law on Administrative Procedure, the Law on Administrative Penalties, and the State Compensation Law, which created the system that finally allowed Chinese citizens to sue the government. According to him, 'China used to attach importance to making substantive law, defining and regulating rights and duties, instead of procedural law, whose primary concern is the just and efficient enforcement of the substantive law. Societies living in the dark under a feudal system for an extremely a long time (such as pre-liberation China) had less knowledge about such common sense ideas as procedural democracy and justice. A country remains far away from the ideal of rule of law in the real sense, when it is modernised in regard to substantive law but relatively backward in procedural law. Whether or not a government can exercise its powers exactly, according to well-established procedures, is a sign of its level of legal construction' (*Beijing Review* 15-3-1998).

Now, said Luo, under a new regulation on administrative penalties, when an executive body imposes heavy fines on citizens or withdraws their business licenses, the latter have the right to apply for an open hearing to debate and re-examine the case, according. 'According to the Administrative Procedural Law, citizens have the right to sue executive departments, while the latter have no right of counterclaim. The law also stipulates that it is the defendant, the executive body, who must prove it has acted legally' (ibid.).

This, he sees as a major step forward in a society where for thousands of years 'ordinary people saw government officials as a type of parent. So, logically, how could one sue one's parents? Now the Chinese are learning to shrug off the old belief that government consists of angels immune from temptation to commit crime. In 1995, the courts handled 52,596 cases involving citizens suing the government, and the figure rose to 90,000 in 1997. And the citizens won at least 30 per cent of the time'. Nevertheless the Chief Justice acknowledged that China still has a long way to go to realise the ideal of democracy and rule of law. Obstacles remain to the healthy development of the administrative procedural system. 'For example, there are still many executive departments which hate to be

227

brought to the court as defendant because they see this as something shameful. Quite a number of ordinary Chinese dare not to sue government departments, fearing this will damage their future relations. Some courts hesitate to handle the cases involving administrative law because the executive departments of the same level or higher would always interfere with judicial affairs' (ibid.).

Thus, the state, as represented by the CPC, is still firmly in control and intends to remain so. The question is whether it can really adapt itself to the changing environment in which it has to operate, especially the free flow of ideas that have come in from the outside world along with all the foreign investment and the technological trappings of a modernising society. Certainly, as we have seen in this book, China in its third revolution is attempting to modernise dramatically, seeking to change its structure from a mainly closed and parochial agricultural society to a much more open and increasingly sophisticated urban/industrial one.

A key element in this is, as we have seen in Chapters 2 and 3, the restructuring of state-owned enterprises (SOEs). But some of what is being attempted looks suspiciously like 'capitalism', and raises questions as to what place communism has in future economic and industrial development. We are struck by the essential defensiveness of the convoluted arguments produced by party and government propagandists in trying to explain why it isn't capitalism at all, but socialism with Chinese characteristics. The argument seems to be that as the workers are members of the 'public', then the old Communist principle of 'public ownership' has been retained. Thus, one reads that:

'The joint-stock partnership belongs to public ownership. This is for the following reasons: 1. Labour is already allied, and does not work in an isolated way; 2. Although a person in the enterprise owns a portion of its assets and receives dividends according to this share, the means of production of the enterprise have been socialised; 3. Means of production under the alliance system are owned and used by the public. They create wealth for collective welfare; 4. In the process of enterprise development, public accumulation should be retained, forming inseparable assets. Therefore, the joint-stock partnership is an individual ownership based on public ownership. Alliance is the demarcation line between individual and private ownership' (*Beijing Review*, 4-5-1998).

One of the strengths of China is that such models are being tried and tested to provide new opportunities for alternative forms of partnership between the private and public sectors, albeit if logic has to be strangled in the process, as shown in here. However, what we increasingly find is that the strengths are riddled with contradictions, and the opportunities are double-edged. Thus, SOE restructuring is an economic necessity, but throws up the problem of unemployment; investment has to be spatially concentrated for economic efficiency and effectiveness but contributes to regional disparities; the Single Child Family Programme is a major element in demographic 'restructuring' but gives rise to the problems of 'little emperors' and a growing unwillingness or inability of families to look after the growing numbers of elderly population as was once *de rigeur*; and the authorities feel obliged to focus on the successes of the reforms in order to keep them on track and maintain their own position, while at the same time many people are losing faith in the authorities' ability to deal with the growing environmental issues, crime and joblessness discussed in previous chapters.

The latter is shown by the 'spin' of the state media which still maintains the traditional 'look for a silver lining' approach to any social problem in China, as evidenced by the following: 'Only a decade ago, unemployment was still shameful in the eyes of common Chinese workers, who believed that only people who made major mistakes would lose their 'iron rice-bowl'. 'I was totally depressed in 1993 when the director of our factory told me that I was being laid-off,' recalled Zhang Shaoyi, a 43-year-old vegetable salesman who used to work as head of the general office of a medium-sized factory in Tieling, a city in Northeast China's Liaoning Province. Zhang has done really well since then, however, and is proud of his recent success. 'Being laid-off was not something totally bad, since it at least encouraged me to depend on myself to improve my reality,' he said. Zhang is not the only one of many workers who have had to change their attitude toward unemployment, and who have had some success in their new careers. 'As China's old industrial base, Liaoning once had as many as two million laid-off workers, but half of them have found new jobs since 1994. A recent study found that 90 per cent of the laid-off workers do not consider collectively-owned enterprises as inferior to state-owned ones the way they used to. Many are willing to become self-employed if they can make a fortune in their new career. Ding Chunlin, the Secretary-General of the Re-Employment Research Association of Liaoning, said that with the increasing reforms, an increasing number of laid-off workers have come to see getting rid of redundant personnel as something that inevitably happens in factories' (Xinhua, 23-2-1998).

So unemployment is a good thing! As we shall see in the next section, few are as sanguine about this and other issues. Now we shall turn to clear evidence of the weaknesses inherent in China's third revolution, and the many threats that it faces.

China's weaknesses and threats: internal/external

Contrary to the spin of the Xinhua report above, loss of job security is leading to an upsurge in anti-government violence around the country (see Box 10.1), as well as heightening the perception of urban residents that

---

Box 10.1 Alarm Over Unrest

Alarmed by the fact that demonstrators managed to get near the Communist Party and government offices in the Tiananmen Square area mid-November, 1998, President Jiang Zemin immediately ordered security departments to ensure that Beijing was not hit by any form of social unrest. Jiang told them to minimise 'social disruption' caused by unemployed workers or victims of financial scams (the Tiananmen protest was by hundreds of people angered by the Government's failure to help them get compensation from a defunct brokerage firm). 'As soon as a little fire is lit up, it must be extinguished. If possible, unrest should be dispelled or solved where it started and never allowed to spread. On no account should demonstrators be allowed to get near to the party and government headquarters'. Following the lessons of the 1989 crushing of the pro-democracy movement in Tiananmen Square, however, the government is promoting a combination of tough tactics and 'guidance and persuasion'. For example, social welfare or labour organisations could give out emergency relief funds to destitute workers if it helped avert a challenge to the administration by ensuring that 'all workers have rice on the table'.

These moves came at a time when a growing number of Chinese appeared willing to defy a ban on unauthorised protests in order to express their anger over a variety of causes, mostly economic related. In the cities, it tends to be the jobless or workers who have not been paid for several months to vent their anger. In the countryside, farmers are angry at falling incomes that are putting them at an increasing disadvantage in the national drive for affluence, or at the dozens of illegal taxes and 'service' fees extorted by officials at the local level. In a sign that China is becoming increasingly violent, in the first half of 1998 a total of 144 police officers were reported killed and 3,062 wounded while on duty (*People's Daily*, 10-12-1998). The officers were killed dealing with increasingly violent criminals, separatist movements in areas like Xinjiang and in violent incidents staged by the jobless and homeless. The national police headquarters vowed to increase 'armed combat drills under battle conditions' in order to help protect officers (ibid.).

Some anecdotal evidence of the rising tide of protest is provided by the following reports drawn from various sources over a period of several months:

- An explosion believed to be caused by a home-made nail bomb ripped through a farmers' market in Hunan, killing nine people and injuring more than 65 (*Yangchang Evening News* 28-1-1999).
- Bomb explosions around the country have become a frequent occurrence with more than 2,500 reported in 1998 (CASS, 1999).

- Police arrested several organisers of a protest by 500 steel workers who blocked railway lines in Jiangyou city, about 850 miles Southwest of Beijing in protest at not being paid for three months (Associated Press 2-11-1998).
- More than 200 protesters blocked traffic in Changsha, capital of Hunan Province, claiming they had not been paid for more than six months (Associated Press, 18-11-1998).
- Hundreds of machinery workers in Sichuan province blocked a road for three days in protest at not being paid for 14 months (*South China Morning Post*, 19-11-1998).
- Four hundred demonstrators tried to block a major railway line when they rioted over finance companies which allegedly cheated them out of investments, in Zhengzhou, capital of Henan province. Police had to protect the line from Beijing to Guangzhou that runs through the city, eventually arresting two leaders and dispersing the protesters, who lost their money when the government closed down several finance companies for illegal fund fathering (*South China Morning Post*, 14-10-1998).
- Disgruntled workers took to the streets in the Hubei cities of Wuhan and Shiyan in separate incidents. About 200 ex-workers from the defunct Wuhan Comprehensive Materials Factory blocked a major trunk road for several hours in the provincial capital demanding the authorities pay them their monthly stipends. An estimated 1,200 factory workers marched in Shiyan, blocking a major road and paralysing traffic, protesting over a company that applied for bankruptcy in June after having collected 10 million yuan in investments from workers (*Hubei Daily*, 13-10-1998).
- Some 200 workers at a loss-making factory in the Inner Mongolian city of Baotou used trucks to block the plant's main gate for several hours to demand months of unpaid wages, a lawyer and worker said (Associated Press, 18-7-1998).
- More than 200 sales staff and suppliers demonstrated outside Shenzhen's municipal government building demanding compensation over an alleged fraud at a department store. The Bao'an Guangkelong Department Store opened in June, but was closed after just 21 days, leaving unpaid bills running into millions of Yuan (*South China Morning Post*, 6-8-1998).
- Workers at a state-run Shenyang Micro-Electrical Factory, which had run up debts of 37 million Yuan, that was sold to its manager for one yuan took to the streets to protest against the sale and held repeated sit-ins. The workers, who heard of the sale from the television news, had preferred buy out the factory themselves and turn it into a shareholding firm (*South China Morning Post*, 14-8-1998).

- Hundreds of retired workers demonstrated in Wuhan demanding several months' unpaid pensions from the China No 1 Metallurgical Co. Two months earlier, about 2,000 laid-off workers demonstrated, demanding six months' back pay (Agence France Presse, 19-9-1998).
- The Ministry of Labour and Social Insurance admitted it owed almost three million retirees billions of Yuan in pension arrears. Ministry figures showed that, to the end of March, 1998, 2.83 million retirees in thirty provinces, cities and regions were owed 4.67 billion Yuan, including 709,000 who had not been paid for more than six months (*South China Morning Post*, 5-6-1998).
- Five hundred state factory workers in Sichuan broke through a police line during a march to back demands for four months' back pay (*South China Morning Post*, 8-9-1998).

Willy Wo-Lap Lam, a Chinese writer with the *South China Morning Post* regarded as having good mainland contacts, quoted 'sources close to the security establishment', as reporting more than 10,000 'unruly incidents' by farmers in 1997, ranging from demonstrations and petitions to efforts to surround or damage government offices. There were at least 300 attempts to break into banks and post offices (*South China Morning Post*, 18-10-1998). As a result, in mid-1998, the Ministry of Agriculture began co-ordinating a review by governments at all levels aimed at reappraising the taxes and levies imposed on farmers in order to lessen the burden. Lam quoted a Politburo member who cited of one village in a central province which was hit with close to 150 taxes and other levies. Concurrently, an anti-corruption drive more extensive than that in the cities was begun in the countryside. The politburo member reiterated that unless graft was eradicated, 'the survival of the party would be called into question' (ibid.).

Sources: as cited in text.

crime is on the increase. Against this backdrop, holding down unemployment and finding new jobs for laid-off workers was a prime topic of conversation among members of the new government of Prime Minister Zhu Rongji, elected at the first session of the Ninth National People's Congress (NPC) in March 1998. In interviews with the official *Workers' Daily* (17-3-1998), for example, six party secretaries from different parts of the mainland (Jiangsu, Liaoning, Jilin, Shaanxi and Hunan provinces, and the city of Chongqing) put job creation as their top priority, along with guaranteeing a minimum living standard to the unemployed. 'The increasing number of laid off workers has become the No 1 factor to determine whether social stability can be maintained,' declared Li Jianguo, of Shaanxi, and Zhang Delin, from Chongqing City. The six officials said they were aware that unemployment was a necessary consequence of furthering economic structural reform and state-owned enterprise reform. But they were even more keenly aware that, under the present inadequate social security system, the rising number of laid off workers had become the most important problem of China's economic reform. Hunan secretary Wang Maolin asked: 'Where will people go? It is the toughest issue faced by China now'.

In the growing climate of unease and uncertainty, many rural townships have fallen under the influence of doomsday cults and clan associations connected to criminal triad societies. Such manifestations were common in China's past as a prelude to the rural uprisings that on occasions toppled imperial dynasties.

Fear of unrest creates unusual situations. Take the example of a company in Gansu province, which had received a collateral-backed loan from a European bank based in Hong Kong. The loan became overdue, but the company had no means of making repayment. Unable to service this and other loans, the enterprise – which produced inferior construction materials rejected by the market – filed for bankruptcy, subsequently approved by a court. With this, creditors thought they might get their money back. However, the city's mayor, ignoring the court ruling, stepped in and refused to allow the firm to fold (*South China Morning Post*, 23-4-1999). Such disregard for a court decision can be suicidal for politicians in countries where the rule of law is just that, but, on the mainland – and especially in the hinterlands – barely an eyebrow is raised. The factory has about 7,000 workers on its payroll, and is one of the city's largest employers. The mayor could not risk having 7,000 workers protesting against job losses in 1999 – a volatile year, marking the eightieth anniversary of the May 4 protest movement, the fiftieth anniversary of the founding of the People's Republic of China, the fortieth anniversary of the Lhasa Uprising in Tibet, and the tenth anniversary of the June 4th Tiananmen crackdown on student protesters. The convergence of these politically significant events meant the potential for public discontent and social unrest was high, and political leaders preferred to err on the side of caution than be accused of igniting any rebel-rousing spark.

So, while Premier Zhu Rongji and his ministers continue to deny that the tide of state-sector reforms is in retreat, the evidence would appear to suggest it is falling behind, as will be discussed again later in this chapter. By disregarding a court ruling, a lone city mayor was at least trying to stem any potential trouble. Gansu is not a favoured destination of foreign investors and politicians have a hard job finding work for the newly laid off, so the unenthusiastic response to reform is understandable. As shown in Chapter 4, provinces such as Guangxi, Guizhou, Sichuan, Yunnan, Tibet, Shaanxi, Qinghai, Ningxia, and Xinjiang are also not popular with foreign investors. Laying-off workers in these regions is not as easy as in Shanghai, an investor hot spot. Even so, even Shanghai has not entirely embraced the reforms. A small factory in the city wanted to cut staff from 200 to eighty. But the general manager said his retrenchment plans were rejected, declaring: 'They cannot throw every surplus worker out, so the smaller factories will have to wait'. Equally worrying are reports of corrupt officials taking advantage of the reform call to force factory closures in order to siphon off state assets or evade the need to repay loans from state banks.

It is the authors' belief that the mainland is an economic crisis waiting to happen unless the government deals effectively with loss-making state enterprises and reforms the banking system. The government, as already noted, fears that mass unemployment will lead to social unrest and has shied away from cutting the lifelines of millions of workers. But, by propping up industrial loss-makers, the banks have little chance of moving from being mere government funding agencies, their traditional role, to becoming competitive and commercial.

At the time of writing, it was estimated that non-performing loans (NPLs) held by the four main state banks were between 20 and 35 per cent of their total, a crippling amount. The government's answer has been to set up special asset management companies for each bank, with the initial aim of reducing their NPLs by 30 per cent or even one half by the middle of 2001. The idea is to sell off the debts at a discount to investors, whether domestic or foreign, private or state, probably in the form of equity in the restructured ailing SOE. The first bad-debt management company, China Cinda Asset Management, to take over more than 200 billion Yuan of NPLs from China Construction Bank (CCB) for repackaging. If the approach works, asset-management companies will also be set up for the Bank of China, Industrial and Commercial Bank of China, and the Agricultural Bank of China. And the emphasis must be on the phrase 'if it works.' For many, the belief remains strong that until the government is really willing to allow the bad companies to disappear, it is likely to face continued problems in the banking sector. And such a banking system cannot continue indefinitely without running into serious problems. What price stability, then, if, as has happened in powerful Japan, banks start collapsing, thus wiping out the lifetime savings of millions and damaging international confidence in Chinese credit?

Although a 1995 Chinese Academy of Social Sciences report on national conditions ruled out social instability as a serious threat, there is evidence that many cadres at grassroots level now think otherwise. A 1998 internal party document seen by one of the authors revealed that 70 per cent of the nation's factories were unable to pay their workers on a regular basis. They resorted to issuing IOUs not just for basic salaries, but bonuses and medical and overtime benefits.

This is one of the major contradictions in today's China. In the early years of the PRC, everyone worked for the state, private business being considered an exploitative remnant of the capitalist system the Communists were dedicated to destroying. Under the centralised planned economy, employment was monopolised by the government. Enterprises could not recruit workers on their own, but were generally assigned a specific number of bodies each year with little or no input into the selection process.

The life-tenure employment system, in turn, prevented enterprises from divesting themselves of redundant employees. The all-embracing security and welfare system exercised by enterprises, as a form of state social welfare, covered the housing, health care and the pension of their employees. Leaving of one's work unit actually meant losing everything. These traditional practices resulted in a large amount of hidden unemployment. But now that enterprises need to calculate their input and output, lower costs, increase profit and enhance market competitiveness, the problem has been brought out into the open. Dealing with this in the most logical way cutting out the waste entails great political and economic risks if they plan to dismiss redundant workers, especially if the Communist Party wishes to persist in the ideological concept that the workers are the 'masters of the state', and, therefore, of the enterprises for which they work.

At the same time, the unemployment situation in rural areas is becoming ever more acute, and is undoubtedly a bigger headache other two major rural challenges – decline of arable land and population increases. There are six key issues here:

1. Unemployment pressure from an increase in the rural population. Twenty-six percent of the rural labour force is chronically unemployed. Moreover, there will be an annual increase in the rural labour force of 6.66 million from 1997 to 2000. Even if the rural township enterprises can maintain their current growth rate of 15 per cent and, thus, create 2.24 million jobs, there will still be 134 million unemployed at the end of the century.

2. Regional economic disparities generate further unemployment tension. During the first half of the next century, eastern coastal areas, as the most dynamic elements of the country, will still be the major market for the redundant rural labour force. But this market is not big enough to absorb so many farmers in the destitute central and western areas.

3. Unemployment during the process of economic transformation will be serious. While many new, advanced industries appear in cities and there is a shortage of qualified labourers, rural surplus labour forces, mostly unskilled, find it more difficult to get positions. Official calculations put the illiteracy rate among the 450 million rural labourers is 21 per cent, while only 9 per cent have a senior high school education. Unemployment, caused by shifts in the economic structure, is the most difficult to settle. It will co-exist with the country's modernisation progress for at least the first 10 years of the next century.

235

4. With the increasing application of science and technology in the rural economy, many mechanical, manual tasks will be phased out in traditional agriculture and former labour-intensive township enterprises. Also, land and money, basic for agricultural development, are more likely to be used for progressive urbanisation in the next century. As a result, farmers' prospects will be limited.
5. Fifth, more farmers will stay idle as the slack season is prolonged by a rise in agricultural productivity.
6. Periodic economic regression will also reduce rural employment. For example, from 1988 to 1991, among 13 million farmers who temporarily worked in the building industry, five million lost their jobs as a result of the central government's tightening macro control over the scale of infrastructure construction.

Further pressure on those without a job, or facing the imminent prospect of redundancy, is the determination of new Prime Minister Zhu Rongji to push ahead rapidly with his key reforms, including a massive overhaul of the social welfare system. After decades of reliance on the state for their housing and medical care, millions of Chinese workers now face the prospect of having to make their own arrangements and pay for them out of their own pocket. Soon after taking office in March 1998, it became clear that Mr Zhu was determined to see the state no longer providing welfare housing to urban residents within a year, as was discussed in Chapter 8. After this, state employees, including civil servants and workers in state-owned firms, would have to buy their apartments through a government-aided hire purchase scheme, with the prospect of one-eighth of their fairly meagre salaries going on monthly mortgage payments. Workers with 'sufficient funds' would be able to buy a better apartment with the help of their work unit and government loans.

This, however, deals yet another blow to the egalitarianism espoused by Chairman Mao already under strain from the reign of the late Deng Xiaoping who first proposed the idea that even under Communism it was still permissible for some to 'get rich first'. In the days when everyone received essentially the same paltry salary albeit offset by the provision of subsidies in the shape of housing, medical care, coupons to obtain daily necessities and pensions at the employer's expense this problem never arose. Now, however, one of the most common problems is what Chinese call 'red-eye disease', namely, envy at the sight of someone else being better off. Another manifestation is the rampant corruption that has resurfaced in China resulting from the desire to cut corners in the race to get rich.

The reforms may go down more smoothly in relatively rich cities along the coast, where it is estimated workers bank as much as half their salaries. But, there will be resistance in provinces hard-hit by company bankruptcies such as the Northeast, where hundreds of thousands of workers barely earn enough money to eat. As a related issue, one of the worst aspects of 'Old China' which the Communists were determined to eradicate was the appalling gap in health standards between rich and poor the latter, the bulk of the population, being condemned to considerably lower life expectancy and a disease-prone existence. One of the best aspects of 'New China' has been the provision of excellent basic health care for virtually all. Can this survive in an era of commercialised medicine?

The formation of shareholding companies and co-operatives was touted as a panacea for state-owned enterprises at the 15th Communist Party Congress in September 1997, especially with the enthusiastic support of President Jiang Zemin, seeing this as a demonstration of his ability to push the Deng Xiaoping reforms to new heights. Mr Jiang repeatedly told party cadres that, that since joint-stock companies were not the monopoly of capitalist economies, 'we must be bold in going about *gufenhua* (going joint-stock)'. Yet, within six months, *gufenhua* seemed to have passed its high point, especially with Zhu Rongji being a known sceptic of stocks and shares as the answer to the state sector's problems, and a strong believer in the more traditional methods of merger and bankruptcy to salvage the state sector.

From various sources within the government, one can produce several reasons for the Premier's scepticism. Firstly, while cadre-mandarins from the *ancien regime* have donned new hats called chairman of the board or managing director, they operate the new companies in much the same way as before. Particularly in poor areas, the shareholding format has often been used to milk workers of their savings. Employees have been given the Hobson's choice of either being laid off or making contributions of up to 20,000 Yuan to become 'shareholders' of their concerns, which in many cases have no hope of being turned around. Worst, since at least in theory, SOEs that have been converted into shareholding concerns are only answerable to shareholders, Beijing's control over the economy has been weakened.

The worrying aspect of all this is that China now seems bereft of a direction for the reform of SOEs, perhaps the nation's worst problem. If the shareholding system isn't the answer, then what is? One recalls the other famous 1997 slogan on enterprise reform: *zhuada*, or pumping national resources into several hundred elite SOEs in the hope that they will be turned into 'flagship' conglomerates and multinationals. But the *zhuada* concept was based on the South Korean model of developing *chaebols*, and when these Seoul-based behemoths hit the rocks in the Asian financial crisis that began in late 1997, a hasty rethink was ordered in Beijing.

At the time of writing, it seems likely that there will be a return to that somewhat anti-market formula of 'taking a firm grip on large SOEs and setting the small ones free', although at a slower rate than in the past. This 'government knows best' slogan essentially means that while lesser enterprises can be given a free hand to 'sink or swim in the marketplace', major ones should still be steered by senior cadres and state entrepreneurs. The propagandists have claimed that the so-called *jituangongsi* are aircraft-carrier type concerns that are the results of 'the pooling of resources of strong companies with other equally strong ones'. Such conglomerates have been set up in areas including infrastructure, industry, mining and retailing, and hardly a day passes without claims being made by newly-formed conglomerates that they will soon make the exalted ranks of the Fortune 500. But this development looks somewhat suspect in light of the 'negative examples' of the unhappy marriage of government and business in countries including Japan, Indonesia and, in particular, South Korea.

There is a very real sense here of a government thrashing around trying to find the solution to perhaps insoluble problems because, the only real answer would be the abandon the state-owned sector altogether. But then, what remains of socialism? And what need, therefore, for continuation of the 'people's dictatorship' through the Communist Party? These are not just issues of internal interest. They are also crucial to China's ability to continue attracting vast amounts of foreign investment, which have already enabled it to fund much of the dramatic domestic economic expansion seen in the past two decades. In fact, the honeymoon may already be over for foreign businesses investing in China. Bedazzled for years by the sheer size of the market – '1.2 billion consumers' – normally hard-headed business-men have been pouring billions down a bottomless well in search of riches. Now, some are retiring to lick their wounds. The result of this was expected to be a considerable downturn in the amount of foreign direct investment (FDI) in 1999.

One senior trade ministry economist predicted utilised FDI could fall as much as 55 per cent, others saw flat growth or a decline in the low teens. They said Asian economies such as Taiwan, Hong Kong and Japan, which accounted for about 70 per cent of the mainland's FDI, would not recover fast enough to provide strong capital inflows. Ma Yu, director of the Trade Ministry Research Institute's foreign capital department in January forecast utilised FDI of US$20 billion for the year, but by March he had decided even this was too optimistic considering the worsening economic environment appeared. He believed the official FDI figure in 1998 was around US$30 billion, not the officially reported $45.6 billion, which had been inflated by local governments eager to meet the country's eight per cent economic growth target. In fact, at a national conference in February, Premier Zhu Rongji angrily told provincial government leaders that he didn't believe the figures they were presenting. In the first quarter of 1999, direct contractual foreign investment stood at US$8.72 billion, around the same level as the corresponding period of the previous year, but actually amount utilised was 14.6 per cent lower at US$7.34 billion (*China Daily*, 21-4-1999).

238

By the end of 1998, the number of foreign-funded projects in the mainland had reached 324,000, involving contracted investment of $572.52 billion and actual utilised investment of $267.45 billion (Ministry of Foreign Trade and Economic Cooperation). Some early arrivals in the Chinese market have done well – for example, Shanghai Volkswagen, the country's most profitable joint venture run by the German car-maker and Chinese partner, Shanghai Automotive Industry Corp., Coca-Cola and McDonald's. But VW went through almost a decade of nightmare losses before gaining its present profitable position. And, for every winner, there are casualties: Foster's, Whirlpool, Peugeot and Caterpillar, for example, have shut down or reduced operations in late 1998/ early 1999. Heinrich von Pierer, chief executive of German giant Siemens, was candid when he admitted that his group had partly 'over-estimated the China market' and would close some joint ventures. There are thought to be more companies like Siemens, but most will not openly admit their mistakes for fear of losing face or offending mainland authorities.

But any withdrawal or scaling down of operations will spill over into the banking sector, where non-Chinese banks depend heavily on the business they get from foreign corporations. The shrinkage has already had some impact. In June 1999, the Royal Bank of Canada shut its Shanghai branch, becoming the first leading foreign financial institution to leave the city since the market was thrown open to foreign financial institutions. In September, Japan's Daiwa Bank planned to downgrade its operations to a more limited representative office status. Two Korean banks, Hanil and Commercial Bank of Korea merged their Shanghai branches to survive. French banking group Societé Generale scaled down its mainland operations.

There is plenty of hype about the mainland market – where, like anywhere else, there is money to be made or lost – and for years there has been a mad scramble by the big foreign corporate names to avoid 'missing the gravy train'. The dream of untold riches from the mainland market is an old one. During the nineteenth century Industrial Revolution in Britain, one writer enthused: 'If we could only persuade every person in China to lengthen his shirttail by a foot, we could keep the (cotton) mills of Lancashire working around the clock' (quoted by Mann, 1989)! In contrast, in 1853, 10 years after Shanghai and four other Chinese cities were prised open to foreign residence and trade by the British, a certain Mr Mitchell – an assistant magistrate in Hong Kong – wrote a report on the prospects of China trade for the colony's governor, Sir George Bonham. Mitchell's conclusion was unpalatable to most British traders: the market was grossly over-rated as its sheer size touted by the merchants was a figment of their imagination.

Mitchell was largely proved right, for apart from the demand for opium, that great market never materialised. But when the late Deng Xiaoping flung open China's doors to foreign business once again in the early 1960s, the same sort of hyperbole which Mitchell had so deplored began to reappear, with the old fixation of the massive market of endless zeroes – having grown threefold from the 400 million of the Victorian era. Whether out of politeness or belief, a constant stream of foreign business executives and politicians have helped talk up this mouth-watering market prospect as soon as they set foot on Chinese soil. In fact, in the mid-1990s, there were probably no more than sixty-five million Chinese with the economic means to purchase foreign-made goods, and these are primarily located in the rich eastern coastal provinces. Although this number was expected to expand to about 200 million by the turn of the century, it will be decades before the other billion plus translate into an effective purchasing force. Even then, the mainland is not one big market. Eating habits, spending patterns and lifestyle differences vary from one province to another, making product targeting and distribution a nightmare and pushing up the costs of any company wanting to create a national rather than the regional market.

Thus, the sobering up process has begun, and dissatisfaction is being voiced. The fact is that, often, the complexities of operating in the mainland have been ignored. True, the investment environment has improved greatly since the open-door policy began in 1978. Yet, by and large, laws are still poorly enforced, interpretation remains arbitrary, and the bureaucracy can often be unfriendly. Adding to the list of problems is an appalling lack of transparency and accountability. These thorny issues that have often been neglected because investors feared they would miss out on a big market and potential profits if they didn't join the gold rush. Now, it is time for re-appraisal.

Robert Kapp, President of the US-China Business Council (representing around 280 companies operating in the mainland) was unusually out-spoken: foreign businesses are dissatisfied with the worsening operating conditions in the mainland and American companies have demanded action. 'The reorganisation of the government, launched by Premier Zhu Rongji in March last year, has led to administrative confusion and worsening bureaucratic immobility, making navigation difficult for businesses. A tightening of foreign exchange procedures aimed at stopping smuggling and illegal movement of money offshore has resulted in a backlash on foreign firms seeking to claim legitimate foreign-exchange earnings from exports. New measures adopted to keep state firms afloat and prevent raging unemployment have made it harder for foreign firms in several sectors to pursue their normal business development. There is an almost palpable sense that China is moving away in the short run from more energetic business relations with American firms. The mood of the business community on the ground appears both more sombre and impatient than before' (*China Business Review*, February 1999).

After Hong Kong and Taiwan, the US is the biggest foreign investor in the mainland, with more than 25,000 projects and US$28 billion in actual investment. It is also the country's second-biggest trading partner. The mainland is fourth in the ranks of US trade partners. However, US firms were angry about the limited extent of Beijing's market-opening moves – especially in sectors in which they enjoy competitive advantage, such as telecommunications, insurance, banking and farm goods. Beijing had also taken measures against US investment, such as a ban on direct sales, which impacted badly on companies like Amway, Revlon and Avon, an end to guaranteed returns on power projects and to foreign investment in telecommunications. Mr Kapp said US business had to make clear that a continual deterioration of the investment and commercial climate for US firms in the mainland would be adverse to the growth of bilateral commercial relations and that this would ultimately pollute other sectors of the relationship.

The evidence for a turn in the tide of foreign business enthusiasm for China remains somewhat anecdotal, but it is becoming increasingly persuasive. For example, an increasing number of foreign companies are closing their representative offices in Beijing because of financial problems at home and the headaches of dealing with mainland bureaucrats. Official figures show 652 foreign firms opened offices in Beijing in 1997, while 437 closed. It is believed there was a similar pattern in 1998. There are a number of factors involved. Firms from East and Southeast Asia have had to close overseas operations because of their financial crises, or because they found the mainland market too difficult to penetrate, in part because of government policies that protected domestic firms against foreign competition.

Another reason is a rising tide of complaints since the second half of 1996 about irrational government policies, local protectionism and the poor quality of Chinese officials. Foreign firms complain of turf battles between different government departments and increasingly complicated approval procedures, officials' low efficiency and poor quality of service. Further problems included high costs, especially of property, and the difficulty of obtaining qualified local staff with foreign language skills, forcing firms to send expensive expatriates from their home countries. A Japan Export Trade Organisation (JETRO) official said that many Japanese companies had cut the number of Japanese staff and replaced them with Chinese people. 'Even if they speak Japanese or English, it is not so efficient but there is no other way. It is very expensive to keep a Japanese abroad' (author research, January 1999).

One sign of the current hard times is that 47.35 per cent of the foreign ventures in Shanghai reported losses in 1998 totalling 3.9 billion Yuan (Xinhua, 12-2-1999). Despite being tied to world-famous companies, four ventures reported losses of more than 100 million Yuan each. Xinhua actually cited the data to warn foreigners against indiscriminately pouring capital into the mainland, adding they could improve their prospects by bringing in advanced technologies – in line with Chinese policy. An annual study by the Shanghai government's Bureau of Industrial and Commercial Administration released previously had anticipated the poor annual results, predicting foreign firms would on average report US$368,500 of losses. However, the bureau study also claimed the losses were fake, as two-thirds of the loss-making ventures were either illegally shifting profits overseas or depressing revenue for long-term strategic reasons. One-third – most often ventures set up by large foreign corporations – were taking the strategic approach, the study said. Typically, these firms hold down prices of products sold domestically and spend heavily on advertising in the short term to penetrate the mainland's huge potential market, it said (*Study of Trends in Foreign Investment in Shanghai 1998*).

Some foreign investors push such a strategy even further to obtain greater control over Sino-foreign joint ventures. After years of losses, they declared an intention of boosting investment. The weakened mainland partner, lacking capital to match the new funds, then sees its equity share scaled back. The other one-third of the 'loss-making' foreign firms are healthy, but doctor their books, sending profits home and evading tax, the study said. The authorities find it especially hard to control international movement of funds by such firms, as many are constantly importing manufacturing inputs and exporting goods.

One outcome of the current difficulties faced by foreign companies is for them to take a long and often critical look at the state of their 'marriage' with their domestic joint venture partner. If they are not happy with performance, the result may be a divorce, especially if the foreign side is strong enough to risk establishing a wholly-owned local subsidiary – if it is in a sector where this is permitted by Chinese law – or at least renegotiations to change the terms of the original equity arrangement. One of the largest legal firms working on the mainland, Baker and McKenzie, stated that about half of its commercial business in the mainland now involved 'restructuring' joint ventures. Those facing the greatest problems tend to be at least five years old. They are often in manufacturing and the venture may be heavily overstaffed. After five years, if they are not making money, they know they never will unless they take action (author research, January 1999).

Many foreign ventures complained that their Chinese partners were reluctant to invest profits in upgrading machinery, expanding production or seeking greater market share. In return, the Chinese partner often lacked the deep pockets of its partner to make new investments and resented the drain on profit caused by expatriate salaries. To overcome such deadlocks, many foreign investors have been increasing their stake in joint ventures to 70 per cent or more, giving them control of the boardroom and speeding up decision-making. For example, Xerox Corp. increased its share in Shanghai Xerox from 51 per cent to 80 per cent, while General Electric raised its stake in its GE-Jiabao lighting factory to 89 per cent. Newcomers nowadays often prefer to seek this dominance from the start, no matter how prolonged the negotiations. Eastman Kodak wanted to be 'as fleet-footed as possible' in its latest investments, and spent nearly three years negotiating a deal that gave it 70–80 per cent of two new joint ventures.

Human resources consultant Yung Ling Beiman, of Hewitt Associates, said many joint ventures older than five years were finding their performance hindered by staff more accustomed to the authoritarian approach of their older state enterprises. 'People didn't really pay attention to the human resources challenges,' she said. In most cases, dealing with employees was one of the functions most commonly entrusted to the Chinese partner. 'Now they have to renegotiate'. Changes in the market are pushing the pace of restructuring forward. As the government relaxes its control of the market, competition is heating up for the older joint ventures. Many joint ventures, which drew on the customer base of the local partner originally, are seeing their protected markets disappear as the government permits more open competition. A more mature market, and greater government openness, is also making it less important for foreign companies to have a local partner to cut through the bureaucracy, which used to be the latter's strong selling point. Others discovered too late that the mainland is not a single market but many, composed of several regional and sub-regional markets, with the infrastructure under-equipped and ill prepared to handle the demands of modern logistics and distribution (interview, 14-1-1999).

In 1994, one of the authors identified some of the problems facing Sino-foreign joint ventures as follows:

a) The purpose of establishing the joint venture is dubious. Some local governments have considered only the number of joint ventures they could attract, this being the key criteria by which their performance could be assessed.

b) Although shared goals between joint venture partners were essential, in many cases, they were are not operating on the same wavelength, eventually leading to grief.

c) Local governments often did not possess the expertise to weigh the advantages of disadvantages of a specific investment proposal, which led them into mistakes.

d) Co-operation between provinces was poor with the result that it was often difficult to take advantage of economies of scale, for example.

e) Many areas went ahead with creating development zones without fully considering the burden that would be imposed on local transportation, telecommunications systems, water and electricity supply. Additional levies of various kinds imposed by local authorities to try and make up the deficiencies have become a heavy burden for joint ventures in some places.

f) The investment boom had developed so quickly that quality control systems had not been able to keep up with the influx of technology and equipment needed for China's modernisation (Murray , 1994, pp.159, 171–2).

Examining the situation again in 1999, one can see great efforts being made by the central government to deal with these and other deficiencies, but the same grumbles can still be heard. Overall, a growing number of foreign businessmen feel the best approach for newcomers to China today is a cautious investment strategy that demands limited exposure and a well-defined business plan, while existing investors should concentrate on consolidation of business and market share, pushing harder on localisation and indigenisation, building up local content and sinking deeper roots ready for better times.

For foreign investors, another key issue is prospects for this leads naturally into consideration of the prospects for change in China's political system. The management 'guru' Peter Drucker has argued that in a Communist system of government, decisions are invariably made at the highest possible level. As a result, 'no one is in the habit of decision-making, trained in it, tested in it. Nothing so much frightens people in former Communist countries ... as to be asked to make a decision. They are paralysed by fear of making a mistake. They hold endless meetings, call for more and more studies and in the end find a good reason why someone higher up should take the responsibility' (Drucker, 1992, p.121).

Interestingly, similar sentiments were expressed at a Politburo meeting in August 1980 by Deng Xiaoping, who accused party cadres and government officials of 'indulging in empty talk; sticking to rigid ways of thinking; being hidebound by convention; overstaffing administrative organs ... circulating documents endlessly without solving problems; shifting responsibility to others ... being arbitrary and despotic; practising favouritism; participating in corrupt practices in violation of the law and so on' (Wang, 1995, p.141). Deng said there was 'a close relationship between bureaucratism and 'highly centralised management in economic, political, cultural and social fields'. He observed that 'when the entire decision-making process is highly individualised in the hands of a few, the results are inefficiency and inability to make decisions' (ibid.).

During the third phase of his political reform programme, one regular theme was that the party needed leaders at every level who were 'more revolutionary, younger, better educated and more competent professionally' (Evans, 1993, p.258). Another was that the party was trying to do too much, duplicating the work and cramping the style of the government and preventing experts from contributing as much as they could to develop-ment. There was a need to develop 'socialist democracy' by allowing 'grassroots units' and individuals to participate more actively in decision-making and management. In June 1986, Deng told the visiting Japanese Prime Minister that one of the key targets of reform was to 'eliminate bureaucratism and increase efficiency' and to 'stimulate the initiative of grass roots units and of workers, peasants and intellectuals' by letting them participate in management (ibid., p.279).

Such a view is strongly reformist. More recently, President Jiang Zemin fuelled reformist cadres' hopes for a more relaxed environment to promote change with remarks he made to a meeting of the Central Committee of Discipline Inspection in March 1998 that corruption was rampant in Southeast Asian countries because they were feudalistic therefore, 'it is important to be anti-feudalistic and be democratic'. In the same month, Jiang also told a group of top scientists that a more ideologically and politically relaxed environment should be provided for them to conduct meaningful research needed for the country's modernisation.

Meanwhile, reform-minded officials and intellectuals in the capital were closely watching the fate of a book that harshly attacks conservative ideologues. The book, 'Cross Swords', published in 1998 during the NPC session, for the first time exposed to the public a series of heated debates among leaders and senior cadres on market reform as well as privatisation issues, referred to earlier in this chapter. The book also covers the four 10,000-character letters circulated by leftists among senior cadres for the past two years. The letters violently attack the deep penetration of negative Western influence, 'bourgeois liberalisation' and rampant corruption, which the conservative camp says are caused by market reforms. The book is rumoured to have won the support of some reform-minded leaders since its text was published in advance in January by Gaige Bao, a publication under the former State Commission on Restructuring Economy.

At the same time, another book appeared which reaffirmed Marxism's central role, despite all the dismantling of the communist social system, *Marxism in China Over the Past 100 Years*, written by scholars from all the country, was 'the most systematic look at the subject to date', editorial adviser Ding Shouhe was quoted as saying (Xinhua, 4-8-1998). It reaffirms that, even as it moves toward a market economy, the present government continues to define itself by the founding philosophy of Mao Zedong's revolution. 'The theory is the guiding ideology of the state and the Communist Party of China, which is the largest communist organisation in the world,' Xinhua said. 'The book illustrates the validity of the truths of Marxism'.

These two books, at least, serve as a barometer of the political climate in a year of significant sensitive anniversaries. China in 1998 marked both the centenary of the country's first reform movement, launched by Kang Youwei and Liang Qichao in the last days of the Qing dynasty, along with the twentieth anniversary of the launching of Deng Xiaoping's reforms after he came to power in October 1978. Both provided a platform for those unhappy with the slow pace of change to press for political reforms to be speeded up – or, equally, to be slowed down.

Overall, however, the political pendulum appears to be swinging back towards caution and conservatism. At the end of 1998, President Jiang Zemin made it quite clear what the nation could expect in the following year – a continued crackdown on dissent. And this has been borne out by events in 1999. In a major speech to cadres attending the National Meeting on Political and Legal Work, he used uncompromising language heard less frequently over the previous past 18 months as the Chinese leadership sought to improve relations abroad. He vowed to crush any challenges to Communist Party rule and preserve 'social stability'.

The speech was delivered in the same week as the summary trials and convictions of dissidents Wang Youcai , Qin Yongmin and Xu Wenli who tried to form the opposition China Democracy Party. Jiang said stability was crucial over the next year. He noted two key events on the political calendar: the fiftieth anniversary of Communist Party rule on 1 October and Macao's handover on 20 December. 'We must strengthen the ideological and political education of officials and raise their awareness of, and resistance to, the sabotaging acts of hostile domestic and foreign forces. Whenever any element that undermines stability raises its head, it must be resolutely nipped in the bud'.

He ticked off a list of potentially volatile problems – inefficient state industries, legions of laid-off workers, stagnating farmers' incomes and corrupt officials. The emphasis on stability and warnings to those who would disrupt it were reminiscent of party pronouncements in the waning years of Mr Jiang's mentor, Deng Xiaoping. Prior to making this speech, the president had been under pressure from two sides. Leftists, or quasi-Maoist conservatives, for some time had been petitioning the party leadership on the threat posed by economic globalisation to Chinese autonomy and security, and their fear that further market reforms would result in China becoming a 'vassal' of the capitalist West. They cited Deng's 'four cardinal principles' of orthodox Marxism, including the 'dictatorship of the proletariat' and 'both fists be tough' policy, meaning free-thinking views must be suppressed even as the economy is being restructured. On the other side, liberal academics, legislators and government consultants urged a faster pace in the 'democratising decision-making'. Some avant-garde intellectuals and non-communist politicians even urged that China should follow the 'South Korean and Taiwan experience' in political liberalisation.

Members of the National People's Congress and the Chinese People's Political Consultative Conference also complained that the party had dragged its feet on reform. There were reports that some NPC and CPPCC members had written to the leadership warning that China would 'become like Indonesia and Malaysia' if it did not proceed with political liberalisation. But, at least at the time of writing, it seemed the leftist voice was being paid more heed

Commemorating the twentieth anniversary of Deng's great achievement – the reform and opening up programme – Jiang delivered another tough speech showing he was eschewing radical or 'Westernised' methods in economic or political reform. Instead, the emphasis of the televised address was on maintaining stability and curtailing signs of unrest, which, he said, must be 'nipped in the bud'. Although repeating the standard line that Deng's reforms would be upheld for at least 100 years, he echoed the views of conservatives, such as ex-premier Li Peng, that reform must not jeopardise political stability, the leadership's codewords for one-party dictatorship. The President gave strong hints that bold reforms pioneered by Premier Zhu Rongji less than a year earlier might be toned down. He said the speed of reform must be adjusted to 'the people's ability to accept them'. Mr Jiang also tried to reassure the nation's mushrooming army of unemployed that the state would not throw them overboard. 'Polarisation between rich and poor is not socialism,' the President said. This was tantamount to saying that many enterprise reform measures entailing laying-off more workers would have to be held up.

The President was even more conservative on political reform. He decried 'Western-style models of democracy', saying they 'must never be copied' in China. He claimed that the Communist Party and the socialist system could be rendered better and less corrupt by 'self-improvement' and no structural overhaul was needed. One indication of the harder political line was the reactivation of a secretive Crisis Management Leading Group within the Party Central Committee to handle challenges to the administration posed by dissidents and laid-off workers. One of the group's central tasks is to prevent different 'unstable' sectors such as workers and radical intellectuals from joining forces. Another indicator was the ruling out by the Politburo of any immediate reconsideration of the verdict on the student movement of 1989, officially characterised as 'counter-revolutionary turmoil'. There has, at times, been quite vocal lobbying for the verdict to be overturned and for compensation to be paid the victims. At the same time, the General Office of the Party Central Committee issued a circular to regional officials asking them to raise their guard against challenges to the administration, along with promoting an education campaign emphasising national stability and fighting Western influences. Similar instructions were given to university authorities.

The media is also the focus of the intensified drive against dissent. Publishers, authors and artists were united in fearing an across-the-board crackdown following publication in December 1998 of a judicial interpretation of 'subversion' and 'splitting the country'. Under new rules carried in the official media, book and magazine publishers as well as music producers and film makers face life in prison if they are found guilty of 'inciting to subvert state power'. Publishers are barred from knowingly allowing publication, printing, reproduction, circulation or dissemination of written or recorded works with subversive content, the latest Supreme People's Court interpretations showed. The maximum punishment is life in prison. The new rules cover writing, music, films, television, video recordings and computer software. They outlaw material that 'endangers social order' the catchall phrase for words or deeds that challenge the Communist Party.

The 18 articles also ban material aimed at 'splitting the nation', a reference to separatist activities in Tibet and the Muslim region of Xinjiang, sabotaging reunification with Taiwan and overthrowing the socialist system. Politically sensitive books by reformist authors have slipped through the cracks in recent years and found their way into bookshops in the wake of economic reforms that have forced state publishing houses to sink or swim in the marketplace. This may not be so easy from now on. For example, the authorities ordered a best-selling book '*Political China: Facing the Era of Choosing a New Structure*' removed from the shelves and banned any reprints (*South China Morning Post*, 19-12-1998). At least two television journalists were disciplined for hosting a programme on the controversial book, while one of its co-editors, Shi Binhai, was still under detention at the time of writing for allegedly maintaining connections with ousted party chief Zhao Ziyang.

But the leadership has been forced to face the reality that in many parts of rural China, the Party's word is no longer law. According to a 'party source' quoted by the *South China Morning Post*, a survey of 10 provinces showed rural party cells had lost legitimacy and power. 'The survey finds real power in the villages resides with heads of clans or even leaders of underground churches and cults,' the source said. 'Jiang was alarmed on hearing that clan and cult leaders in relatively remote hamlets can often take the law into their own hands'. By contrast, party committees in villages, which are supposed to lay down the rules, fail to command the respect of the people (*South China Morning Post*, 9-10-1998).

During the 1990s, the central government has both surrendered some of its power to provincial authorities in the interests of efficiency, and then tried to regain them. But it has discovered that it is easier to give than to take back. Some key decisions on how to run the economy can no longer be enforced by Beijing and, to the extent that managing economic success is an important part of the regime's legitimacy and hence a key part of its political power, the decentralisation of economic power is also a decentralisation of political power. Power has been devolved to a range of actors, including township and village enterprises, individuals and even overseas Chinese and other outsiders. Thus there is no simple struggle for control between centre and province. Inter-provincial protectionism, trade wars and the refusal to accept central decisions on the economy; these all suggest that real disputes exist and that real power has increased at the provincial level.

Alternative futures; towards a post-Communist society?

In the light of such concerns, we can ask where are China and its political system heading? As we saw in Chapter 1, when Mao Zedong entered Beijing in 1949 to declare the foundation of the People's Republic of China, the country was utterly devastated. The economy was in ruins due to decades of war feuds between various warlords, civil war, war against the invading Japanese. Generally, the advent of Communism was welcomed in offering hope of an end to the slaughter and an end to the oppression and exploitation of venal landlords and officials of the corrupt Nationalist regime.

In the past fifty years, China has been transformed. Much of this reflects great credit on Mao and his successors, despite the extremes of the Great Leap Forward and the Great Proletarian Cultural Revolution. Dire poverty, which was the inevitable lot of the peasantry from time immemorial, has largely been eliminated. Illiteracy too, is now considerably reduced. There is almost universal education, and the majority of young Chinese today have a chance of not only completing secondary education but even of going further. Public health programmes down to grassroots level have almost doubled life expectancy in the past five decades.

China at the turn of century is the world's third largest economic power behind the United States and Japan (World Bank, 1997). Within the next thirty years, it may overhaul both. It is among the world's top 10 trading nations (World Trade Organisation, 1997). Billions of dollars of foreign investment pour into the country each month. As we have seen in this book, cities like Beijing, Shanghai and Guangzhou are typified by forests of high rise office buildings sporting the names of the world's best known conglomerates. Looking at the latest model cars clogging the streets, and the fashionable clothing of the passers-by, one can see many signs of growing affluence.

At the same time, on these same streets one can see beggars for virtually the first time since the advent of the PRC. Some seem organised in professional gangs, but be that as it may, in winter there is no more heart-rending sight than to see elderly men and women, bound up in filthy rags, kow-towing (their foreheads touching the ground) in front of a tin can placed on the pavement; and peasant women with babes in arms, ragged young children, pestering the passers-by night and day. The egalitarianism espoused by Mao everyone eating out of the same pot meant that, if nobody was literally rich, at least no-one was dirt-poor. That perspective has been abandoned in the dash for economic growth. There is a growing gap between rich and poor in both the cities and the rural areas; there is a growing gap between East and West, North and South China, as was discussed in Chapters 4 and 5. Many Chinese are now beginning to worry that their society is returning to the bad old days that Communism was supposed to have eradicated for ever.

Even for the Chinese, it is hard to see exactly which way the country will go. As Murray notes in the conclusion to his previous book (1998), a 500,000-word novel *Yellow Peril* was published in 1997, written under a pseudonym by a mainland Chinese author. The novel 'gives a flavour of the kind of doomsday ideas spinning around Beijing' (Murray, 1998, p.208) in this time of rapid change and attendant insecurity. 'It describes a civil war between north and south China – with Taiwan supporting the south – ending in nuclear conflict and millions of starving refugee spilling across the borders into neighbouring states to trigger fresh unrest there. The message is that the demise of Communist ideology, and the passing of old guard leaders whose revolutionary credentials gave them a certain legitimacy, poses new problems. It also raises the question of whether the Chinese Communist Party survives to 2020. No feast lasts forever, say some intellectuals in Beijing. There is only one powerful Communist Party, and if one day it fails society will be thrown into disorder. China, they say, has only two futures: control or loss of control' (ibid.).

The civil war noted above is similar to Cook and Li's (1996) 'nightmare scenario' mentioned in Chapter 4. This is the 'loss of control' outcome, the spectre which haunts Chinese feast. It presents a return to the Old China, of humiliation, degradation and disaster. The CPC is desperate to avoid such a future; hence the increasing crackdown on dissent noted above. As it gropes for the right formula to update Maoism, the party leadership has still to find a new model and a new vocabulary to describe what they seek to create. 'Socialism with Chinese characteristics', which is constantly espoused as the way forward, is essentially a catchall concept. Similarly, the idea that China is at the 'primary stage of socialism' which the leadership use to lend Marxist legitimacy to reform policies, does not seriously confront the issue of preserving the core of the socialist enterprise through a long historical detour. There is a loss of direction, with the vacuum left by the demise of communism as a utopian but achievable goal filled by a descent into the pursuit of personal, local and regional self-interest.

One of the key elements in the future of China will be the role of the People's Liberation Army, the PLA. In the 1990s, the PLA were known to be involved in many commercial activities, and were rumoured to be involved in some which were dubious, including smuggling in South China and running a trade in gold. Whatever the truth of these charges, in August 1998 the Chinese leadership passed an order for the PLA to divest itself of all commercial activities. Since then, the PLA's effort to cut ties with its commercial enterprises continues to hit problems despite repeated instructions from senior leaders. The army's leading group overseeing the divestiture admitted at a plenary session in early July 1999, that problems included finding jobs for laid-off workers, bad debts, and financial liabilities (*Liberation Army Daily*, 7-7-1999).

The group received briefings from six major inspection teams which made spot checks and identified problems over the transfer at all regional commands in April and May. Problems remained in the management of enterprises kept by the PLA. The same was true for eleven quasi-commercial services the army was allowed to maintain. The army paper reported that inertia and timidity in carrying out the change existed alongside problems in transferring former military assets to private accounts, overcharging and the spending of official funds during the handover process. PLA chief commissar General Yu Yongbo, who chaired the meeting, outlined the work for the next phase based on 'numerous important instructions by Jiang Zemin, chairman of the Central Military Commission, and the commission's talks since this year over the major problems of decommercialising the PLA'. One objective of the campaign appeared to be to crack down on interest groups, especially those involving the children of senior cadres, in an effort to consolidate Jiang's position. This ties in with earlier policies of ensuring that the centre retains a tight control over the armed forces (Cook and Li, 1996, op.cit., p.206)

Another potential challenge to party supremacy may lie in the revival of the feudalistic clans, undermining the authority of the party in the countryside: 'Rural cadres complain that clan activities have siphoned off badly needed funds for agriculture and education. The security departments cited villages in Hunan as having clan units so powerful they had refused to pay taxes or implement family planning measures. At the same time, since only males can join clans, their revival has fuelled families' desires for male children in rural areas' (Murray, 1998, p.146). Further, he notes that 'One clan in central China boasts more than 30,000 members from three generations' (ibid.).

Also, numerous cults and folk religions, along with more traditional beliefs such as Christianity and Buddhism, are filling a spiritual void in society as China abandons socialism. One such is the Falun-Gong, a *qi gong* (martial art that allows practitioners to develop their 'inner energy') movement promising to cure sickness and reverse a tide of evil sweeping mankind to the brink of catastrophe, which, in April 1999, staged a remarkable silent protest involving an estimated 15,000 followers outside Zhongnanhai, the Communist Party headquarters in central Beijing to demand it be given the status of a religion. The so-called 'Buddhist Law' cult is rooted in the notion of karma, which holds that people's good and bad deeds determine their fate in the next life. Society is in such steep decline that humans are actually being reincarnated as demons, many disguised as monks, according to its leader, Li Hongzhi, who has written five books, regarded by devotees as sacred. Some followers believe the end of the world is near. And, like the Boxer rebels a century ago, many claim they have acquired superhuman powers through training their minds and bodies in line with ancient Chinese martial arts practices. The movement had grown rapidly in the late 1990s, and was officially said to have two million members, although there were some Chinese who thought the figure was far higher, apparently tapping into deep public resentment, and fear of the unknown, as China undergoes wrenching social change and upheaval. An undetermined number of Party cadres were among the members.

Surprisingly, given the authoritarian image of China in the West where memories of the 1989 Tiananmen Square incident remain vivid, the protesters outside Zhongnanhai, in April were allowed to carry out their protest unmolested – and actually gained many of the concessions sought from the government through negotiations. This proved deceptive. On July 22, the government banned the sect, which it clearly regarded as a serious threat to party rule. The official announcement said: 'The Falun Gong Research Society conducted illegal activities, spreading superstitious, evil thinking to blind people, to stir up trouble and sabotage social stability' (Xinhua, 22-7-1999). The state media accused it of causing deaths and serious injuries among its followers, and some had died after refusing to take medicine in the belief that their self-proclaimed Buddha leaders would heal them. The announcement came after three days of protests by as many as 30,000 people in many Chinese cities, over the arrests of some 70 leading members of the sect (ibid.).

Analysing this, it would seem the government was caught unawares by the April protest and was forced to bide its time while building up a true picture of the nature of the sect and the seriousness of the threat it posed. In part, this suggests that there is a growing sense of a leadership that is confused over how to deal with dissent – whether to be placatory, or wield the big stick as in 1989. The fear that the party is losing control comes through quite clearly in an editorial published by an official newspaper, which issued a rallying call to the people to help security departments 'expose hidden enemies' threatening state security'. It went on: 'Enemies outside the country have never stopped their activities of endangering China's state security. The special organs of the Government should get the people's support and assistance to expose our enemies and give them no place to hide. At a time when we are focused on economic construction and face various challenges arising from reforms, leaders at all levels within the party, especially high-level cadres, should consistently keep high vigilance and make state sovereignty and security top priority.'

In contrast to overseas' criticism of China's tightened social control and the crackdown on dissent, the paper actually attacked the low awareness of state security among mainlanders. 'Some people block the state security organs from carrying out their lawful duties. Some people leak state security secrets and cause severe damage to the Government's work, and some engage in illegal activities, endangering state security in exchange for private gain' (*Legal Daily*, 3-3-1999).

All this suggests that this 'third revolution' which the PRC is still undergoing, is even more complex and challenging than the first one led by Dr. Sun which helped set the preconditions for Mao's victory half a century ago, and as dramatic as that fundamental second revolution. In tackling this challenge, China will not be an easy country for the rest of the world to deal with. The government in Beijing watched with horror the disintegration of the Soviet Union from its own economic reform program, and are determined that same thing will not happen to them. The accidental bombing by NATO of the Chinese embassy in Belgrade during the Kosovan conflict in 1999, coupled with the contemporary controversy over the alleged stealing of US nuclear secrets, brought new pressures to bear on the leadership, as has a new book by Taiwan's leader, Lee Teng Hui, which advocates autonomy for China's 'peripheral' regions. As noted in Chapter 4, Lee's call for state-to-state relations has further inflamed tensions, as will such views as:

> 'I also want to see the mainland enhance political reforms and expand the breadth and depth of democratization so that our fellow Chinese on the continent will be able to apply fully their ingenuity and abilities in building a multifaceted, open and modern society' (Lee Teng-Hui, 1999, p.8).

We shall, along with other China watchers, await the PRC's response with considerable interest and some trepidation. Communism's survival in the twenty-first century is not assured, certainly in its current form. The Chinese government has yet to find the right formula to ensure that its own survival in the face of those tensions analysed in this book, along with others still to come, is a foregone conclusion. The environmental stopwatch is still ticking away, never mind the many other internal and external tensions noted here. A post-Communist China may still be a distant dream; but that dream remains a potent vision. In our view, the CPC, contrary to many of its instincts, would be better advised to more firmly grasp and nurture the democracy nettle, encouraging a higher level of informed debate even if this sometimes seems like dissent, to thus avoid the worst of its sting.

References

Chapter 1

Blecher, M. (1986), *China: Politics, Economics and Society: Iconoclasm and Innovation in a Revolutionary Socialist Country*, London: Frances Pinter.

Bloodworth, D. (1966), *The Chinese Looking Glass*, New York: Farrar, Strauss & Giroux.

Cannon, T. and Zhang, L-Y (1996), 'Inter-region Tension and China's Reforms', Chapter 4 in Cook, I.G., Doel, M.A. and Li, R. (eds), *Fragmented Asia: Regional Integration and National Disintegration in Pacific Asia*, Aldershot, England: Avebury, pp.75–101.

Chen, Jerome (1965), *Mao and the Chinese Revolution*, Oxford: Oxford University Press.

China Daily, 15-7-1999.

Fitzgerald, C.P. (1977), *Mao Tse-Tung and China*, Harmondsworth, Middlesex, England: Penguin.

Forney, M. (1996), 'Party Line: Beijing Plenum Backs Jiangist Ideology', *Far Eastern Economic Review*, 24th October, p.28.

Goodman, D. (1990), *Makers of the Twentieth Century: Deng Xiaoping*, London: Cardinal.

—— (1994), *Deng Xiaoping and the Chinese Revolution*, London: Routledge.

Han Suyin (1976), *Wind In The Tower: Mao Tsetung and the Chinese Revolution 1949–1975*, New York: Little Brown & Co..

Hsu, I.C.Y. (1990), *The Rise of Modern China*, Oxford: Oxford University Press, Fourth Edition.

Hughes, E.R. (1937), *The Invasion of China by the Western World*, London: Adam and Charles Black.

Lattimore, O. (1940/1998), *Inner Asian Frontiers of China*, Hong Kong: Oxford University Press.

Mackeras, C. and Yorke, A. (1991), *The Cambridge Handbook of Contemporary China*, Cambridge: Cambridge University Press.

Mao Zedong (1954), *Selected Works of Mao Tse-Tung*, London: Lawrence and Wishart, Four Volumes.

—— (1971), *Selected Readings from the Works of Mao Zedong*, Beijing: Foreign Languages Press.

Murray, G. (1994), *China: The Last Great Market*, London: China Library and New York: St. Martin's Press.

—— (1998), *China The Next Superpower: Dilemmas in Change and Continuity*, London: China Library and New York: St. Martin's Press.

Nolan, P. and Dong Fureng (eds) (1990), *The Chinese Economy And Its Future*, Cambridge: Polity Press.

Parker, J. (1987), 'China's Economy: The Biggest Developer of All', *The Economist*, 1st August, pp.3–22.

Petras, J. (1988), 'Contradictions of Market Socialism in China (Part II), *Journal of Contemporary Asia*, 18, 2, pp.234–244.

Saich, A. (1995), 'China's Political Structure', Chapter 3 in Benewick, R. and Wingrove, P. (eds), *China in the 1990s*, London: Macmillan.

Salisbury, H. (1992), *The New Emperors: Mao & Deng, A Dual Biography*, London: Harper Collins.

Schaller, M. (1979), *The US Crusade in China 1938–45*, New York: Columbia University Press.

Short, P. (1982), *The Dragon and the Bear*, London: Hodder and Stoughton.

Snow, E. (1941), *Scorched Earth*, London: Victor Gollancz.

—— (1970), *Red China Today: The Other Side of the River*, Harmondsworth, Middlesex, England: Penguin.

Spence, J. (1982), *The Gate Of Heavenly Peace: The Chinese and Their Revolution 1895–1980*, London: Faber and Faber.

State Statistics Bureau Annual Report 1998, Beijing.

Terrill, R. (1984), *The White-Boned Demon: A Biography of Madame Mao Zedong*, New York: William Morrow & Co..

Wiethoff, B. (1975), *Introduction to Chinese History*, London: Thames and Hudson.

World Bank (1997a). '*China 2020: Development Challenges in the New Century*', Washington.

—— (1997b) '*China Engaged: Integration with the Global Economy*', Washington.

Xu, Dixin (ed.) (1982), *China's Search For Economic Growth*, Beijing: New World Press.

Yang, D.L. (1994), 'Reform and the Restructuring of Central-Local Relations', Chapter 3 in Goodman, D.S.G. and Segal, G. (eds), *China Deconstructs: Politics, Trade and Regionalism*, London: Routledge, pp.59–98.

Chapter 2

Associated Press, 25-1-1998.

Beijing Review, 16-8-1993; 12-10-1996; 16-6-1997.

Bukharin and Preobrazhensky (1969), *The ABC of Communism*, Harmondsworth, Middlesex, England: Penguin.

Business Weekly, 16-11-1997, 21-11-1997.

China Daily, 17-2-1998, 3-5-1998, 14-12-1998, 14-4-1999 and 26-6-1999.

China Internet Information Centre, www.chinanews.org.

China Labour News, 12-2-1998.

Chinese Academy of Social Science (1995). '*Market Orientation, Decision-Making Power and Enterprise Performance – A Statistical and Analytical Report on the Sample Data of 795 State-Owned Enterprises*', Economic Institute of the Chinese Academy of Social Science, Beijing.

Etheridge, J. (1988), *Changing China*, Beijing: New World Press.

Murray, G. (1994), *China: The Last Great Market*, London: China Library and New York: St Martins Press.

—— (1998), *China The Next Superpower: Dilemmas in Change and Continuity*, London: China Library and New York: St Martins Press.

Nolan, P. and Dong Fureng (eds) (1990), *The Chinese Economy And Its Future*, Cambridge: Polity Press.

Outlook, 22-2-1998.

Shanghai Liberation Daily, 3-11-1997.

South China Morning Post, 31-12-1998.

World Bank, *World Development Report 1996*, Oxford: Oxford University Press.

Xinhua, 6-8-1997, 21-3-1998.

Chapter 3

Bannister, N. (1999), 'Steel deal raises job fears', *Guardian*, 8th June.

Baosteel Annual Report 1996, Baoshan: Baoshan Iron and Steel Corporation.

Byrd, W.A. (1992), 'The Anshan Iron and Steel Company', in Byrd, W.A. (ed.) *Chinese Industrial Firms Under Reform*, Oxford: Oxford University Press for the World Bank, pp.303–370.

Cannon, T. (1990), 'Regions, Spatial Inequality and Regional Policy', in Cannon, T. and Jenkins, A. (eds), *The Geography of Contemporary China: The Impact of Deng Xiaoping's Decade*, London: Routledge, pp.28–60.

Cheng Guang (1997), 'Baosteel Business Strategy in Market Economy', in Guan Zhian and Liu Kexun (eds), *International Symposium on Steel Industry Development and Management Proceedings*, Beijing: Metallurgical Industry Press, pp.27–32.

Chi Fulin (1996), *Pressing Tasks of China's Economic Transition*, Beijing: Foreign Languages Press.

—— (1997), *Several Issues Arising During the Retracking of the Chinese Economy*, Studies on the Chinese Market Economy Series, Gao Shangquang and Chi Fulin (eds), Beijing: Foreign Languages Press.

China Daily (1998), 'Shougang Moves Mill for Capital's Environment', 18th June.

Cook, I.G. (1997), *Contextualising Steel: Changing Locational Factors in the Steel Industry*, International Symposium on Steel Industry Development and Management, Baoshan, May 1997.

—— and Murray, G. (1999), *Some Contradictions in the Process of China's Economic Reform*, Paper Presented to the 10th Chinese Economic Association, UK, Conference on 'The Chinese Economy and Industry in the 21st Century', Middlesex Business School, 29–30 March 1999.

Cooke, K. (1993), 'Baoshan Steelworks: Leading Supplier of Quality Products, *Financial Times*, June 2, p.34.

D'Costa (1993), 'State-Sponsored Internationalization: Restructuring and Development of the Steel Industry', in Noponen, H., Graham, J. and Markusen, A.R. (eds), *Trading Industries, Trading Regions: International Trade, American Industry and Regional Economic Development*, London: Guilford Press.

Dong Liming (1988), 'Beijing: The Development of a Socialist Capital', in Sit, V.F.S. (ed.), *Chinese Cities*, Oxford: Oxford University Press, pp.67–93.

Harding, J. (1997), 'Chinese Steelmaker Takes a National Role: James Harding on a State group Allowed to Manage its Own Business – For the Time Being', *Financial Times*, June 11, p.4.

Hodder, R. (1994), 'State, Collective and Private Industry in China's Evolving Economy', in Dwyer, D. (ed.), *China: The Next Decades*, Harlow, Essex, England: Longman Scientific and Technical, pp.116–127.

Jing Can (1996), 'Resurrection of a Dinosaur: Angang Thrives', *Beijing Review*, Oct.28-Nov.3, pp.10–13.

Howe, C. (1978), *China's Economy: A Basic Guide*, London: Paul Elek.

Kirkby, R.J.R. (1994), 'Dilemmas of Urbanization: Review and Prospects', in Dwyer, D. (ed.), *China: The Next Decades*, Harlow, Essex, England: Longman Scientific and Technical, pp.128–155.

Liu, Fu-Kuo (1996), 'Industrial Development and the Impetus to Regional Economic Integration in Pacific Asia', Chapter 6 in Cook, I.G., Doel, M.A. and Li, R. (eds), *Fragmented Asia: Regional Integration and National Disintegration in Pacific Asia*, Aldershot, England: Avebury, pp.137–166.

Linge, G.J.R. and Forbes, D.K. (1990), 'The Space Economy of China', in Linge, G.J.R. and Forbes, D.K. (eds), *China's Spatial Economy*, Oxford: Oxford University Press, pp.10–34.

Lucas, L. (1997), 'Angang Seeks HKDollars 1.75 billion', *Financial Times*, 10th July.

Luo Bing-Sheng (1997), 'Internationalized Business of Chinese Steel Industry Judged by the Practice of Shougang Group Company', in Guan Zhian and Liu Kexun (eds), *International Symposium on Steel Industry Development and Management Proceedings*, Beijing: Metallurgical Industry Press, pp.75–8.

Miller, R.R. (1991), 'The Changing Economics of Steel', *Finance and Development*, 28, 2. pp.38–40.

Straits Times (1999), '46,000 China firm workers not paid', 5th April.

Taylor, M. (1996), 'Industrialisation, Enterprise Power, and Environmental Change: An Exploration of Concepts', *Environment and Planning A*, 28, pp.1035–1051.

Tregear, T.R. (1980), *China: A Geographical Survey*, Sevenoaks, Kent, England: Hodder and Stoughton.

Zhao Songqiao (1994), *Geography of China: Environment, Resources, Population and Development*, New York: Wiley.

Chapter 4

Blecher, M. (1986), *China: Politics, Economics and Society*, London: Frances Pinter.

Bramall, C. and Jones, M.E. (1993), 'Rural Income Inequality in China Since 1978', *Journal of Peasant Studies*, 21, 1, pp.41–70.

Bray, J. (1996), 'Burma: Prospects for Regional Integration', Chapter 8 in Cook, I.G., Doel, M.A. and Li, R. (eds), *Fragmented Asia: Regional Integration and National Disintegration in Pacific Asia*, Aldershot, England: Avebury.

Buchanan, K. (1970), *Transformation of the Chinese Earth*, London: Bell.

Cannon, T. (1990), 'Regions: Spatial Inequality and Regional Policy', in Cannon, T. and Jenkins, A. (eds), *The Geography of Contemporary China: The Impact of Deng Xiaoping's Decade*, London: Routledge, 1990, pp.28–60.

—— and Zhang, L-Y. (1996), 'Inter-region Tension and China's Reforms', in I.G., Doel, M., and Li, R. (eds), *Fragmented Asia:Regional Integration and National Disintegration in Pacific Asia*, Aldershot, England: Avebury, pp.75–101.

Chai, J.C.H. (1996), 'Divergent Development and Regional Income Gap in China', *Journal of Contemporary Asia*, 26, 1, pp.46–58.

Chen, Xiangming (1995), 'The Evolution of Free Economic Zones and the Recent Development of Cross-National Growth Zones', *International Journal of Urban and Regional Research*, 19, pp.593–621.

Cho-Oon Khong (1996), 'Pacific Asia as a Region: A View From Business', in Cook, I.G., Doel, M., and Li, R. (eds), *Fragmented Asia:Regional Integration and National Disintegration in Pacific Asia*, Aldershot, England: Avebury, pp.167–180.

Cook, I.G. (2000), 'Urban and Regional Pressures of Development', Chapter 2 in Cannon, T. (ed.), *China's Economic Growth: The Impact on Regions, Migration and the Environment*, London: Macmillan.

—— and Li, R. (1994a), *The Future of China: Unity or Division?*, Paper presented to the British Pacific Rim Research Group, School of Oriental And African Studies, University of London, May.

—— and Li, R. (1996), The Rise of Regionalism and the Future of China, Chapter 9 in Cook, I.G., Doel, M., and Li, R. (eds) *Fragmented Asia: Regional Integration and National Disintegration in Pacific Asia*, Aldershot, England: Avebury.

Foreign Investment Administration and China Economic and Trade Consultants Corp., (1993), *Investment in China*, Beijing: Ministry of Foreign Trade and Economic Co-operation.

Freeberne, M. (1971), 'The People's Republic of China', Chapter 5 in East, W.G., Spate, O.H.K. and Fisher, C.A. (eds), *The Changing Map of Asia: A Political Geography*, London: Methuen, Fifth Edition, pp.341–447.

Fu-Kuo Liu (1996), 'Industrial Development and the Impetus to Regional Economic Integration in Pacific Asia', Chapter 6 in Cook, I.G., Doel, M.A. and Li, R. (eds), *Fragmented Asia: Regional Integration and National Disintegration in Pacific Asia*, Aldershot, England: Avebury.

Goodman, D.S.G. (1994), 'The Politics of Regionalism: Economic Development, Conflict and Negotiation', Chapter 1 in Goodman, D.S.G. and Segal, G. (eds), *China Deconstructs: Politics, Trade and Regionalism*, London: Routledge, pp.1–20.

—— and Feng Chongyi (1994), 'Guangdong: Greater Hong Kong and the New Regionalist Future', Chapter 6 in Goodman, D.S.G. and Segal, G. (eds), *China Deconstructs: Politics, Trade and Regionalism*, London: Routledge, pp.177–201.

Hook, G. (1996), 'Japan and Contested Regionalism', Chapter 1 in Cook, I.G., Doel, M.A. and Li, R. (eds), *Fragmented Asia: Regional Integration and National Disintegration in Pacific Asia*, Aldershot, England: Avebury.

Hussain, A. (1994), 'The Chinese Economic Reforms: An Assessment', Chapter Two in Dwyer, D. (ed.), *China: The Next Decades*, Harlow, Essex, England: Longman Scientific and Technical.

Li, R. (1997), 'China's Investment Environment: The Security Dimension', *Asia Pacific Business Review*, 4, 1, pp.39–62.

Phillips, D.R. and Yeh, A. G-O (1990), 'Foreign Investment and Trade: Impact on Spatial Structure of the Economy', in Cannon, T. and Jenkins, A. (eds), *The Geography of Contemporary China: The Impact of Deng Xiaoping's Decade*, London: Routledge, pp.224–248.

Tsang Shu-Ki (1996), 'The Political Economy of Greater China', Chapter 2 in Rowley, C. and Lewis, M. (eds), *Greater China: Political Economy, Inward Investment and Business Culture*, London: Frank Cass.

Uri Dadush and Dong He (1995), 'China: A New Power in World Trade', *Finance and Development*, June, pp.36–8.

Yabuki, S. (1995) *China's New Political Economy: The Giant Awakes*, Oxford: Westview Press.

Zhang Ping (1998), *Analysis of Inequality Distribution of Rural Residents in Different Regions*, with the Institute of Economics, Chinese Academy of Social Sciences, Beijing.

Zhou Shunwu (1992), *China Provincial Geography*, Beijing: Foreign Languages Press.

Chapter 5

Beijing Review, 10-5-1993, 18-7-1994, 26-10-1996 and 24-3-1997.
CASS (1997), '*1991–2010: Policy Choices of China's Economic Development*', Chinese Academy of Social Sciences, Beijing.
China Daily, 18-4-1993, 8-4-1999 and 27-4-1999.
China Today, 'The Floating Population', February 1999.
Gao Shangquan and Chi Fulin (1997), *The Reform and Development of China's Rural Economy*, Studies on the Chinese Market Economy Series, Beijing: Foreign Languages Press.
Grant. P. (1988), *Celestial Empire: China in the 20th Century*, London: Queen Anne Press.
Hinton, W. (1966), *Fenshan. A Documentary of Revolution in a Chinese Village*, New York: Vintage Books.
—— (1983), *Shenfan*, London: Secker & Warburg.
Mao Zedong (1954), Selected Works of Mao Tse-Tung, Volume One, London: Lawrence and Wishart.
Murray, G. (1998), *China The Next Superpower: Dilemmas in Change and Continuity*, London: China Library and New York: St. Martin's Press.
People's Daily, 'Survey Shows Worsening Poverty', 10-9-1998.
Snow, E. (1963), *The Other Side Of The River*, London: Victor Gollancz.
China Statistical Almanac 1996, Beijing
State Statistics Bureau, *Annual Reports*, Beijing.
—— (1998), *Survey of the Status of Rural Migrants in Key Cities*, Beijing.
Xinhua News Agency, 22-4-1999.
Zhang Xinmin and Tang Ping (1998), Market and Demographic Analysis, State Statistics Bureau, September, published in the December 1998 issue of *China Population Today*.

Chapter 6

Agence France Press, 20-4-1999.
Amnesty International, April 1999.
Annual Statistical Report of the State Statistics Bureau, 1996.
Beijing Review, 9-3-1998, 30-3-1998 and 5-11 October, 1998.
Bell, Sir C. (1924), *Tibet Past & Present*, Oxford: Clarendon Press.
Bishop, P. (1989), *The Myth Of Shangri-La. Tibet, Travel Writing and the Western Creation of Sacred Landscape*, London: Athlone Press.
Bista, D.B. (1979), *Report From Lhasa*, Kathmandu: Sahja Prakashan.
China Daily, 15-11-1997 and 13-3-1998.
China's Tibet, February 1998, p.16.
Clark, L. (1955), *The Marching Wind*, London: Hutchinson.
Cook, I.G. and Li, R. (1996), The Rise of Regionalism and the Future of China, in Cook, I.G., Doel, M., and Li, R. (eds) *Fragmented Asia:Regional Integration and National Disintegration in Pacific Asia*, Aldershot, England: Avebury, pp. 200–219.
Cotterell, A. (1995), *China. A History*, London: Pimlico (Random House).
Dalai Lama (1962), *My Land and My People*, London: Weidenfeld & Nicolson.
Fleming, P. (1936), *News From Tartary*, London: Jonathan Cape.
—— (1961), *Bayonets To Lhasa*, London: Readers Union.
Gelder, S and R. (1964), *The Timely Rain. Travels in New Tibet*, London: Hutchinson.

259

Goldstein, M. 'The Dalai Lama's Dilemma', *Foreign Affairs*, Vol. 77, No.1. January/ February 1998, pp. 83–93.

Han Suyin (1972), *The Morning Deluge*, London: Jonathan Cape.

Harrer, H. (1953), *Seven Years in Tibet*, London: Reprint Society.

—— (1988), *Return To Tibet*, Harmondsworth, Middlesex, England: Penguin.

Huc, E. *Souvenirs of a Journey Through Tartary, Tibet and China During the Years 1844, 1845 and 1846 Vols 1 and 2*. Annotated Version edited by Planchet, J-M., Beijing: Lazarist Press, 1931. Original English Version, *Recollections Of A Journey Through Tartary and Thibet and The Chinese Empire*, London: Longman, Brown, Green, Longmans and Roberts, 1859.

Landon, P. (1905). *Lhasa Vol.1*, London: Hurst & Blackett Ltd.

Lattimore, O. (1940/1998). *Inner Asian Frontiers of China*, Hong Kong: Oxford University Press. First published by the American Geographical Society, Boston.

Liao Pin (ed.) (1991), *Life Among the Minority Nationalities in Northwest Yunnan*, Beijing: Foreign Languages Press.

Lowe, J. (1986), *Into China*, London: John Murray.

Ma Yin (ed.) (1994), *China's Minority Nationalities*, Beijing: Foreign Languages Press.

McGovern, W.M. (1924), *To Lhasa In Disguise*, London and New York: The Century Co..

Patterson, G.N. (1954), *Tibetan Journey*, London: Faber and Faber.

Snow, E. (1963), *The Other Side of the River*, London: Victor Gollancz.

South China Morning Post, 4-8-1998, 15-8-1998 and 24-6-1999.

Spence, J. (1990), *The Search For Modern China*. London: Hutchinson.

Tibetan Government-In-Exile, www.tibet.com.

Tsering Shakya (1999), *The Dragon in the Land of the Snows. A History of Modern Tibet Since 1947*, London: Pimlico.

Wang Gui (1997), *Discussion of the Historical Status of Tibet*, Beijing: Foreign Languages Press.

Wang, C.F. (1992), *Contemporary Chinese Politics, An Introduction*, New Jersey: Prentice Hall, Fourth Edition.

Wilby. S. (1988), *Journey Across Tibet*, Chicago: Contemporary Books.

Xinhua, 13-10-1997 and 8-3-1998.

Younghusband, Sir F. (1910), *India and Tibet*, London: John Murray.

Zhang Zhirong (1995), *The International Relation and the Tibet Issue*, Beijing: Xinhua Publishing House.

Chapter 7

Armstrong, W and McGee, T. (1985), *Theatres of Accumulation*, London: Methuen.

Blecher, M. (1986), *China: Politics, Economics and Society: Iconoclasm and Innovation in a Revolutionary Socialist Country*, London: Frances Pinter.

Business Beijing (1996), 'Back and Beyond: Beijing in '95 and '96', Vol. 9, January, pp.16–18.

Business Weekly, 16-5-1999.

Cao Min (1996), 'Beijing Seeks More Overseas Investment', *China Daily*, 17th February.

Chan, Kam Wing (1994), *Cities with Invisible Walls: Reinterpreting Urbanization in Post-1949 China*, Oxford: Oxford University Press.

China Mail (1996), 'An Overstock of Commodity Property in China', Vol.9, No.1, January-February 1996, p.76.

China Mainland Market Research Company (1999), *Survey on Current Consumption Habits among Beijing Residents and Future Trends*, Beijing, January.

Cook, I.G. (1993), *Urban Issues in the West Pacific Rim*, Paper presented to the British Pacific Rim Research Group, Liverpool John Moores University, May.

—— (1995), *Reflections on Pressures of Development in China's Large Cities*, Paper presented to the Symposium on International Urbanization in China, Shunde City, Guangdong Province, August 28th-September 1st 1995.

—— (2000), 'Urban and Regional Pressures of Development', Chapter 2 in Cannon, T. (ed.), *China's Economic Growth. The Impact on Regions, Migration and the Environment*, London: Macmillan.

—— and Li, R. (1994a), *The Transformation of China's Cities: The International Dimension*, Paper presented at the Rotal United Services Institute Asia Forum, Whitehall, London, January.

—— and Wang, Y. (1998), 'Foreign Direct Investment in China: Patterns, Processes, Prospects', Chapter 6 in Cook, I.G., Doel, M. A., Li, R. and Wang, Y. (eds), *Dynamic Asia: Business, Trade and Economic Development in Pacific Asia*, Aldershot, England: Ashgate.

Cooke, K. (1993), 'Pudong Development Zone: New Tiger Will Pace the East Bank', *Financial Times*, June 2nd.

Croll, E. (1995), 'Women in China: Experience and Action', *China Review*, No.1, Summer, pp.12–15.

Foreign Investment Administration and China Economic and Trade Consultants Corp., (1993), *Investment in China*, Beijing: Ministry of Foreign Trade and Economic Co-operation.

Gallup Organisation (1999), *Survey of Chinese Consumer Attitudes and Lifestyles, 1998*, Beijing.

Gao Shangquan and Chi Fulin (eds) (1997), *New Progress in China's Special Economic Zones*, Beijing: Foreign Languages Press.

Gaubatz, P.R. (1995), 'Urban Transformation in Post-Mao China: Impacts of the Reform Era on China's Urban Form', Chapter Two in Davis, D.S., Kraus, R., Naughton, B. and Perry, E.J. (eds), *Urban Spaces in Contemporary China: The Potential for Autonomy and Community in Post-Mao China*, Washington: Woodrow Wilson Center Press and Cambridge: Cambridge University Press.

Gittings, J. (1999a), 'Beijing: City of Secrets and Shopping', *Guardian*, 3rd May.

—— (1999b), 'China's City of Dreams and Extremes', *Guardian*, 5th May.

Hanes, J.E. (1993), From Megalopolis to Megaroporisu, *Journal of Urban History*, 19, 2, February 1993, pp.56–94.

Hu Piyun et.al. (eds) (1995), *Historical Photos of Old Beijing*, Beijing: Beijing Publishing House.

Hua Yequan et.al. (eds) (1996), *Guide to Trade and Investment in Shanghai*, Shanghai: Shanghai Scientific and Technological Literature Publishing House.

Johnston, T. (1994), 'Disappearing Shanghai', *Britain-China*, No.54, pp.4–5.

Kirkby, R.J.R. (1985), *Urbanization in China: Town and Country in a Developing Economy 1949–2000 AD*, London: Croom Helm.

—— (1994), 'Dilemmas of Urbanization: Review and Prospects', Chapter Eight in Dwyer, D. (ed.), *China: The Next Decades*, Harlow, Essex, England: Longman Scientific and Technical.

Liu Yingiang (1996), 'Women Expanding Their Role in Society', *China Daily*, 28th February.

Mirsky, J. (1992), 'China's Baby Girls 'Killed by the Million'' *Observer*, 26th January.

Rai, S.M. (1995), 'Gender in China', Chapter 15 in Benewick, R. and Wingrove, P. (eds), *China in the 1990s*, London: Macmillan, pp.181–192.

Ridding, J. (1996), 'China's Fledgling Export Base Takes Off: But Shenzhen Economic Zone Finds the Future Insecure', *Financial Times*, August 16th.

Riley, N.E. (1996), 'China's^Missing Girls¤: Prospects and Policy', *Population Today*, February, pp.4–5.

Sender, H. (1992), 'Eastern Promise: Hongkong Developers Flock to Shanghai', *Far Eastern Economic Review*, 17-9-1992, p.72.

Shen Yahong (1992), Enlightenment From the Development of Ancient City Planning in China in the Ancient Times, *China City Planning Review*, 8, 1, 1992, pp.65–75.

Shi Min (1991), China's Human Resource Development in the 1990's, *Asia-Pacific Studies*, No. 1, 1991, pp.78–85.

Solinger, D. J. (1995), 'The Floating Population in the Cities: Chances for Assimilation?', Chapter Five in Davis, D.S., Kraus, R., Naughton, B. and Perry, E.J. (eds), *Urban Spaces in Contemporary China: The Potential for Autonomy and Community in Post-Mao China*, Washington: Woodrow Wilson Center Press and Cambridge: Cambridge University Press.

State Information Centre (1999), *Topic Group Report On Consumption Supply and Demand*, March, Beijing.

Sudjic, D. (1992), Birth of the Brave New City, *Guardian*, 2nd December, pp.2–3.

Wheatley, P. (1971), *The Pivot of the Four Quarters: A Preliminary Enquiry into the Origins and Character of the Ancient Chinese City*, Edinburgh: Edinburgh University Press.

Xin Zhou (1997), 'Shanghai at Night', *China National Day 1997*, Beijing: China Intercontinental Press, pp.52–7.

Yan Mingfu (1995), *Modern Civilization and China's Urbanization Toward the 21st Century*, Paper presented to the Symposium on International Urbanization in China, Shunde City, Guangdong Province, August 28th-September 1st 1995.

Zhang Zaoji et.al. (eds) (1993), *Hutongs of Beijing*, Beijing: Beijing Arts and Photography Publishing House.

Zou Deci (1995), 'The Introduction of Urban Development in China', *China City Planning Review*, 11, 1, March, pp.25–32.

Chapter 8

Author research (1996–9), Part of the material in this chapter is based on articles contributed by Geoffrey Murray from 1996 onwards to *Property Review*, a monthly magazine published in Singapore by Magazine Inc. on behalf of the Real Estate Developers Association of Singapore and used here with permission.

CASS (1997), '*1991–2010: Policy Choices of China's Economic Development*', Chinese Academy of Social Sciences, Beijing.

China Daily, Property section reports published on 20-11-1997, 26-1-1997, 17-5-1997, 23-5-1997, 2-8-1997,3-9-1997, 27-11-1997, 1-12-1997 and 11-12-1997.

Legal Daily, 30-7-1997.

Murray, G. (1993), *The Rampant Dragon*, London: Minerva Press.

Real Estate Newspaper (Ministry of Construction), various reports published throughout 1997 and 1998, Beijing.

State Commission for Economic Restructuring (1997), '*Main Points of Implementation of the 1997 Economic Restructuring*', Beijing.

Xinhua News Agency, 4-12-1997.

Chapter 9

Bei Jingshi (1999), 'Capital cleans up', *Business Beijing*, Issue 38, p.22.

Beijing Review, 22nd–27th October 1996, 14th–20th September 1998, 12-7-1999.

Business Beijing, January 1996 and February 1999.

Bradbury, I. and Kirkby, R. (1995), 'Prospects for Conservation in China', *Ecos*, 16, 3, 4, pp.64–71

Brown, L. (1995), *Who Will Feed China: Wake Up Call for a Small Planet*, Washington: Worldwatch Institute.

Buchanan, K. (1970), *Transformation of the Chinese Earth*, London: Bell.

Chao, P.K.I. (1990), *The Changing Geography of China: A Synoptic View*, Hong Kong: Commercial Press.

China Daily, 21-11-1997, 22-12-1997, 4-6-1998.

China Daily Business Weekly, 6-6-1998.

Cook, I.G. (1993), *Urban Issues in the West Pacific Rim*, Paper presented to the British Pacific Rim Research Group, Liverpool John Moores University, May.

—— (1995), *Reflections on Pressures of Development in China's Large Cities*, Paper presented to the International Symposium on International Urbanization in China, Shunde City, Guangdong Province, August 28th-September 1st.

—— (2000), 'Urban and Regional Pressures of Development', Chapter 2 in Cannon, T. (ed.), *China's Economic Growth: The Impact on Regions, Migration and the Environment*, London: Macmillan.

Dai Qing (1998), *The River Dragon Has Come! The Three Gorges Dam and the Fate of China's Yangtze River and its People*, (edited by Thibodeau, J.G. and Williams, P.B.; tr. Yi Ming), New York: M.E.Sharpe.

Derbyshire, E. (1994), 'Environment: Understanding and Transforming the Physical Environment', Chapter 4 in Dwyer, D. (ed.), *China: The Next Decades*, Harlow, Essex, England: Longman Scientific and Technical.

Douglas, I., Gu Hengyue and He Min (1994), 'Water Resources and Environmental Problems of China's Great Rivers', Chapter 10 in Dwyer, D. (ed.), *China: The Next Decades*, Harlow, Essex, England: Longman Scientific and Technical.

Edmonds, R.L. (1994a), *Patterns of China's Lost Harmony: A Survey of the Country's Environmental Degradation and Protection*, London: Routledge.

—— (1994b), 'China's Environment: Problems and Prospects', Chapter 9 in Dwyer, D. (ed.), *China: The Next Decades*, Harlow, Essex, England: Longman Scientific and Technical.

Fisher, A. (1996), 'China's Three Gorges Dam: Is the 'Progress' Worth the Ecological Risk?', *Popular Science*, August.

Gittings, J. (1996), 'In Restless China, Deng's Death Is Not the Only Threat', *Guardian*, 19th July.

—— (1999), 'Floods Threaten Millions in China', *Guardian*, 5th July.

Hardoy, J.E., Mitlin, D. and Satterthwaite, D. (1992), *Environmental Problems in Third World Cities*, London: Earthscan.

Information Office of the State Council (1996), *Environmental Protection in China*, Beijing.

Li Wen (1999), 'China's Environmental Conditions in 1998', *Beijing Review*, 12th July, pp.13–18.

Mao Zedong (1971), *Selected Readings from the Works of Mao Zedong*, Beijing: Foreign Languages Press.

Ming Wan (1998), 'China's Economic Growth and the Environment in the Asia-Pacific Region', *Asian Survey*, 38, pp.365–378.

Muldavin, J.S.S. (1996), 'Impact of Reform on Environmental Sustainability in Rural China', *Journal of Contemporary Asia*, 26, 3, pp.289–321.

—— (1997), 'Environmental Degradation in Heilongjiang: Policy Reform and Agrarian Dynamics in China's New Hybrid Economy', *Annals of the Association of American Geographers*, 87, 4, pp.579–613.

Murray, G. (1998), *China The Next Superpower: Dilemmas in Change and Continuity*, London: China Library and New York: St. Martin's Press.

Pang Bo (1998), 'Dam Needed to Prevent Flood', *Chinafrica*, 85, January.

Qu Geping (1992), 'Technology to Tackle Pollution Problems', *China City Planning Review*, 8, 1, March, p.64.

Rees, W.E. (1992), 'Ecological Footprints and Appropriated Carrying Capacity: What Urban Economics Leaves Out', *Environment and Urbanisation*, 4,2.

Shen Yahong (1992), 'Enlightenment From the Development of Ancient City Planning in China in the Ancient Times', *China City Planning Review*, 8, 1, 1992, pp.65–75.

Shi Min (1991), 'China's Human Resource Development in the 1990's', *Asia-Pacific Studies*, No. 1, 1991, pp.78–85.

Smil, V. (1993), *China's Environmental Crisis: An Inquiry Into the Limits of National Development*, New York: M.E. Sharpe.

South China Morning Post, 21-3-1997, 13-1-1998, 7-4-1998, 7-4-1999.

Topping, A.R. (1998), 'Foreword: The River Dragon Has Come', in Dai Qing, *The River Dragon Has Come! The Three Gorges Dam and the Fate of China's Yangtze River and its People*, (edited by Thibodeau, J.G. and Williams, P.B.; tr. Yi Ming), New York: M.E.Sharpe.

WWF (1992), *International Country Profile: China*.

—— (1998), Hong Kong Factsheet, no. 49.

Wu Bian (1997), 'Damming of the Yangtse', *Beijing Review*, 15th December.

Wu Fang (1997), Chongqing Ready to Make a Fresh Start, *China National Day 1997*,

Beijing: China Intercontinental Press, pp.74–77.

Wu Ming (1998), 'Resettlement Problems of the Three Gorges Dam', www.

Zhao Sonqiao (1994), *Geography of China: Environment, Resources, Population, and Development*, New York: Wiley.

Zhou Bian (1998), 'Hydropower to Cut Greenhouse Gases', *Chinafrica*, 85, January.

Chapter 10

Associated Press, 18-7-1998, 2-11-1998, 18-11-1998.

Agence France Press, 19-9-1998.

Beijing Review, 15-3-1998, 4-5-1998.

CASS (1999), *Annual Social Report for 1998*, Chinese Academy of Social Sciences, Beijing.

China Daily, 21-4-1998.

Cook, I.G. and Li, R. (1996), The Rise of Regionalism and the Future of China, Chapter 9 in Cook, I.G., Doel, M., and Li, R. (eds) *Fragmented Asia: Regional Integration and National Disintegration in Pacific Asia*, Aldershot, England: Avebury.

Drucker, P. (1992), *Age of Discontinuity: Guidelines To Our Changing Society*, New York: Transactional Press.

Evans, R. (1993), *Deng Xiaoping and the Making of Modern China*, Harmondsworth, Middlesex, England: Penguin Books.

Hubei Daily, 13-10-1998.
Lee, Teng-Hui (1999), 'The Road to Democracy', *Asia 21*, August, pp.6-8.
Legal Daily, 3-3-1999.
Mann, J. (1989), *Beijing Jeep. The Short, Unhappy Romance of American Business in China*, New York: Simon and Schuster.
Murray, G. (1994), *China: The Last Great Market*, London: China Library and New York: St. Martin's Press.
—— (1998), *China: The Next Superpower: Dilemmas in Change and Continuity*, London: China Library and New York: St. Martin's Press.
People's Daily, 10-12-1998.
South China Morning Post, 5-6-1998, 18-7-1998, 6-8-1998, 14-8-1998, 8-9-1998, 4-10-1998, 9-10-1998, 14-10-1998, 2-11-1998, 18-11-1998, 19-11-1998, 19-12-1998 and 23-4-1999.
Wang, C.F. (1995), *Contemporary Chinese Politics: An Introduction*, New Jersey: Prentice Hall.
Workers' Daily, 17-3-1998.
Xinhua, 23-2-1998; 4-8-1998, 22-7-1999.
Yangchang Evening News, 28-1-1999.

Bibliography

Amnesty International, April 1999.

Armstrong, W and McGee, T. (1985), *Theatres of Accumulation*, London: Methuen.

Bannister, N. (1999), 'Steel deal raises job fears', *Guardian*, 8th June.

Baosteel Annual Report 1996, Baoshan: Baoshan Iron and Steel Corporation.

Bei Jingshi (1999), 'Capital cleans up', *Business Beijing*, Issue 38, p.22.

Bell, Sir C. (1924), *Tibet Past & Present*, Oxford: Clarendon Press.

Bishop, P. (1989), *The Myth Of Shangri-La. Tibet, Travel Writing and the Western Creation of Sacred Landscape*, London: Athlone Press.

Bista, D.B. (1979), *Report From Lhasa*, Kathmandu: Sahja Prakashan.

Blecher, M. (1986), *China: Politics, Economics and Society*, London: Frances Pinter. Blecher, M. (1986), *China: Politics, Economics and Society: Iconoclasm and Innovation in a Revolutionary Socialist Country*, London: Frances Pinter.

Bloodworth, D. (1966), *The Chinese Looking Glass*, New York: Farrar, Strauss & Giroux.

Bradbury, I. and Kirkby, R. (1995), 'Prospects for Conservation in China', *Ecos*, 16, 3, 4, pp.64–71

Bramall, C. and Jones, M.E. (1993), 'Rural Income Inequality in China Since 1978', *Journal of Peasant Studies*, 21, 1, pp.41–70.

Bray, J. (1996), 'Burma: Prospects for Regional Integration', Chapter 8 in Cook, I.G., Doel, M.A. and Li, R. (eds), *Fragmented Asia: Regional Integration and National Disintegration in Pacific Asia*, Aldershot, England: Avebury.

Brown, L. (1995), *Who Will Feed China: Wake Up Call for a Small Planet*, Washington: Worldwatch Institute.

Buchanan, K. (1970), *Transformation of the Chinese Earth*, London: Bell.

Bukharin and Preobrazhensky (1969), *The ABC of Communism*, Harmondsworth, Middlesex, England: Penguin.

Business Beijing (1996), 'Back and Beyond: Beijing in '95 and '96', Vol. 9, January, pp.16–18.

Byrd, W.A. (1992), 'The Anshan Iron and Steel Company', in Byrd, W.A. (ed.) *Chinese Industrial Firms Under Reform*, Oxford: Oxford University Press for the World Bank, pp.303–370.

Cannon, T. (1990), 'Regions, Spatial Inequality and Regional Policy', in Cannon, T.

and Jenkins, A. (eds), *The Geography of Contemporary China: The Impact of Deng Xiaoping's Decade*, London: Routledge, pp.28–60.

—— and Zhang, L-Y (1996), 'Inter-region Tension and China's Reforms', Chapter 4 in Cook, I.G., Doel, M.A. and Li, R. (eds), *Fragmented Asia: Regional Integration and National Disintegration in Pacific Asia*, Aldershot, England: Avebury, pp.75–101.

Cao Min (1996), 'Beijing Seeks More Overseas Investment', *China Daily*, 17th February.

Chai, J.C.H. (1996), 'Divergent Development and Regional Income Gap in China', *Journal of Contemporary Asia*, 26, 1, pp.46–58.

Chan, Kam Wing (1994), *Cities with Invisible Walls: Reinterpreting Urbanization in Post-1949 China*, Oxford: Oxford University Press.

Chao, P.K.I. (1990), *The Changing Geography of China: A Synoptic View*, Hong Kong: Commercial Press.

Chen, Jerome (1965), *Mao and the Chinese Revolution*, Oxford: Oxford University Press.

Chen, Xiangming (1995), 'The Evolution of Free Economic Zones and the Recent Development of Cross-National Growth Zones', *International Journal of Urban and Regional Research*, 19, pp.593–621.

Cheng Guang (1997), 'Baosteel Business Strategy in Market Economy', in Guan Zhian and Liu Kexun (eds), *International Symposium on Steel Industry Development and Management Proceedings*, Beijing: Metallurgical Industry Press, pp.27–32.

Chi Fulin (1996), *Pressing Tasks of China's Economic Transition*, Beijing: Foreign Languages Press.

—— (1997), *Several Issues Arising During the Retracking of the Chinese Economy*, Studies on the Chinese Market Economy Series, Gao Shangquang and Chi Fulin (eds), Beijing: Foreign Languages Press.

China Daily (1998), 'Shougang Moves Mill for Capital's Environment', 18th June.

China Mail (1996), 'An Overstock of Commodity Property in China', Vol.9, No.1, January-February 1996, p.76.

China Mainland Market Research Company (1999), *Survey on Current Consumption Habits among Beijing Residents and Future Trends*, Beijing, January.

China Statistical Almanac 1996, Beijing

China Today, 'The Floating Population', February 1999.

Chinese Academy of Social Science (CASS) (1995). '*Market Orientation, Decision-Making Power and Enterprise Performance – A Statistical and Analytical Report on the Sample Data of 795 State-Owned Enterprises*', Economic Institute of the Chinese Academy of Social Science, Beijing.

—— (1997), '*1991–2010: Policy Choices of China's Economic Development*', Chinese Academy of Social Sciences, Beijing.

—— (1999), *Annual Social Report for 1998*, Chinese Academy of Social Sciences, Beijing.

Cho-Oon Khong (1996), 'Pacific Asia as a Region: A View From Business', in Cook, I.G., Doel, M., and Li, R. (eds), *Fragmented Asia:Regional Integration and National Disintegration in Pacific Asia*, Aldershot, England: Avebury, pp.167–180.

Clark, L. (1955), *The Marching Wind*, London: Hutchinson.

Cook, I.G. (1993), *Urban Issues in the West Pacific Rim*, Paper presented to the British Pacific Rim Research Group, Liverpool John Moores University, May.

—— (1995), *Reflections on Pressures of Development in China's Large Cities*, Paper presented to the International Symposium on International Urbanization in China, Shunde City, Guangdong Province, August 28th-September 1st.

—— (1997), *Contextualising Steel: Changing Locational Factors in the Steel Industry*, International Symposium on Steel Industry Development and Management, Baoshan, May 1997.

—— (2000), 'Urban and Regional Pressures of Development', Chapter 2 in Cannon, T. (ed.), *China's Economic Growth: The Impact on Regions, Migration and the Environment*, London: Macmillan.

—— and Li, R. (1994a), *The Future of China: Unity or Division?*, Paper presented to the British Pacific Rim Research Group, School of Oriental And African Studies, University of London, May.

—— and Li, R. (1994a), *The Transformation of China's Cities: The International Dimension*, Paper presented at the Rotal United Services Institute Asia Forum, Whitehall, London, January.

—— and Li, R. (1996), The Rise of Regionalism and the Future of China, Chapter 9 in Cook, I.G., Doel, M., and Li, R. (eds) *Fragmented Asia:Regional Integration and National Disintegration in Pacific Asia*, Aldershot, England: Avebury.

—— and Murray, G. (1999), *Some Contradictions in the Process of China's Economic Reform*, Paper Presented to the 10th Chinese Economic Association, UK, Conference on 'The Chinese Economy and Industry in the 21st Century', Middlesex Business School, 29–30 March 1999.

—— and Wang, Y. (1998), 'Foreign Direct Investment in China: Patterns, Processes, Prospects', Chapter 6 in Cook, I.G., Doel, M. A., Li, R. and Wang, Y. (eds), *Dynamic Asia: Business, Trade and Economic Development in Pacific Asia*, Aldershot, England: Ashgate.

Cooke, K. (1993), 'Baoshan Steelworks: Leading Supplier of Quality Products, *Financial Times*, June 2, p.34.

—— (1993), 'Pudong Development Zone: New Tiger Will Pace the East Bank', *Financial Times*, June 2nd.

Cotterell, A. (1995), *China. A History*, London: Pimlico (Random House).

Croll, E. (1995), 'Women in China: Experience and Action', *China Review*, No.1, Summer, pp.12–15.

D'Costa (1993), 'State-Sponsored Internationalization: Restructuring and Development of the Steel Industry', in Noponen, H., Graham, J. and Markusen, A.R. (eds), *Trading Industries, Trading Regions: International Trade, American Industry and Regional Economic Development*, London: Guilford Press.

Dai Qing (1998), *The River Dragon Has Come! The Three Gorges Dam and the Fate of China's Yangtze River and its People*, (edited by Thibodeau, J.G. and Williams, P.B.; tr. Yi Ming), New York: M.E.Sharpe.

Dalai Lama (1962), *My Land and My People*, London: Weidenfeld & Nicolson.

Derbyshire, E. (1994), 'Environment: Understanding and Transforming the Physical Environment', Chapter 4 in Dwyer, D. (ed.), *China: The Next Decades*, Harlow, Essex, England: Longman Scientific and Technical.

Dong Liming (1988), 'Beijing: The Development of a Socialist Capital', in Sit, V.F.S. (ed.), *Chinese Cities*, Oxford: Oxford University Press, pp.67–93.

Douglas, I., Gu Hengyue and He Min (1994), 'Water Resources and Environmental Problems of China's Great Rivers', Chapter 10 in Dwyer, D. (ed.), *China: The Next Decades*, Harlow, Essex, England: Longman Scientific and Technical.

Drucker, P. (1992), *Age of Discontinuity: Guidelines To Our Changing Society*, New York: Transactional Press.

Edmonds, R.L. (1994a), *Patterns of China's Lost Harmony: A Survey of the Country's Environmental Degradation and Protection*, London: Routledge.

—— (1994b), 'China's Environment: Problems and Prospects', Chapter 9 in Dwyer,

D. (ed.), *China: The Next Decades*, Harlow, Essex, England: Longman Scientific and Technical.

Etheridge, J. (1988), *Changing China*, Beijing: New World Press.

Evans, R. (1993), *Deng Xiaoping and the Making of Modern China*, Harmondsworth, Middlesex, England: Penguin Books.

Fisher, A. (1996), 'China's Three Gorges Dam: Is the 'Progress' Worth the Ecological Risk?,' *Popular Science*, August.

Fitzgerald, C.P. (1977), *Mao Tse-Tung and China*, Harmondsworth, Middlesex, England: Penguin.

Fleming, P. (1936), *News From Tartary*, London: Jonathan Cape.

—— (1961), *Bayonets To Lhasa*, London: Readers Union.

Foreign Investment Administration and China Economic and Trade Consultants Corp., (1993), *Investment in China*, Beijing: Ministry of Foreign Trade and Economic Co-operation.

Forney, M. (1996), 'Party Line: Beijing Plenum Backs Jiangist Ideology', *Far Eastern Economic Review*, 24th October, p.28.

Freeberne, M. (1971), 'The People's Republic of China', Chapter 5 in East, W.G., Spate, O.H.K. and Fisher, C.A. (eds), *The Changing Map of Asia: A Political Geography*, London: Methuen, Fifth Edition, pp.341–447.

Fu-Kuo Liu (1996), 'Industrial Development and the Impetus to Regional Economic Integration in Pacific Asia', Chapter 6 in Cook, I.G., Doel, M.A. and Li, R. (eds), *Fragmented Asia: Regional Integration and National Disintegration in Pacific Asia*, Aldershot, England: Avebury.

Gallup Organisation (1999), *Survey of Chinese Consumer Attitudes and Lifestyles, 1998*, Beijing.

Gao Shangquan and Chi Fulin (1997), *The Reform and Development of China's Rural Economy*, Studies on the Chinese Market Economy Series, Beijing: Foreign Languages Press.

—— and —— (eds) (1997), *New Progress in China's Special Economic Zones*, Beijing: Foreign Languages Press.

Gaubatz, P.R. (1995), 'Urban Transformation in Post-Mao China: Impacts of the Reform Era on China's Urban Form', Chapter Two in Davis, D.S., Kraus, R., Naughton, B. and Perry, E.J. (eds), *Urban Spaces in Contemporary China: The Potential for Autonomy and Community in Post-Mao China*, Washington: Woodrow Wilson Center Press and Cambridge: Cambridge University Press.

Gelder, S and R. (1964), *The Timely Rain. Travels in New Tibet*, London: Hutchinson.

Gittings, J. (1996), 'In Restless China, Deng's Death Is Not the Only Threat', *Guardian*, 19th July.

—— (1999a), 'Beijing: City of Secrets and Shopping', *Guardian*, 3rd May.

—— (1999), 'Floods Threaten Millions in China', *Guardian*, 5th July.

—— (1999b), 'China's City of Dreams and Extremes', *Guardian*, 5th May.

Goldstein, M. 'The Dalai Lama's Dilemma', *Foreign Affairs*, Vol. 77, No.1. January/February 1998, pp. 83–93.

Goodman, D. (1990), *Makers of the Twentieth Century: Deng Xiaoping*, London: Cardinal.

—— (1994a), *Deng Xiaoping and the Chinese Revolution*, London: Routledge.

—— (1994b), 'The Politics of Regionalism: Economic Development, Conflict and Negotiation', Chapter 1 in Goodman, D.S.G. and Segal, G. (eds), *China Deconstructs: Politics, Trade and Regionalism*, London: Routledge, pp.1–20.

—— and Feng Chongyi (1994), 'Guangdong: Greater Hong Kong and the New Regionalist Future', Chapter 6 in Goodman, D.S.G. and Segal, G. (eds), *China Deconstructs: Politics, Trade and Regionalism*, London: Routledge, pp.177–201.

Grant. P. (1988), *Celestial Empire: China in the 20th Century*, London: Queen Anne Press.

Han Suyin (1972), *The Morning Deluge*, London: Jonathan Cape.

—— (1976), *Wind In The Tower: Mao Tsetung and the Chinese Revolution 1949–1975*, New York: Little Brown & Co..

Hanes, J.E. (1993), From Megalopolis to Megaroporisu, *Journal of Urban History*, 19, 2, February 1993, pp.56–94.

Harding, J. (1997), 'Chinese Steelmaker Takes a National Role: James Harding on a State group Allowed to Manage its Own Business – For the Time Being', *Financial Times*, June 11, p.4.

Hardoy, J.E., Mitlin, D. and Satterthwaite, D. (1992), *Environmental Problems in Third World Cities*, London: Earthscan.

Harrer, H. (1953), *Seven Years in Tibet*, London: Reprint Society.

—— (1988), *Return To Tibet*, Harmondsworth, Middlesex, England: Penguin.

Hinton, W. (1966), *Fenshan. A Documentary of Revolution in a Chinese Village*, New York: Vintage Books.

—— (1983), *Shenfan*, London: Secker & Warburg.

Hodder, R. (1994), 'State, Collective and Private Industry in China's Evolving Economy', in Dwyer, D. (ed.), *China: The Next Decades*, , Harlow, Essex, England: Longman Scientific and Technical, pp.116–127.

Hook, G. (1996), 'Japan and Contested Regionalism', Chapter 1 in Cook, I.G., Doel, M.A. and Li, R. (eds), *Fragmented Asia: Regional Integration and National Disintegration in Pacific Asia*, Aldershot, England: Avebury.

Howe, C. (1978), *China's Economy: A Basic Guide*, London: Paul Elek.

Hsu, I.C.Y. (1990), *The Rise of Modern China*, Oxford: Oxford University Press, Fourth Edition.

Hu Piyun et.al. (eds) (1995), *Historical Photos of Old Beijing*, Beijing: Beijing Publishing House.

Hua Yequan et.al. (eds) (1996), *Guide to Trade and Investment in Shanghai*, Shanghai: Shanghai Scientific and Technological Literature Publishing House.

Huc, E. *Souvenirs of a Journey Through Tartary, Tibet and China During the Years 1844, 1845 and 1846 Vols 1 and 2.* Annotated Version edited by Planchet, J-M., Beijing: Lazarist Press, 1931. Original English Version, *Recollections Of A Journey Through Tartary and Thibet and The Chinese Empire*, London: Longman, Brown, Green, Longmans and Roberts, 1859.

Hughes, E.R. (1937), *The Invasion of China by the Western World*, London: Adam and Charles Black.

Hussain, A. (1994), 'The Chinese Economic Reforms: An Assessment', Chapter Two in Dwyer, D. (ed.), *China: The Next Decades*, Harlow, Essex, England: Longman Scientific and Technical.

Information Office of the State Council (1996), *Environmental Protection in China*, Beijing.

Jing Can (1996), 'Resurrection of a Dinosaur: Angang Thrives', *Beijing Review*, Oct.28-Nov.3, pp.10–13.

Johnston, T. (1994), 'Disappearing Shanghai', *Britain-China*, No.54, pp.4–5.

Kirkby, R.J.R. (1985), *Urbanization in China: Town and Country in a Developing Economy 1949–2000 AD*, London: Croom Helm.

—— (1994), 'Dilemmas of Urbanization: Review and Prospects', in Dwyer, D. (ed.), *China: The Next Decades*, Harlow, Essex, England: Longman Scientific and Technical, pp.128–155.

Landon, P. (1905). *Lhasa Vol.1*, London: Hurst & Blackett Ltd.

Lattimore, O. (1940/1998). *Inner Asian Frontiers of China*, Hong Kong: Oxford

University Press. First published by the American Geographical Society, Boston.

Lee, Teng-Hui (1999), 'The Road to Democracy', *Asia 21*, August, pp.6–8.

Li Wen (1999), 'China's Environmental Conditions in 1998', *Beijing Review*, 12th July, pp.13–18.

Li, R. (1997), 'China's Investment Environment: The Security Dimension', *Asia Pacific Business Review*, 4, 1, pp.39–62.

Liao Pin (ed.) (1991), *Life Among the Minority Nationalities in Northwest Yunnan*, Beijing: Foreign Languages Press.

Linge, G.J.R. and Forbes, D.K. (1990), The Space Economy of China', in Linge, G.J.R. and Forbes, D.K. (eds), *China's Spatial Economy*, Oxford: Oxford University Press, pp.10–34.

Liu, Fu-Kuo (1996), 'Industrial Development and the Impetus to Regional Economic Integration in Pacific Asia', Chapter 6 in Cook, I.G., Doel, M.A. and Li, R. (eds), *Fragmented Asia: Regional Integration and National Disintegration in Pacific Asia*, Aldershot, England: Avebury, pp.137–166.

Liu, Yingiang (1996), 'Women Expanding Their Role in Society', *China Daily*, 28th February.

Lowe, J. (1986), *Into China*, London: John Murray.

Lucas, L. (1997), 'Angang Seeks HKDollars 1.75 billion', *Financial Times*, 10th July.

Luo Bing-Sheng (1997), 'Internationalized Business of Chinese Steel Industry Judged by the Practice of Shougang Group Company', in Guan Zhian and Liu Kexun (eds), *International Symposium on Steel Industry Development and Management Proceedings*, Beijing: Metallurgical Industry Press, pp.75–8.

Ma Yin (ed.) (1994), *China's Minority Nationalities*, Beijing: Foreign Languages Press.

Mackeras, C. and Yorke, A. (1991), *The Cambridge Handbook of Contemporary China*, Cambridge: Cambridge University Press.

Mann, J. (1989), *Beijing Jeep. The Short, Unhappy Romance of American Business in China*, New York: Simon and Schuster.

Mao Zedong (1954), *Selected Works of Mao Tse-Tung*, London: Lawrence and Wishart, Four Volumes.

—— (1971), *Selected Readings from the Works of Mao Zedong*, Beijing: Foreign Languages Press.

McGovern, W.M. (1924), *To Lhasa In Disguise*, London and New York: The Century Co..

Miller, R.R. (1991), 'The Changing Economics of Steel', *Finance and Development*, 28, 2. pp.38–40.

Ming Wan (1998), 'China's Economic Growth and the Environment in the Asia-Pacific Region', *Asian Survey*, 38, pp.365–378.

Mirsky, J. (1992), 'China's Baby Girls 'Killed by the Million" *Observer*, 26th January.

Muldavin, J.S.S. (1996), 'Impact of Reform on Environmental Sustainability in Rural China', *Journal of Contemporary Asia*, 26, 3, pp.289–321.

—— (1997), 'Environmental Degradation in Heilongjiang: Policy Reform and Agrarian Dynamics in China's New Hybrid Economy', *Annals of the Association of American Geographers*, 87, 4, pp.579–613.

Murray, G. (1993), *The Rampant Dragon*, London: Minerva Press.

—— (1994), *China: The Last Great Market*, London: China Library and New York: St. Martin's Press.

—— (1998), *China The Next Superpower: Dilemmas in Change and Continuity*, London: China Library and New York: St. Martin's Press.

Nolan, P. and Dong Fureng (eds) (1990), *The Chinese Economy And Its Future*, Cambridge: Polity Press.

Pang Bo (1998), 'Dam Needed to Prevent Flood', *Chinafrica*, 85, January.

Parker, J. (1987), 'China's Economy: The Biggest Developer of All', *The Economist*, 1st August, pp.3–22.

Patterson, G.N. (1954), *Tibetan Journey*, London: Faber and Faber.

People's Daily, 'Survey Shows Worsening Poverty', 10-9-1998.

Petras, J. (1988), 'Contradictions of Market Socialism in China (Part II), *Journal of Contemporary Asia*, 18, 2, pp.234–244.

Phillips, D.R. and Yeh, A. G-O (1990), 'Foreign Investment and Trade: Impact on Spatial Structure of the Economy', in Cannon, T. and Jenkins, A. (eds), *The Geography of Contemporary China: The Impact of Deng Xiaoping's Decade*, London: Routledge, pp.224–248.

Qu Geping (1992), 'Technology to Tackle Pollution Problems', *China City Planning Review*, 8, 1, March, p.64.

Rai, S.M. (1995), 'Gender in China', Chapter 15 in Benewick, R. and Wingrove, P. (eds), *China in the 1990s*, London: Macmillan, pp.181–192.

Rees, W.E. (1992), 'Ecological Footprints and Appropriated Carrying Capacity: What Urban Economics Leaves Out', *Environment and Urbanisation*, 4,2.

Ridding, J. (1996), 'China's Fledgling Export Base Takes Off: But Shenzhen Economic Zone Finds the Future Insecure', *Financial Times*, August 16th.

Riley, N.E. (1996), 'China's^Missing Girls¤: Prospects and Policy', *Population Today*, February, pp.4–5.

Saich, A. (1995), 'China's Political Structure', Chapter 3 in Benewick, R. and Wingrove, P. (eds), *China in the 1990s*, London: Macmillan.

Salisbury, H. (1992), *The New Emperors: Mao & Deng, A Dual Biography*, London: Harper Collins.

Schaller, M. (1979), *The US Crusade in China 1938–45*, New York: Columbia University Press.

Sender, H. (1992), Eastern Promise: Hongkong Developers Flock to Shanghai, *Far Eastern Economic Review*, 17-9-1992, p.72.

Shen Yahong (1992), 'Enlightenment From the Development of Ancient City Planning in China in the Ancient Times', *China City Planning Review*, 8, 1, 1992, pp.65–75.

Shi Min (1991), 'China's Human Resource Development in the 1990's', *Asia-Pacific Studies*, No. 1, 1991, pp.78–85.

Short, P. (1982), *The Dragon and the Bear*, London: Hodder and Stoughton.

Smil, V. (1993), *China's Environmental Crisis: An Inquiry Into the Limits of National Development*, New York: M.E. Sharpe.

Snow, E. (1941), *Scorched Earth*, London: Victor Gollancz.

—— (1963), *The Other Side Of The River*, London: Victor Gollancz.

—— (1970), *Red China Today: The Other Side of the River*, Harmondsworth, Middlesex, England: Penguin.

Solinger, D. J. (1995), 'The Floating Population in the Cities: Chances for Assimilation?', Chapter Five in Davis, D.S., Kraus, R., Naughton, B. and Perry, E.J. (eds), *Urban Spaces in Contemporary China: The Potential for Autonomy and Community in Post-Mao China*, Washington: Woodrow Wilson Center Press and Cambridge: Cambridge University Press.

Spence, J. (1982), *The Gate Of Heavenly Peace: The Chinese and Their Revolution 1895–1980*, London: Faber and Faber.

—— (1990), *The Search For Modern China*. London: Hutchinson.

State Commission for Economic Restructuring (1997), *Main Points of Implementation of the 1997 Economic Restructuring*, Beijing.

State Information Centre (1999), *Topic Group Report On Consumption Supply and Demand*, March, Beijing.

State Statistics Bureau, *Annual Reports*, Beijing.

—— (1998), *Survey of the Status of Rural Migrants in Key Cities*, Beijing.

Straits Times (1999), '46,000 China firm workers not paid', 5th April.

Sudjic, D. (1992), Birth of the Brave New City, *Guardian*, 2nd December, pp.2–3.

Taylor, M. (1996), 'Industrialisation, Enterprise Power, and Environmental Change: An Exploration of Concepts', *Environment and Planning A*, 28, pp.1035–1051.

Teirill, R. (1984), *The White-Boned Demon: A Biography of Madame Mao Zedong*, New York: William Morrow & Co..

Topping, A.R. (1998), 'Foreword: The River Dragon Has Come', in Dai Qing, *The River Dragon Has Come! The Three Gorges Dam and the Fate of China's Yangtze River and its People*, (edited by Thibodeau, J.G. and Williams, P.B.; tr. Yi Ming), New York: M.E.Sharpe.

Tregear, T.R. (1980), *China: A Geographical Survey*, Sevenoaks, Kent, England: Hodder and Stoughton.

Tsang Shu-Ki (1996), 'The Political Economy of Greater China', Chapter 2 in Rowley, C. and Lewis, M. (eds), *Greater China: Political Economy, Inward Investment and Business Culture*, London: Frank Cass.

Tsering Shakya (1999), *The Dragon in the Land of the Snows. A History of Modern Tibet Since 1947*, London: Pimlico.

Uri Dadush and Dong He (1995), 'China: A New Power in World Trade', *Finance and Development*, June, pp.36–8.

WWF (1992), *International Country Profile: China*.

—— (1998), Hong Kong Factsheet, no. 49.

Wang Gui (1997), *Discussion of the Historical Status of Tibet*, Beijing: Foreign Languages Press.

Wang, C.F. (1992), *Contemporary Chinese Politics, An Introduction*, New Jersey: Prentice Hall, Fourth Edition.

—— (1995), *Contemporary Chinese Politics: An Introduction*, New Jersey: Prentice Hall, Fifth Edition.

Wheatley, P. (1971), *The Pivot of the Four Quarters: A Preliminary Enquiry into the Origins and Character of the Ancient Chinese City*, Edinburgh: Edinburgh University Press.

Wiethoff, B. (1975), *Introduction to Chinese History*, London: Thames and Hudson.

Wilby. S. (1988), *Journey Across Tibet*, Chicago: Contemporary Books.

World Bank (1997a), *China 2020: Development Challenges in the New Century*, Washington.

—— (1997b), *China Engaged: Integration with the Global Economy*, Washington.

—— (1997c), *World Development Report 1996*, Oxford: Oxford University Press.

Wu Bian (1997), 'Damming of the Yangtse', *Beijing Review*, 15th December.

Wu Fang (1997), Chongqing Ready to Make a Fresh Start, *China National Day 1997*,

Wu Ming (1998), '*Resettlement Problems of the Three Gorges Dam*', www.

Xin Zhou (1997), 'Shanghai at Night', *China National Day 1997*, Beijing: China Intercontinental Press, pp.52–7.

Xu, Dixin (ed.) (1982), *China's Search For Economic Growth*, Beijing: New World Press.

Yabuki, S. (1995) *China's New Political Economy: The Giant Awakes*, Oxford: Westview Press.

Yan Mingfu (1995), *Modern Civilization and China's Urbanization Toward the 21st*

Century, Paper presented to the Symposium on International Urbanization in China, Shunde City, Guangdong Province, August 28th-September 1st 1995.

Yang, D.L. (1994), 'Reform and the Restructuring of Central-Local Relations', Chapter 3 in Goodman, D.S.G. and Segal, G. (eds), *China Deconstructs: Politics, Trade and Regionalism,* London: Routledge, pp.59–98.

Younghusband, Sir F. (1910), *India and Tibet,* London: John Murray.

Zhang Ping (1998), *Analysis of Inequality Distribution of Rural Residents in Different Regions,* with the Institute of Economics, Chinese Academy of Social Sciences, Beijing.

Zhang Xinmin and Tang Ping (1998), Market and Demographic Analysis, State Statistics Bureau, September, published in the December 1998 issue of *China Population Today.*

Zhang Zaoji et.al. (eds) (1993), *Hutongs of Beijing,* Beijing: Beijing Arts and Photography Publishing House.

Zhang Zhirong (1995), *The International Relation and the Tibet Issue,* Beijing: Xinhua Publishing House.

Zhao Songqiao (1994), *Geography of China: Environment, Resources, Population and Development,* New York: Wiley.

Zhou Bian (1998), 'Hydropower to Cut Greenhouse Gases', *Chinafrica,* 85, January.

Zhou Shunwu (1992), *China Provincial Geography,* Beijing: Foreign Languages Press.

Zou Deci (1995), 'The Introduction of Urban Development in China', *China City Planning Review,* 11, 1, March, pp.25–32.

Other Sources

Agence France Press
Associated Press
Beijing Review
Business Beijing
Business Weekly (Beijing)
China Daily
China Internet Information Centre, www.chinanews.org.
China Labour News
China's Tibet
China Today
Hubei Daily
Legal Daily
Outlook
People's Daily
Property Review (Singapore)
Real Estate Newspaper (Ministry of Construction, Beijing)
Shanghai Liberation Daily
South China Morning Post
Tibetan Government-In-Exile, www.tibet.com.
Workers' Daily
Xinhua
Yangchang Evening News

Index